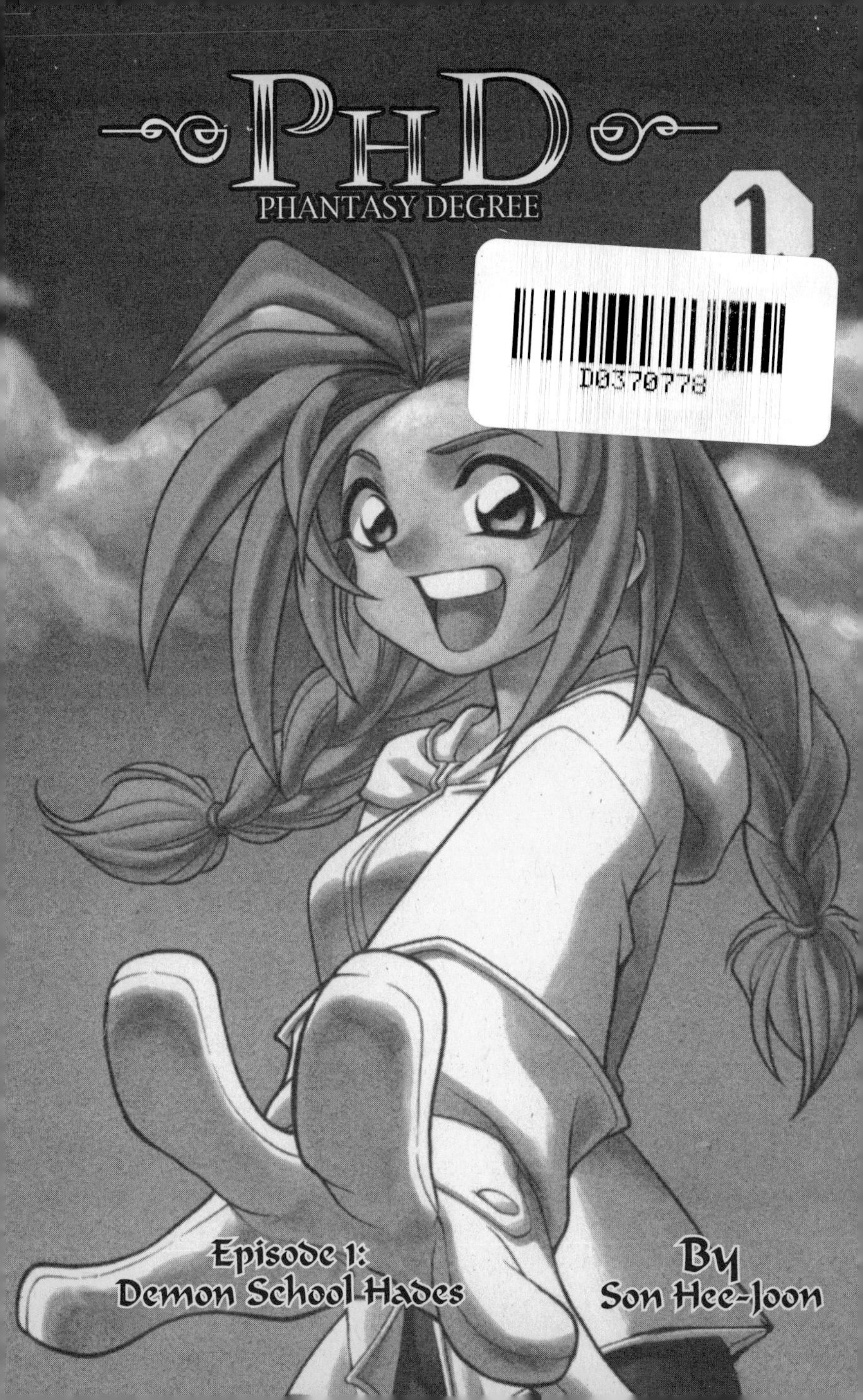
PhD
PHANTASY DEGREE
1
Episode 1:
Demon School Hades
By
Son Hee-Joon

PhD: Phantasy Degree Vol. 1
Created by Son Hee-Joon

Translation - Sarah Kim
English Adaptation - Paul Morrissey
Copy Editor - Adam Arnold
Retouch and Lettering - Eva Han
Production Artists - Jason Milligan and James Lee
Cover Design - Raymond Makowski

Editor - Paul Morrissey
Digital Imaging Manager - Chris Buford
Pre-Press Manager - Antonio DePietro
Production Managers - Jennifer Miller and Mutsumi Miyazaki
Art Director - Matt Alford
Managing Editor - Jill Freshney
VP of Production - Ron Klamert
President and C.O.O. - John Parker
Publisher and C.E.O. - Stuart Levy

A **TOKYOPOP** Manga

TOKYOPOP Inc.
5900 Wilshire Blvd. Suite 2000
Los Angeles, CA 90036

E-mail: info@TOKYOPOP.com
Come visit us online at www.TOKYOPOP.com

ISBN: 1-59532-319-8

First TOKYOPOP printing: January 2005
10 9 8 7 6 5 4 3
Printed in the USA

PhD
PHANTASY DEGREE

Volume 1

By
SON HEE-JOON

HAMBURG // LONDON // LOS ANGELES // TOKYO

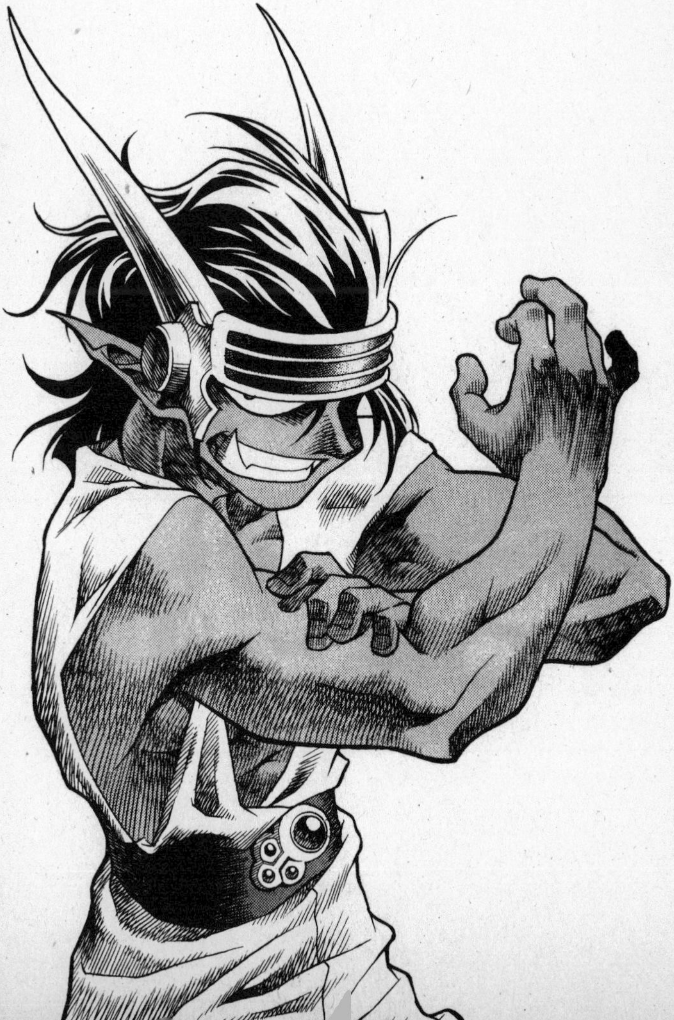

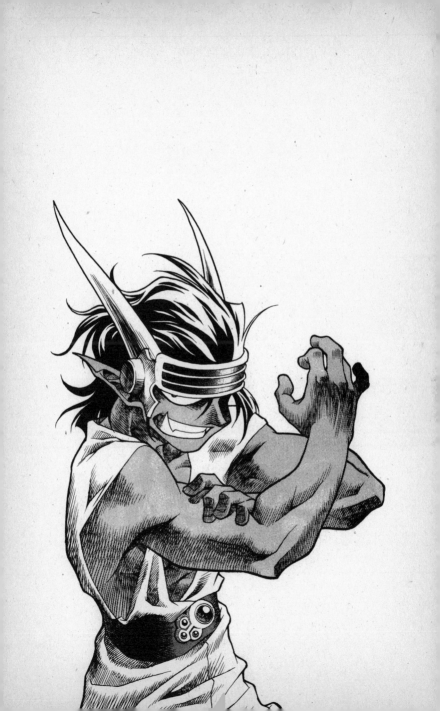

PhD
PHANTASY DEGREE

Table of Contents

Demon School Hades

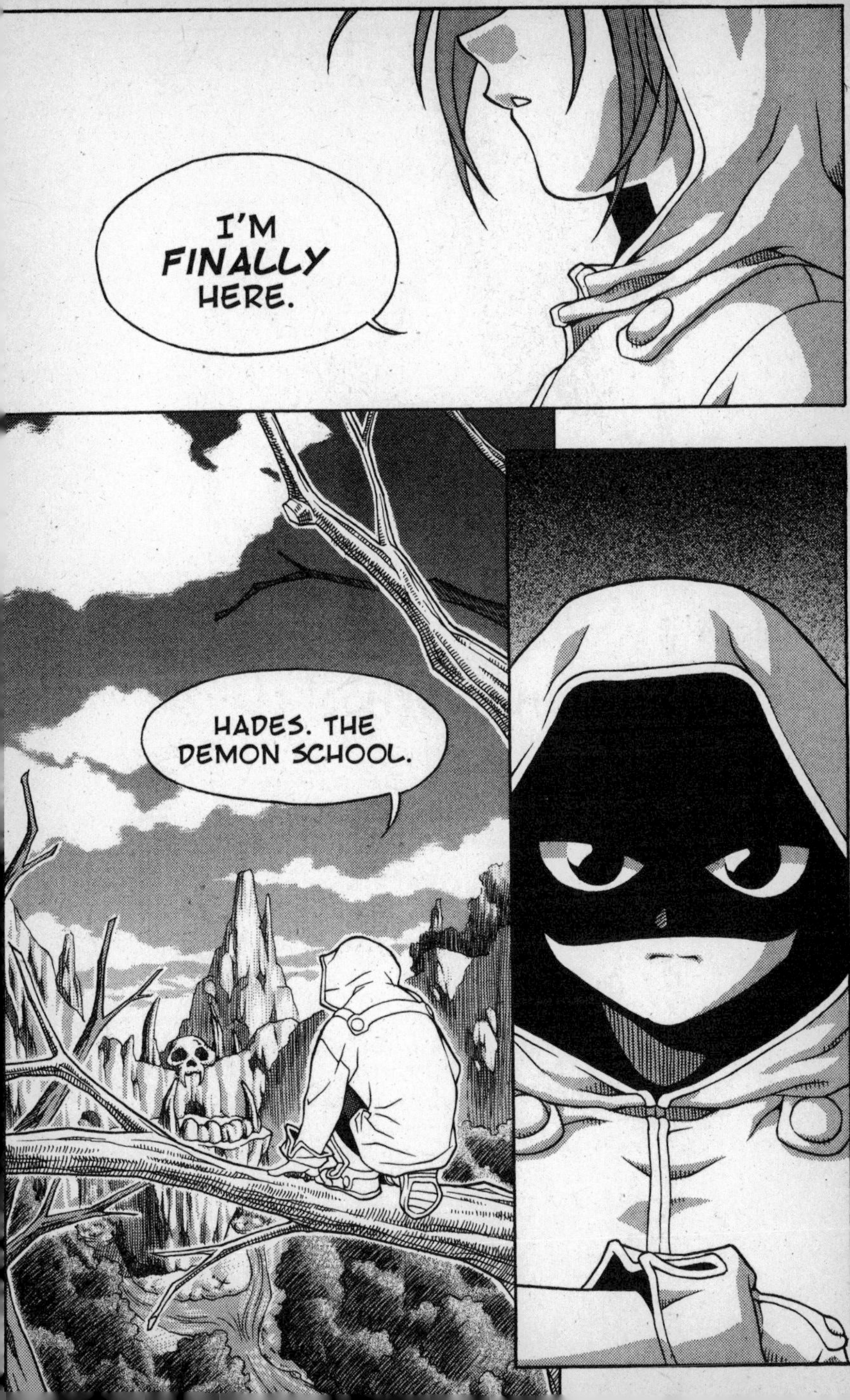
I'M *FINALLY* HERE.
HADES. THE DEMON SCHOOL.

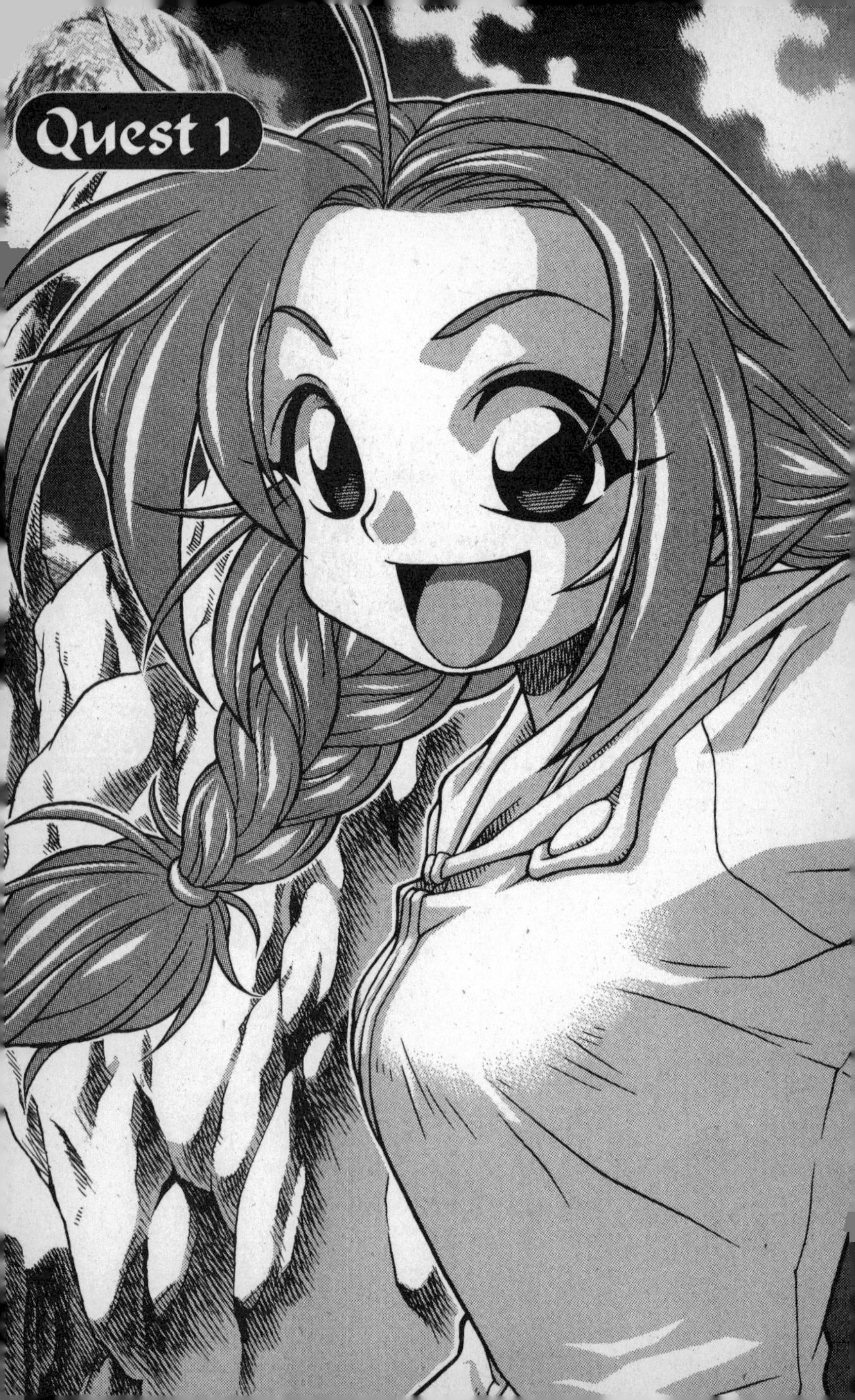
Quest 1

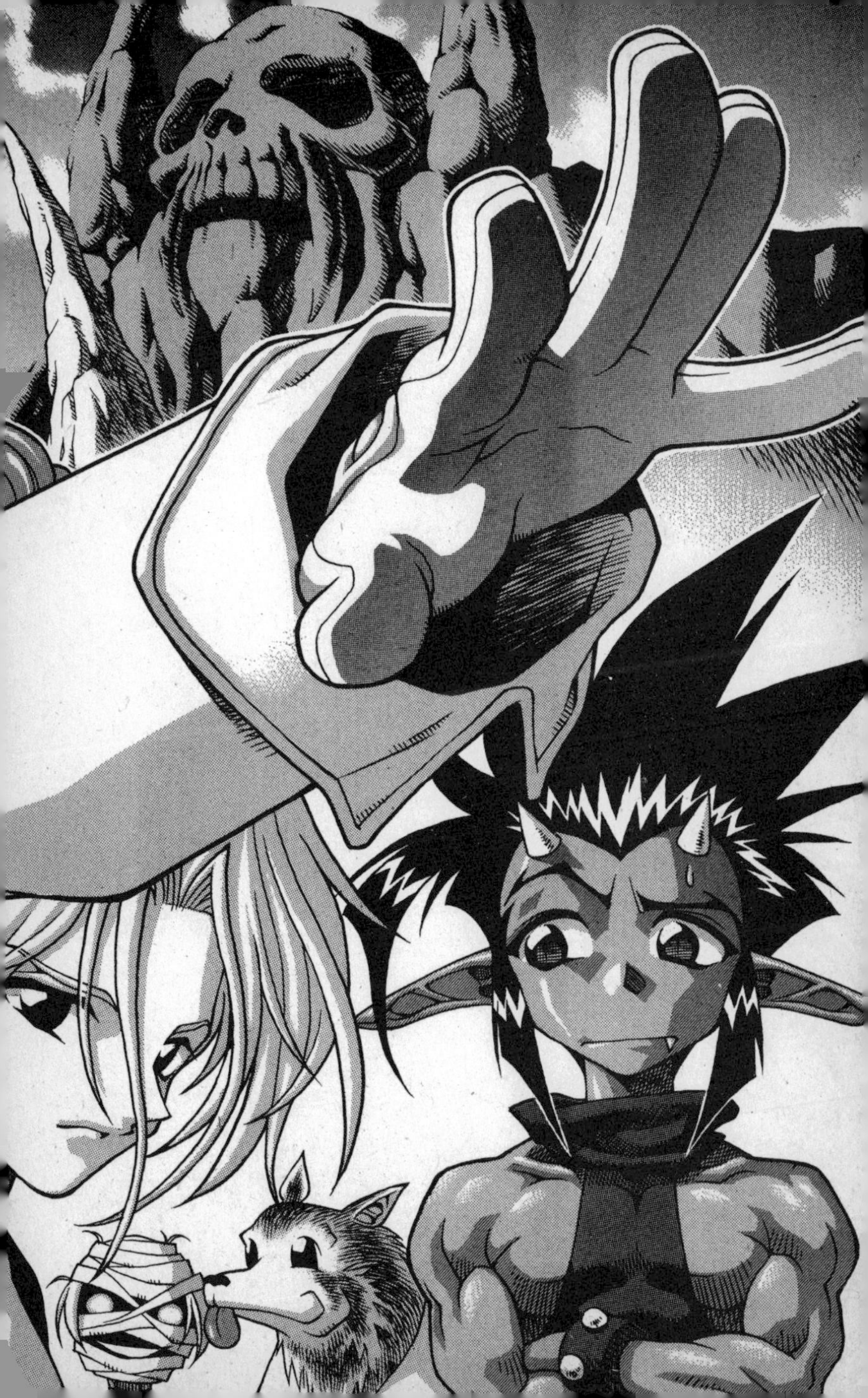

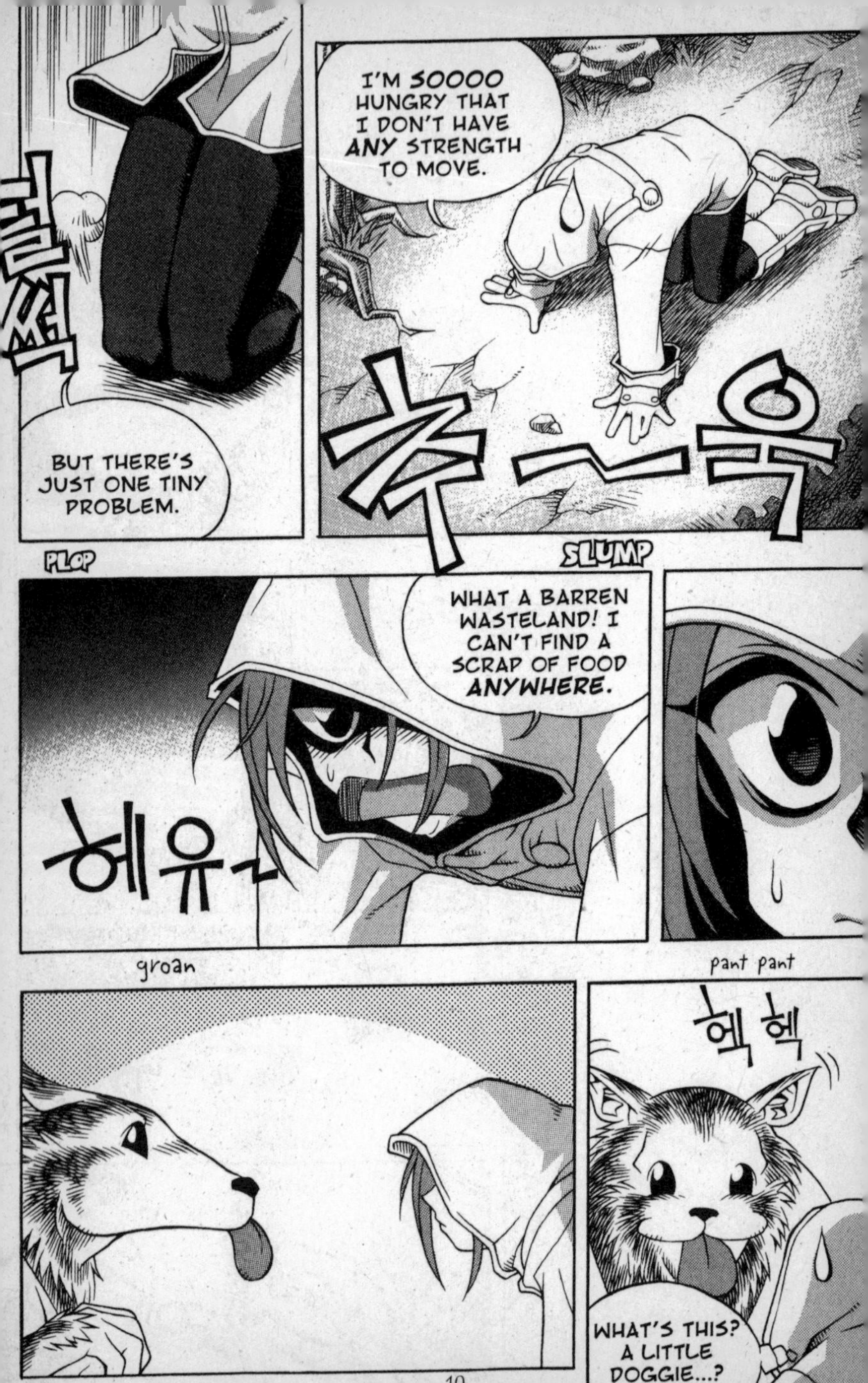
털썩
BUT THERE'S JUST ONE TINY PROBLEM.
PLOP
I'M SOOOO HUNGRY THAT I DON'T HAVE ANY STRENGTH TO MOVE.
추~욱
SLUMP
WHAT A BARREN WASTELAND! I CAN'T FIND A SCRAP OF FOOD ANYWHERE.
헤유~
groan
pant pant
헥헥
WHAT'S THIS? A LITTLE DOGGIE...?

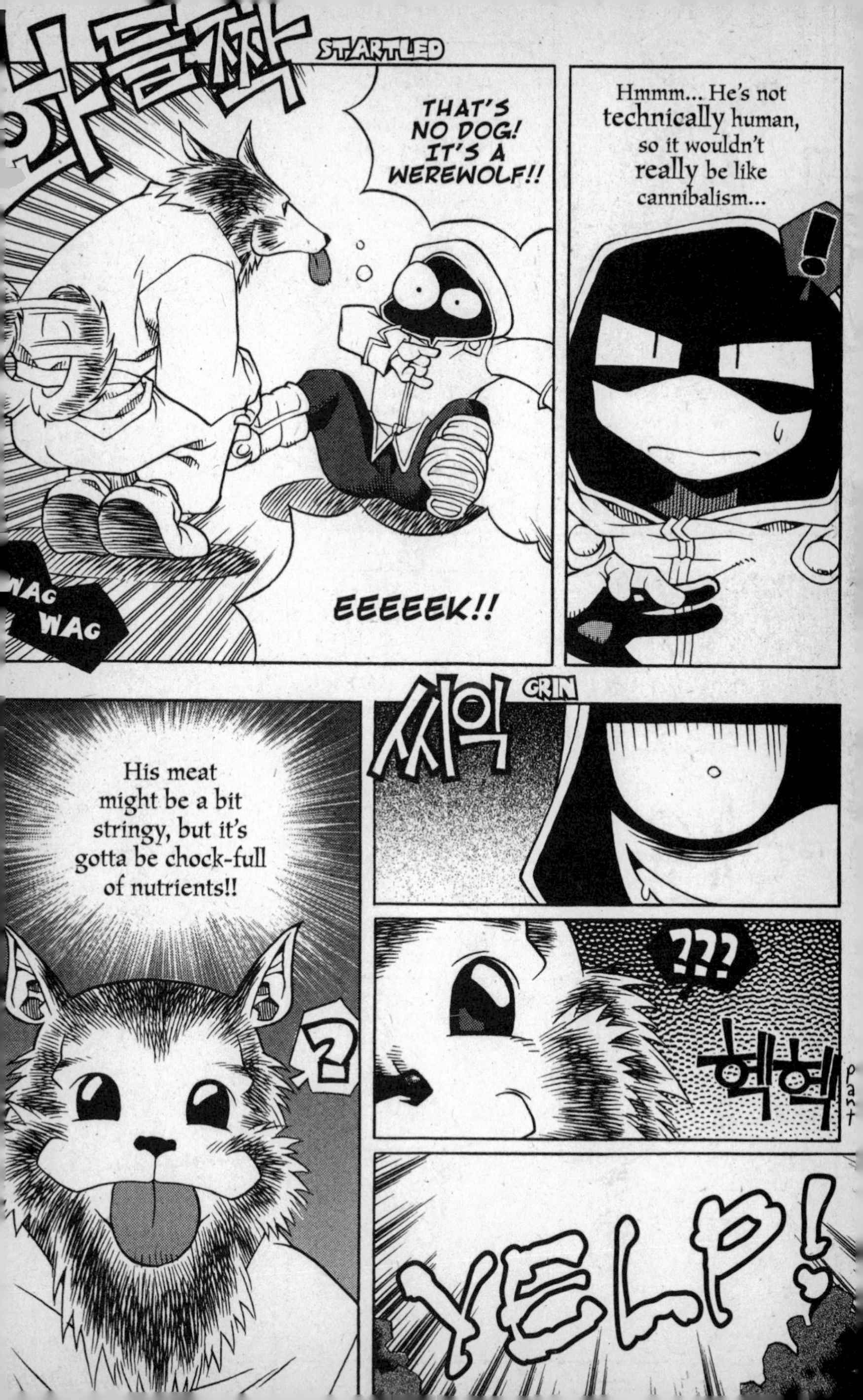
STARTLED
THAT'S NO DOG! IT'S A WEREWOLF!!
WAG
WAG
EEEEEK!!
Hmmm... He's not technically human, so it wouldn't really be like cannibalism...
!
His meat might be a bit stringy, but it's gotta be chock-full of nutrients!!
?
씨익
GRIN
???
헥헥
Pant
YELP!

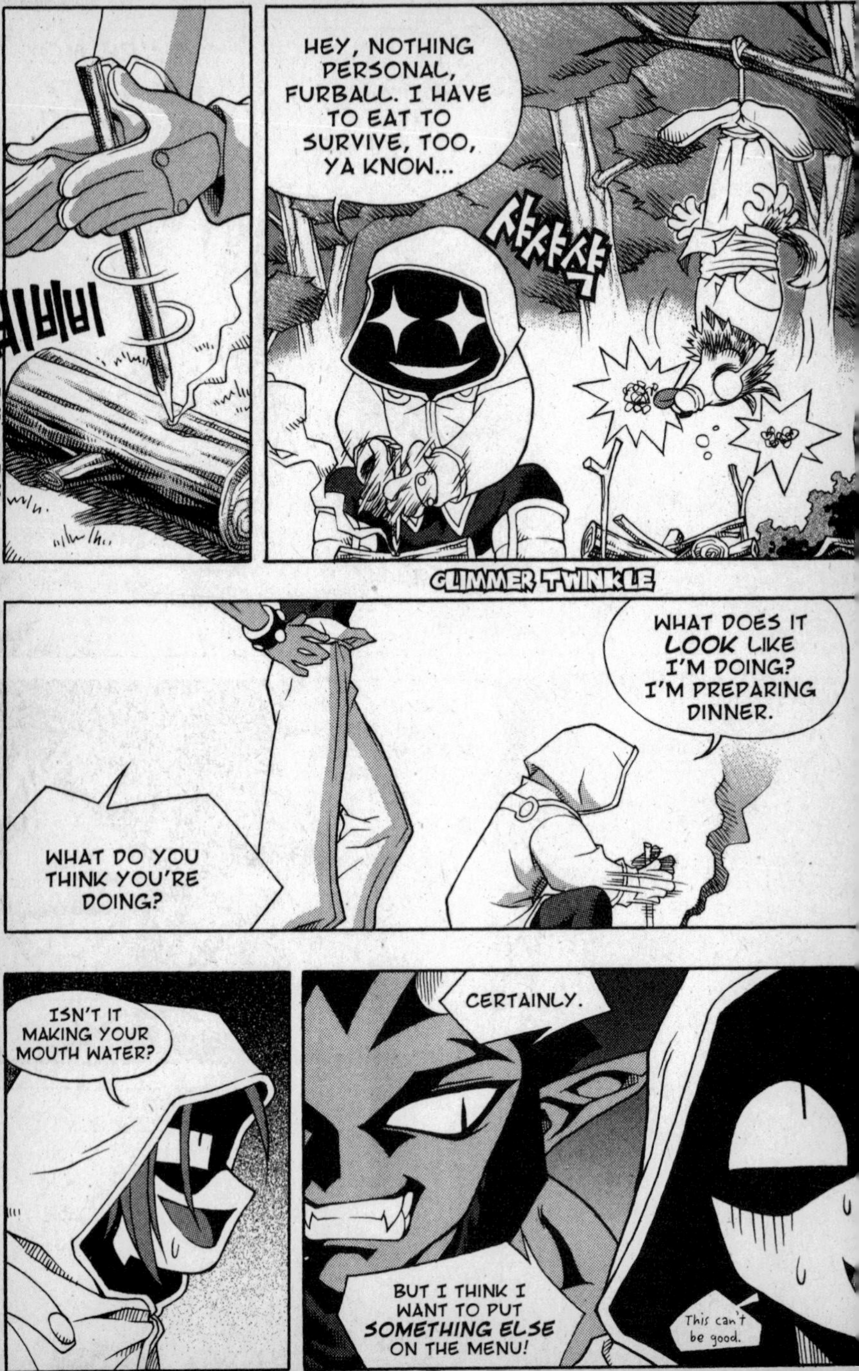
RUB RUB
HEY, NOTHING PERSONAL, FURBALL. I HAVE TO EAT TO SURVIVE, TOO, YA KNOW...
GLIMMER TWINKLE
WHAT DO YOU THINK YOU'RE DOING?
WHAT DOES IT *LOOK* LIKE I'M DOING? I'M PREPARING DINNER.
ISN'T IT MAKING YOUR MOUTH WATER?
CERTAINLY.
BUT I THINK I WANT TO PUT *SOMETHING ELSE* ON THE MENU!
This can't be good.

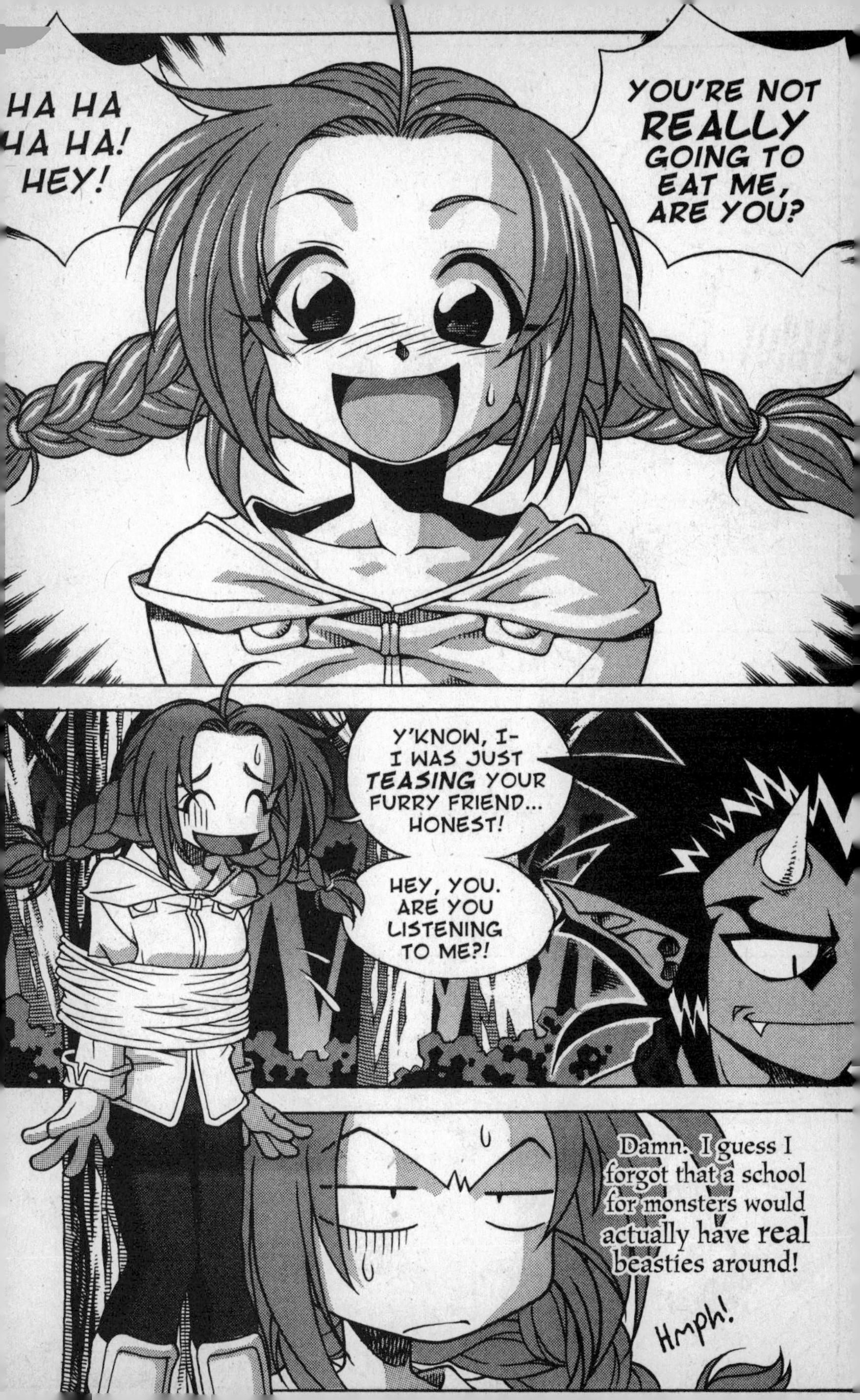
HA HA HA HA! HEY!
YOU'RE NOT REALLY GOING TO EAT ME, ARE YOU?
Y'KNOW, I- I WAS JUST TEASING YOUR FURRY FRIEND... HONEST!
HEY, YOU. ARE YOU LISTENING TO ME?!
Damn. I guess I forgot that a school for monsters would actually have real beasties around!
Hmph!

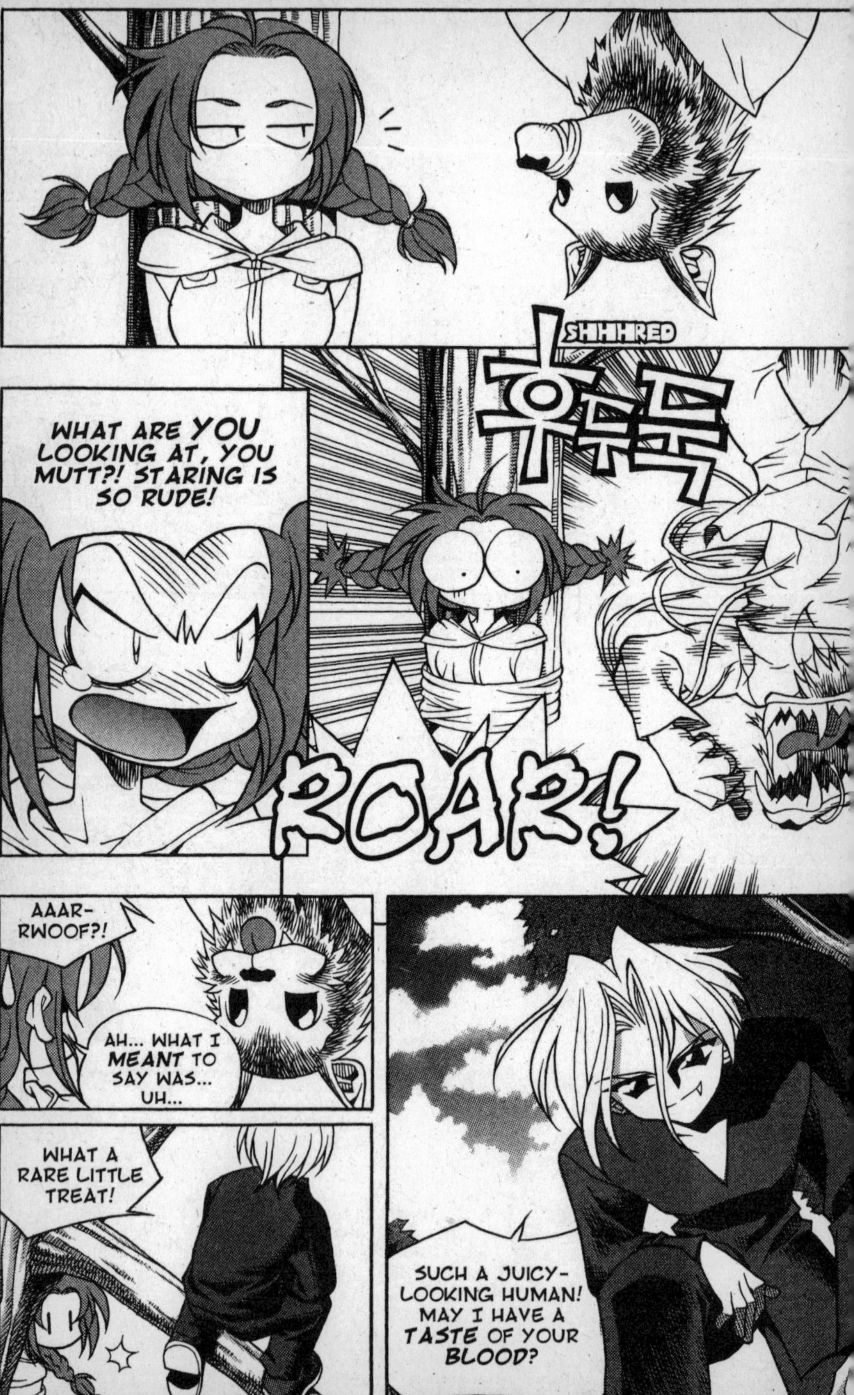
WHAT ARE YOU LOOKING AT, YOU MUTT?! STARING IS SO RUDE!
SHHHRED
후드득
ROAR!
AAAR-RWOOF?!
AH... WHAT I MEANT TO SAY WAS... UH...
WHAT A RARE LITTLE TREAT!
SUCH A JUICY-LOOKING HUMAN! MAY I HAVE A TASTE OF YOUR BLOOD?

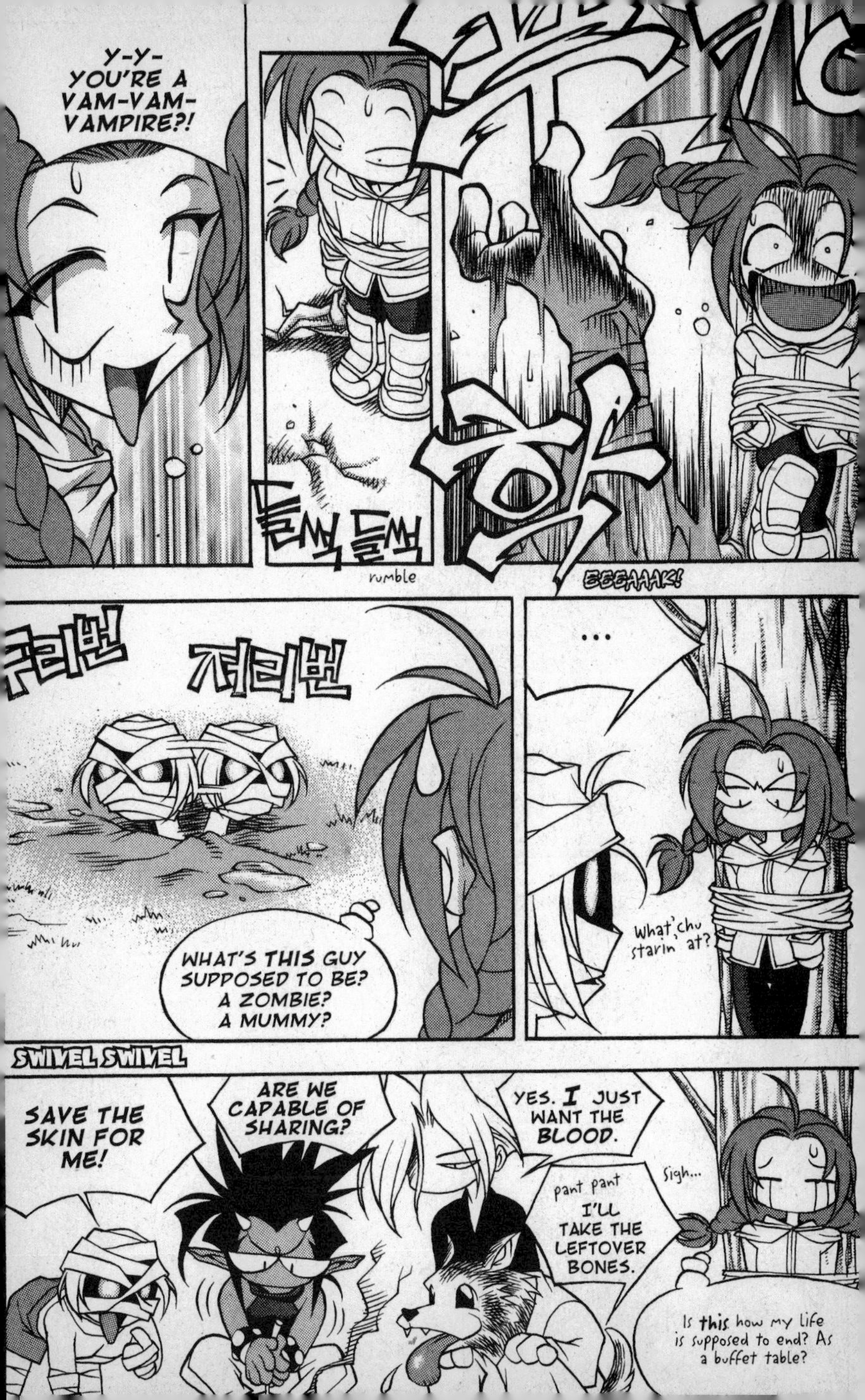
Y-Y-YOU'RE A VAM-VAM-VAMPIRE?!
들썩 들썩
rumble
EEEAAAK!
WHAT'S THIS GUY SUPPOSED TO BE? A ZOMBIE? A MUMMY?
SWIVEL SWIVEL
...
What'chu starin' at?
SAVE THE SKIN FOR ME!
ARE WE CAPABLE OF SHARING?
YES. I JUST WANT THE BLOOD.
pant pant
I'LL TAKE THE LEFTOVER BONES.
Sigh...
Is this how my life is supposed to end? As a buffet table?

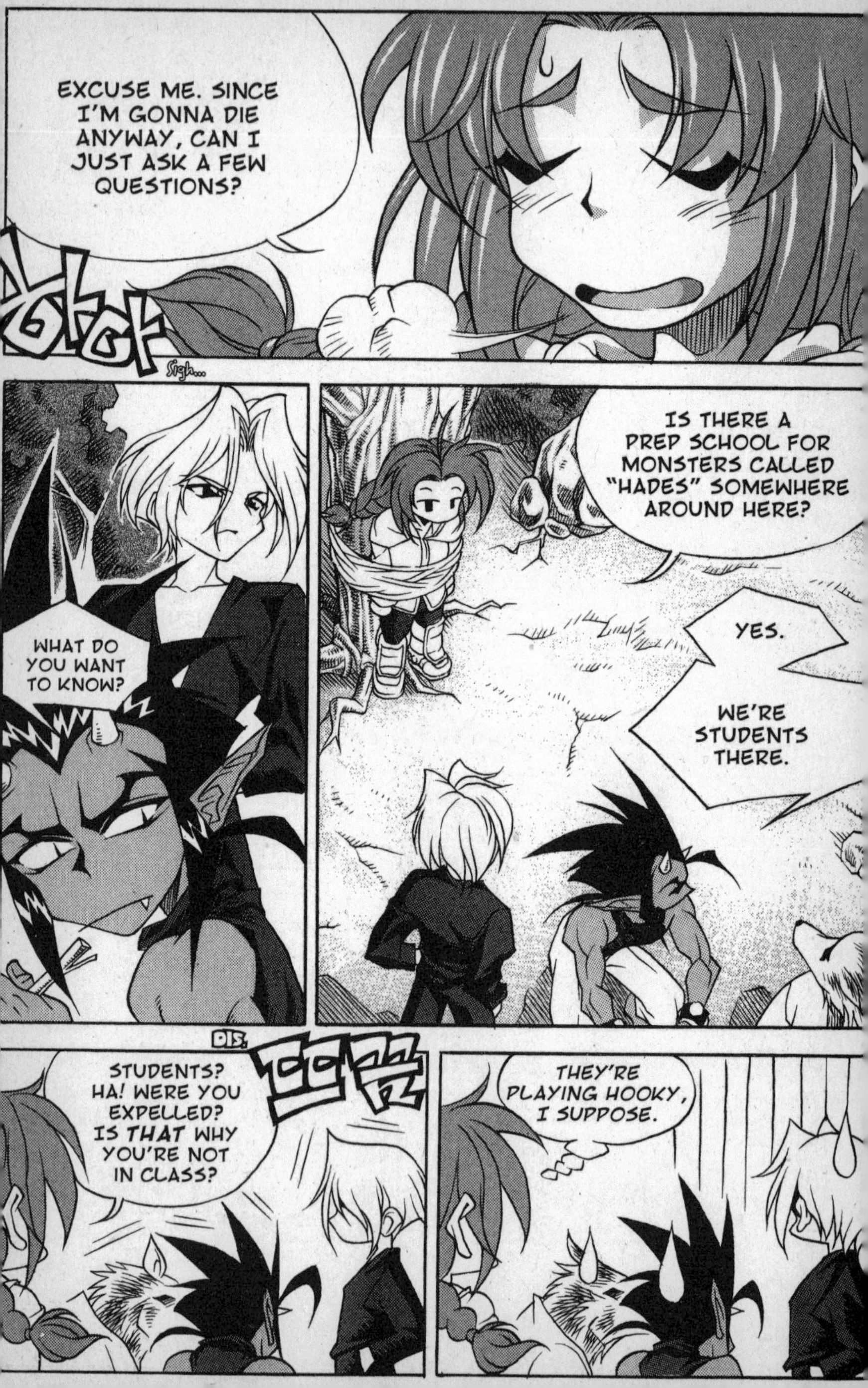
EXCUSE ME. SINCE I'M GONNA DIE ANYWAY, CAN I JUST ASK A FEW QUESTIONS?
Sigh...
WHAT DO YOU WANT TO KNOW?
IS THERE A PREP SCHOOL FOR MONSTERS CALLED "HADES" SOMEWHERE AROUND HERE?
YES.
WE'RE STUDENTS THERE.
STUDENTS? HA! WERE YOU EXPELLED? IS THAT WHY YOU'RE NOT IN CLASS?
DIS.
THEY'RE PLAYING HOOKY, I SUPPOSE.

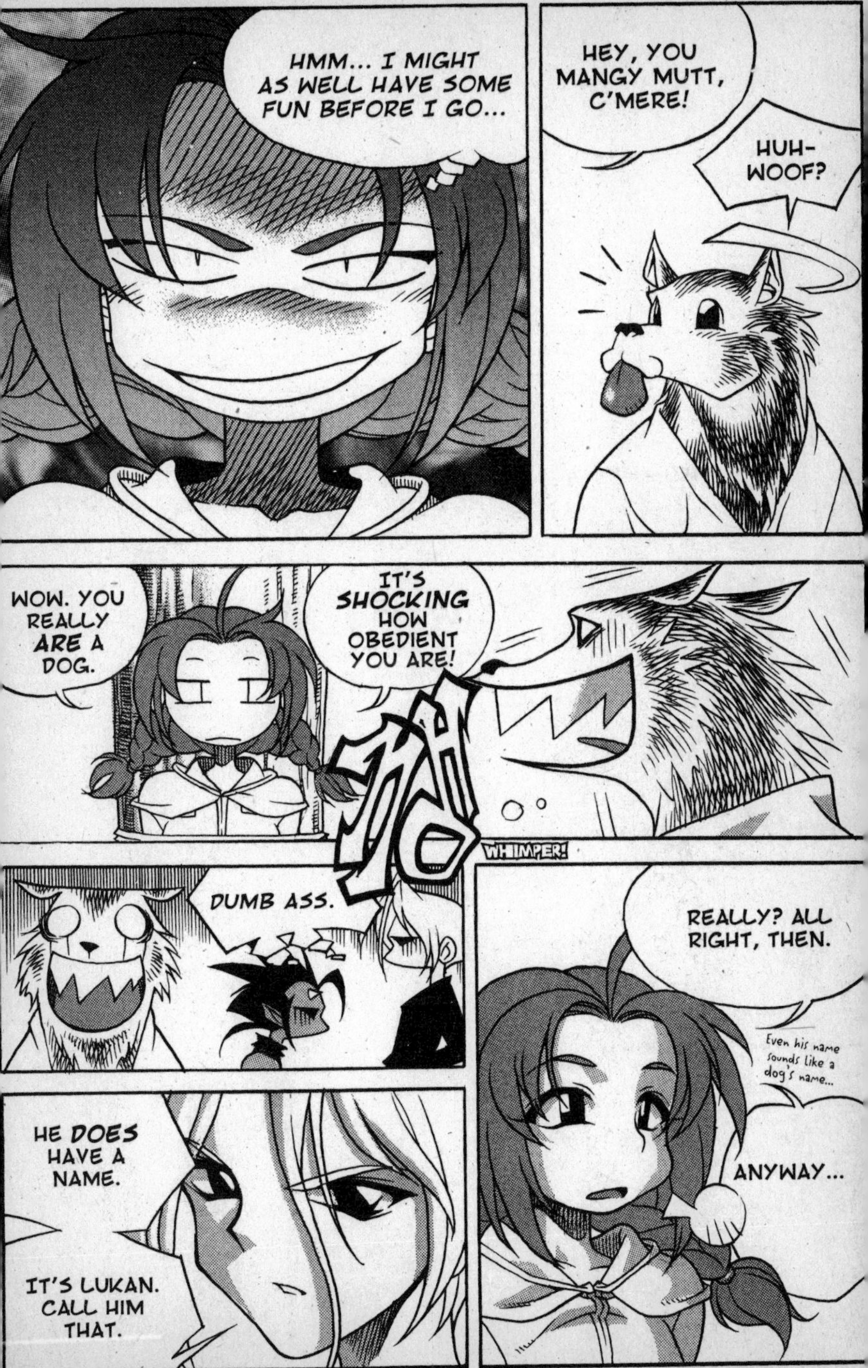
HMM... I MIGHT AS WELL HAVE SOME FUN BEFORE I GO...
HEY, YOU MANGY MUTT, C'MERE!
HUH-WOOF?
WOW. YOU REALLY ARE A DOG.
IT'S SHOCKING HOW OBEDIENT YOU ARE!
WHIMPER!
DUMB ASS.
REALLY? ALL RIGHT, THEN.
Even his name sounds like a dog's name...
ANYWAY...
HE DOES HAVE A NAME.
IT'S LUKAN. CALL HIM THAT.

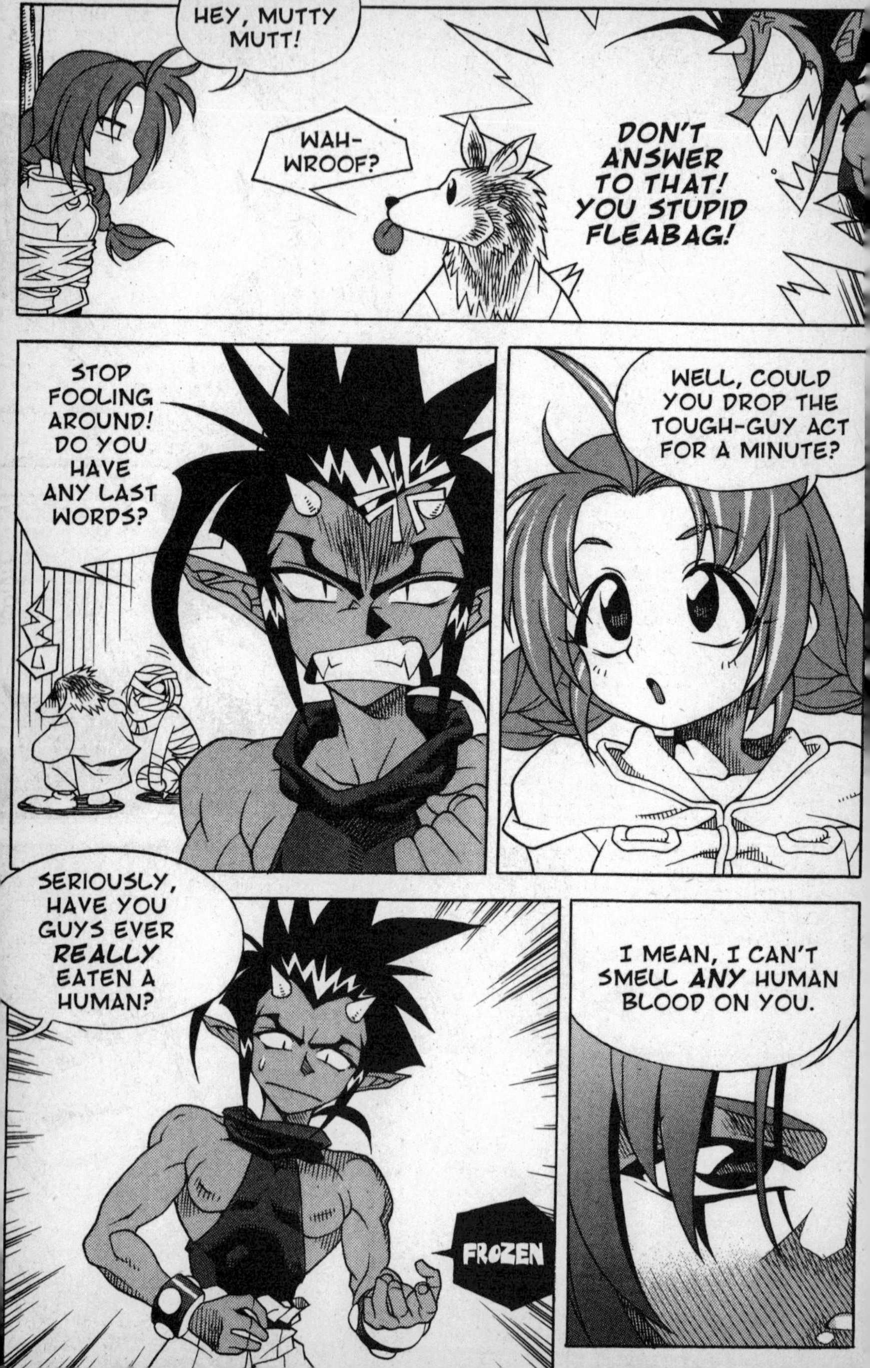
HEY, MUTTY MUTT!
WAH-WROOF?
DON'T ANSWER TO THAT! YOU STUPID FLEABAG!
STOP FOOLING AROUND! DO YOU HAVE ANY LAST WORDS?
WELL, COULD YOU DROP THE TOUGH-GUY ACT FOR A MINUTE?
SERIOUSLY, HAVE YOU GUYS EVER REALLY EATEN A HUMAN?
FROZEN
I MEAN, I CAN'T SMELL ANY HUMAN BLOOD ON YOU.

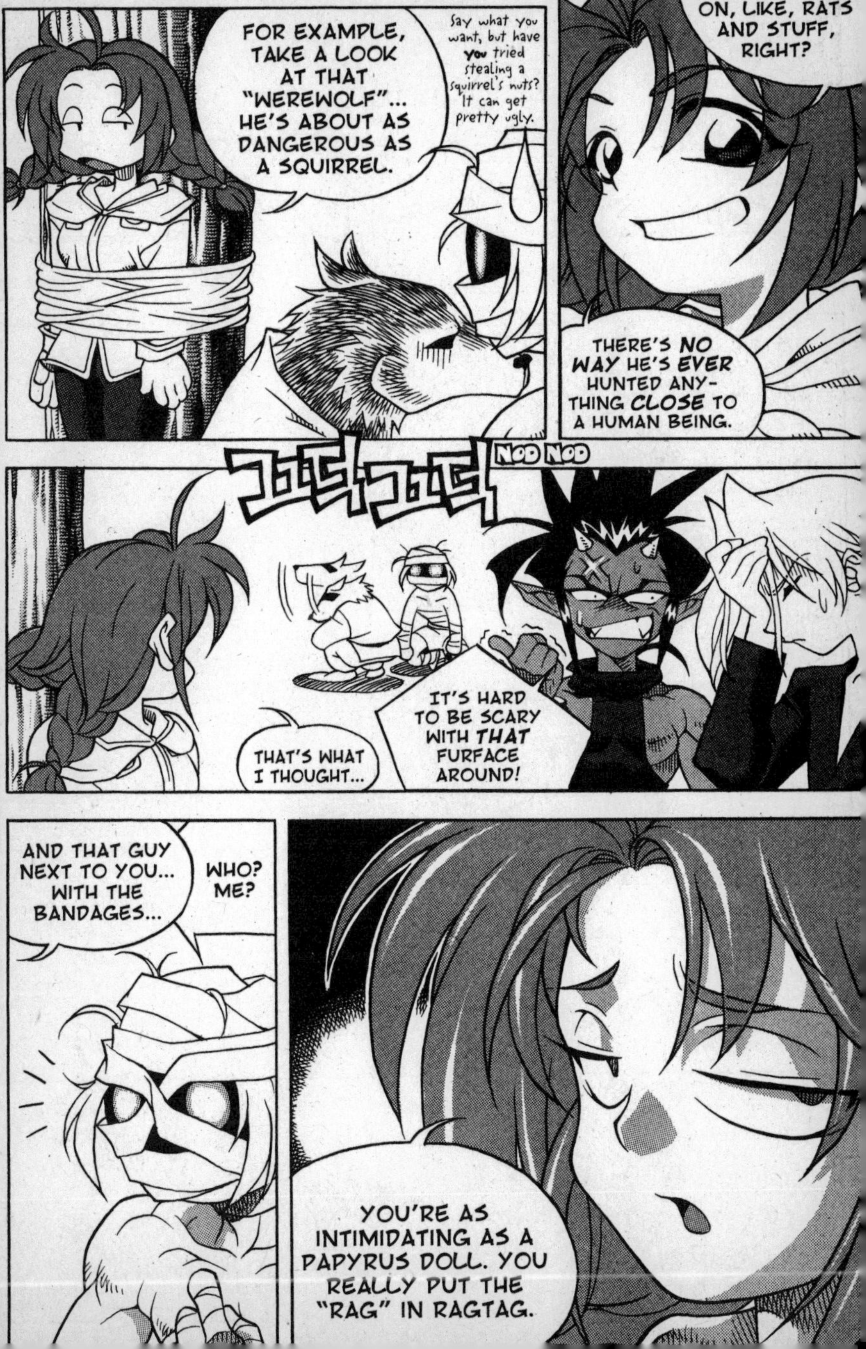

FOR EXAMPLE, TAKE A LOOK AT THAT "WEREWOLF"... HE'S ABOUT AS DANGEROUS AS A SQUIRREL.
Say what you want, but have **you** tried stealing a squirrel's nuts? It can get pretty ugly.
SO...HE LIVES ON, LIKE, RATS AND STUFF, RIGHT?
THERE'S **NO WAY** HE'S **EVER** HUNTED ANY-THING **CLOSE** TO A HUMAN BEING.
NOD NOD
IT'S HARD TO BE SCARY WITH ***THAT*** FURFACE AROUND!
THAT'S WHAT I THOUGHT...
AND THAT GUY NEXT TO YOU... WITH THE BANDAGES...
WHO? ME?
YOU'RE AS INTIMIDATING AS A PAPYRUS DOLL. YOU REALLY PUT THE "RAG" IN RAGTAG.

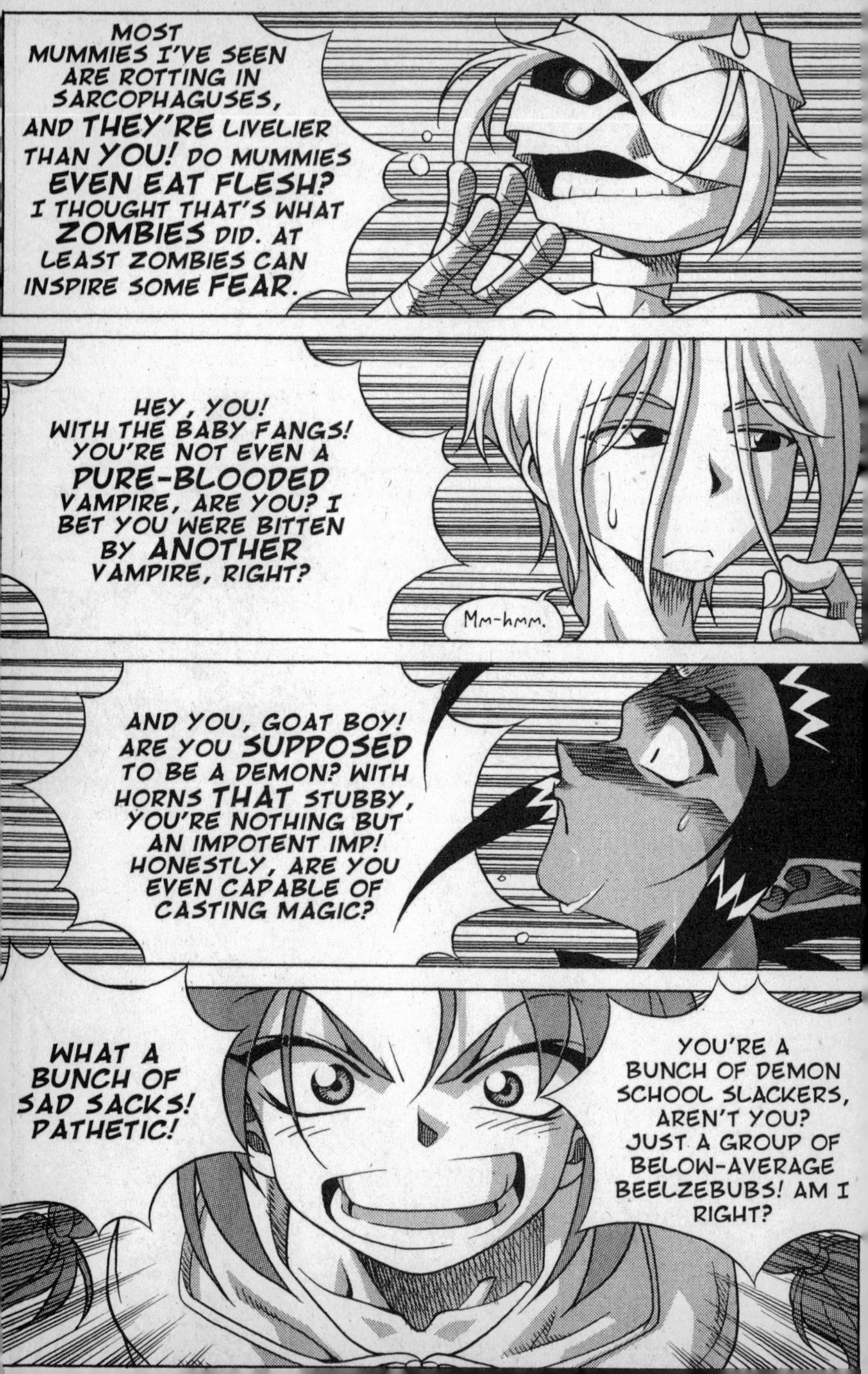
MOST MUMMIES I'VE SEEN ARE ROTTING IN SARCOPHAGUSES, AND THEY'RE LIVELIER THAN YOU! DO MUMMIES EVEN EAT FLESH? I THOUGHT THAT'S WHAT ZOMBIES DID. AT LEAST ZOMBIES CAN INSPIRE SOME FEAR.
HEY, YOU! WITH THE BABY FANGS! YOU'RE NOT EVEN A PURE-BLOODED VAMPIRE, ARE YOU? I BET YOU WERE BITTEN BY ANOTHER VAMPIRE, RIGHT?
Mm-hmm.
AND YOU, GOAT BOY! ARE YOU SUPPOSED TO BE A DEMON? WITH HORNS THAT STUBBY, YOU'RE NOTHING BUT AN IMPOTENT IMP! HONESTLY, ARE YOU EVEN CAPABLE OF CASTING MAGIC?
WHAT A BUNCH OF SAD SACKS! PATHETIC!
YOU'RE A BUNCH OF DEMON SCHOOL SLACKERS, AREN'T YOU? JUST A GROUP OF BELOW-AVERAGE BEELZEBUBS! AM I RIGHT?

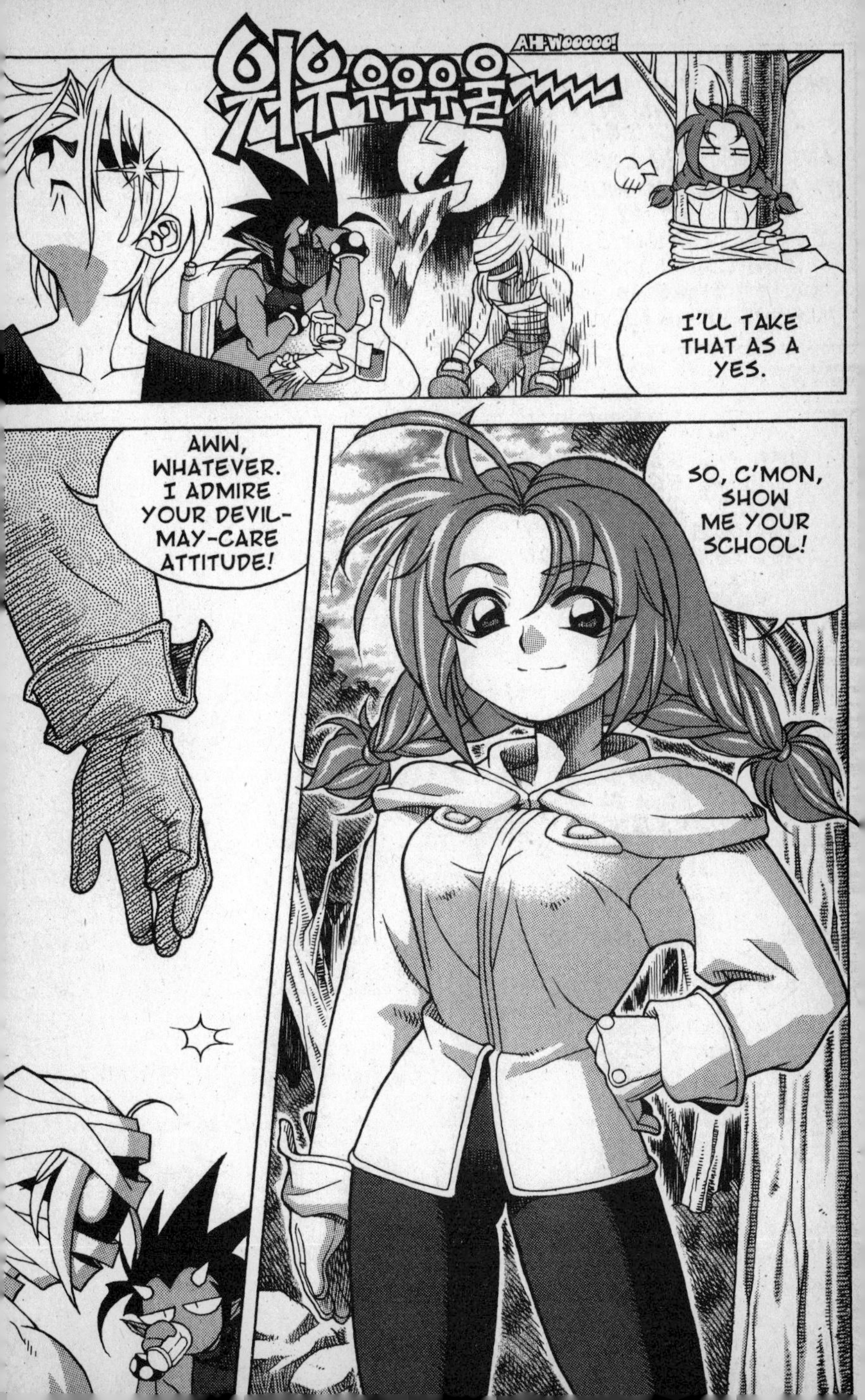
AH-WOOOOO!
I'LL TAKE THAT AS A YES.
AWW, WHATEVER. I ADMIRE YOUR DEVIL-MAY-CARE ATTITUDE!
SO, C'MON, SHOW ME YOUR SCHOOL!

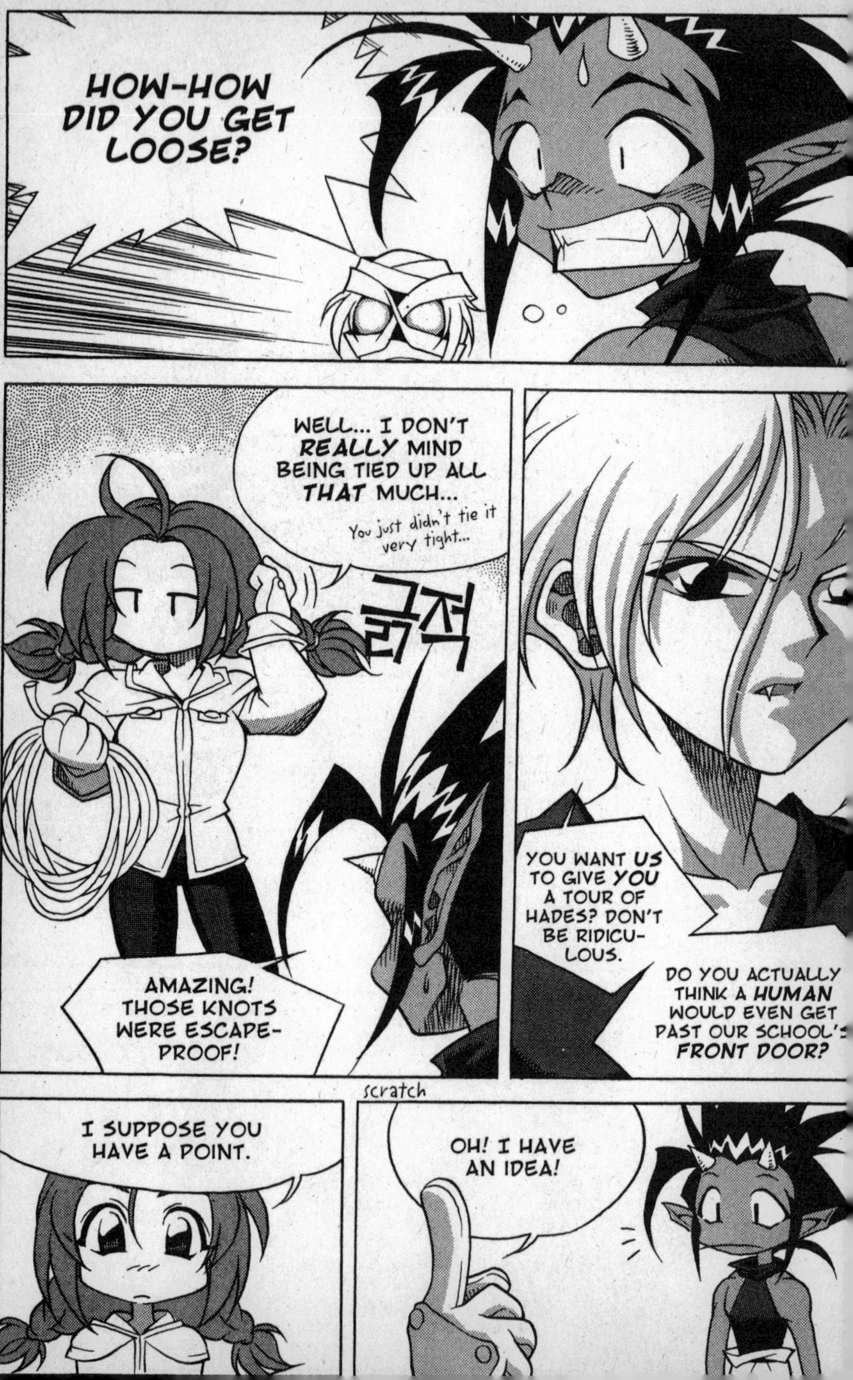
HOW-HOW DID YOU GET LOOSE?
WELL... I DON'T REALLY MIND BEING TIED UP ALL THAT MUCH...
You just didn't tie it very tight...
긁적
AMAZING! THOSE KNOTS WERE ESCAPE-PROOF!
YOU WANT US TO GIVE YOU A TOUR OF HADES? DON'T BE RIDICULOUS.
DO YOU ACTUALLY THINK A HUMAN WOULD EVEN GET PAST OUR SCHOOL'S FRONT DOOR?
scratch
I SUPPOSE YOU HAVE A POINT.
OH! I HAVE AN IDEA!

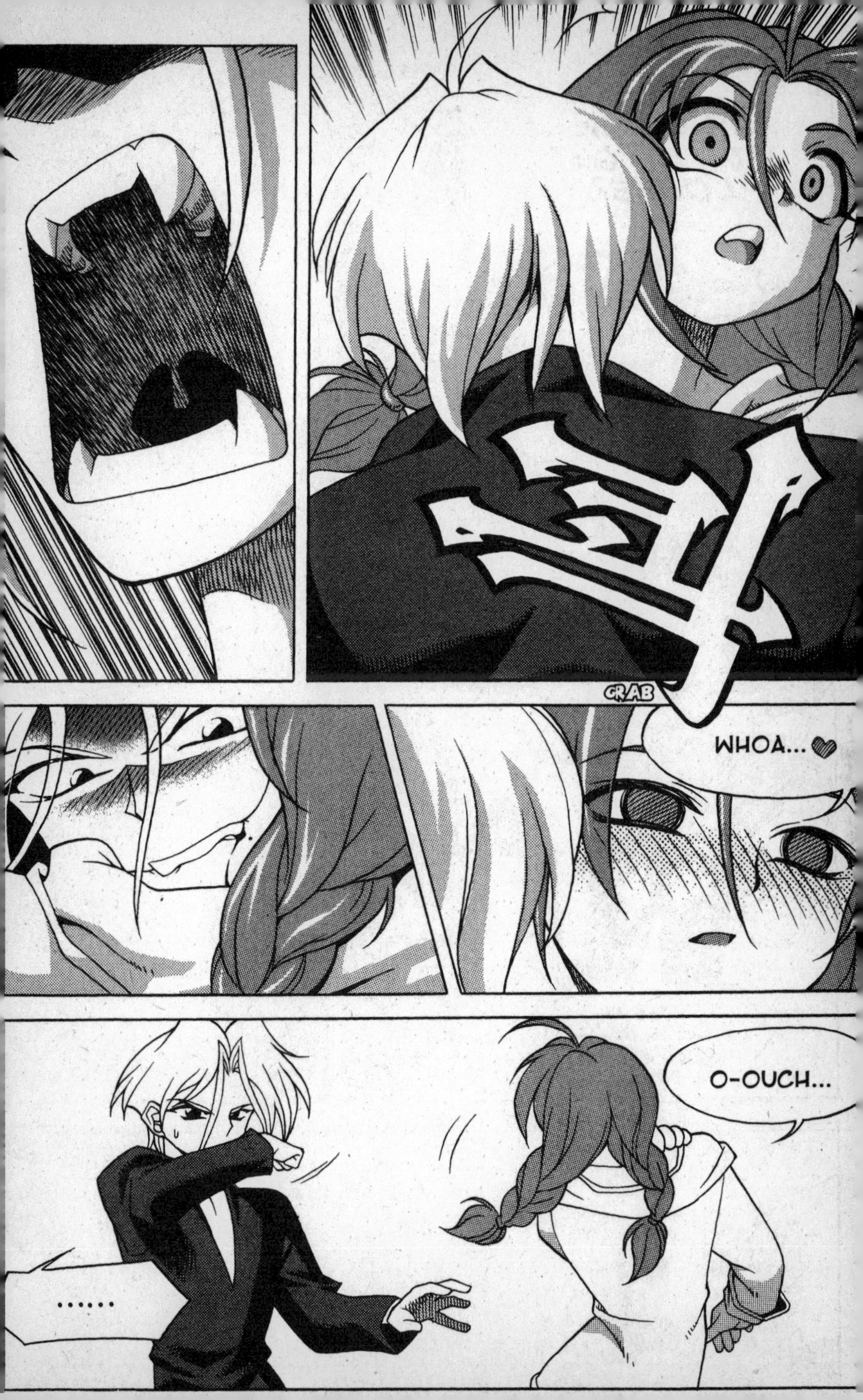
GRAB
WHOA...♥
......
O-OUCH...

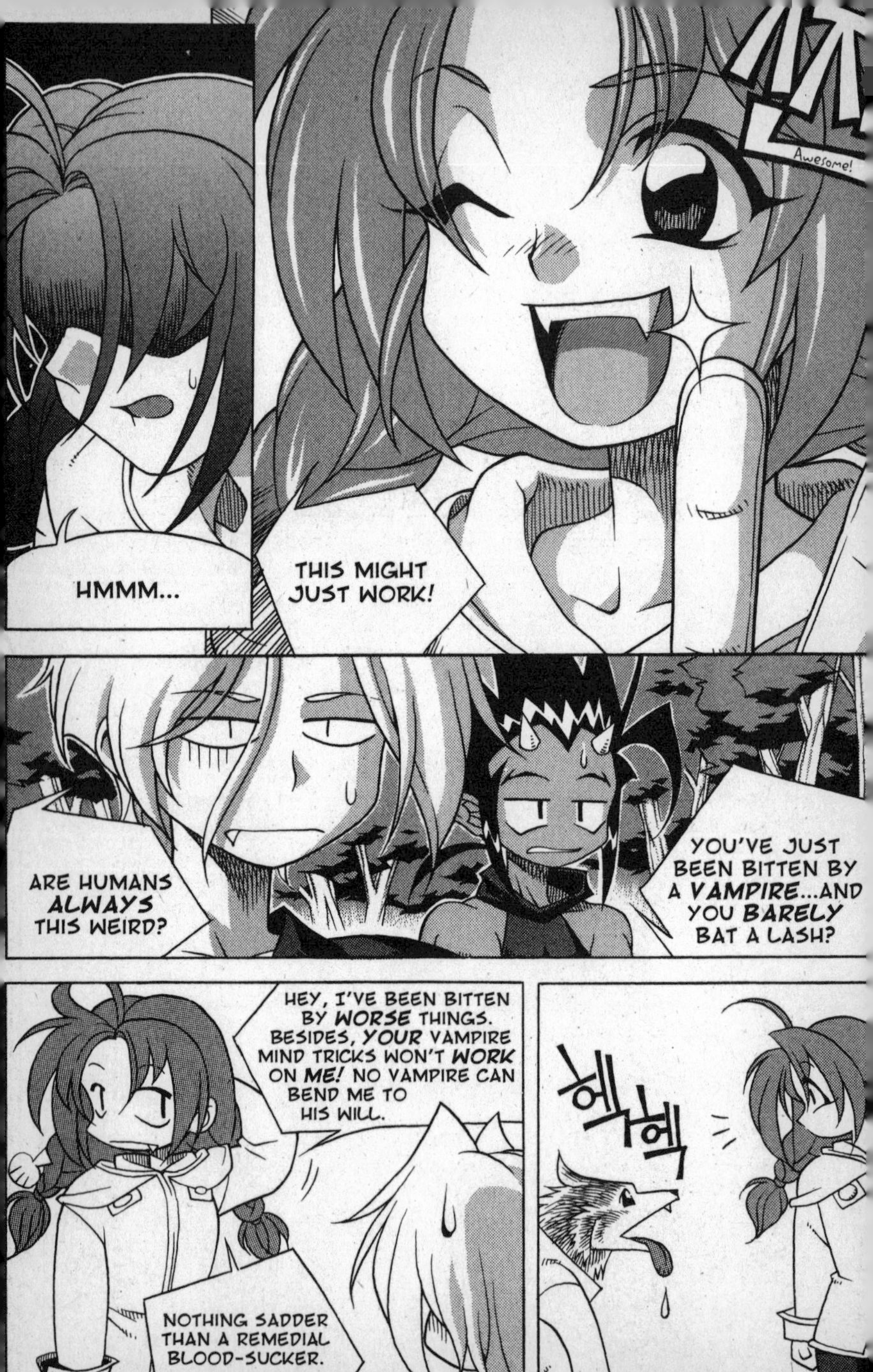
HMMM...
Awesome!
THIS MIGHT JUST WORK!
ARE HUMANS ALWAYS THIS WEIRD?
YOU'VE JUST BEEN BITTEN BY A VAMPIRE...AND YOU BARELY BAT A LASH?
HEY, I'VE BEEN BITTEN BY WORSE THINGS. BESIDES, YOUR VAMPIRE MIND TRICKS WON'T WORK ON ME! NO VAMPIRE CAN BEND ME TO HIS WILL.
NOTHING SADDER THAN A REMEDIAL BLOOD-SUCKER.
헥헥

Vampire mind tricks: Powerful vampires can make their bite victims completely subservient,

PANT PANT

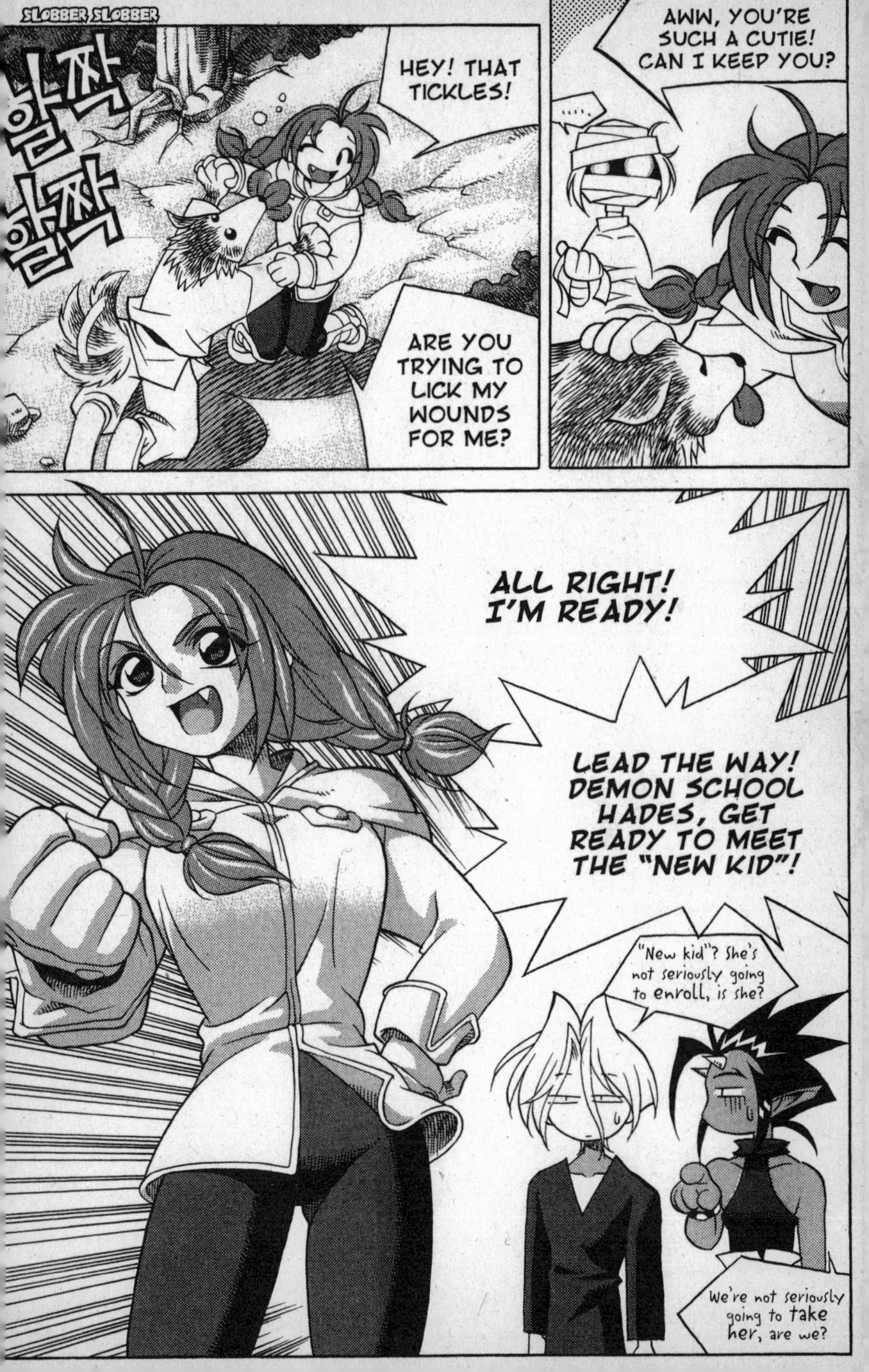
SLOBBER SLOBBER
할짝 할짝
HEY! THAT TICKLES!
ARE YOU TRYING TO LICK MY WOUNDS FOR ME?
AWW, YOU'RE SUCH A CUTIE! CAN I KEEP YOU?
....
ALL RIGHT! I'M READY!
LEAD THE WAY! DEMON SCHOOL HADES, GET READY TO MEET THE "NEW KID"!
"New kid"? She's not seriously going to enroll, is she?
We're not seriously going to take her, are we?

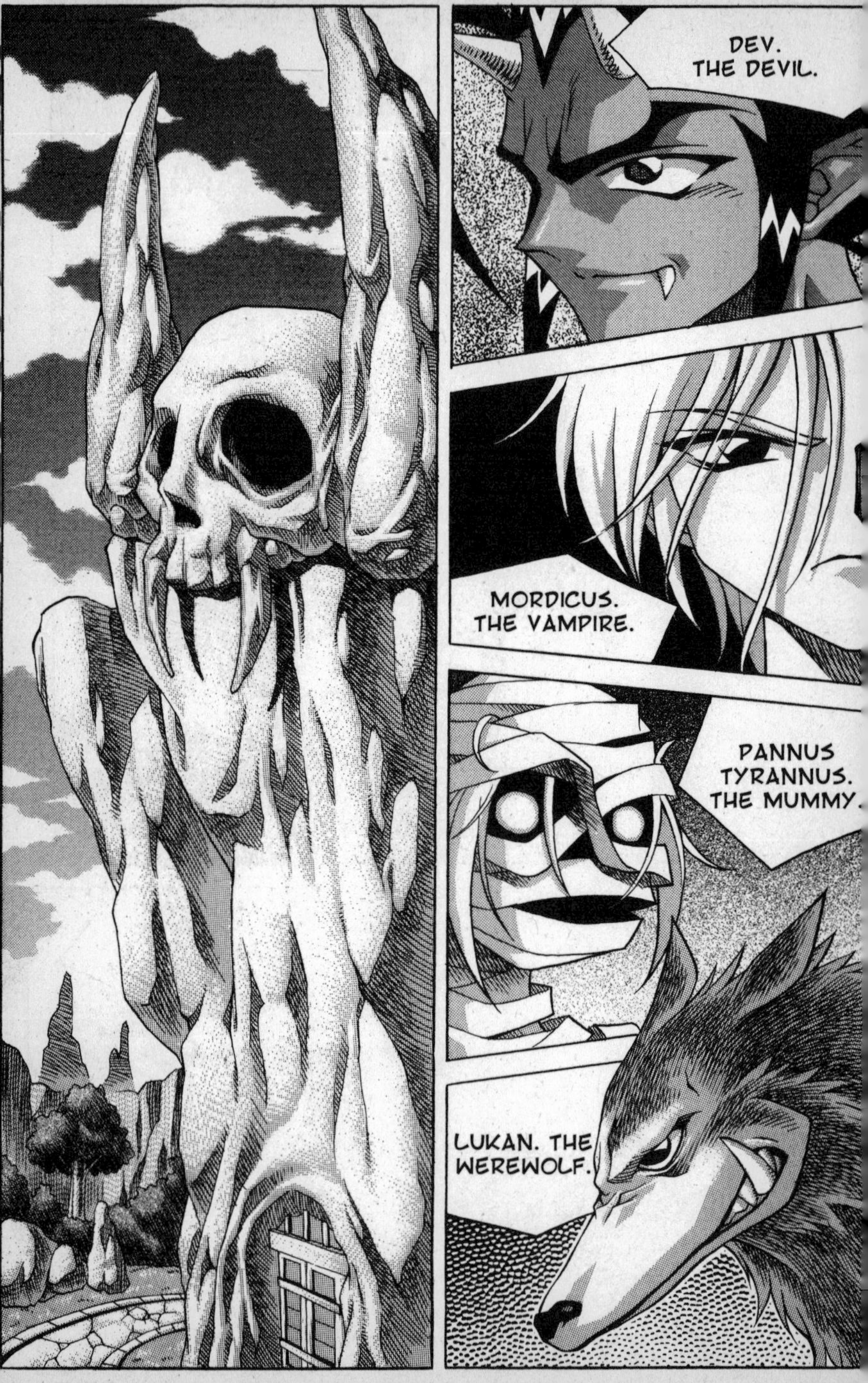
DEV. THE DEVIL.
MORDICUS. THE VAMPIRE.
PANNUS TYRANNUS. THE MUMMY.
LUKAN. THE WEREWOLF.

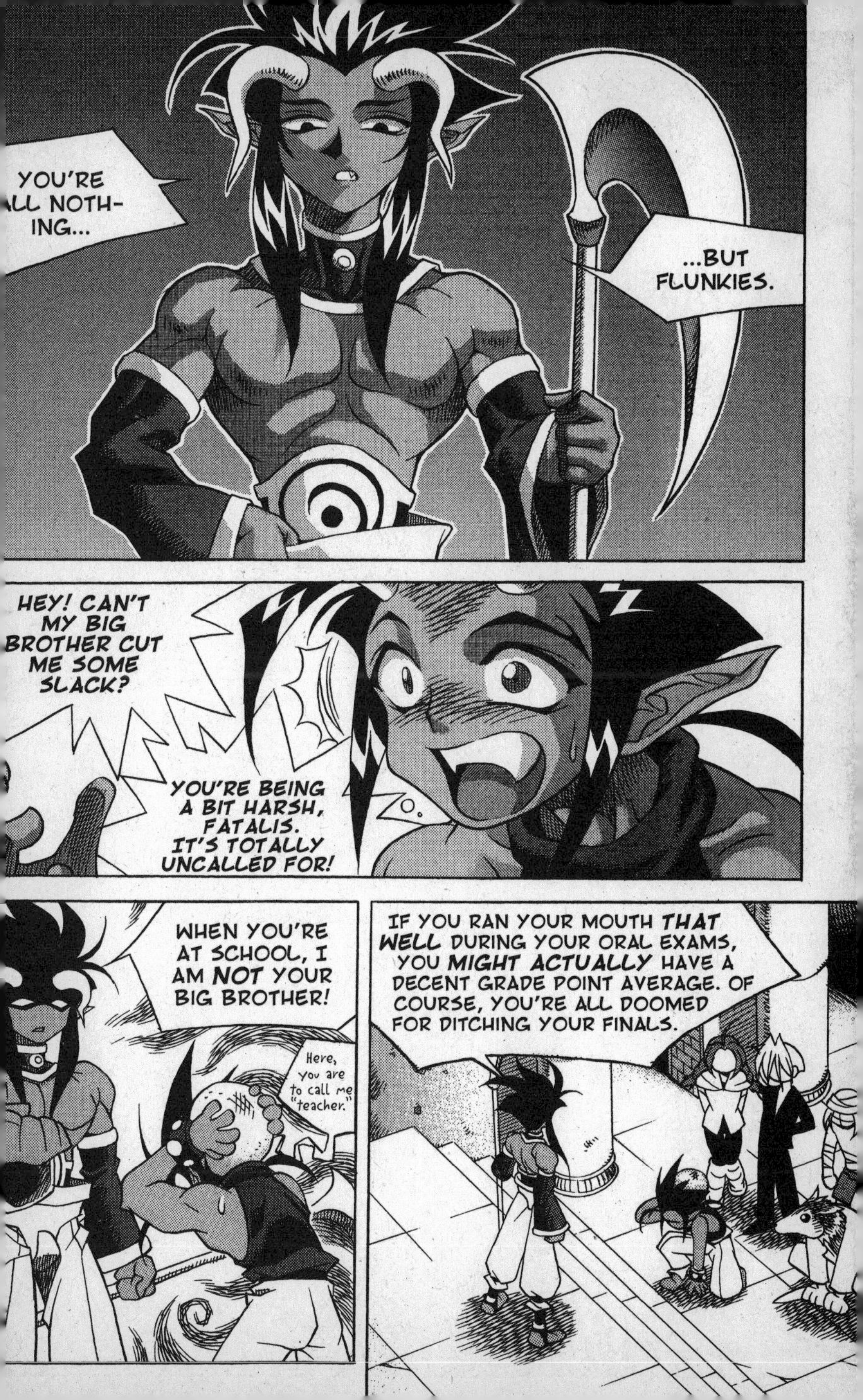
YOU'RE ALL NOTHING...
...BUT FLUNKIES.
HEY! CAN'T MY BIG BROTHER CUT ME SOME SLACK?
YOU'RE BEING A BIT HARSH, FATALIS. IT'S TOTALLY UNCALLED FOR!
WHEN YOU'RE AT SCHOOL, I AM NOT YOUR BIG BROTHER!
Here, you are to call me "teacher."
IF YOU RAN YOUR MOUTH THAT WELL DURING YOUR ORAL EXAMS, YOU MIGHT ACTUALLY HAVE A DECENT GRADE POINT AVERAGE. OF COURSE, YOU'RE ALL DOOMED FOR DITCHING YOUR FINALS.

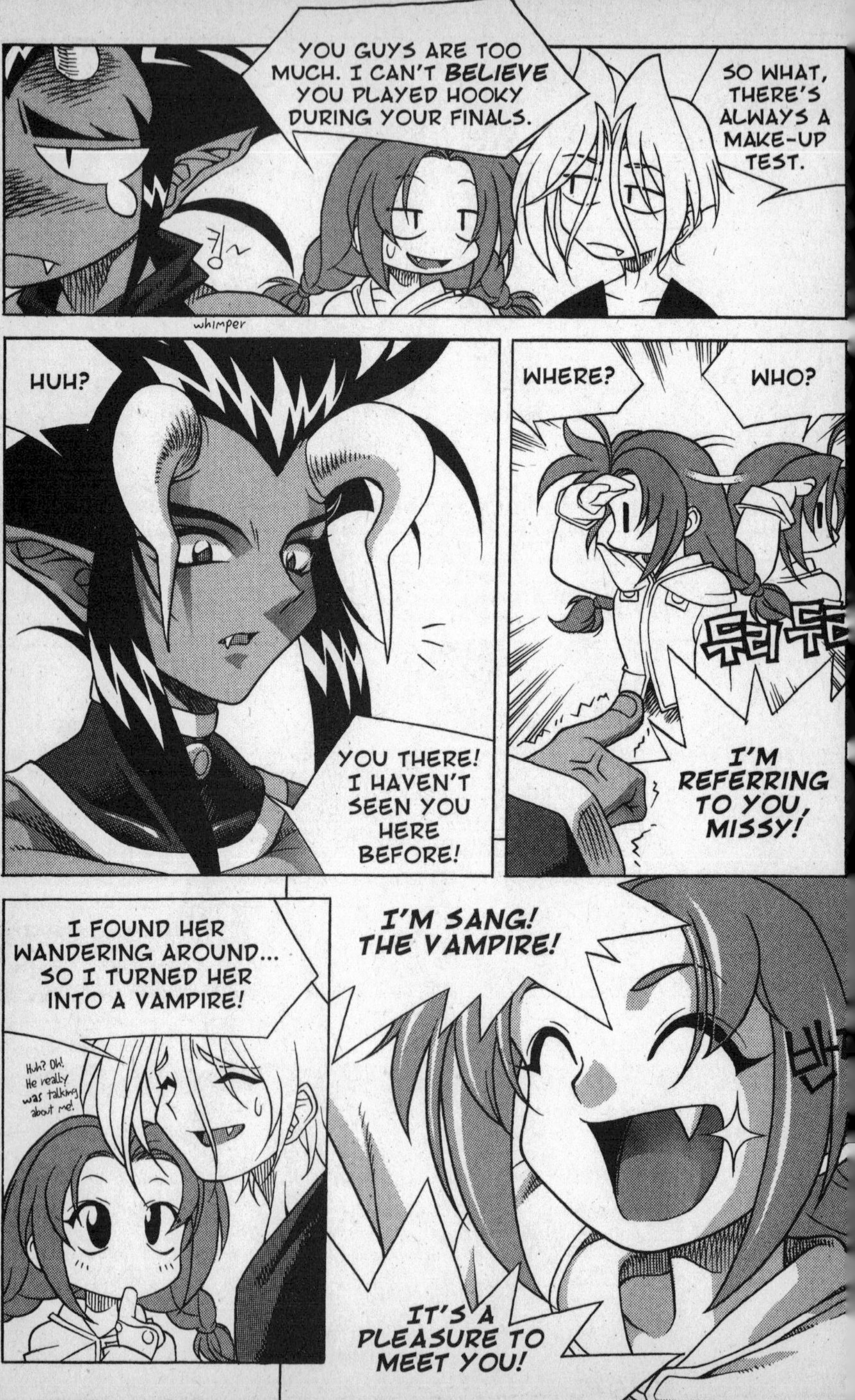
YOU GUYS ARE TOO MUCH. I CAN'T *BELIEVE* YOU PLAYED HOOKY DURING YOUR FINALS.
SO WHAT, THERE'S ALWAYS A MAKE-UP TEST.
whimper
HUH?
YOU THERE! I HAVEN'T SEEN YOU HERE BEFORE!
WHERE?
WHO?
I'M REFERRING TO YOU, MISSY!
I FOUND HER WANDERING AROUND... SO I TURNED HER INTO A VAMPIRE!
Huh? Oh! He really was talking about me!
I'M SANG! THE VAMPIRE!
IT'S A PLEASURE TO MEET YOU!

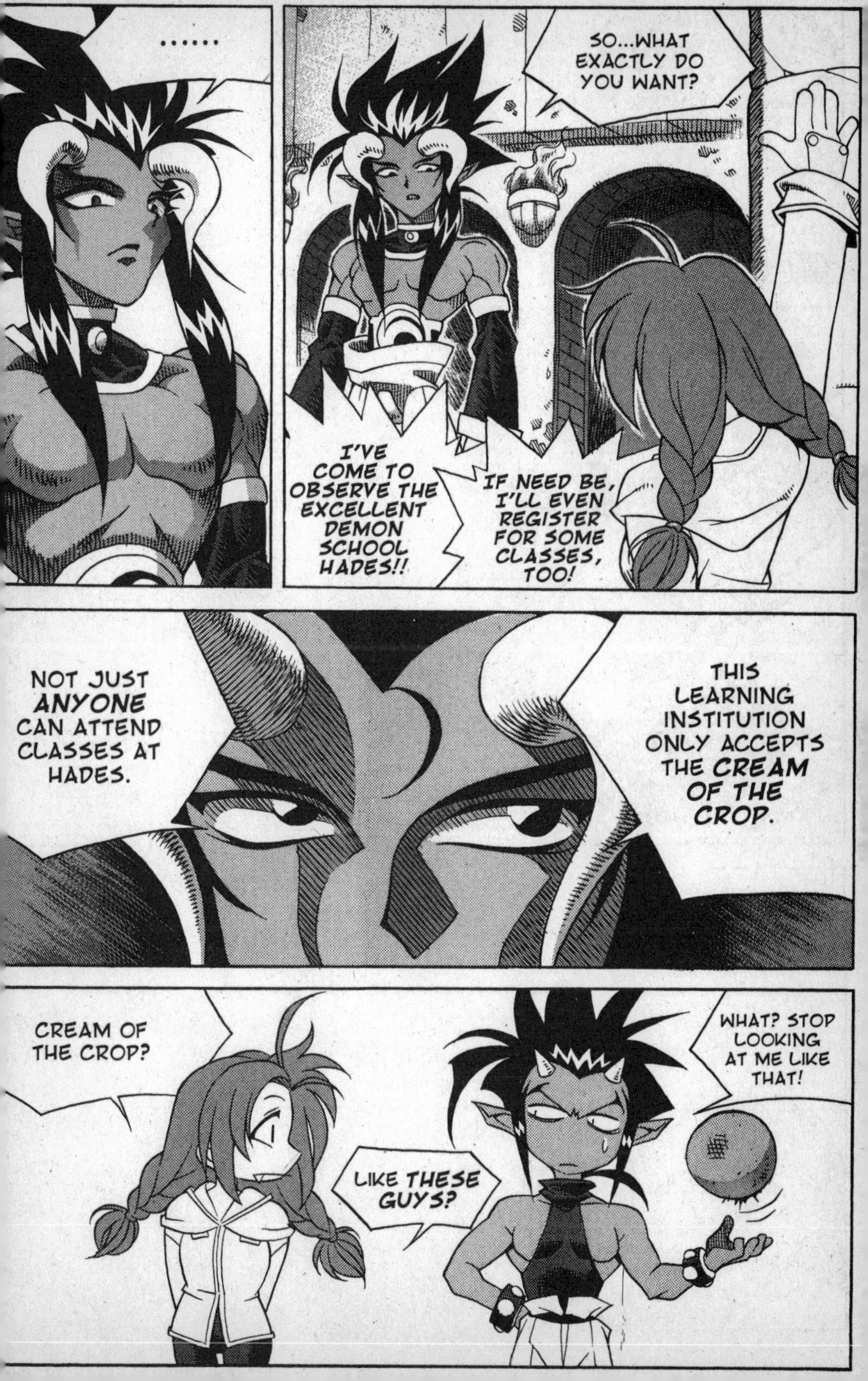
......
SO...WHAT EXACTLY DO YOU WANT?
I'VE COME TO OBSERVE THE EXCELLENT DEMON SCHOOL HADES!!
IF NEED BE, I'LL EVEN REGISTER FOR SOME CLASSES, TOO!
NOT JUST ANYONE CAN ATTEND CLASSES AT HADES.
THIS LEARNING INSTITUTION ONLY ACCEPTS THE CREAM OF THE CROP.
CREAM OF THE CROP?
LIKE THESE GUYS?
WHAT? STOP LOOKING AT ME LIKE THAT!

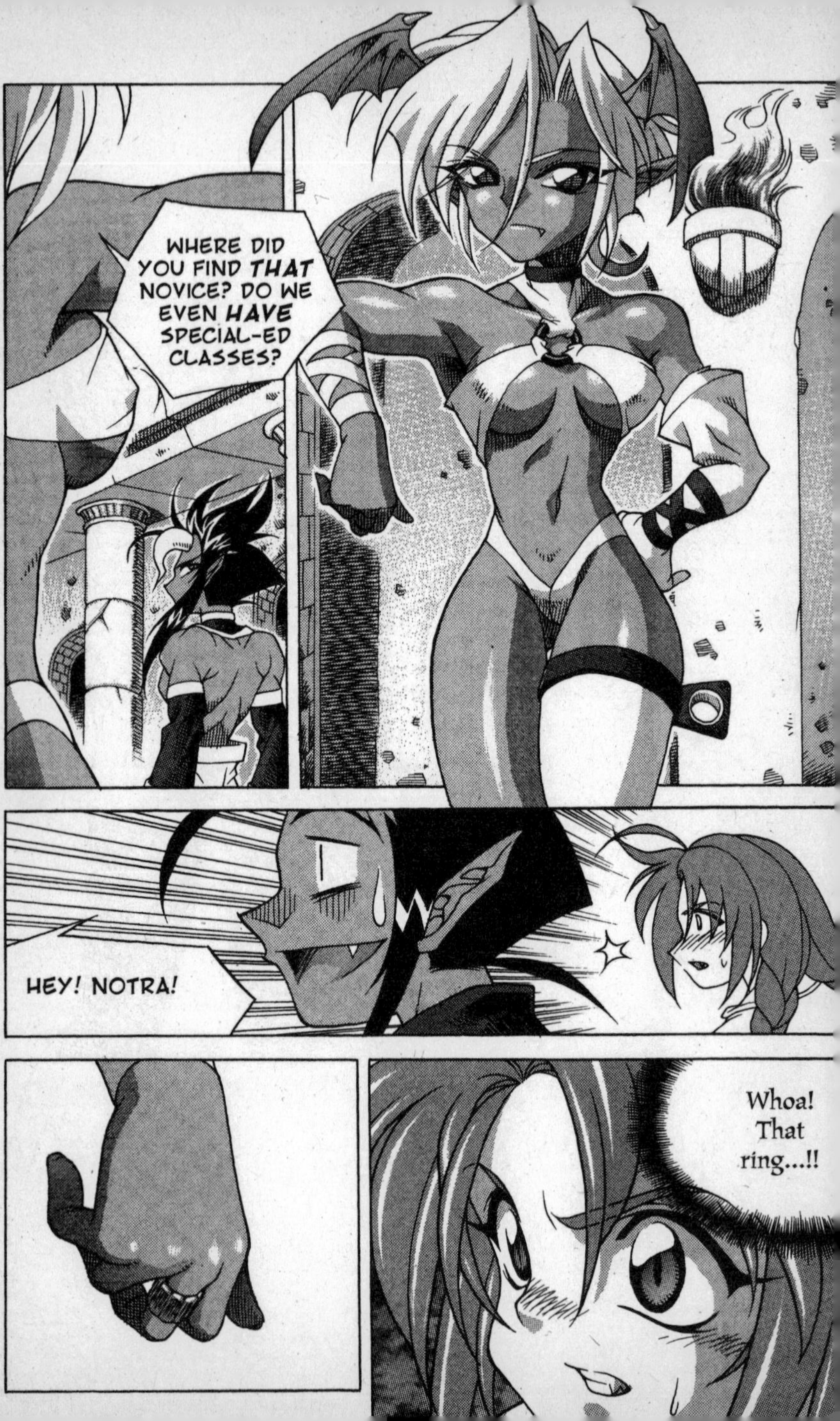
WHERE DID YOU FIND THAT NOVICE? DO WE EVEN HAVE SPECIAL-ED CLASSES?
HEY! NOTRA!
Whoa! That ring...!!

Quest 2

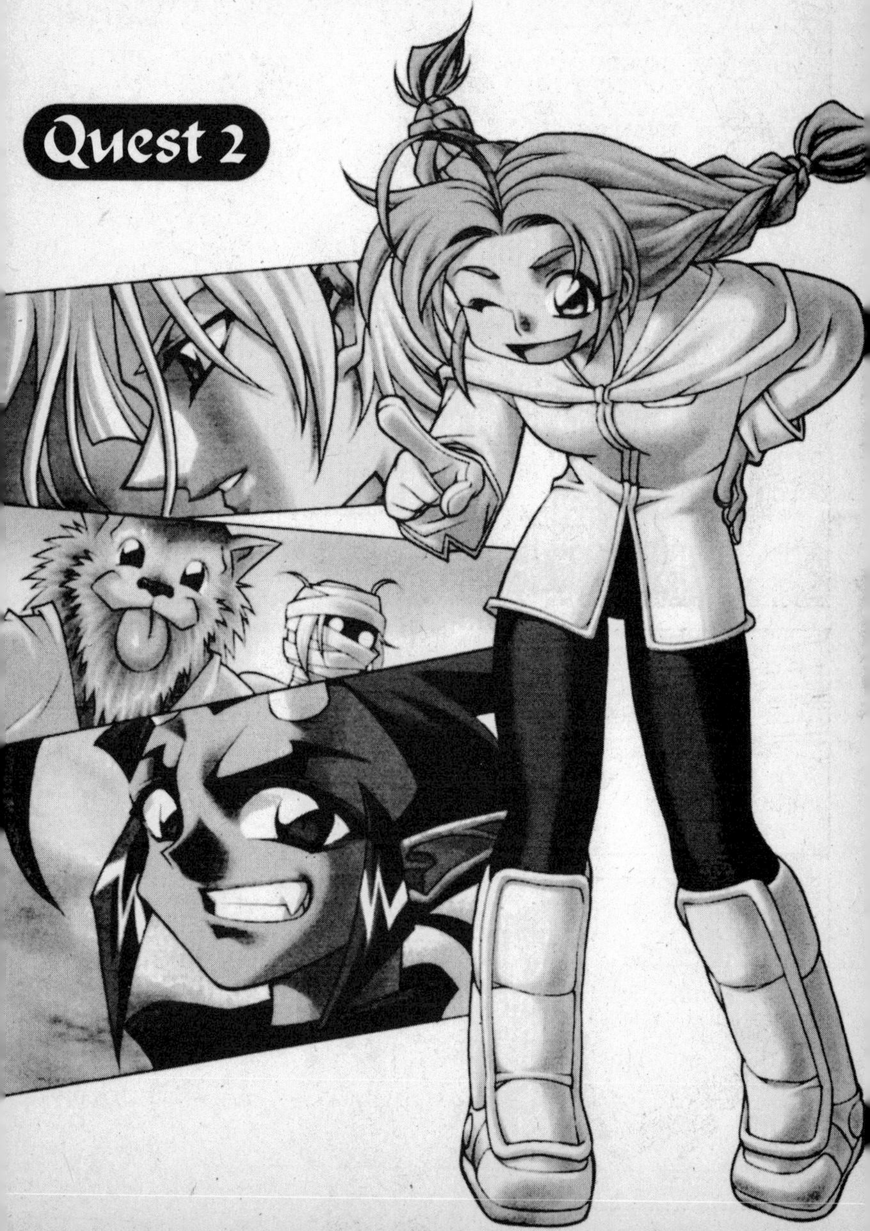

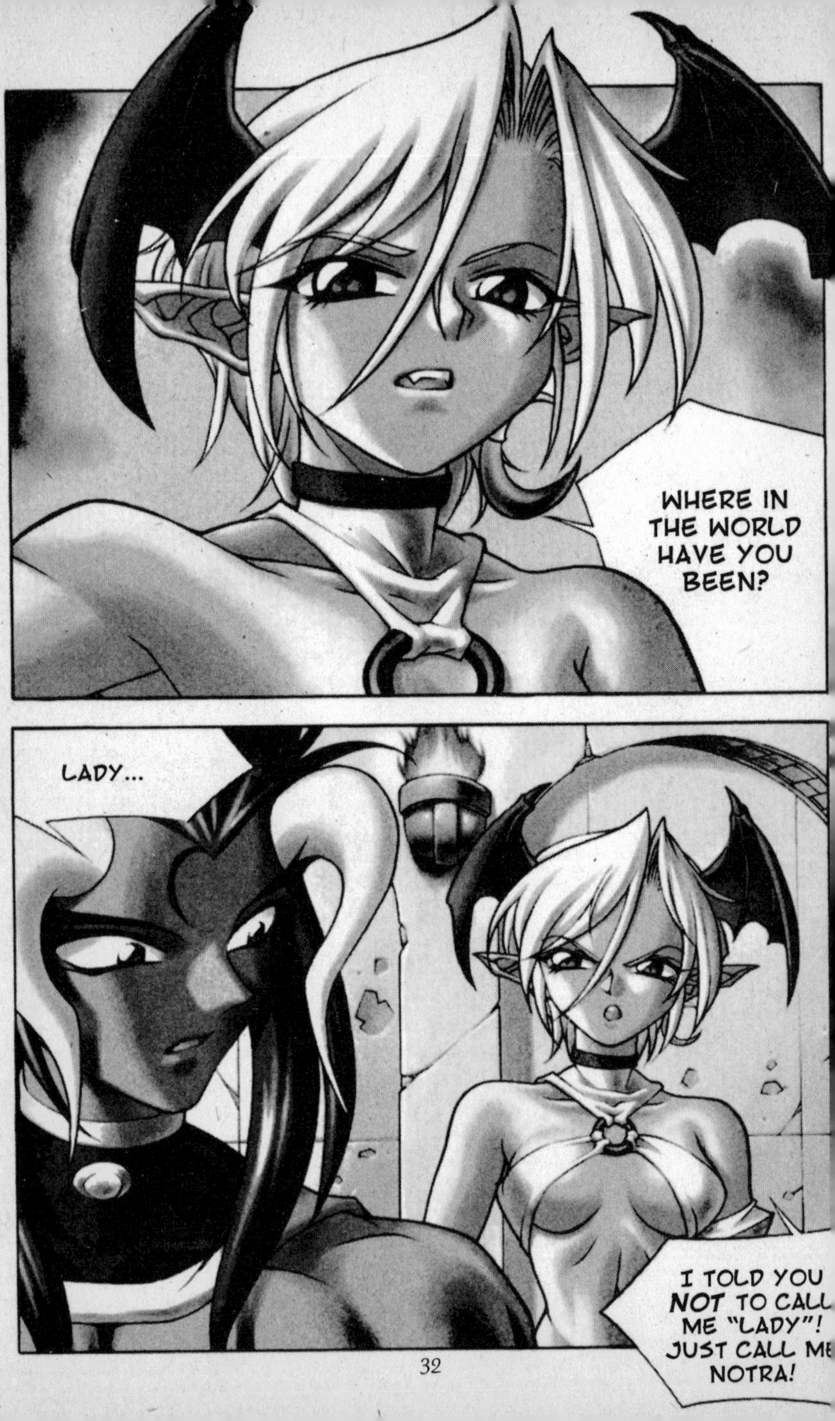
WHERE IN THE WORLD HAVE YOU BEEN?
LADY...
I TOLD YOU *NOT* TO CALL ME "LADY"! JUST CALL ME NOTRA!

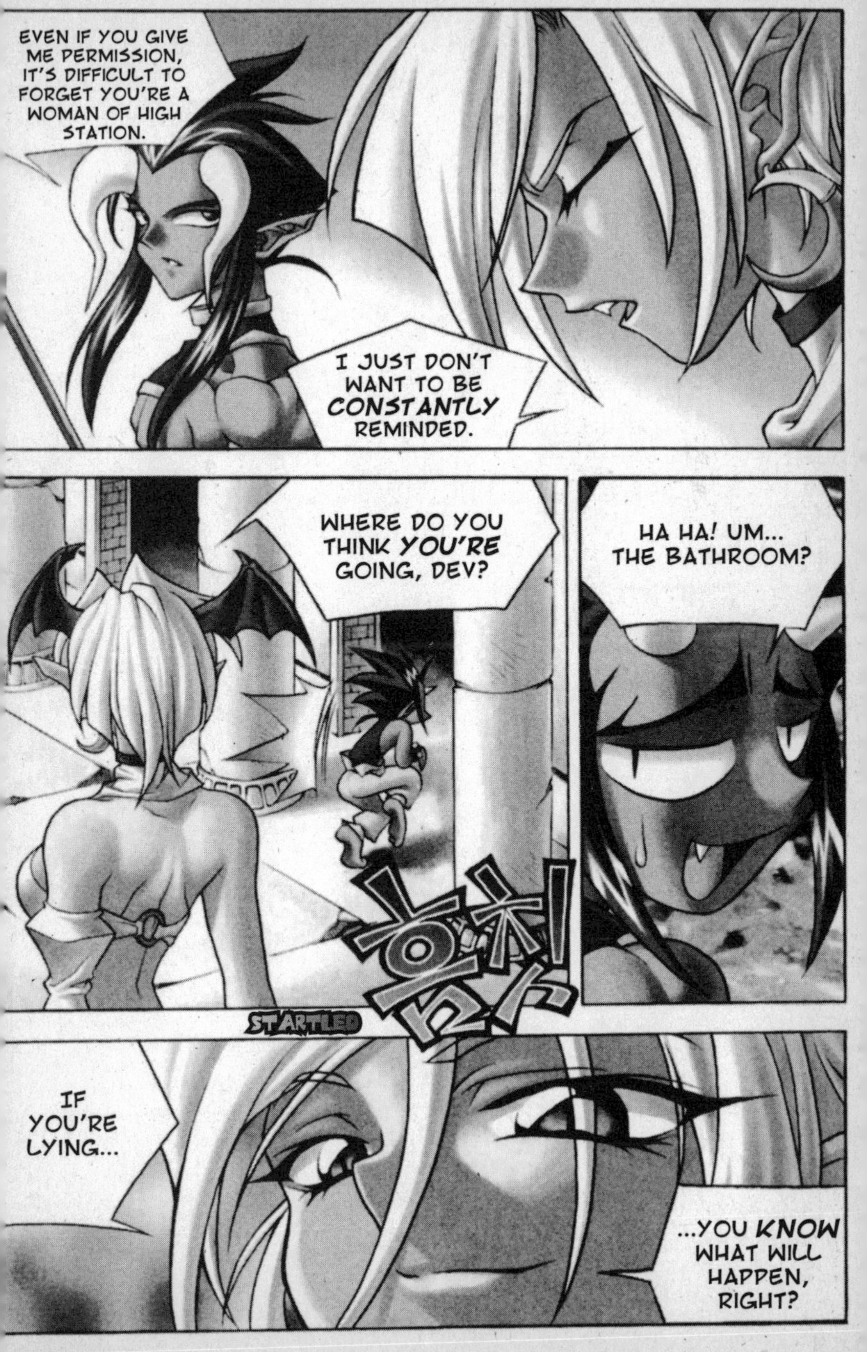
EVEN IF YOU GIVE ME PERMISSION, IT'S DIFFICULT TO FORGET YOU'RE A WOMAN OF HIGH STATION.
I JUST DON'T WANT TO BE CONSTANTLY REMINDED.
WHERE DO YOU THINK YOU'RE GOING, DEV?
HA HA! UM... THE BATHROOM?
STARTLED
IF YOU'RE LYING...
...YOU KNOW WHAT WILL HAPPEN, RIGHT?

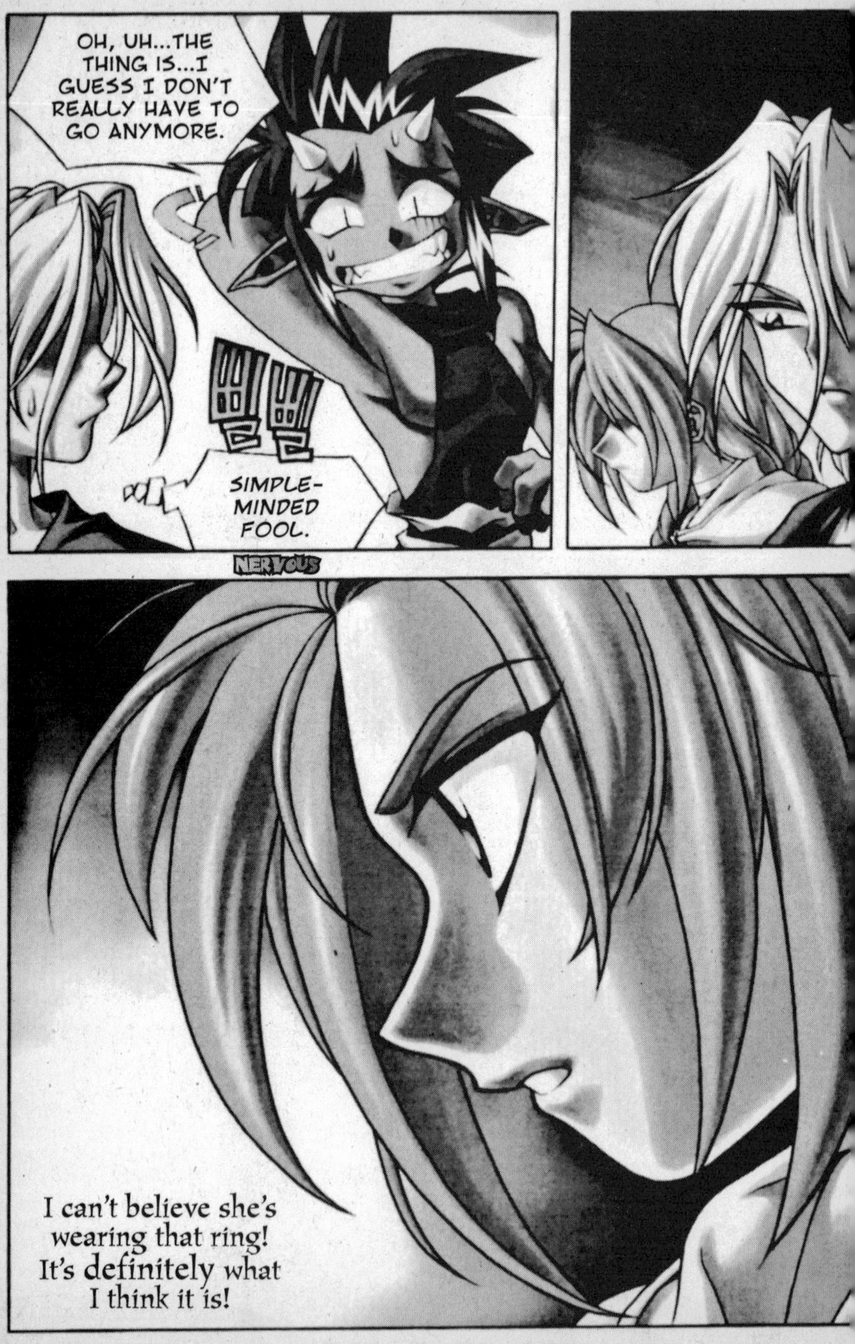
OH, UH...THE THING IS...I GUESS I DON'T REALLY HAVE TO GO ANYMORE.
SIMPLE-MINDED FOOL.
NERVOUS
I can't believe she's wearing that ring! It's definitely what I think it is!

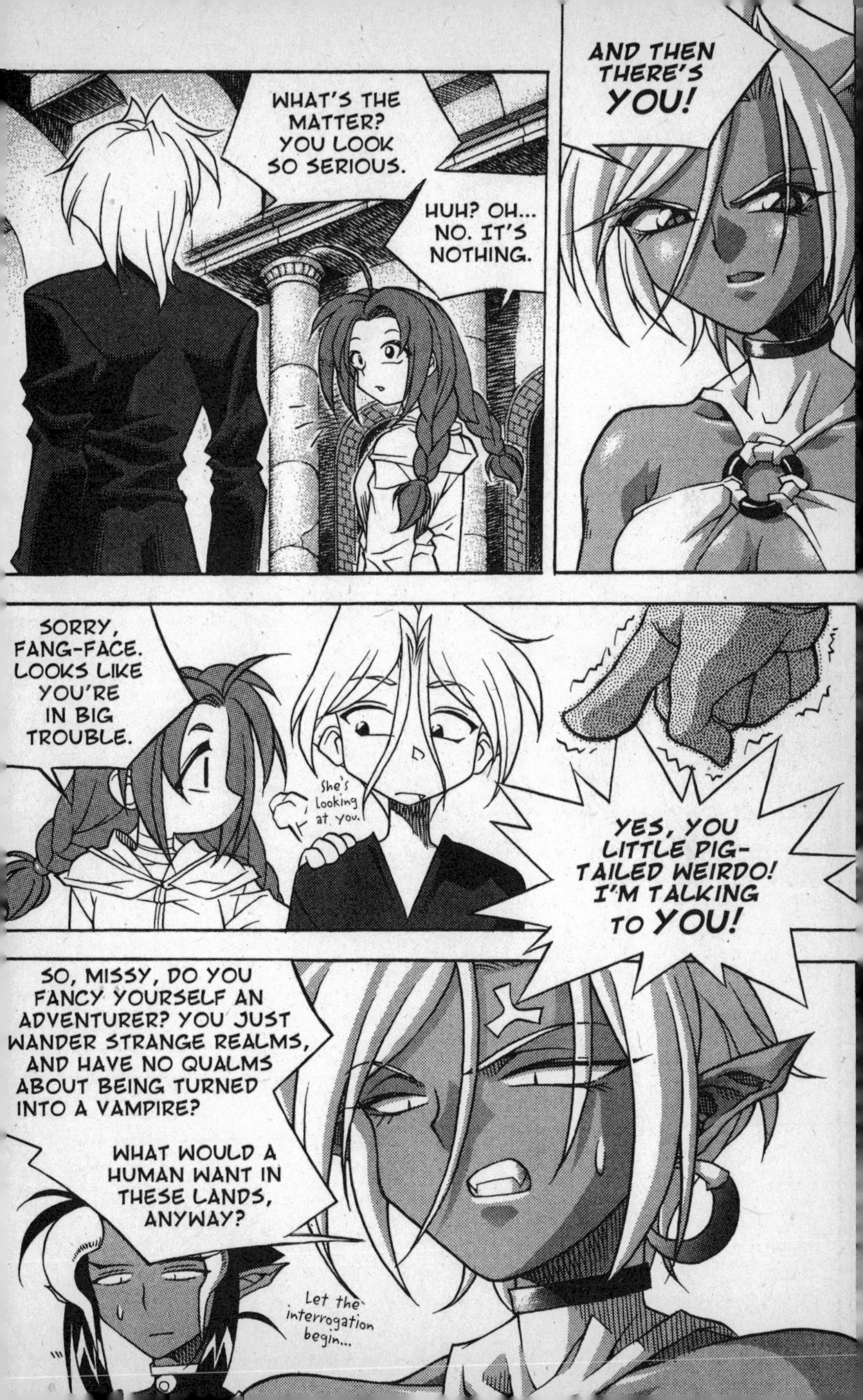

WHAT'S THE MATTER? YOU LOOK SO SERIOUS.
HUH? OH... NO. IT'S NOTHING.
AND THEN THERE'S YOU!
SORRY, FANG-FACE. LOOKS LIKE YOU'RE IN BIG TROUBLE.
She's looking at you.
YES, YOU LITTLE PIG-TAILED WEIRDO! I'M TALKING TO YOU!
SO, MISSY, DO YOU FANCY YOURSELF AN ADVENTURER? YOU JUST WANDER STRANGE REALMS, AND HAVE NO QUALMS ABOUT BEING TURNED INTO A VAMPIRE?
WHAT WOULD A HUMAN WANT IN THESE LANDS, ANYWAY?
Let the interrogation begin...

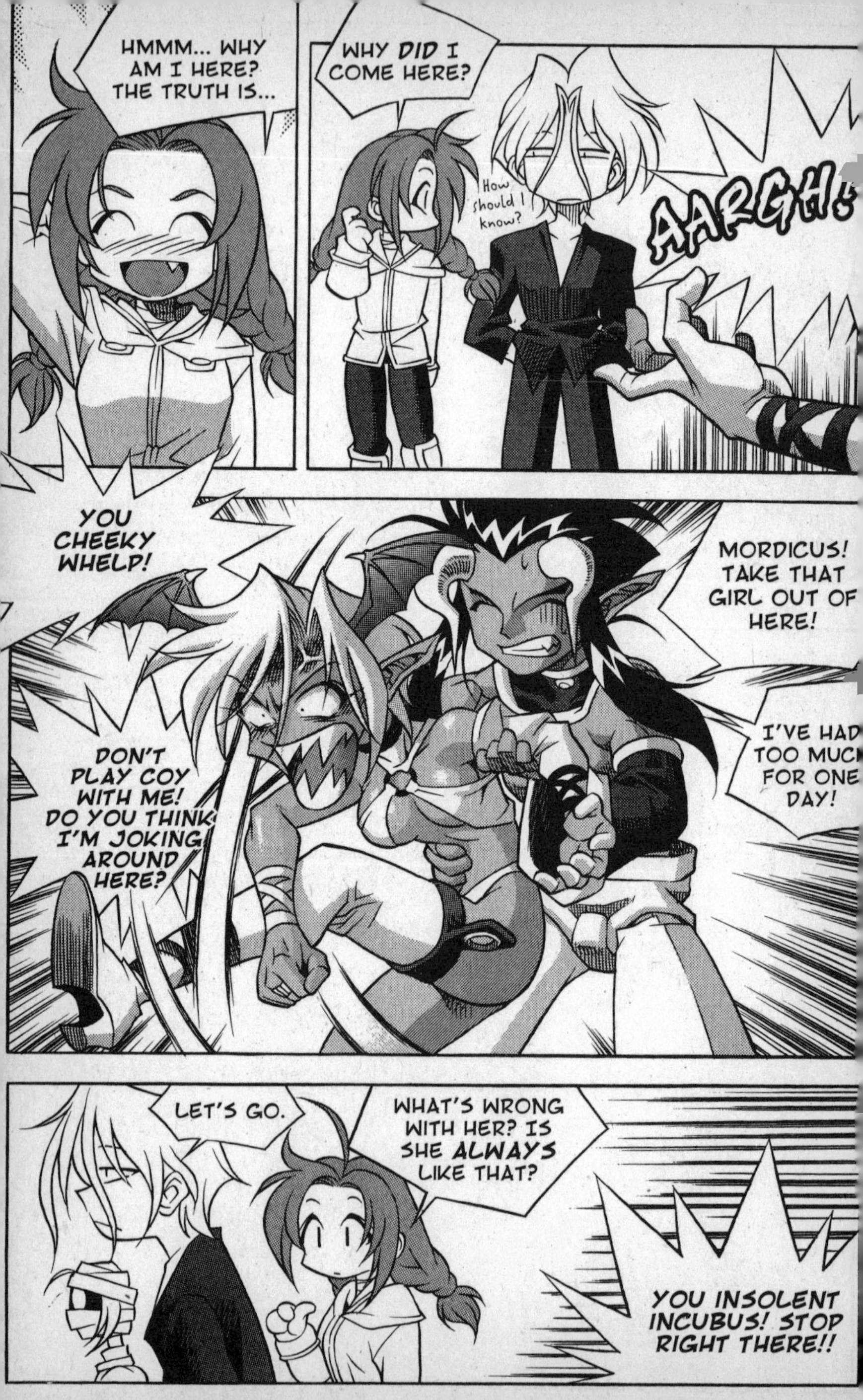
HMMM... WHY AM I HERE? THE TRUTH IS...
WHY DID I COME HERE?
How should I know?
AARGH!
YOU CHEEKY WHELP!
MORDICUS! TAKE THAT GIRL OUT OF HERE!
DON'T PLAY COY WITH ME! DO YOU THINK I'M JOKING AROUND HERE?
I'VE HAD TOO MUCH FOR ONE DAY!
LET'S GO.
WHAT'S WRONG WITH HER? IS SHE ALWAYS LIKE THAT?
YOU INSOLENT INCUBUS! STOP RIGHT THERE!!

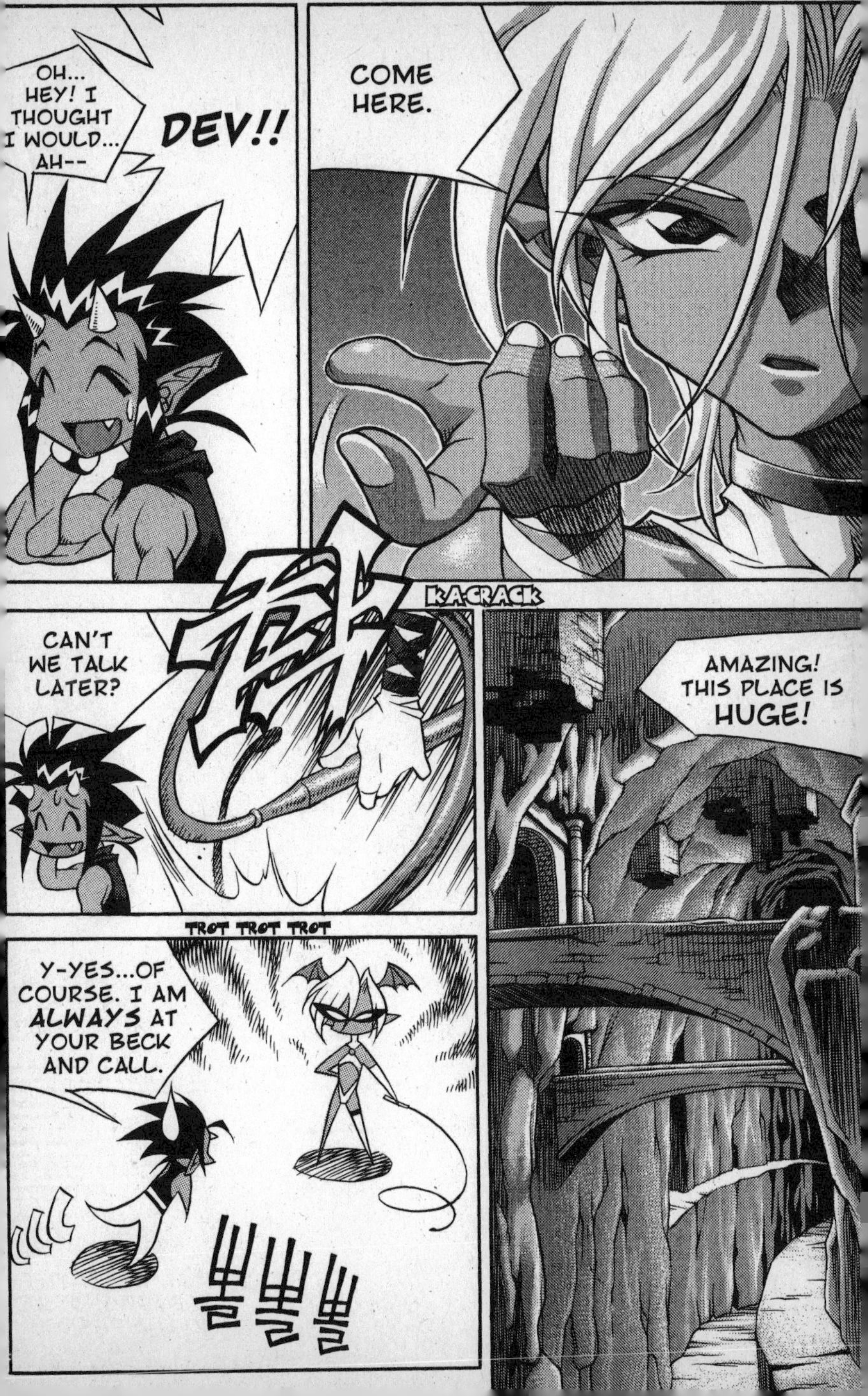
OH... HEY! I THOUGHT I WOULD... AH--
DEV!!
COME HERE.
KA-CRACK
CAN'T WE TALK LATER?
TROT TROT TROT
Y-YES...OF COURSE. I AM ALWAYS AT YOUR BECK AND CALL.
AMAZING! THIS PLACE IS HUGE!

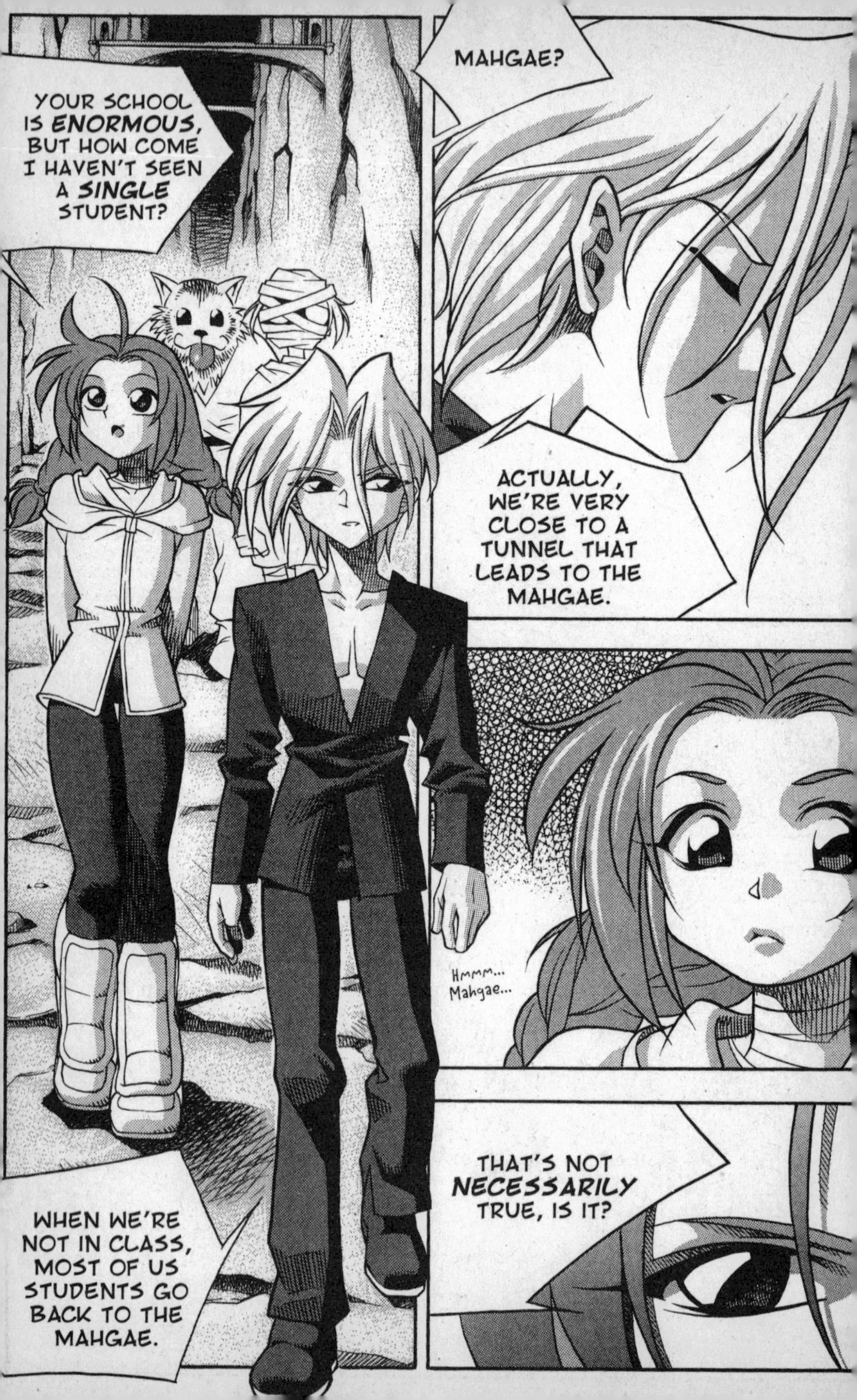
YOUR SCHOOL IS ENORMOUS, BUT HOW COME I HAVEN'T SEEN A SINGLE STUDENT?
WHEN WE'RE NOT IN CLASS, MOST OF US STUDENTS GO BACK TO THE MAHGAE.
MAHGAE?
ACTUALLY, WE'RE VERY CLOSE TO A TUNNEL THAT LEADS TO THE MAHGAE.
Hmmm... Mahgae...
THAT'S NOT NECESSARILY TRUE, IS IT?

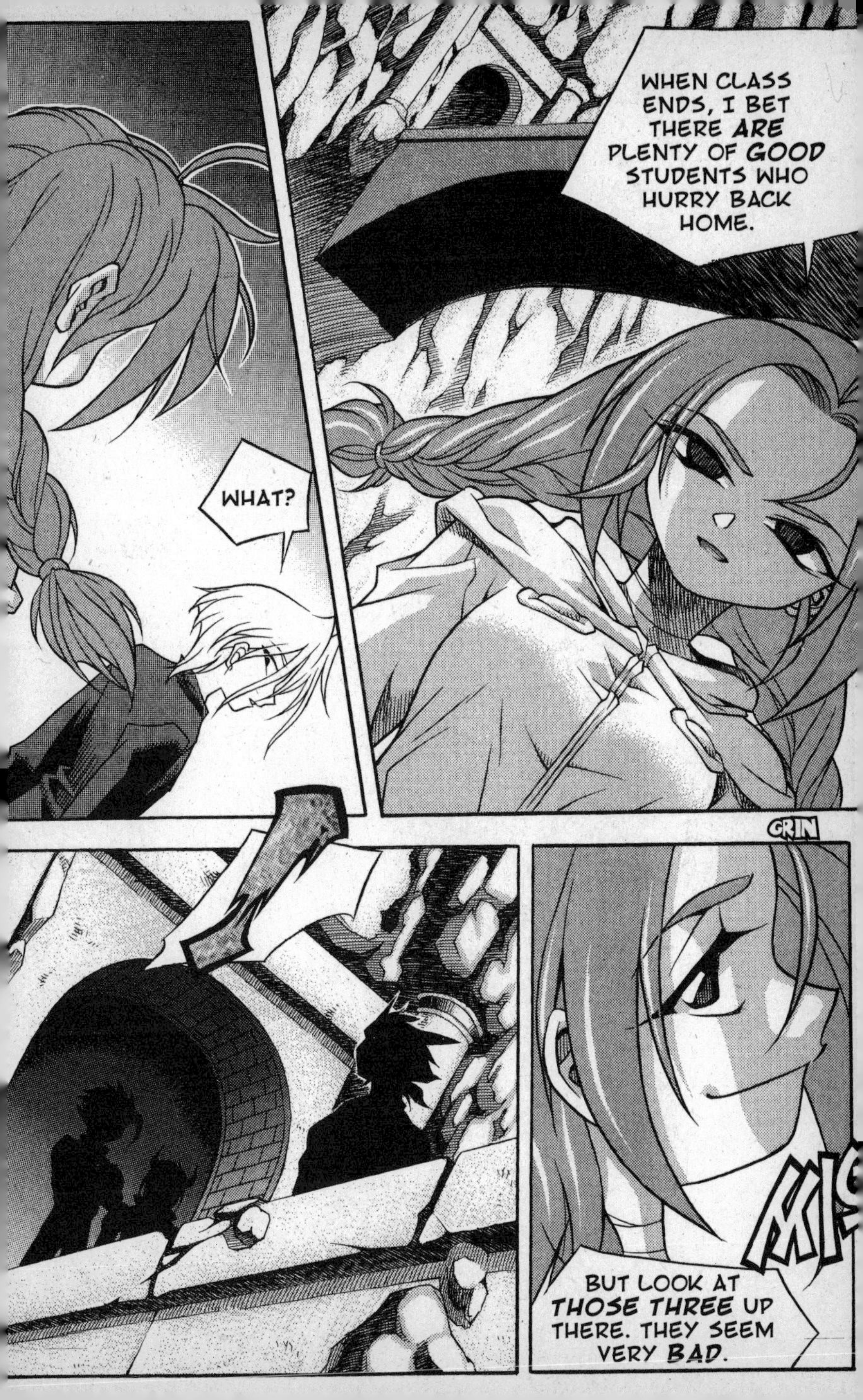
WHAT?
WHEN CLASS ENDS, I BET THERE ARE PLENTY OF GOOD STUDENTS WHO HURRY BACK HOME.
GRIN
BUT LOOK AT THOSE THREE UP THERE. THEY SEEM VERY BAD.

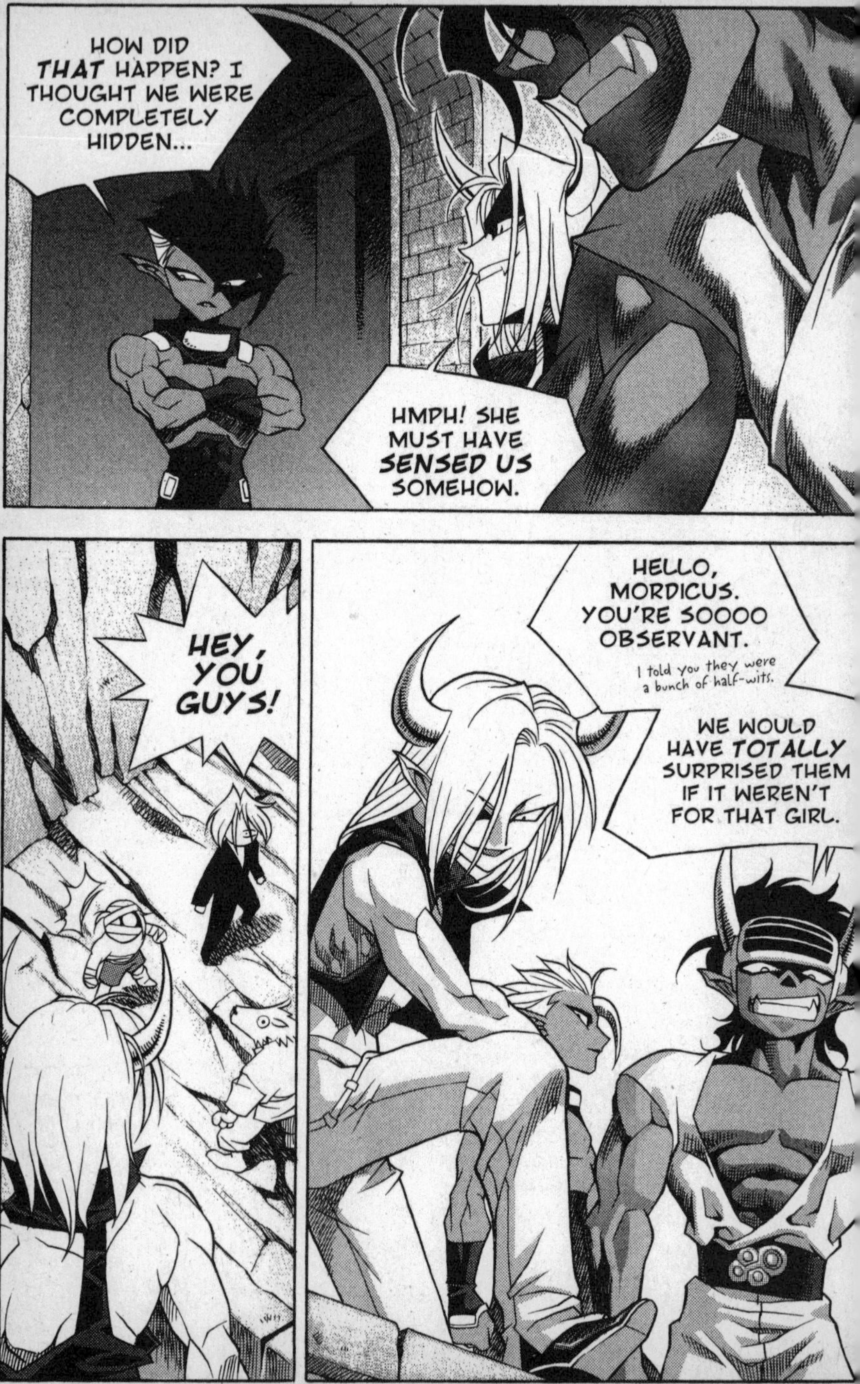
HOW DID THAT HAPPEN? I THOUGHT WE WERE COMPLETELY HIDDEN...
HMPH! SHE MUST HAVE SENSED US SOMEHOW.
HEY, YOU GUYS!
HELLO, MORDICUS. YOU'RE SOOOO OBSERVANT.
I told you they were a bunch of half-wits.
WE WOULD HAVE TOTALLY SURPRISED THEM IF IT WEREN'T FOR THAT GIRL.

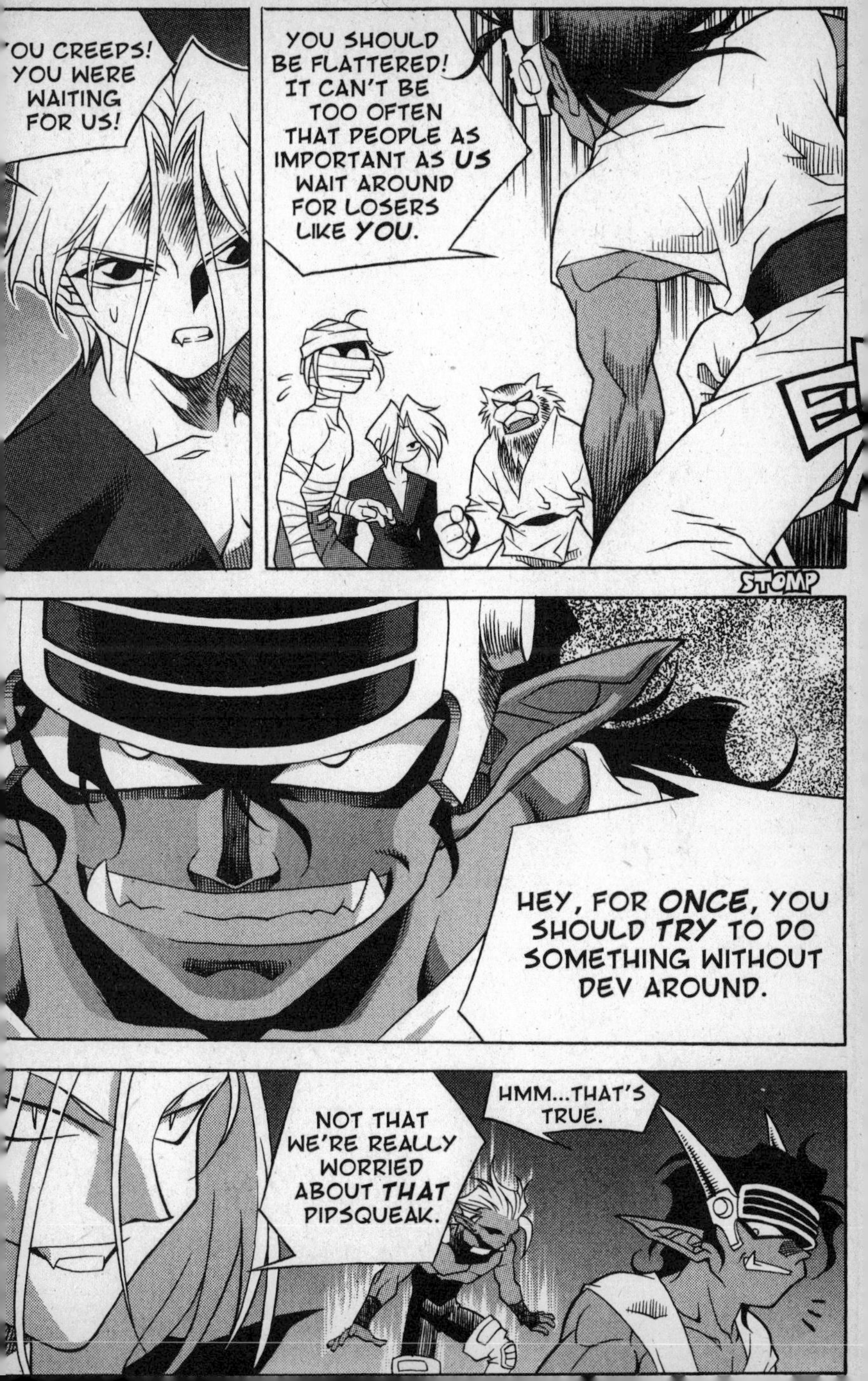
'OU CREEPS! YOU WERE WAITING FOR US!
YOU SHOULD BE FLATTERED! IT CAN'T BE TOO OFTEN THAT PEOPLE AS IMPORTANT AS US WAIT AROUND FOR LOSERS LIKE YOU.
STOMP
HEY, FOR ONCE, YOU SHOULD TRY TO DO SOMETHING WITHOUT DEV AROUND.
NOT THAT WE'RE REALLY WORRIED ABOUT THAT PIPSQUEAK.
HMM...THAT'S TRUE.

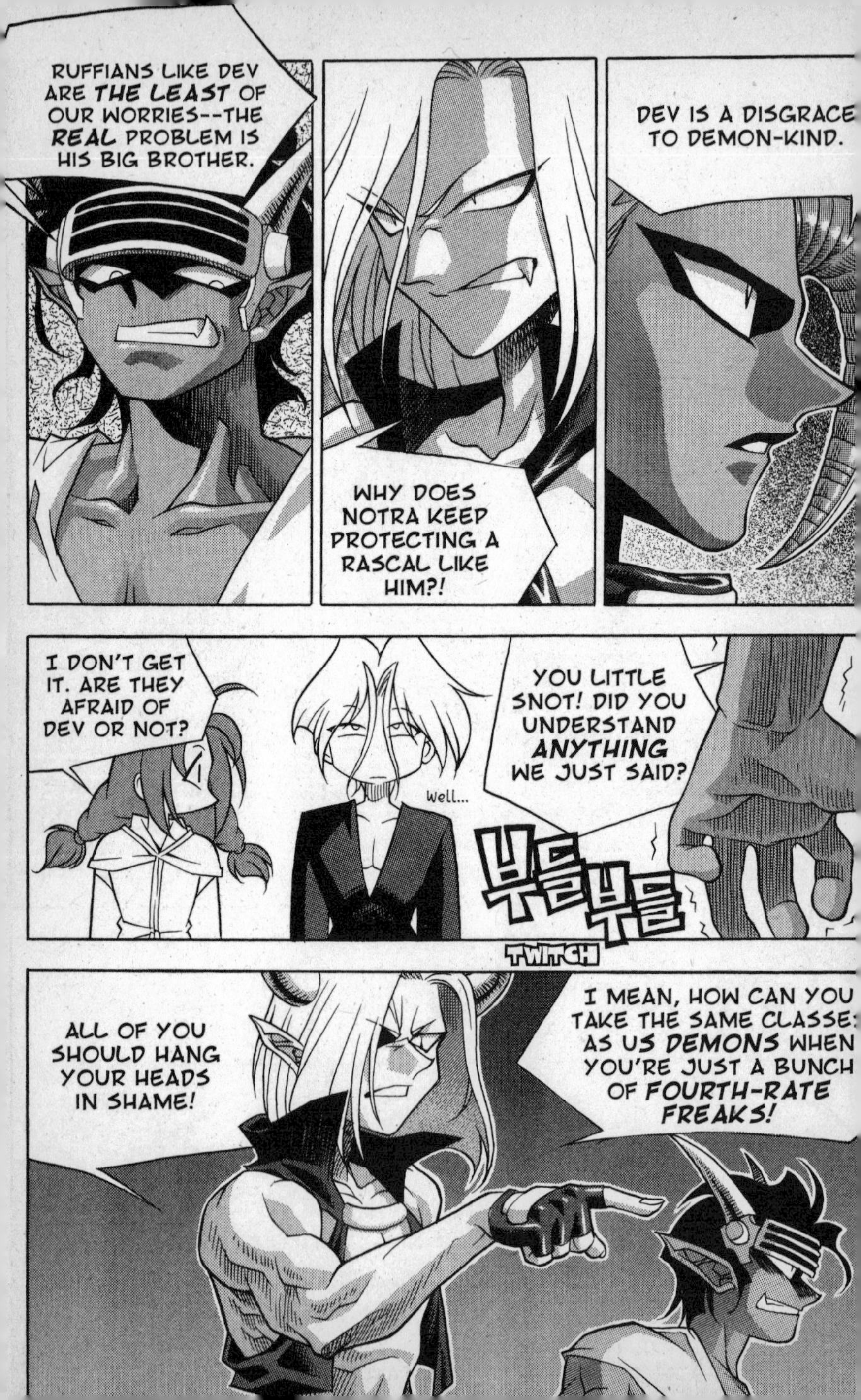
RUFFIANS LIKE DEV ARE *THE LEAST* OF OUR WORRIES--THE *REAL* PROBLEM IS HIS BIG BROTHER.
WHY DOES NOTRA KEEP PROTECTING A RASCAL LIKE HIM?!
DEV IS A DISGRACE TO DEMON-KIND.
I DON'T GET IT. ARE THEY AFRAID OF DEV OR NOT?
Well...
YOU LITTLE SNOT! DID YOU UNDERSTAND *ANYTHING* WE JUST SAID?
TWITCH
ALL OF YOU SHOULD HANG YOUR HEADS IN SHAME!
I MEAN, HOW CAN YOU TAKE THE SAME CLASSES AS US *DEMONS* WHEN YOU'RE JUST A BUNCH OF *FOURTH-RATE FREAKS!*

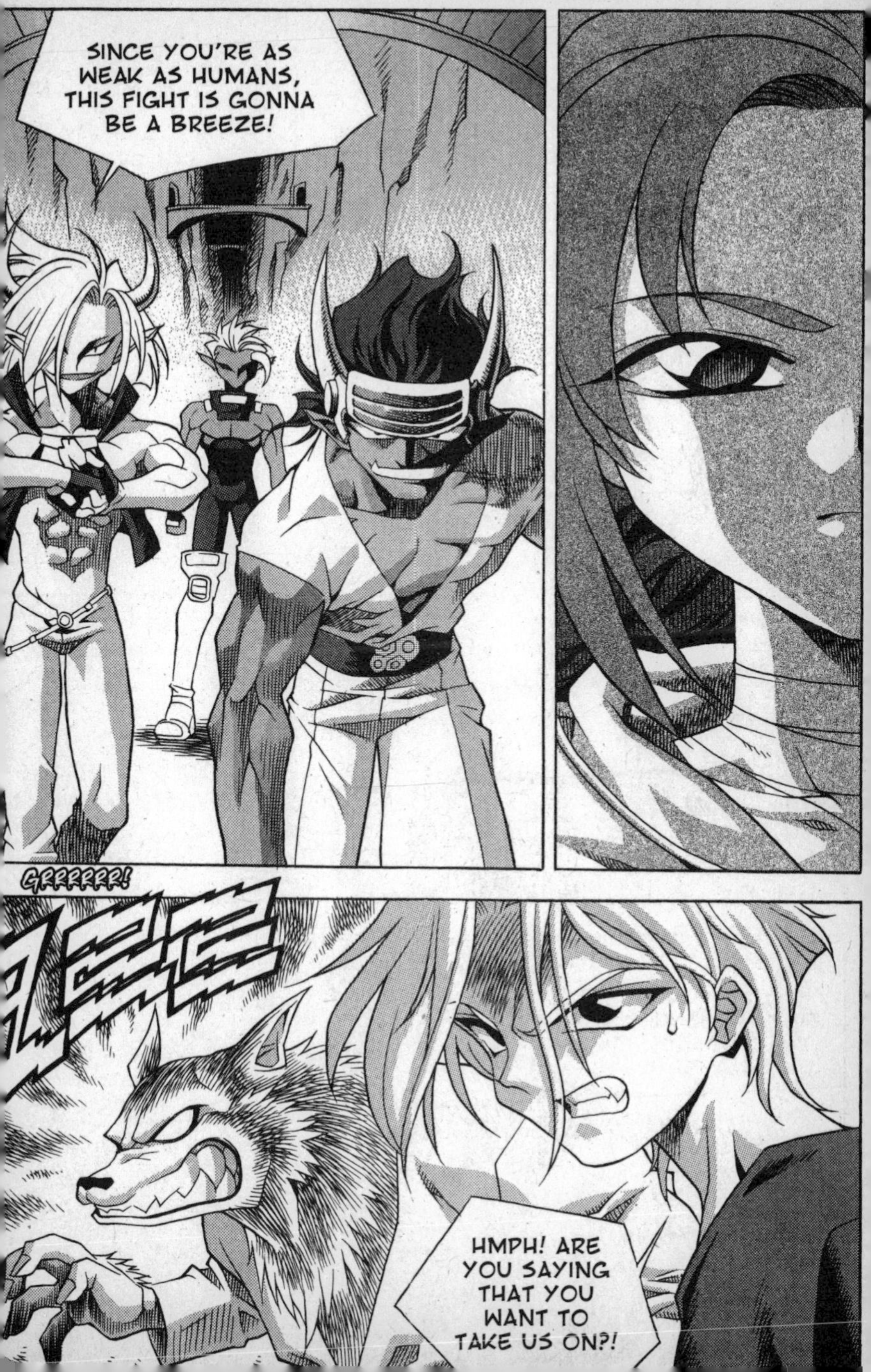
SINCE YOU'RE AS WEAK AS HUMANS, THIS FIGHT IS GONNA BE A BREEZE!
GRRRRRR!
HMPH! ARE YOU SAYING THAT YOU WANT TO TAKE US ON?!

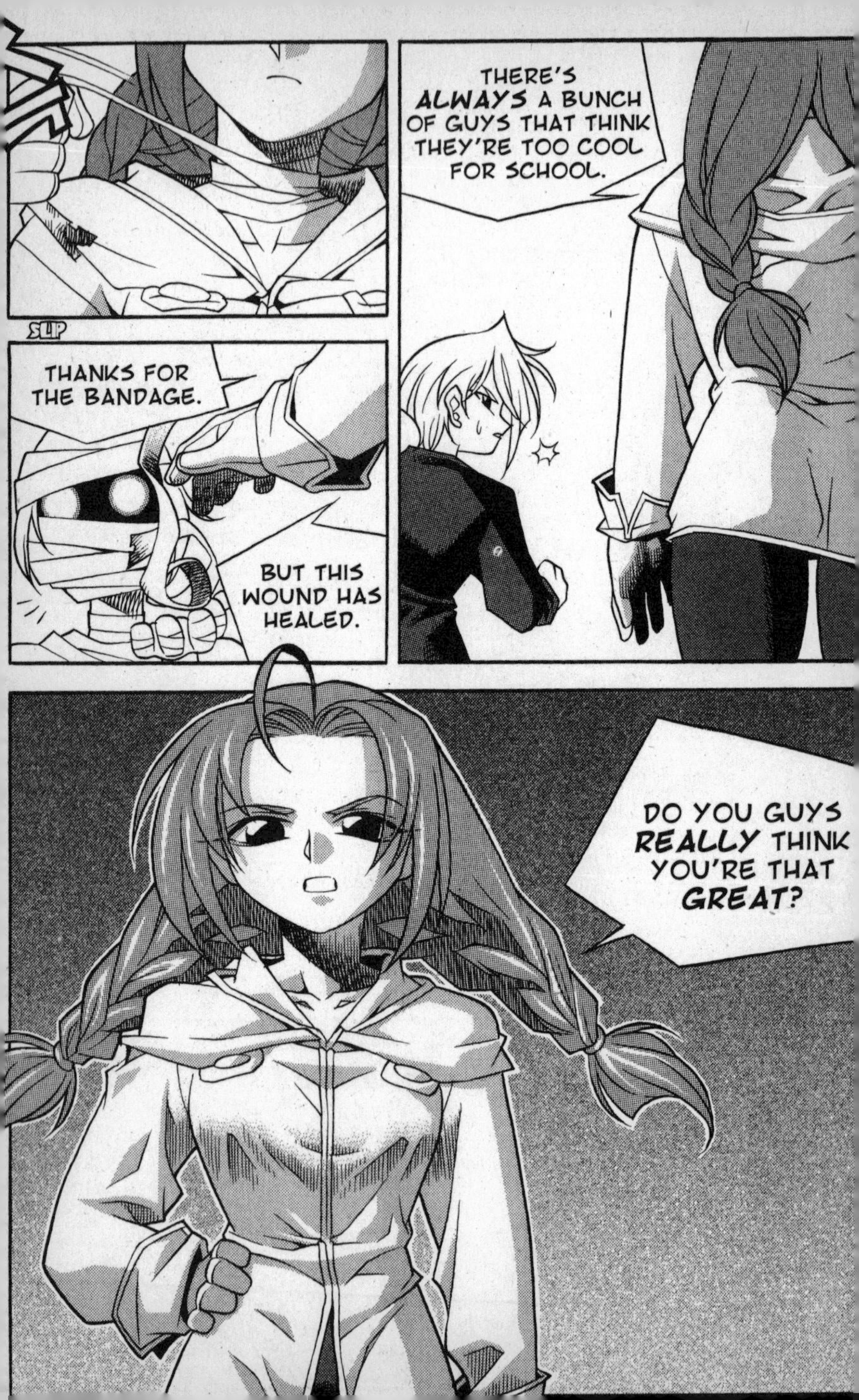
SLIP
THANKS FOR THE BANDAGE.
BUT THIS WOUND HAS HEALED.
THERE'S ALWAYS A BUNCH OF GUYS THAT THINK THEY'RE TOO COOL FOR SCHOOL.
DO YOU GUYS REALLY THINK YOU'RE THAT GREAT?

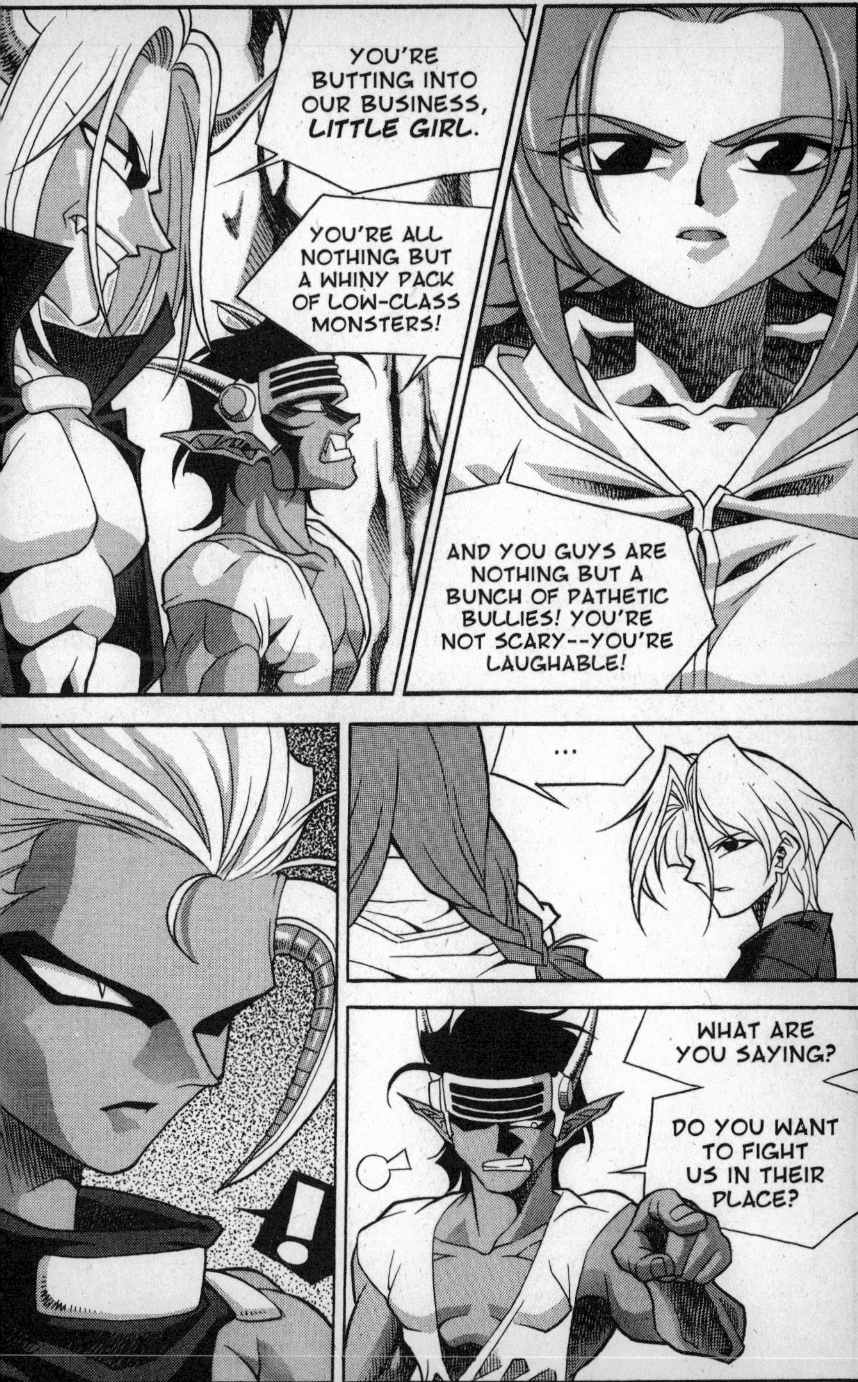
YOU'RE BUTTING INTO OUR BUSINESS, LITTLE GIRL.
YOU'RE ALL NOTHING BUT A WHINY PACK OF LOW-CLASS MONSTERS!
AND YOU GUYS ARE NOTHING BUT A BUNCH OF PATHETIC BULLIES! YOU'RE NOT SCARY--YOU'RE LAUGHABLE!
...
WHAT ARE YOU SAYING?
DO YOU WANT TO FIGHT US IN THEIR PLACE?

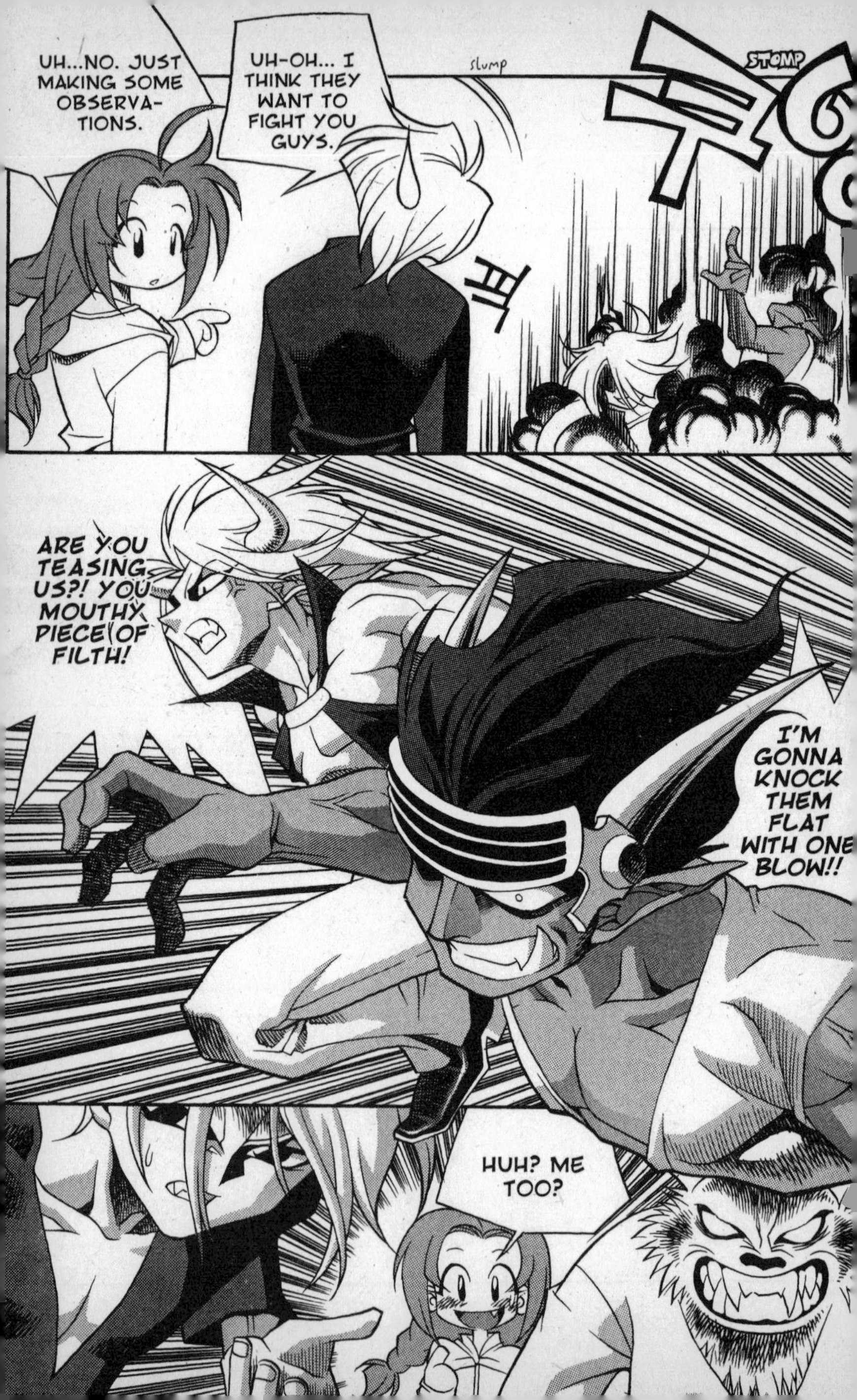
UH...NO. JUST MAKING SOME OBSERVA-TIONS.
UH-OH... I THINK THEY WANT TO FIGHT YOU GUYS.
slump
STOMP
ARE YOU TEASING US?! YOU MOUTHY PIECE OF FILTH!
I'M GONNA KNOCK THEM FLAT WITH ONE BLOW!!
HUH? ME TOO?

Quest 3

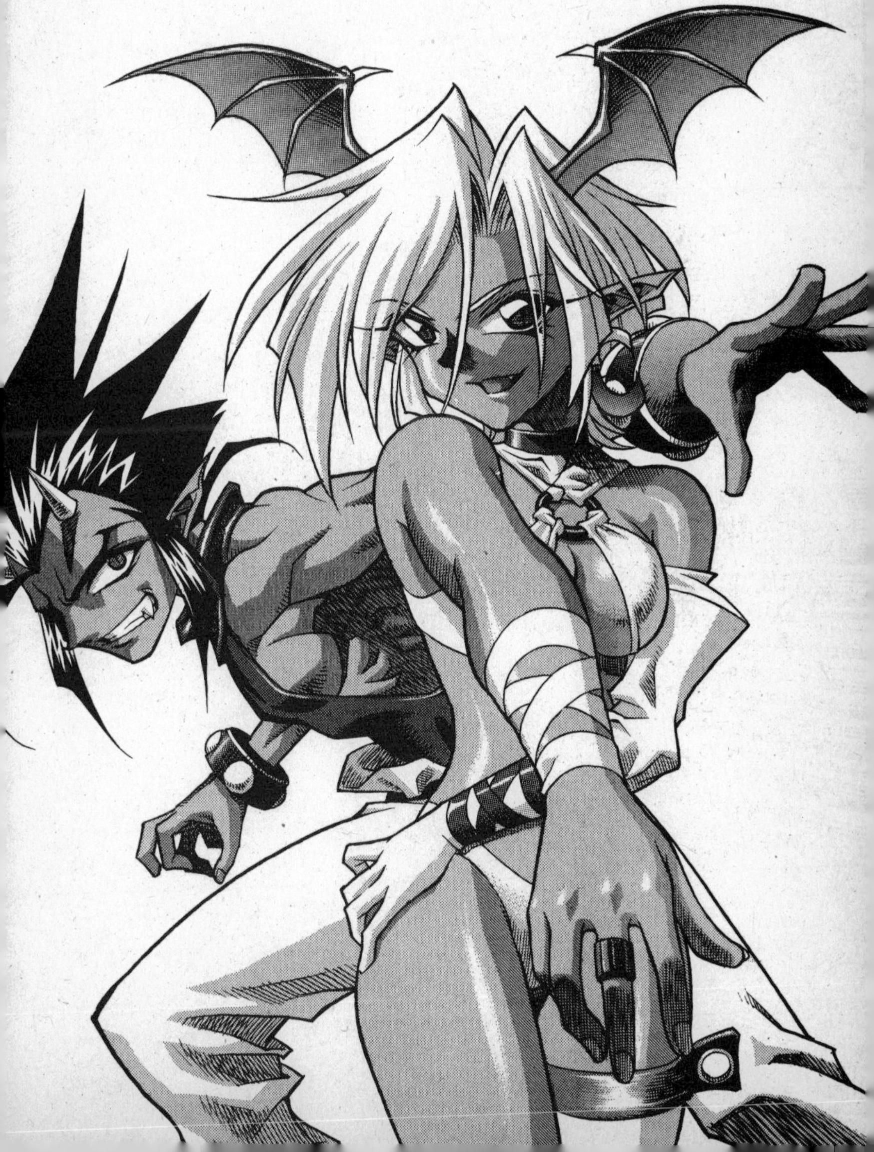

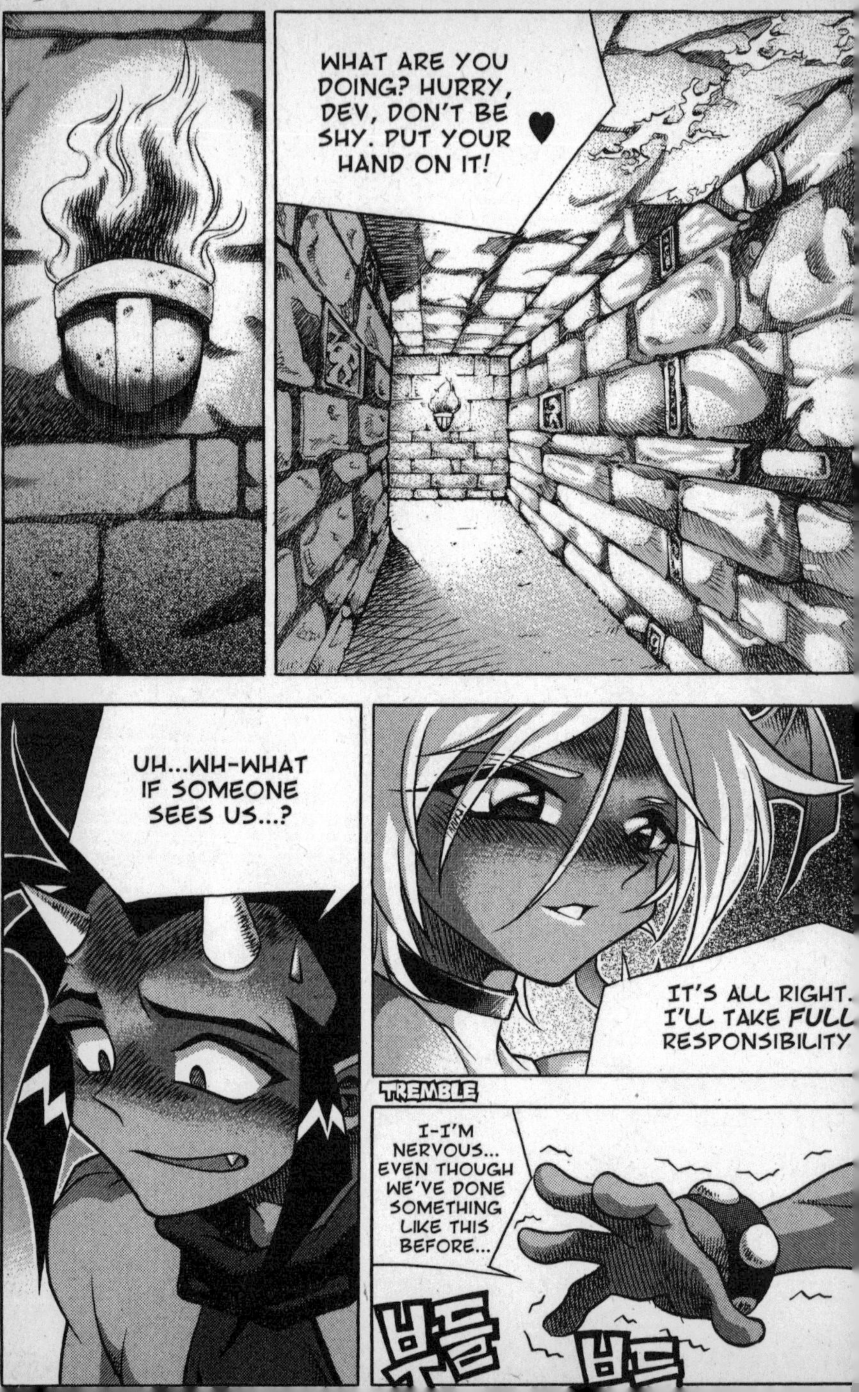
WHAT ARE YOU DOING? HURRY, DEV, DON'T BE SHY. PUT YOUR HAND ON IT!
UH...WH-WHAT IF SOMEONE SEES US...?
IT'S ALL RIGHT. I'LL TAKE FULL RESPONSIBILITY
TREMBLE
I-I'M NERVOUS... EVEN THOUGH WE'VE DONE SOMETHING LIKE THIS BEFORE...

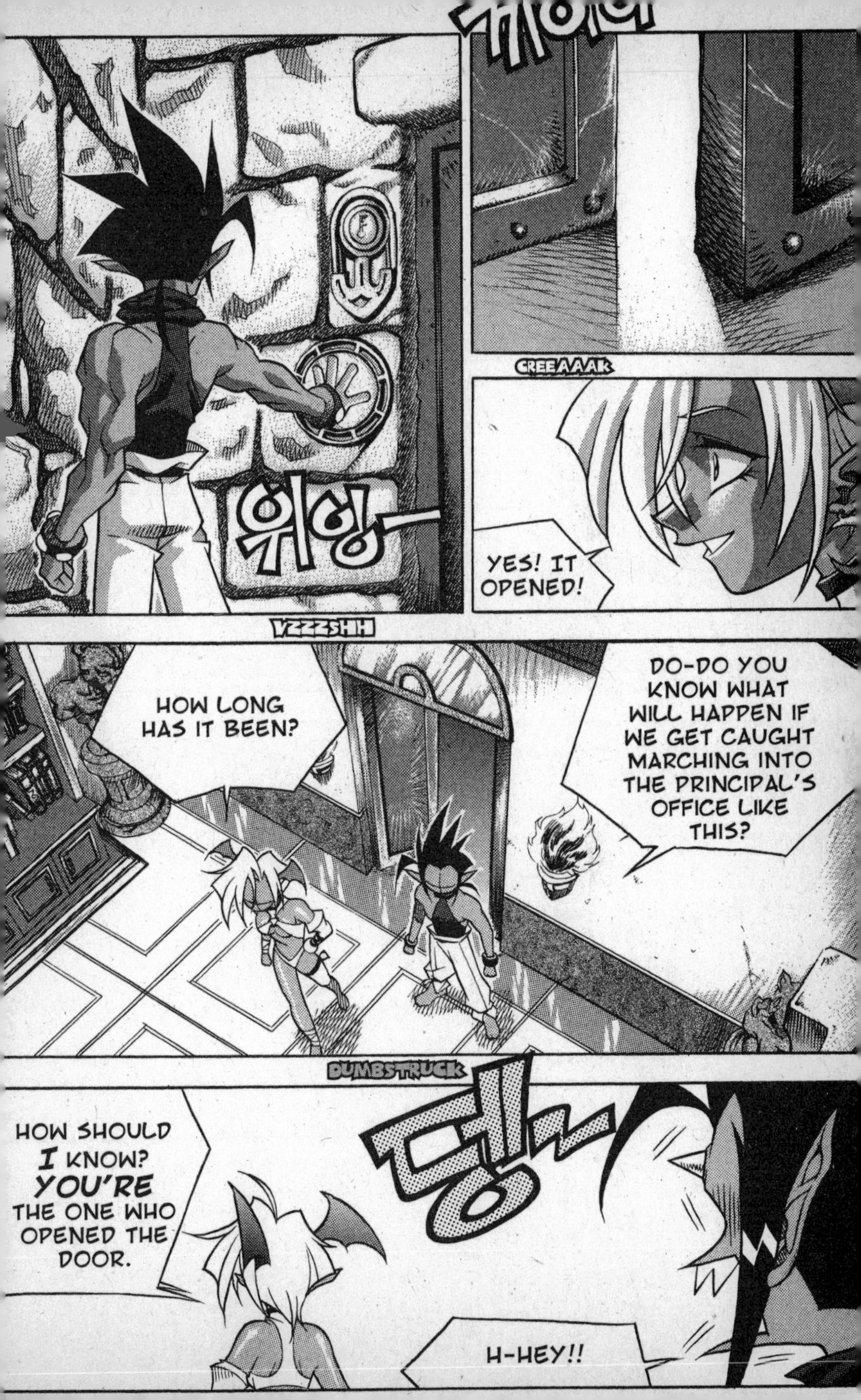

위잉—
VZZZSHH
CREEAAAK
YES! IT OPENED!
HOW LONG HAS IT BEEN?
DO-DO YOU KNOW WHAT WILL HAPPEN IF WE GET CAUGHT MARCHING INTO THE PRINCIPAL'S OFFICE LIKE THIS?
DUMBSTRUCK
멍~
HOW SHOULD *I* KNOW? ***YOU'RE*** THE ONE WHO OPENED THE DOOR.
H-HEY!!

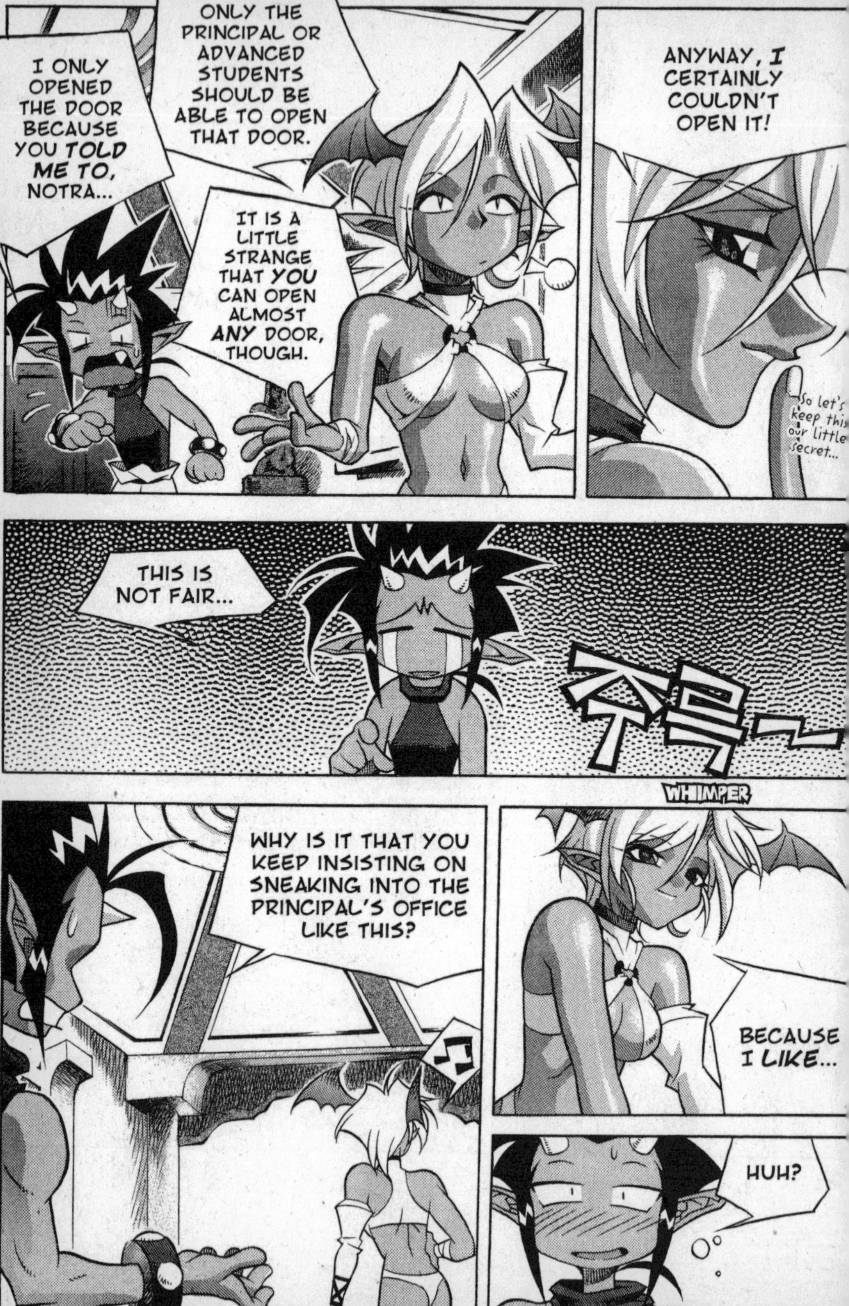
ONLY THE PRINCIPAL OR ADVANCED STUDENTS SHOULD BE ABLE TO OPEN THAT DOOR.
I ONLY OPENED THE DOOR BECAUSE YOU TOLD ME TO, NOTRA...
IT IS A LITTLE STRANGE THAT YOU CAN OPEN ALMOST ANY DOOR, THOUGH.
ANYWAY, I CERTAINLY COULDN'T OPEN IT!
So let's keep this our little secret...
THIS IS NOT FAIR...
WHIMPER
WHY IS IT THAT YOU KEEP INSISTING ON SNEAKING INTO THE PRINCIPAL'S OFFICE LIKE THIS?
BECAUSE I LIKE...
HUH?

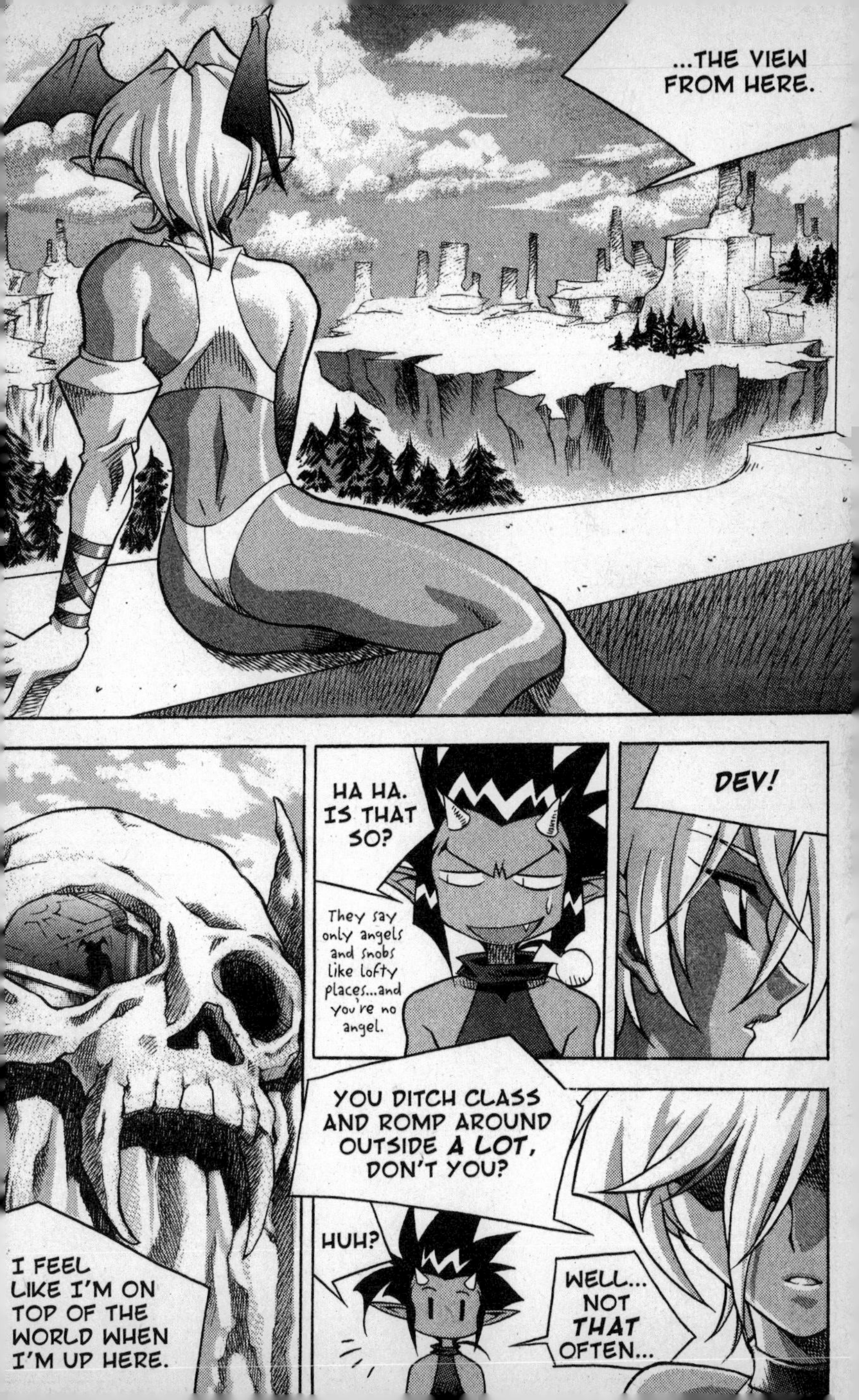
...THE VIEW FROM HERE.
I FEEL LIKE I'M ON TOP OF THE WORLD WHEN I'M UP HERE.
HA HA. IS THAT SO?
They say only angels and snobs like lofty places...and you're no angel.
DEV!
YOU DITCH CLASS AND ROMP AROUND OUTSIDE A LOT, DON'T YOU?
HUH?
WELL... NOT THAT OFTEN...

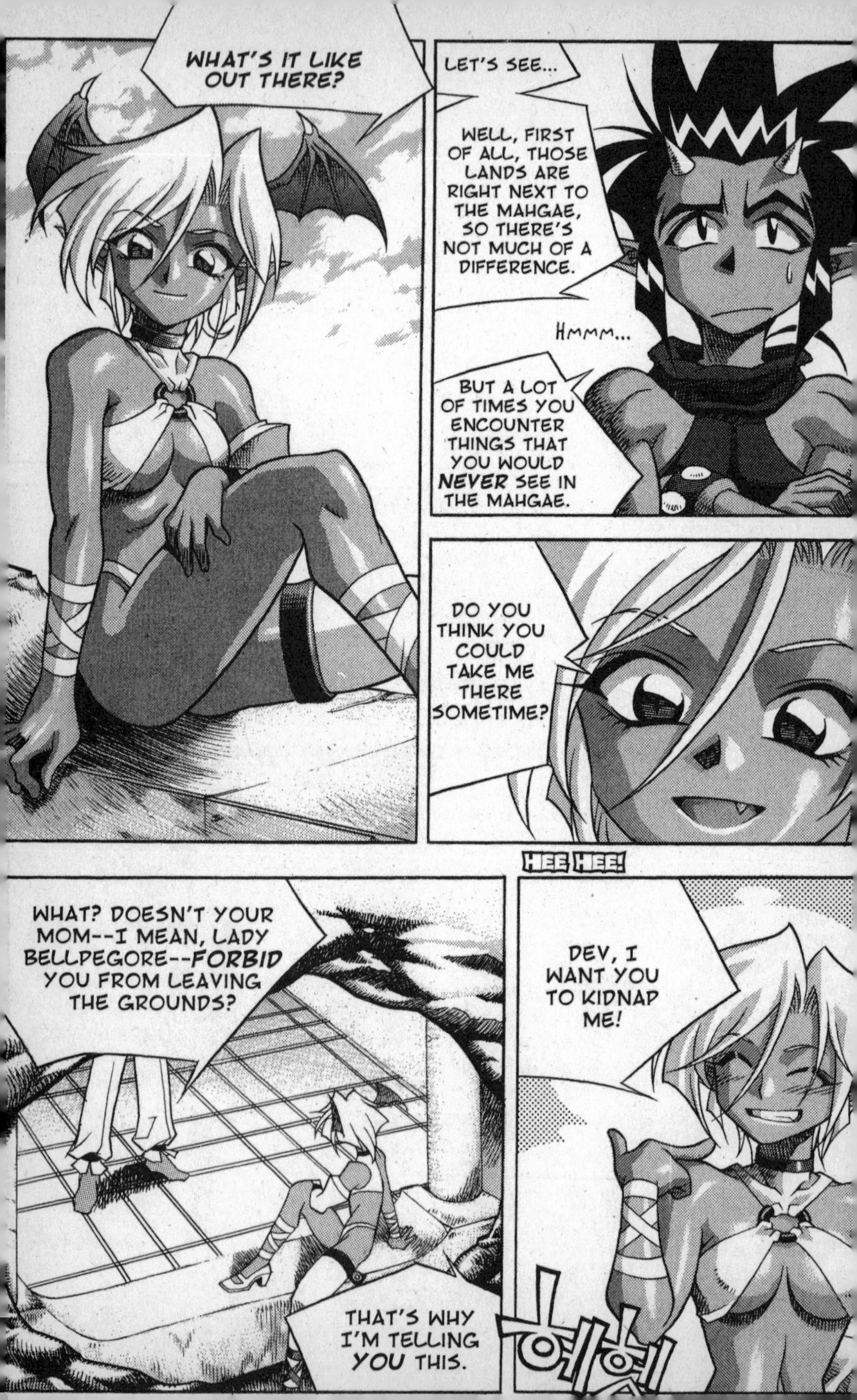
WHAT'S IT LIKE OUT THERE?
LET'S SEE...
WELL, FIRST OF ALL, THOSE LANDS ARE RIGHT NEXT TO THE MAHGAE, SO THERE'S NOT MUCH OF A DIFFERENCE.
HMMM...
BUT A LOT OF TIMES YOU ENCOUNTER THINGS THAT YOU WOULD NEVER SEE IN THE MAHGAE.
DO YOU THINK YOU COULD TAKE ME THERE SOMETIME?
HEE HEE!
WHAT? DOESN'T YOUR MOM--I MEAN, LADY BELLPEGORE--FORBID YOU FROM LEAVING THE GROUNDS?
THAT'S WHY I'M TELLING YOU THIS.
DEV, I WANT YOU TO KIDNAP ME!
해헤

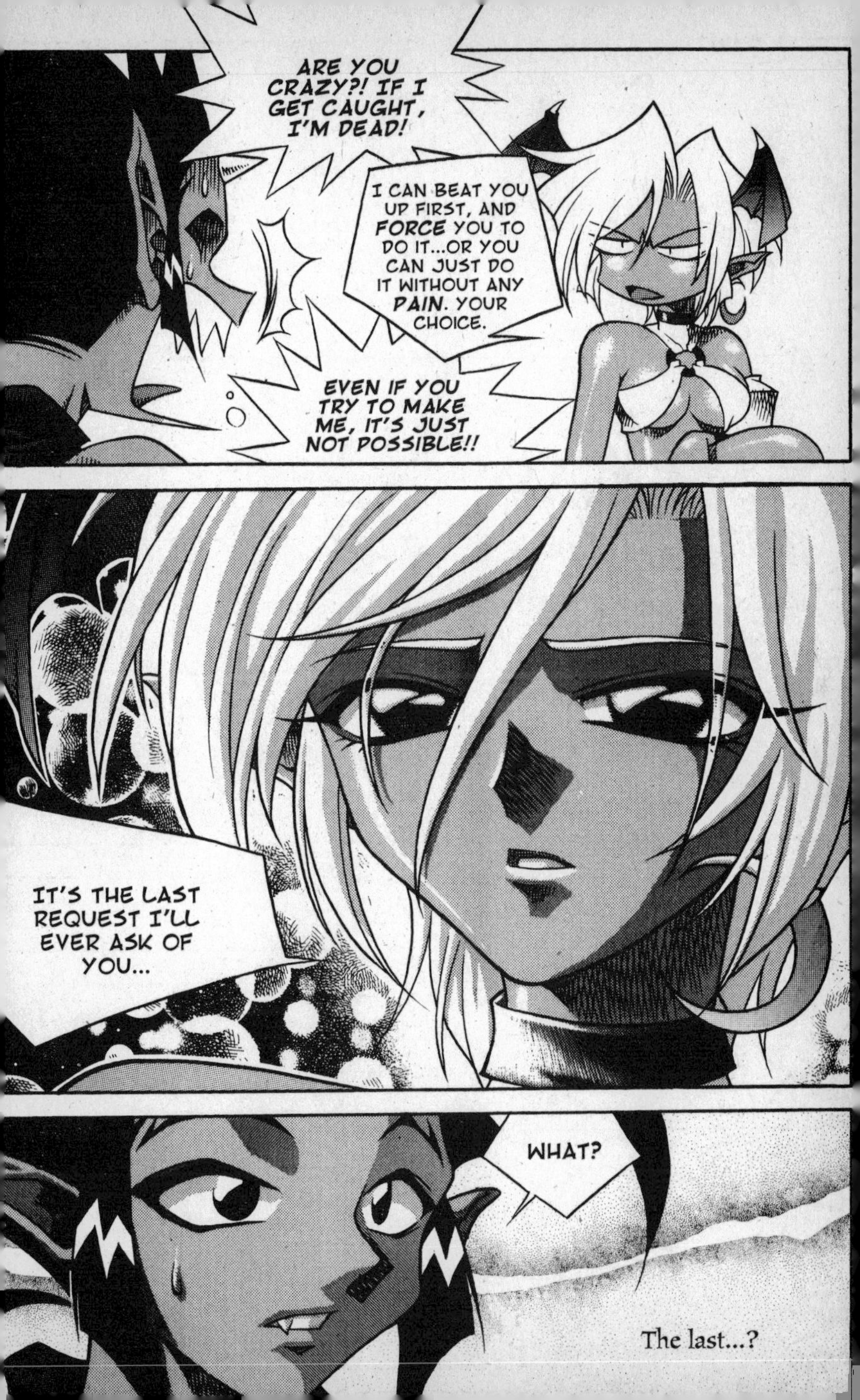

ARE YOU CRAZY?! IF I GET CAUGHT, I'M DEAD!
I CAN BEAT YOU UP FIRST, AND FORCE YOU TO DO IT...OR YOU CAN JUST DO IT WITHOUT ANY PAIN. YOUR CHOICE.
EVEN IF YOU TRY TO MAKE ME, IT'S JUST NOT POSSIBLE!!
IT'S THE LAST REQUEST I'LL EVER ASK OF YOU...
WHAT?
The last...?

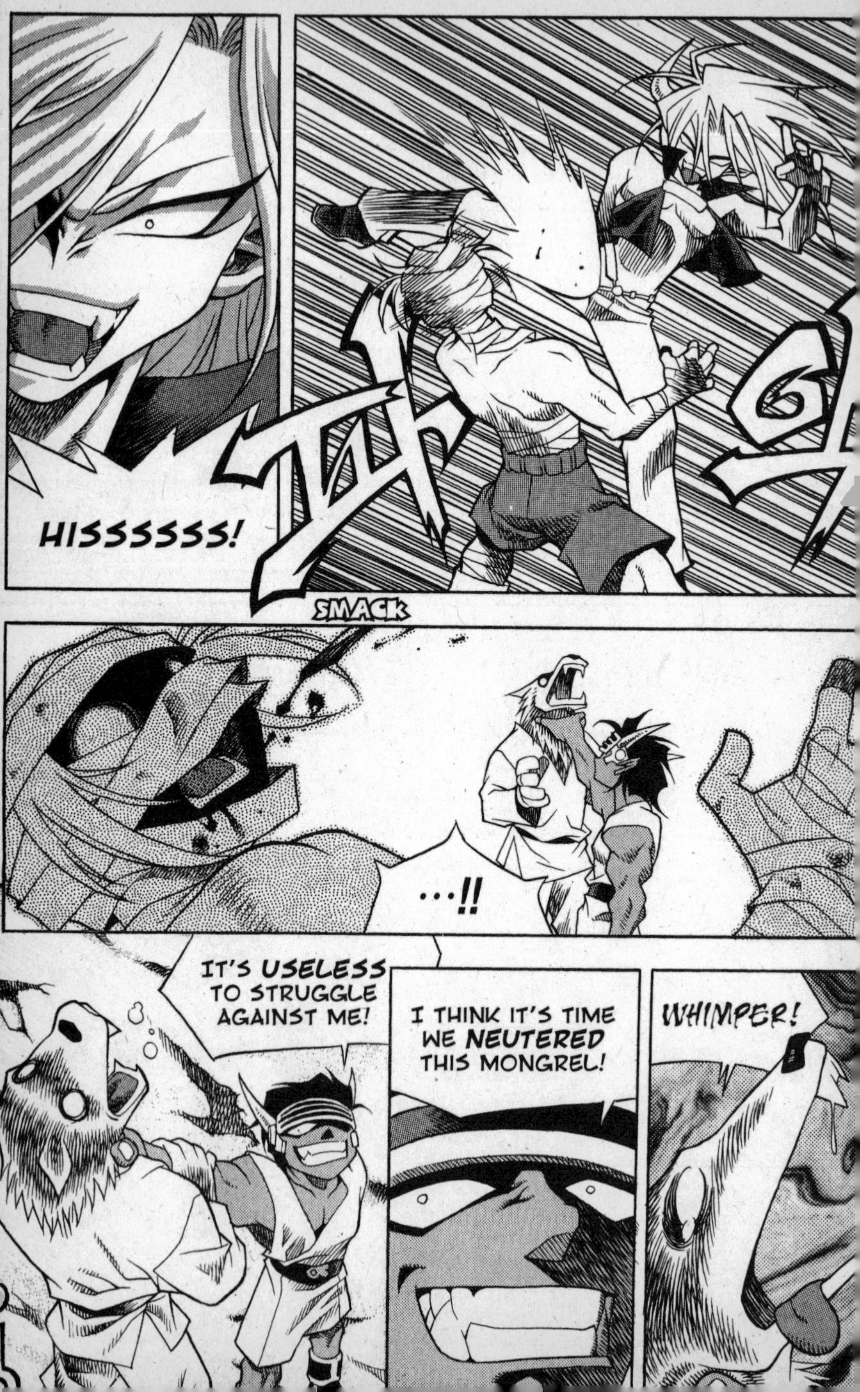
HISSSSSSS!
SMACK
...!!
IT'S USELESS TO STRUGGLE AGAINST ME!
I THINK IT'S TIME WE NEUTERED THIS MONGREL!
WHIMPER!

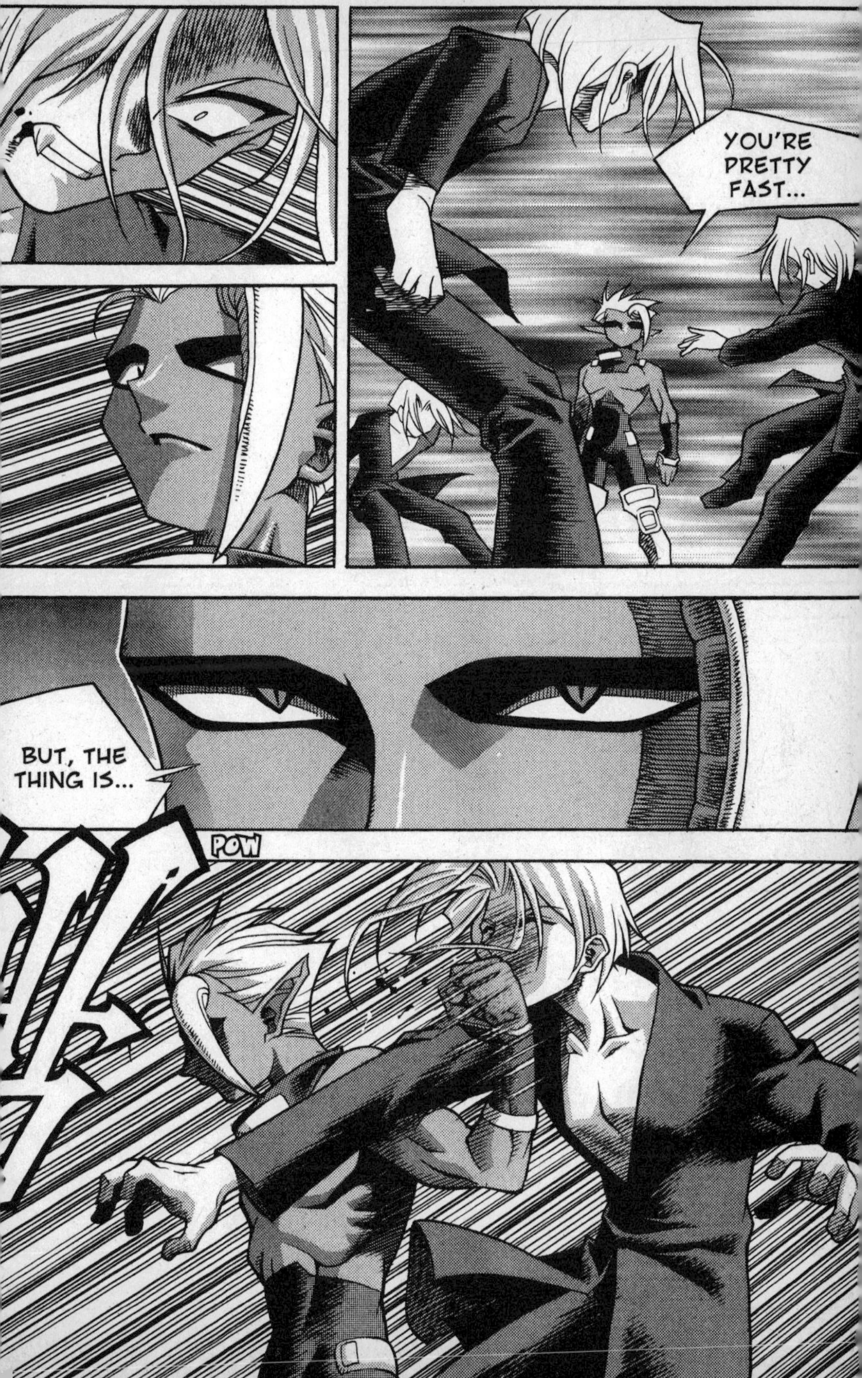
YOU'RE PRETTY FAST...
BUT, THE THING IS...
POW

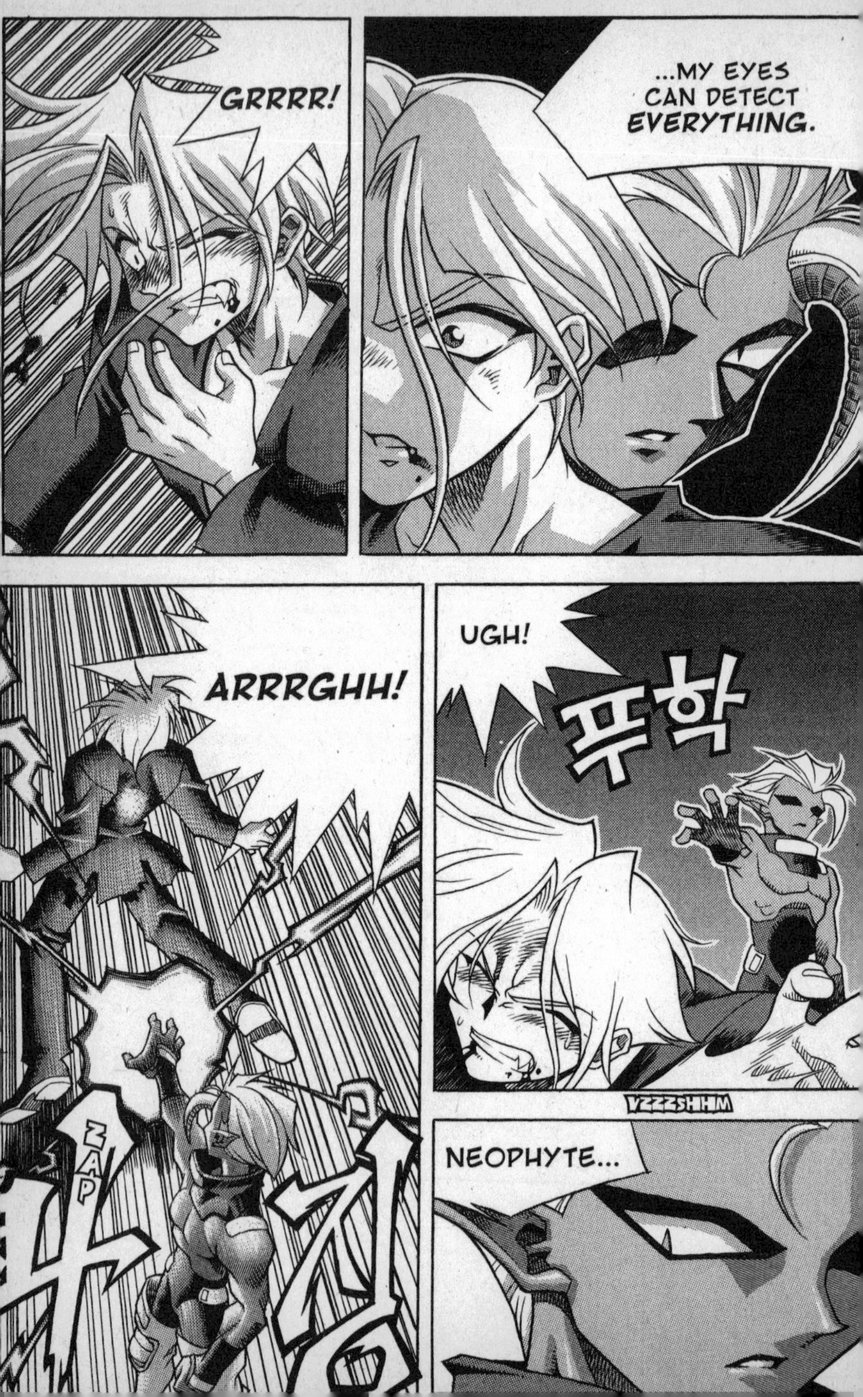
GRRRR!
...MY EYES CAN DETECT EVERYTHING.
ARRRGHH!
ZAP
UGH!
푸학
VZZZSHHM
NEOPHYTE...

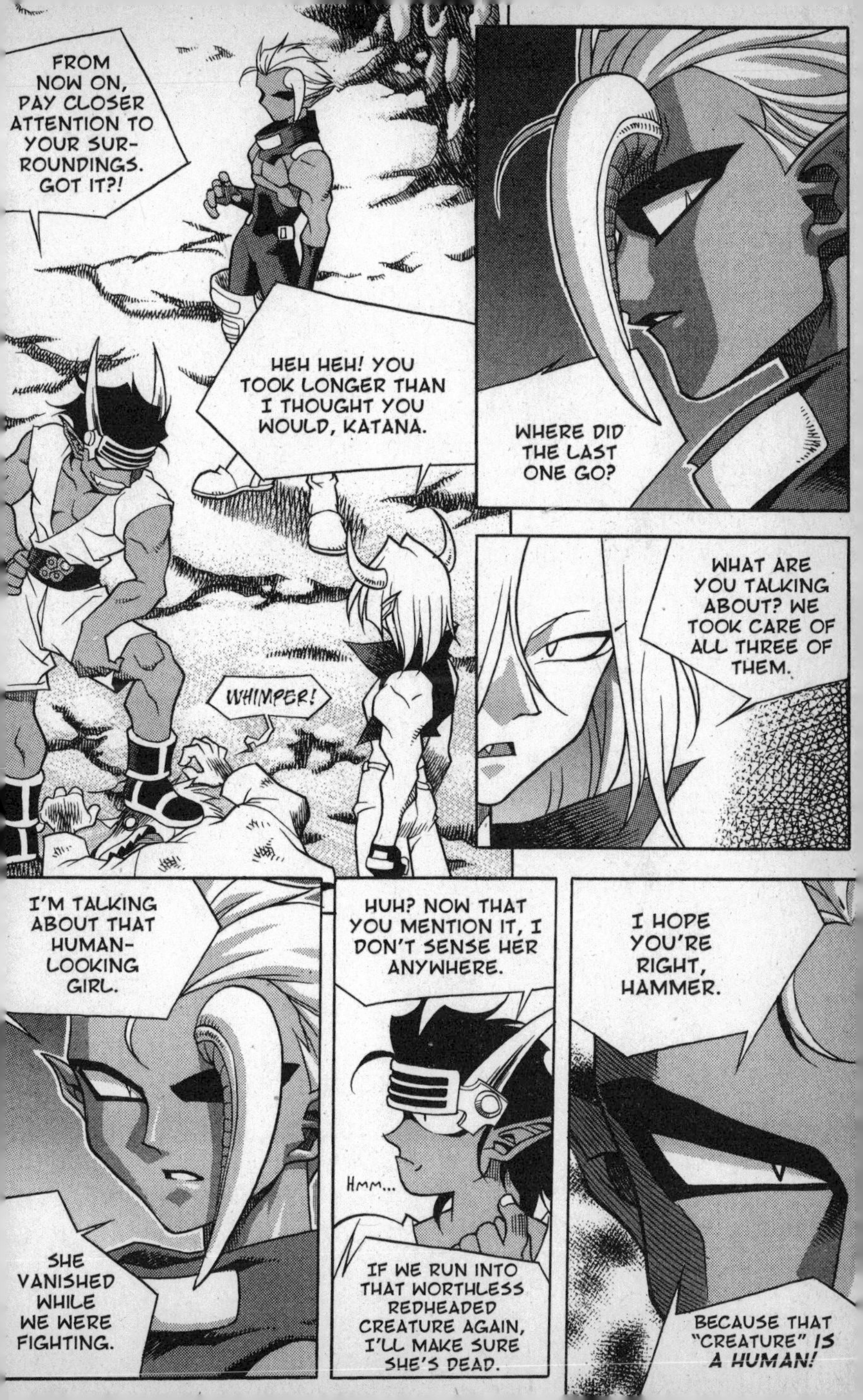
FROM NOW ON, PAY CLOSER ATTENTION TO YOUR SUR-ROUNDINGS. GOT IT?!
HEH HEH! YOU TOOK LONGER THAN I THOUGHT YOU WOULD, KATANA.
WHIMPER!
WHERE DID THE LAST ONE GO?
WHAT ARE YOU TALKING ABOUT? WE TOOK CARE OF ALL THREE OF THEM.
I'M TALKING ABOUT THAT HUMAN-LOOKING GIRL.
SHE VANISHED WHILE WE WERE FIGHTING.
HUH? NOW THAT YOU MENTION IT, I DON'T SENSE HER ANYWHERE.
HMM...
IF WE RUN INTO THAT WORTHLESS REDHEADED CREATURE AGAIN, I'LL MAKE SURE SHE'S DEAD.
I HOPE YOU'RE RIGHT, HAMMER.
BECAUSE THAT "CREATURE" *IS* A *HUMAN!*

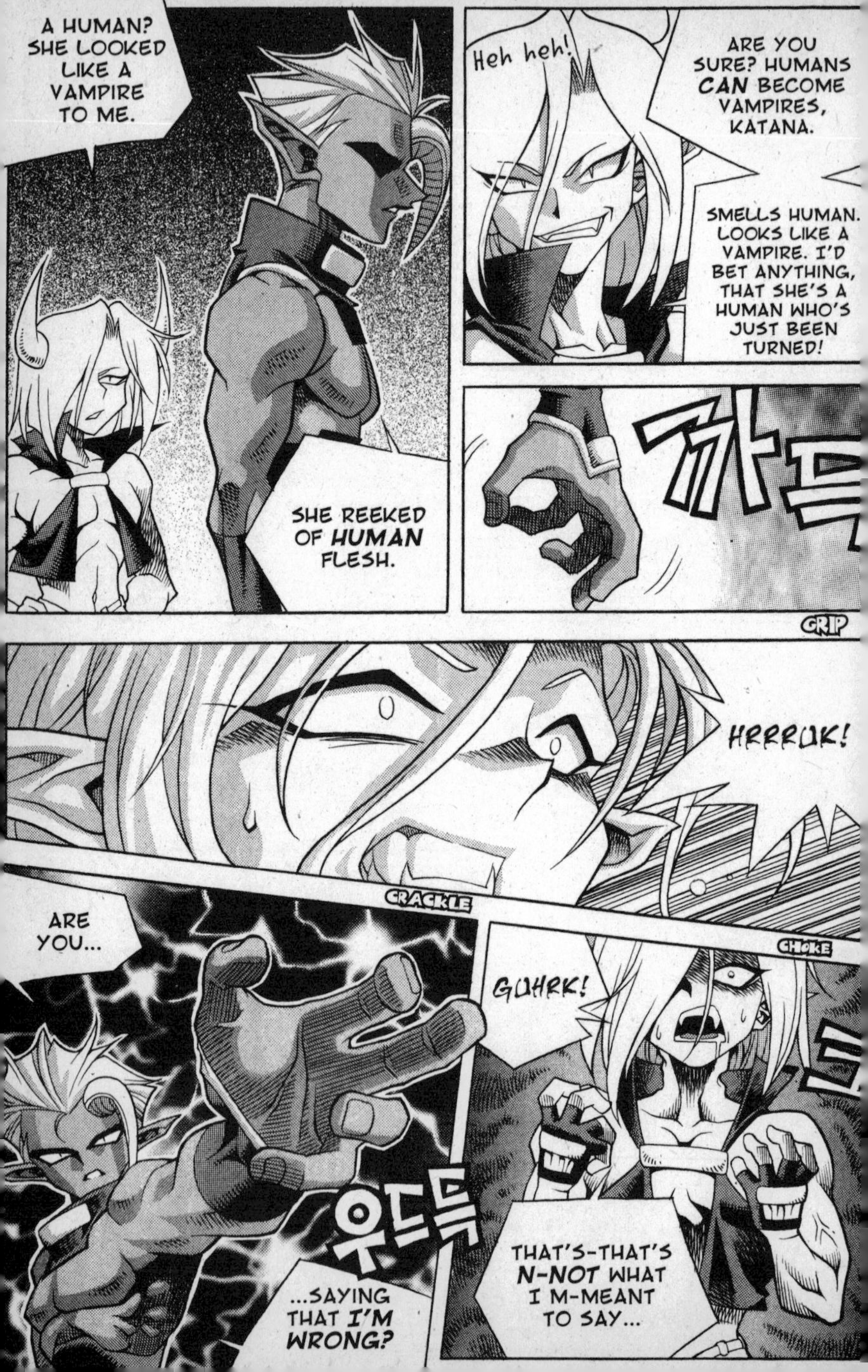
A HUMAN? SHE LOOKED LIKE A VAMPIRE TO ME.
SHE REEKED OF HUMAN FLESH.
Heh heh!
ARE YOU SURE? HUMANS CAN BECOME VAMPIRES, KATANA.
SMELLS HUMAN. LOOKS LIKE A VAMPIRE. I'D BET ANYTHING, THAT SHE'S A HUMAN WHO'S JUST BEEN TURNED!
GRIP
HRRRUK!
CRACKLE
ARE YOU...
...SAYING THAT I'M WRONG?
CHOKE
GUHRK!
THAT'S-THAT'S N-NOT WHAT I M-MEANT TO SAY...

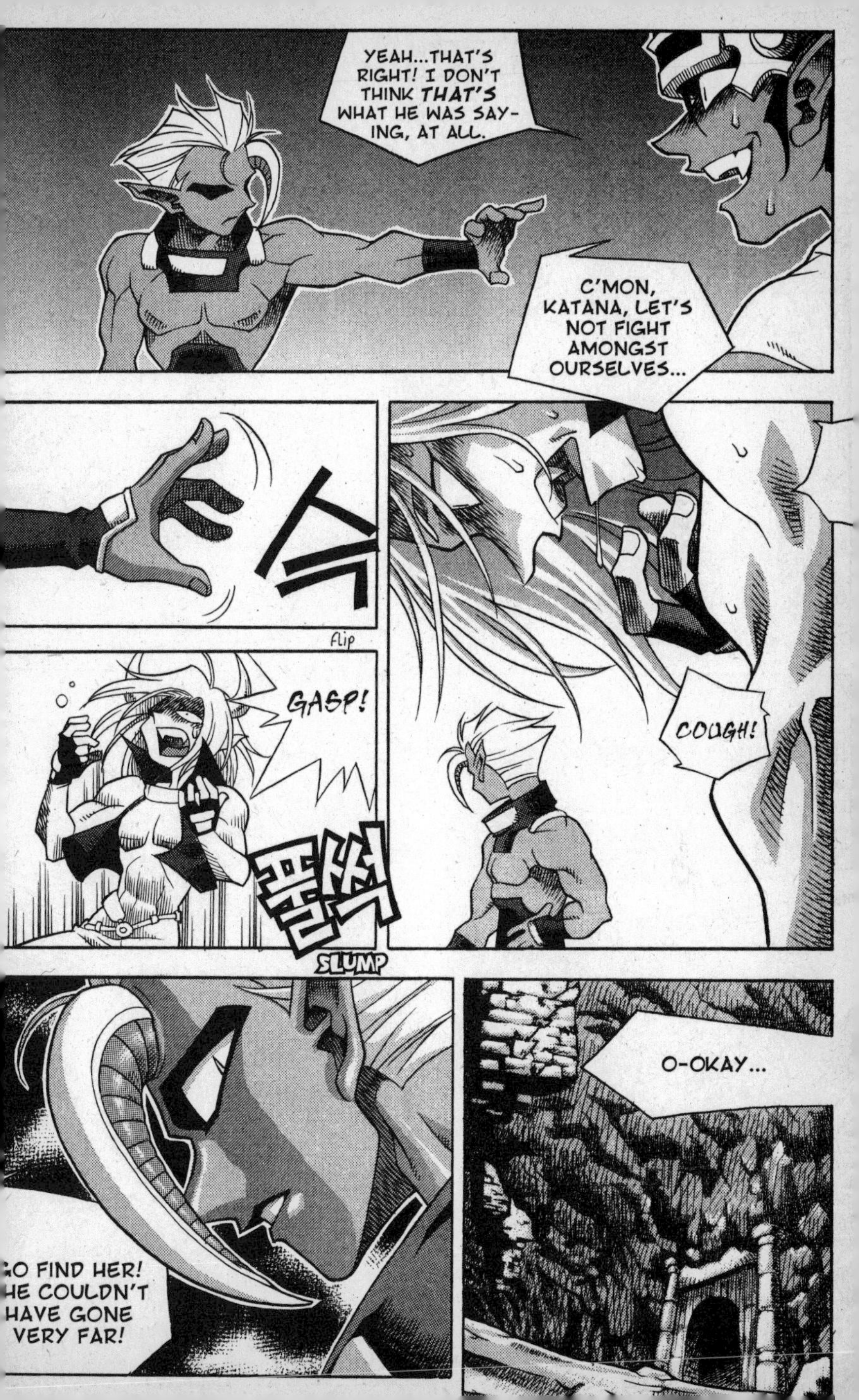
YEAH...THAT'S RIGHT! I DON'T THINK THAT'S WHAT HE WAS SAYING, AT ALL.
C'MON, KATANA, LET'S NOT FIGHT AMONGST OURSELVES...
Flip
GASP!
COUGH!
SLUMP
GO FIND HER! SHE COULDN'T HAVE GONE VERY FAR!
O-OKAY...

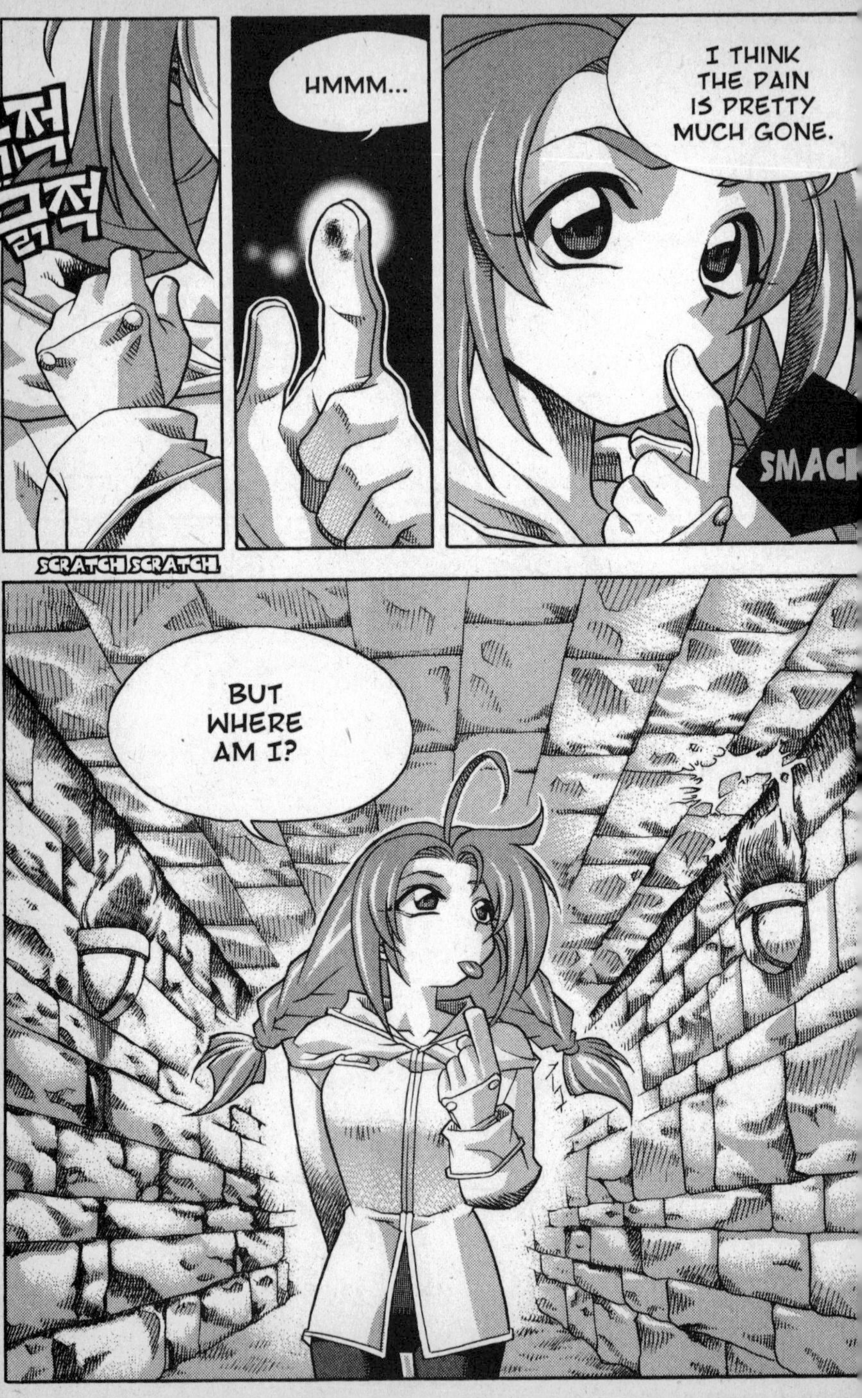
긁적
긁적
SCRATCH SCRATCH
HMMM...
I THINK THE PAIN IS PRETTY MUCH GONE.
SMACK
BUT WHERE AM I?

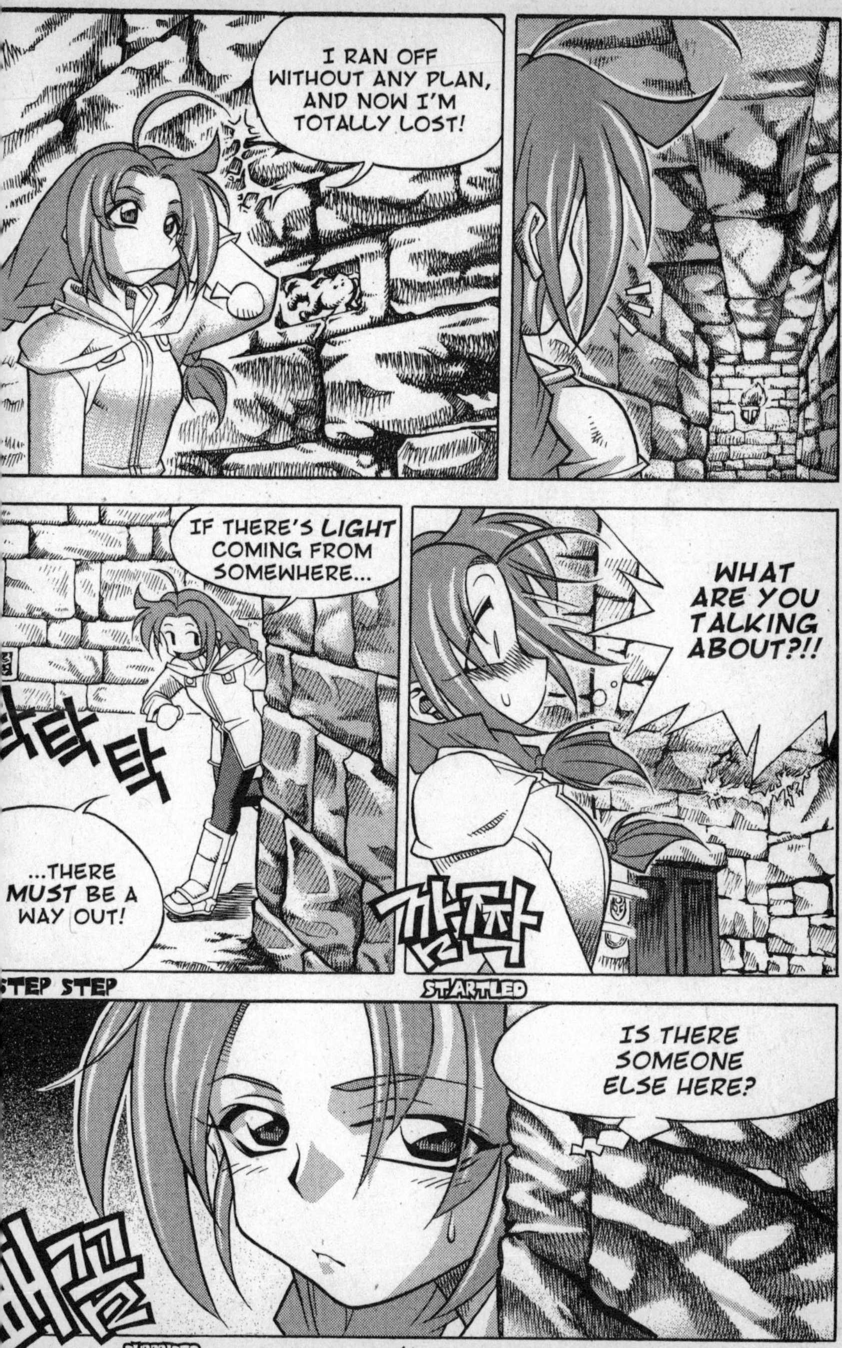
I RAN OFF WITHOUT ANY PLAN, AND NOW I'M TOTALLY LOST!
IF THERE'S LIGHT COMING FROM SOMEWHERE...
...THERE MUST BE A WAY OUT!
STEP STEP
WHAT ARE YOU TALKING ABOUT?!!
STARTLED
IS THERE SOMEONE ELSE HERE?
SURPRISED

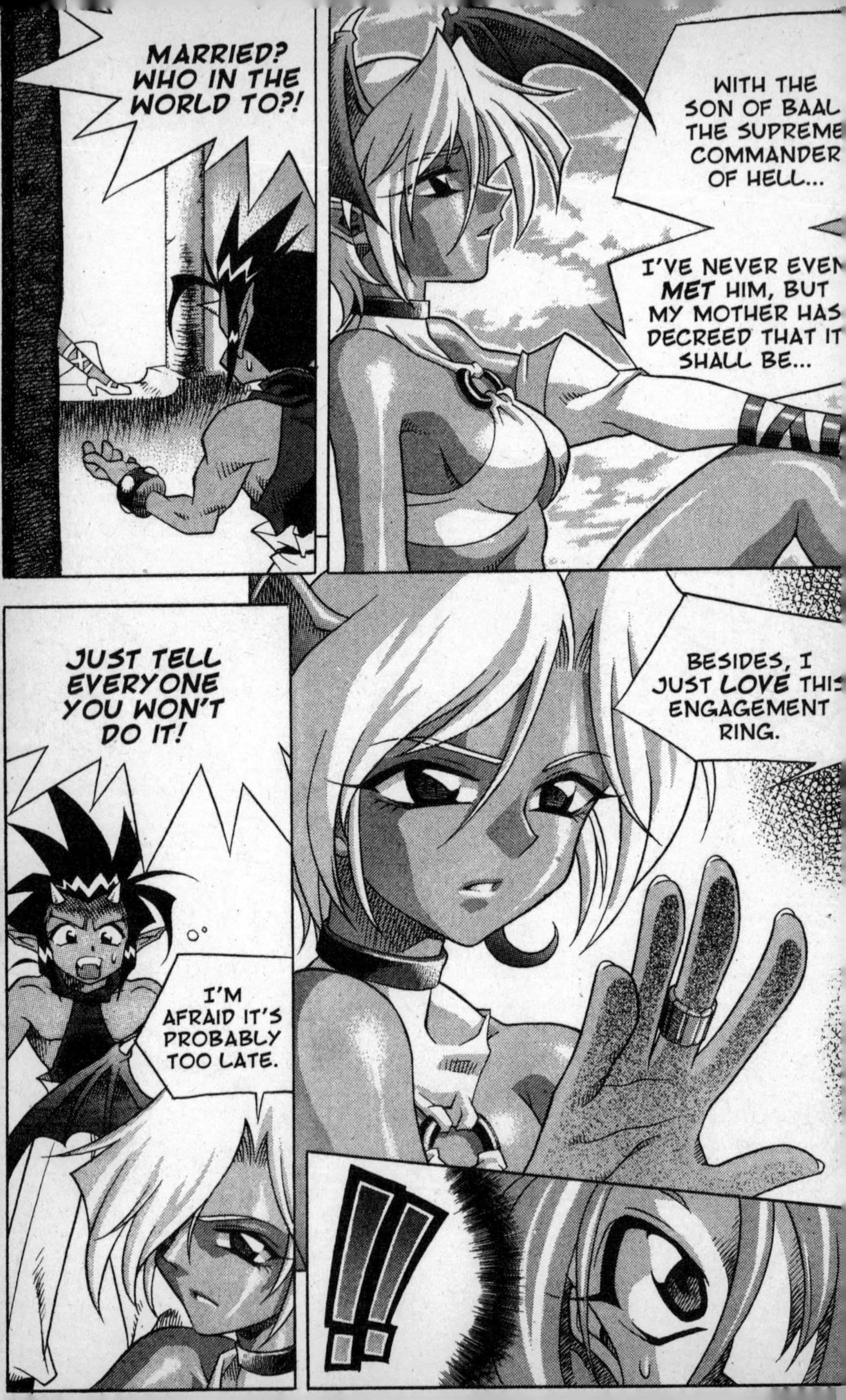
MARRIED? WHO IN THE WORLD TO?!
WITH THE SON OF BAAL THE SUPREME COMMANDER OF HELL...
I'VE NEVER EVEN MET HIM, BUT MY MOTHER HAS DECREED THAT IT SHALL BE...
JUST TELL EVERYONE YOU WON'T DO IT!
I'M AFRAID IT'S PROBABLY TOO LATE.
BESIDES, I JUST LOVE THIS ENGAGEMENT RING.
!!

Quest 4

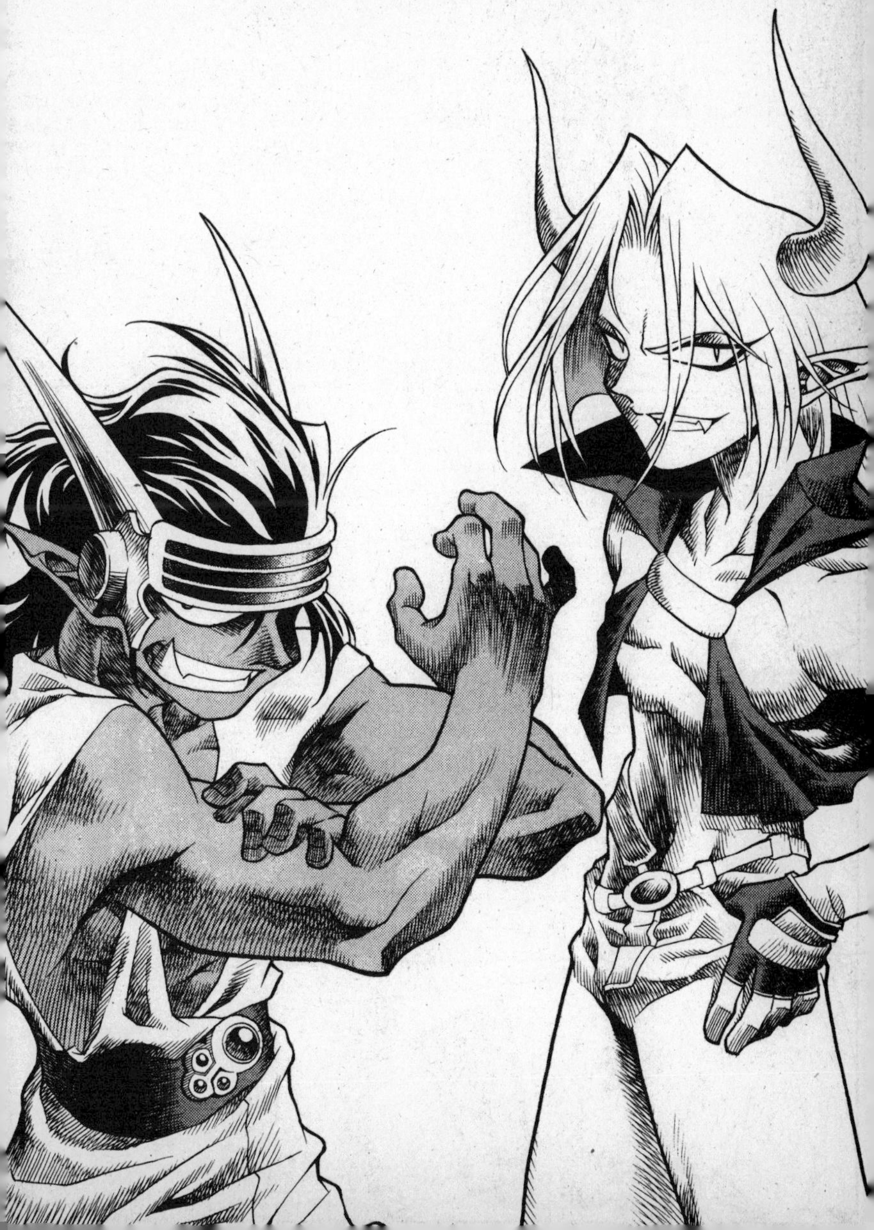

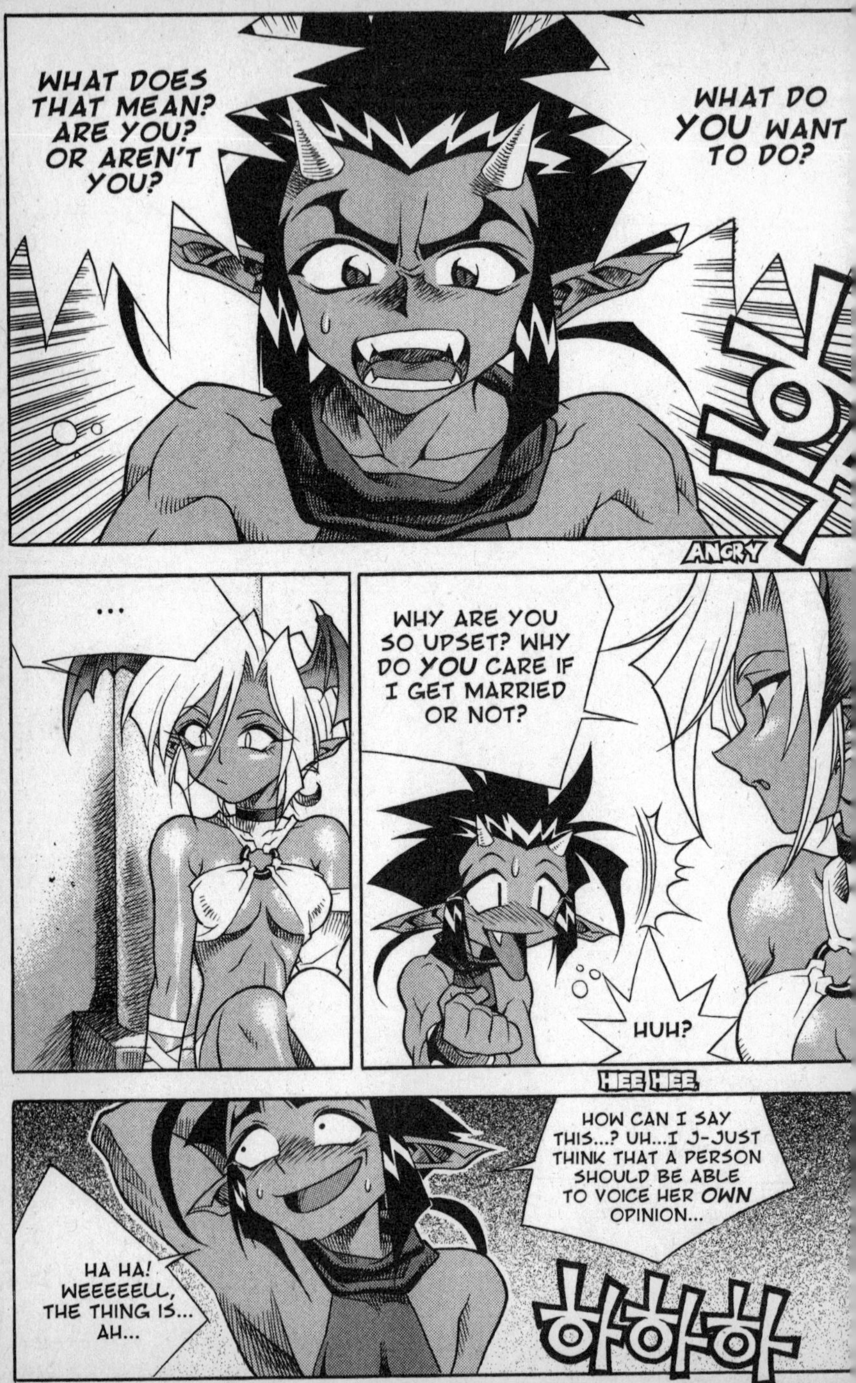
WHAT DOES THAT MEAN? ARE YOU? OR AREN'T YOU?
WHAT DO YOU WANT TO DO?
ANGRY
...
WHY ARE YOU SO UPSET? WHY DO YOU CARE IF I GET MARRIED OR NOT?
HUH?
HEE HEE.
HA HA! WEEEEELL, THE THING IS... AH...
HOW CAN I SAY THIS...? UH...I J-JUST THINK THAT A PERSON SHOULD BE ABLE TO VOICE HER OWN OPINION...
하하하

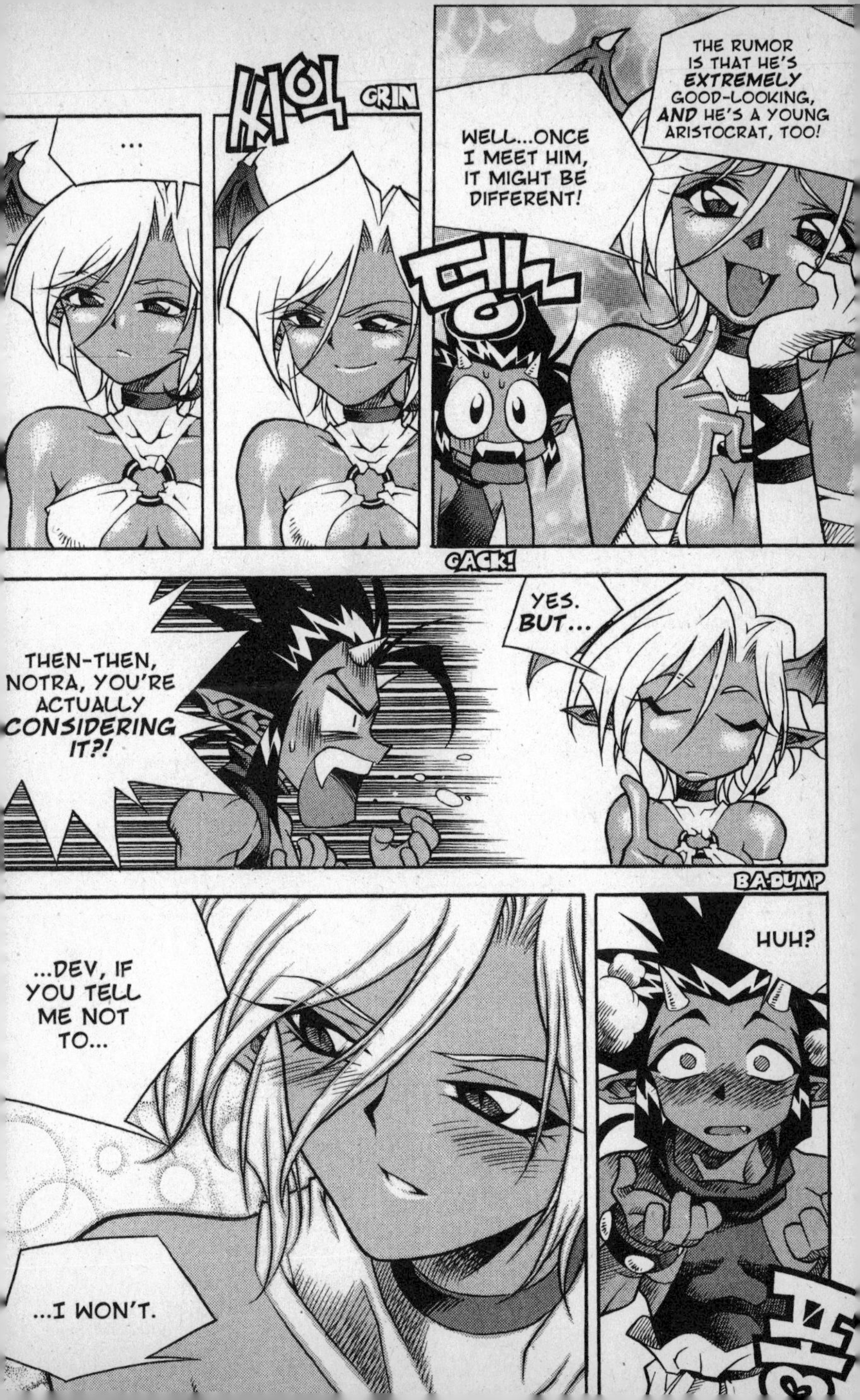
...
히히 GRIN
WELL...ONCE I MEET HIM, IT MIGHT BE DIFFERENT!
THE RUMOR IS THAT HE'S EXTREMELY GOOD-LOOKING, AND HE'S A YOUNG ARISTOCRAT, TOO!
GACK!
THEN-THEN, NOTRA, YOU'RE ACTUALLY CONSIDERING IT?!
YES. BUT...
B-A-DUMP
...DEV, IF YOU TELL ME NOT TO...
...I WON'T.
HUH?

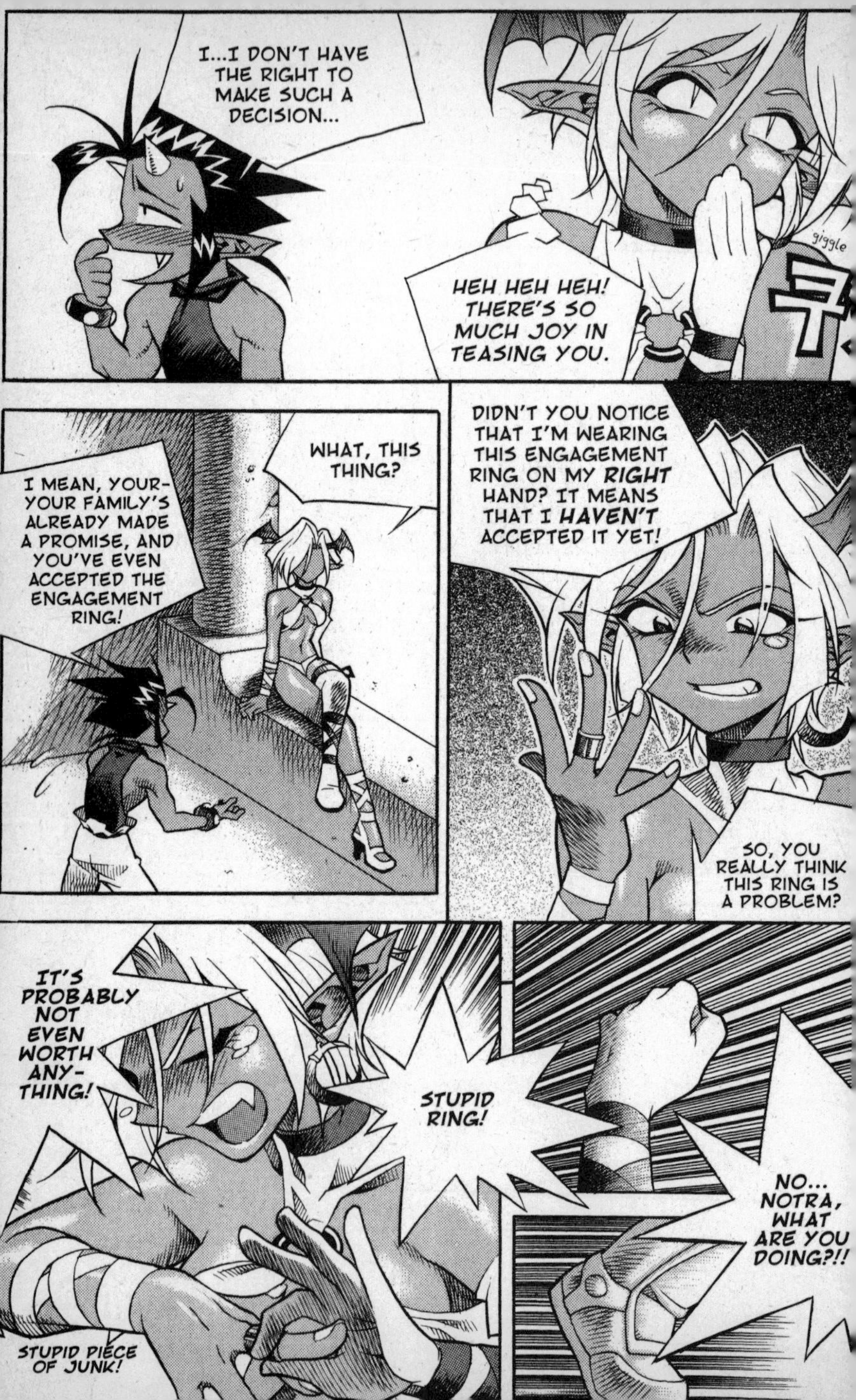
I...I DON'T HAVE THE RIGHT TO MAKE SUCH A DECISION...
giggle
HEH HEH HEH! THERE'S SO MUCH JOY IN TEASING YOU.
I MEAN, YOUR-YOUR FAMILY'S ALREADY MADE A PROMISE, AND YOU'VE EVEN ACCEPTED THE ENGAGEMENT RING!
WHAT, THIS THING?
DIDN'T YOU NOTICE THAT I'M WEARING THIS ENGAGEMENT RING ON MY *RIGHT* HAND? IT MEANS THAT I *HAVEN'T* ACCEPTED IT YET!
SO, YOU REALLY THINK THIS RING IS A PROBLEM?
IT'S PROBABLY NOT EVEN WORTH ANY-THING!
STUPID RING!
STUPID PIECE OF JUNK!
NO... NOTRA, WHAT ARE YOU DOING?!!

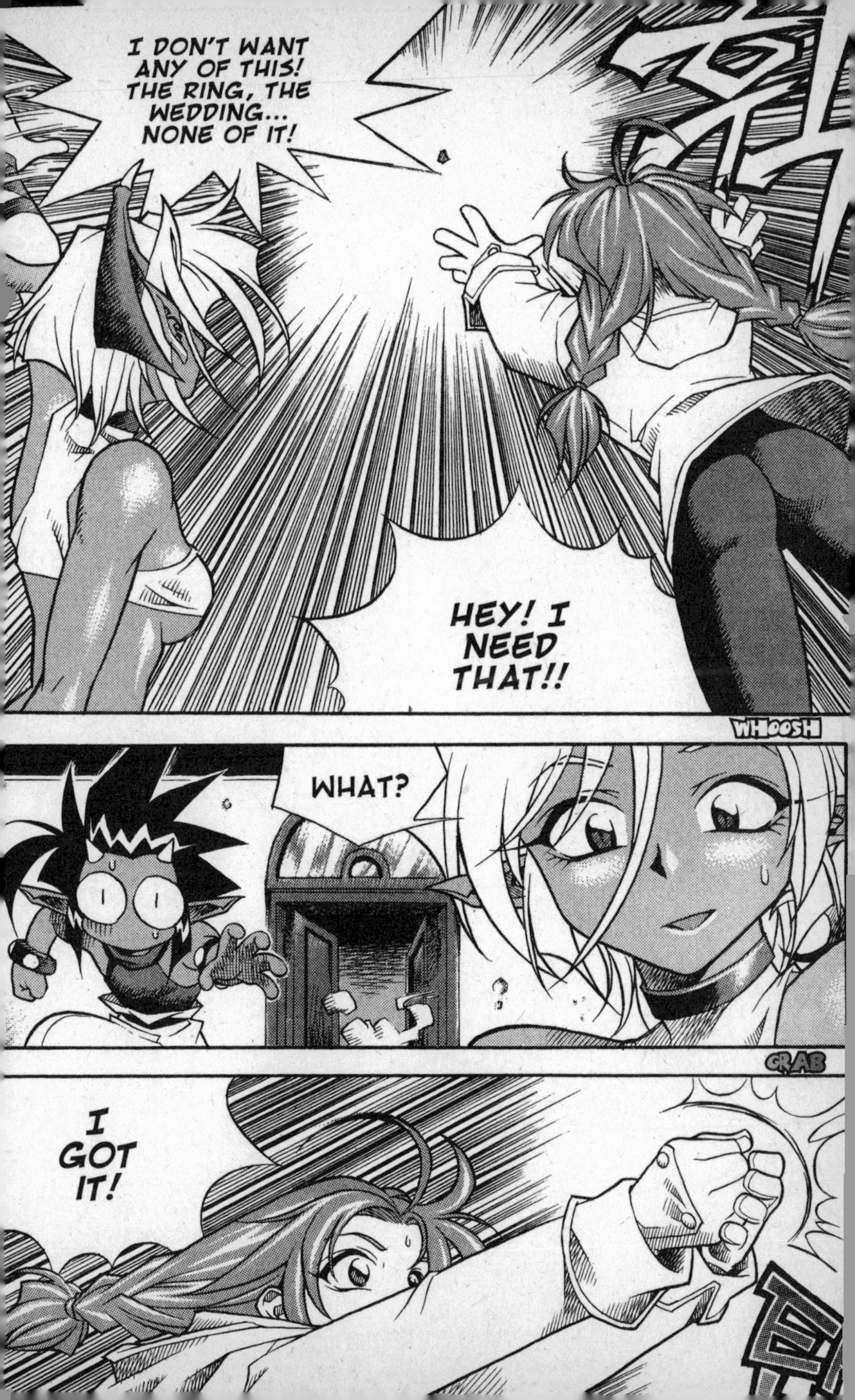
I DON'T WANT ANY OF THIS! THE RING, THE WEDDING... NONE OF IT!
HEY! I NEED THAT!!
WHOOSH
WHAT?
GRAB
I GOT IT!

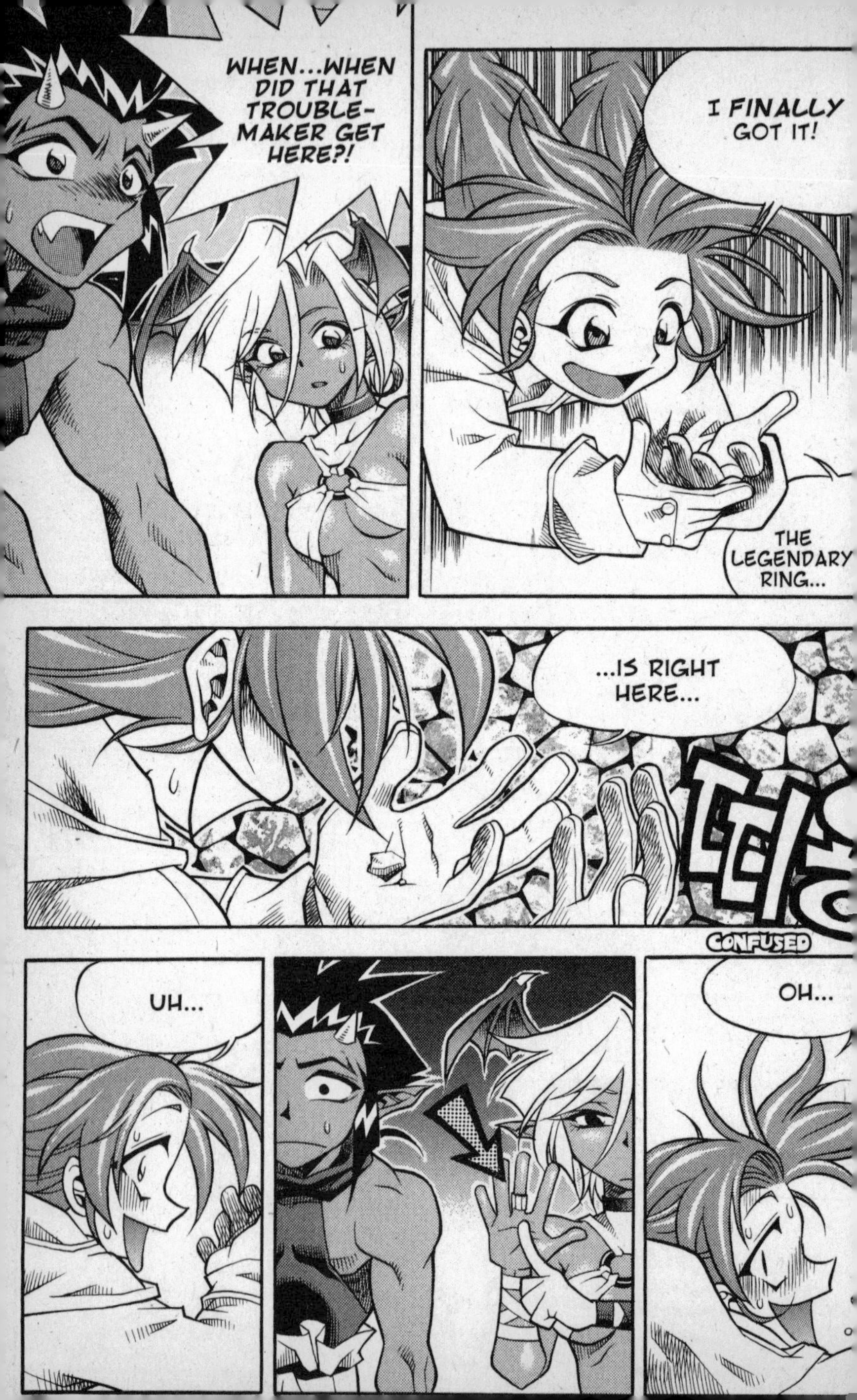

WHEN...WHEN DID THAT TROUBLE-MAKER GET HERE?!
I FINALLY GOT IT!
THE LEGENDARY RING...
...IS RIGHT HERE...
CONFUSED
UH...
OH...

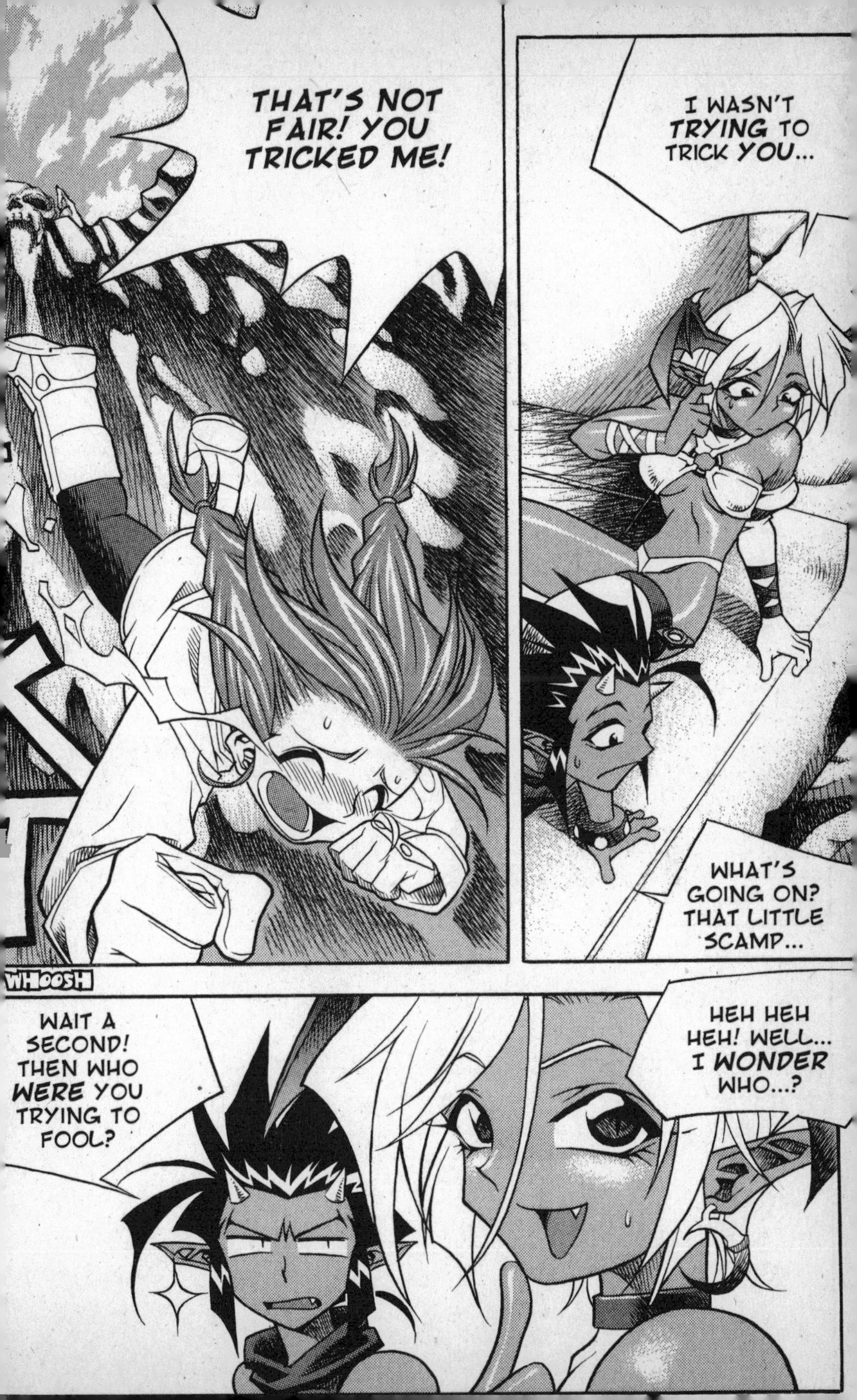
THAT'S NOT FAIR! YOU TRICKED ME!
I WASN'T TRYING TO TRICK YOU...
WHAT'S GOING ON? THAT LITTLE SCAMP...
WHOOSH
WAIT A SECOND! THEN WHO WERE YOU TRYING TO FOOL?
HEH HEH HEH! WELL... I WONDER WHO...?

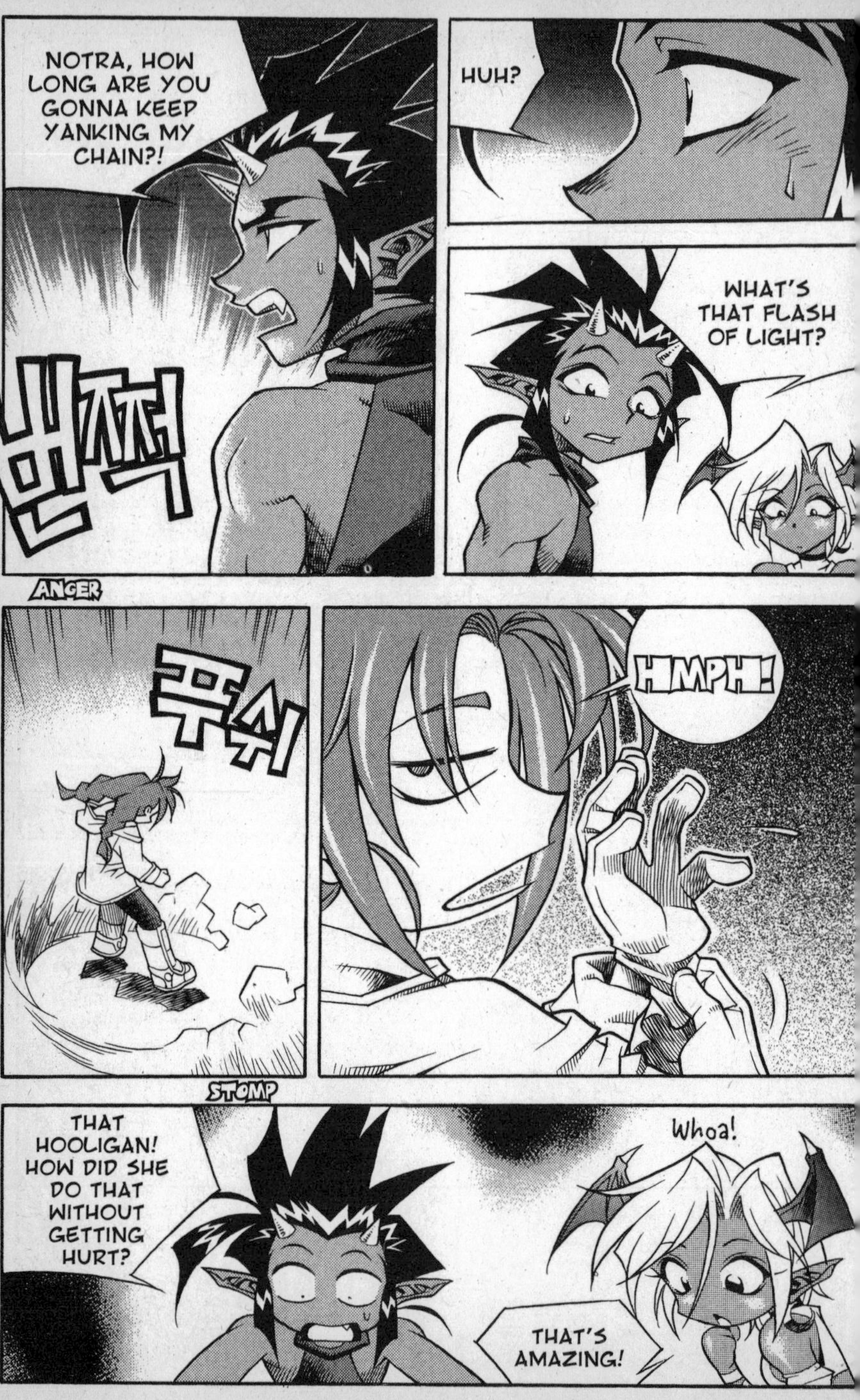
NOTRA, HOW LONG ARE YOU GONNA KEEP YANKING MY CHAIN?!
번쩍
ANGER
HUH?
WHAT'S THAT FLASH OF LIGHT?
STOMP
HMPH!
THAT HOOLIGAN! HOW DID SHE DO THAT WITHOUT GETTING HURT?
Whoa!
THAT'S AMAZING!

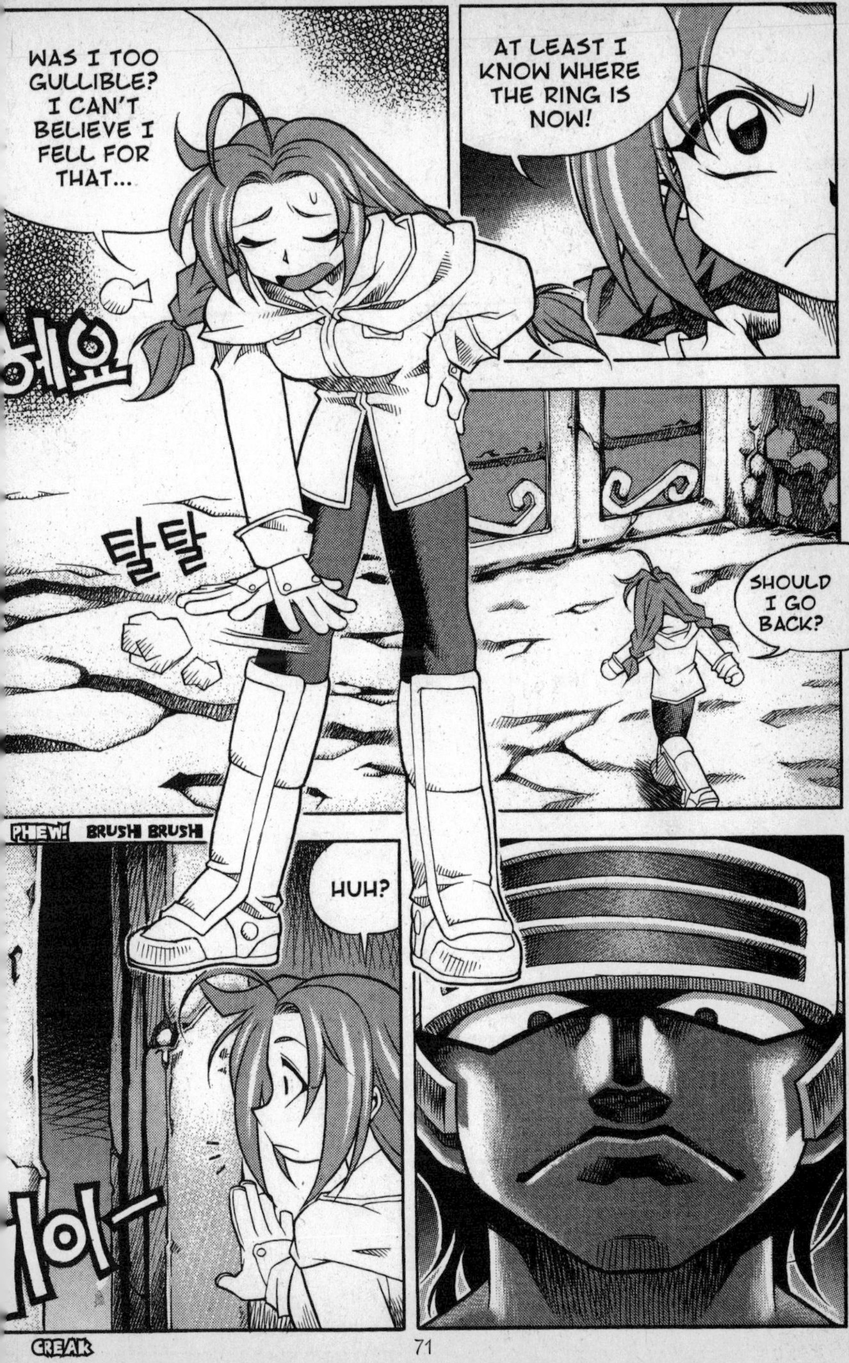

WAS I TOO GULLIBLE? I CAN'T BELIEVE I FELL FOR THAT...
예요
탈탈
PHEW! BRUSH BRUSH
AT LEAST I KNOW WHERE THE RING IS NOW!
SHOULD I GO BACK?
HUH?
이이-
CREAK

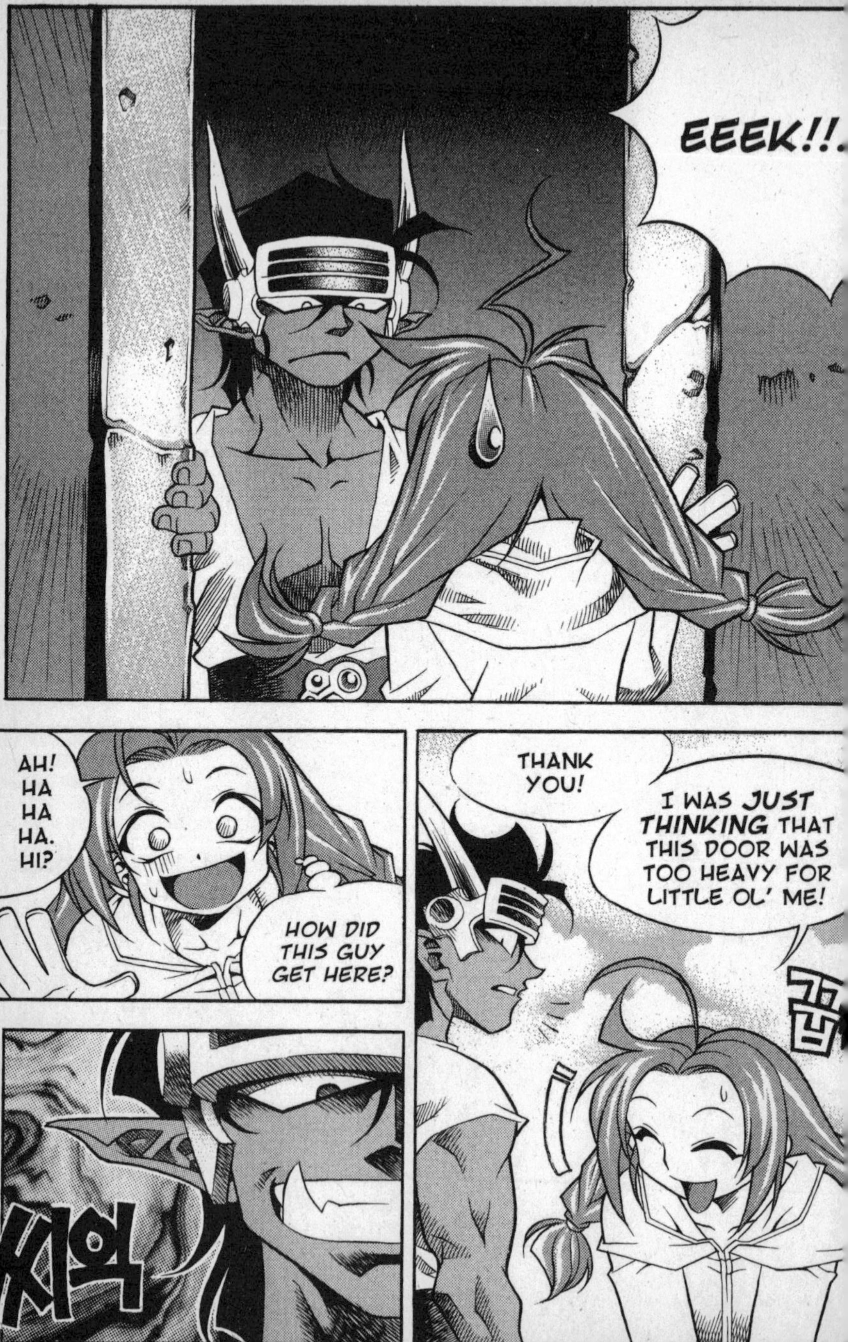
EEEK!!.
AH! HA HA HA. HI?
HOW DID THIS GUY GET HERE?
씨익
THANK YOU!
I WAS *JUST THINKING* THAT THIS DOOR WAS TOO HEAVY FOR LITTLE OL' ME!
꾸벅

GRIN

BOW

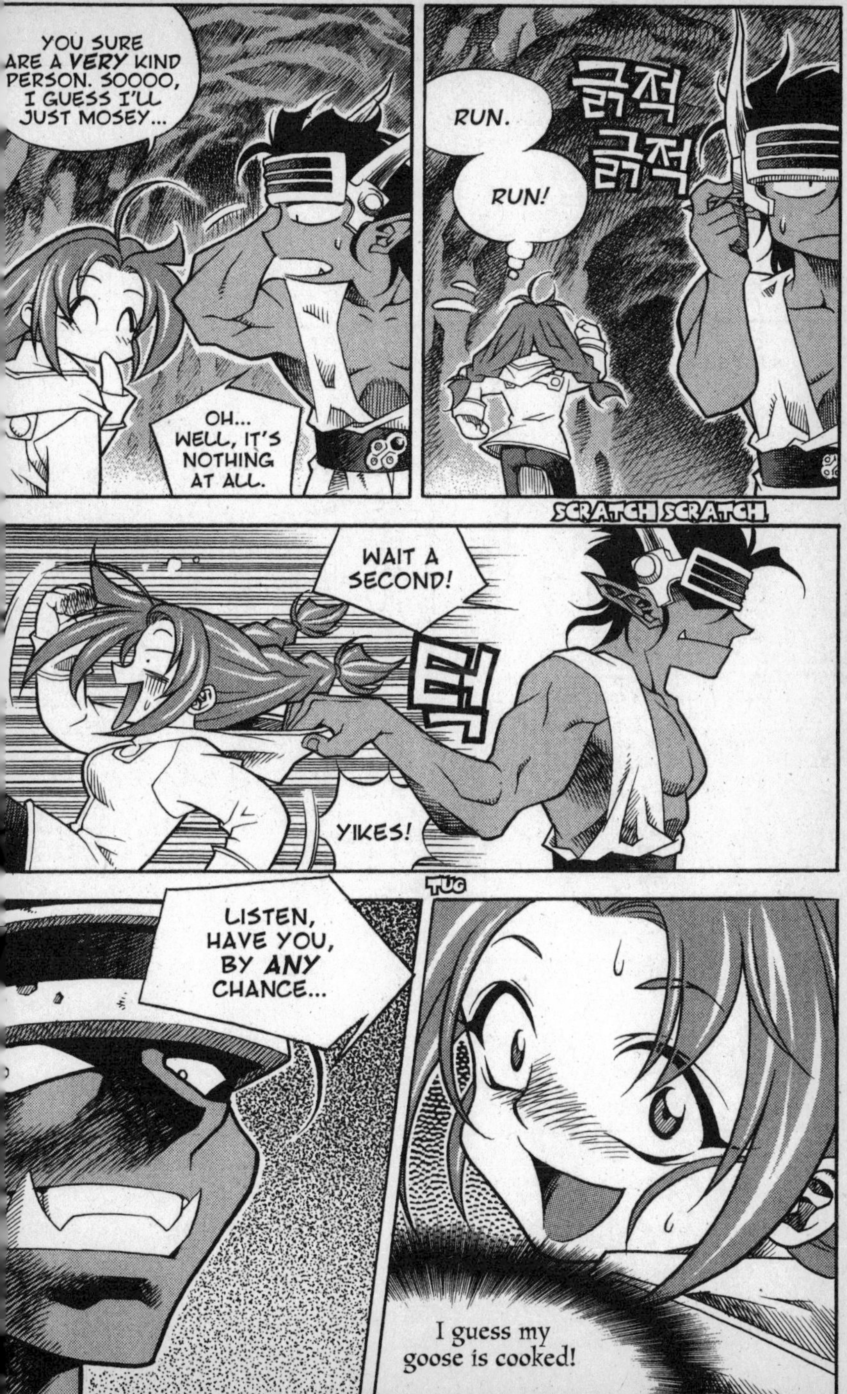
YOU SURE ARE A VERY KIND PERSON. SOOOO, I GUESS I'LL JUST MOSEY...
OH... WELL, IT'S NOTHING AT ALL.
RUN.
RUN!
긁적 긁적
SCRATCH SCRATCH
WAIT A SECOND!
턱
YIKES!
TUG
LISTEN, HAVE YOU, BY ANY CHANCE...
I guess my goose is cooked!

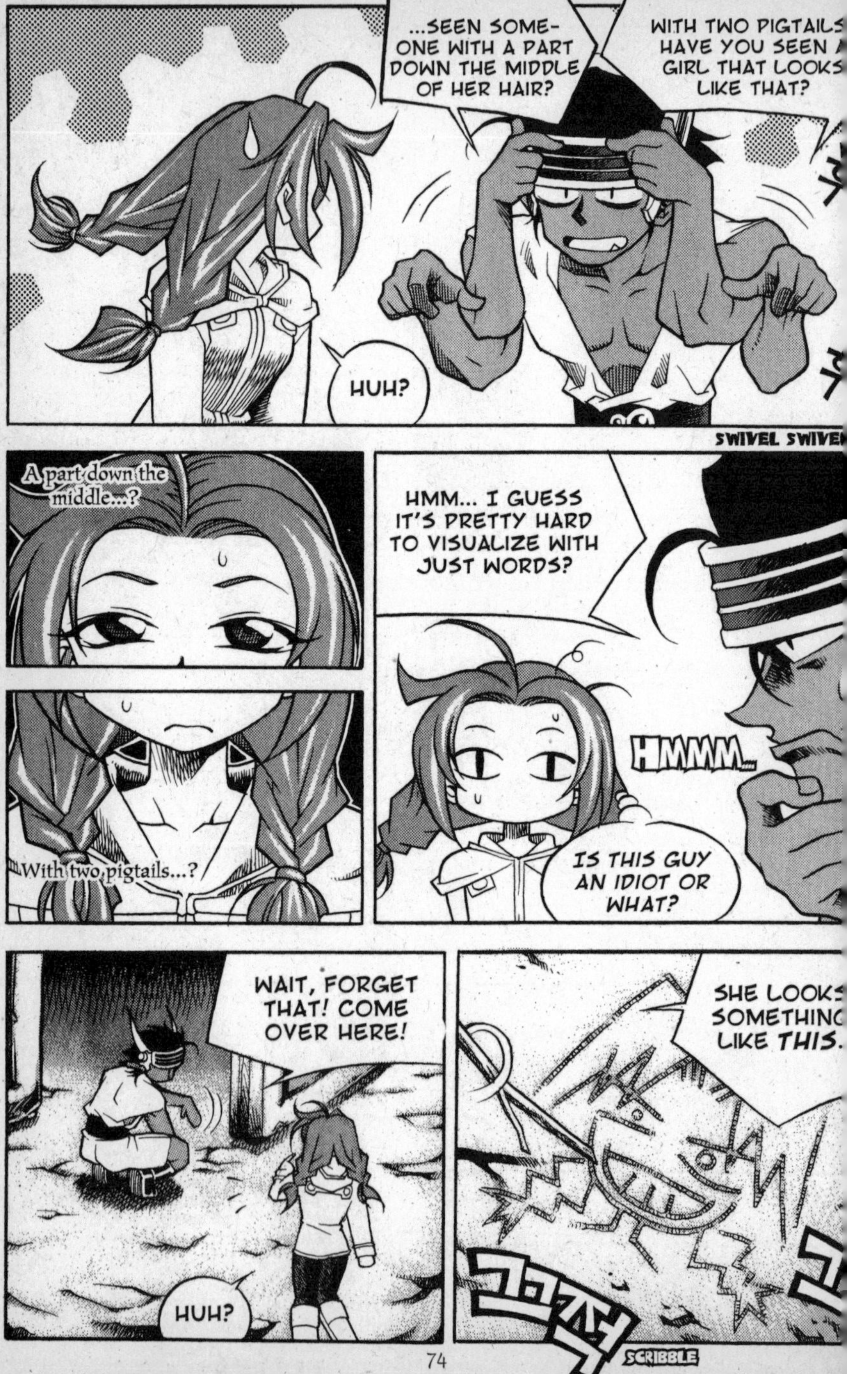

...SEEN SOME-ONE WITH A PART DOWN THE MIDDLE OF HER HAIR?
WITH TWO PIGTAILS HAVE YOU SEEN A GIRL THAT LOOKS LIKE THAT?
HUH?
SWIVEL SWIVEL
A part down the middle...?
With two pigtails...?
HMM... I GUESS IT'S PRETTY HARD TO VISUALIZE WITH JUST WORDS?
HMMM...
IS THIS GUY AN IDIOT OR WHAT?
WAIT, FORGET THAT! COME OVER HERE!
HUH?
SHE LOOKS SOMETHING LIKE THIS.
SCRIBBLE

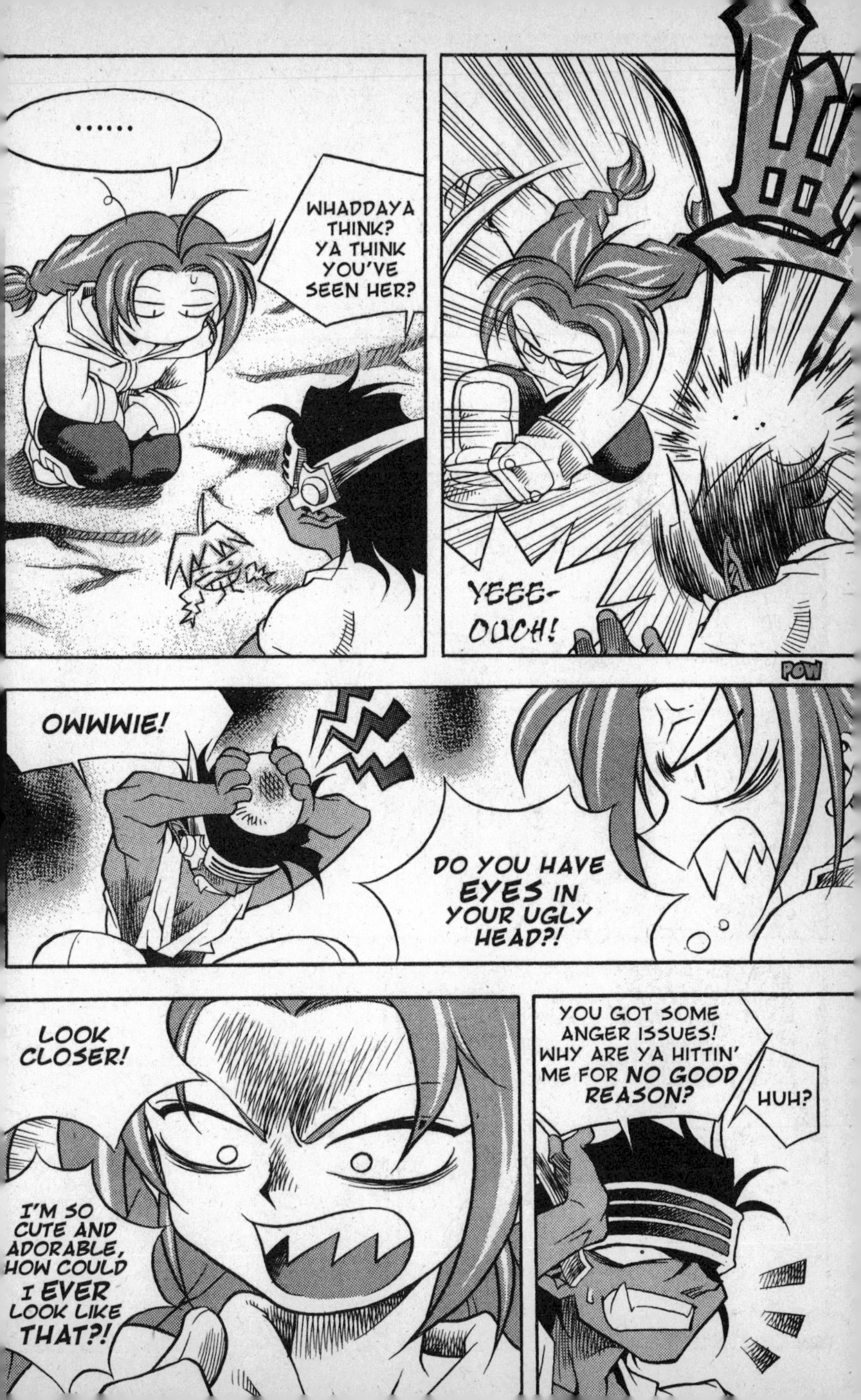
......
WHADDAYA THINK? YA THINK YOU'VE SEEN HER?
YEEE-OUCH!
POW
OWWWIE!
DO YOU HAVE EYES IN YOUR UGLY HEAD?!
LOOK CLOSER!
I'M SO CUTE AND ADORABLE, HOW COULD I EVER LOOK LIKE THAT?!
YOU GOT SOME ANGER ISSUES! WHY ARE YA HITTIN' ME FOR NO GOOD REASON?
HUH?

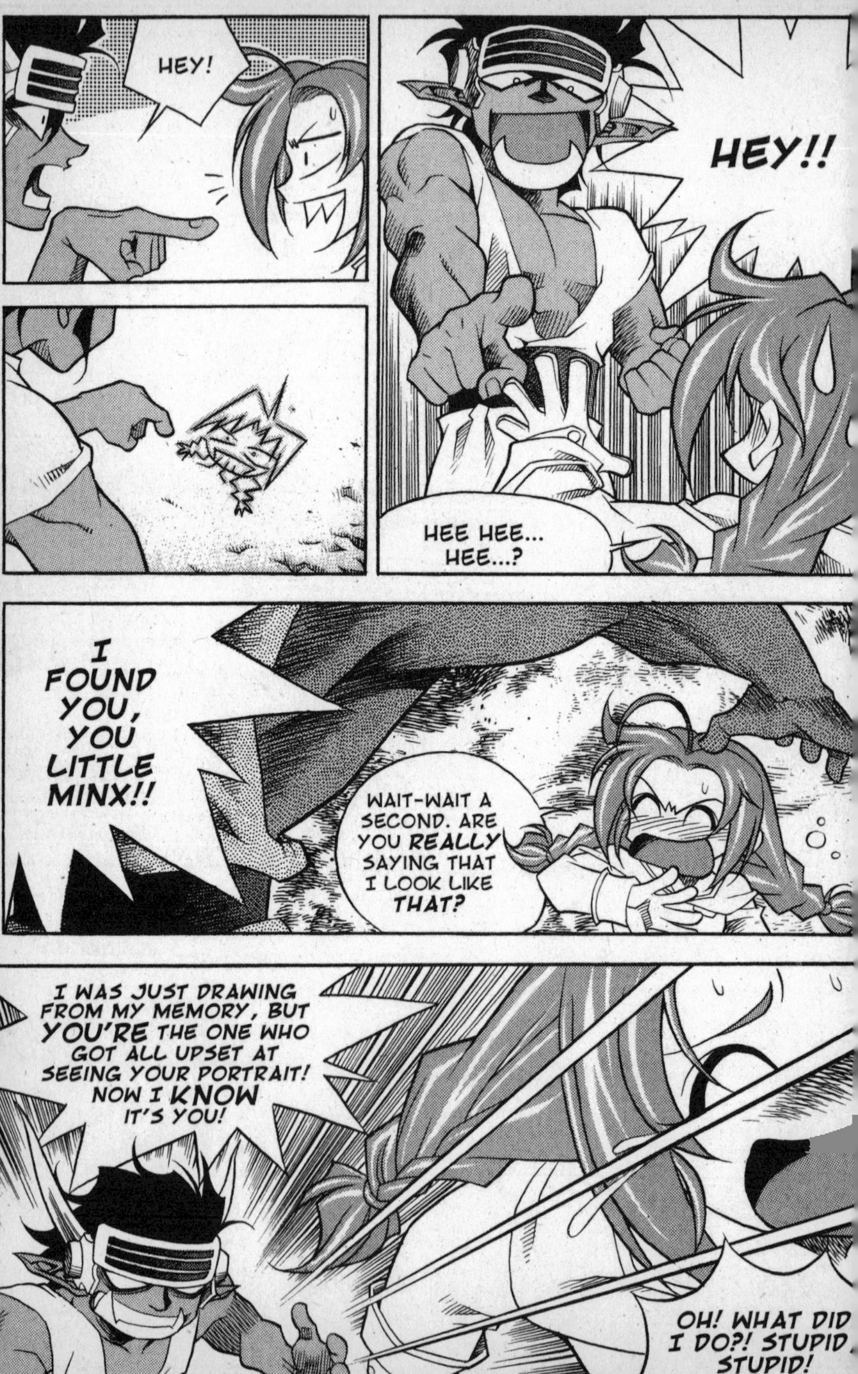

HEY!
HEY!!
HEE HEE... HEE...?
I FOUND YOU, YOU LITTLE MINX!!
WAIT-WAIT A SECOND. ARE YOU REALLY SAYING THAT I LOOK LIKE THAT?
I WAS JUST DRAWING FROM MY MEMORY, BUT YOU'RE THE ONE WHO GOT ALL UPSET AT SEEING YOUR PORTRAIT! NOW I KNOW IT'S YOU!
OH! WHAT DID I DO?! STUPID STUPID STUPID!

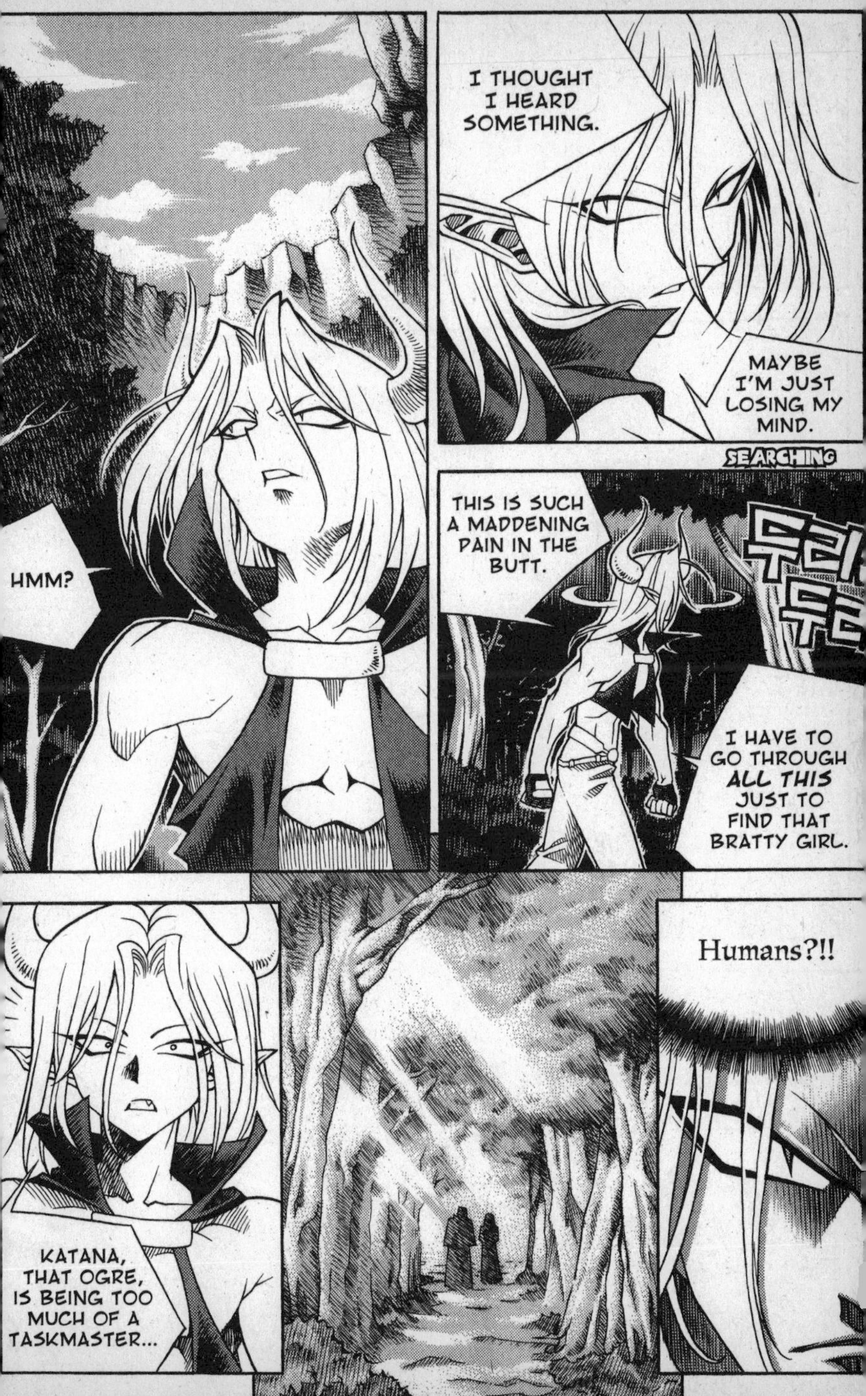
HMM?
I THOUGHT I HEARD SOMETHING.
MAYBE I'M JUST LOSING MY MIND.
SEARCHING
THIS IS SUCH A MADDENING PAIN IN THE BUTT.
I HAVE TO GO THROUGH ALL THIS JUST TO FIND THAT BRATTY GIRL.
KATANA, THAT OGRE, IS BEING TOO MUCH OF A TASKMASTER...
Humans?!!

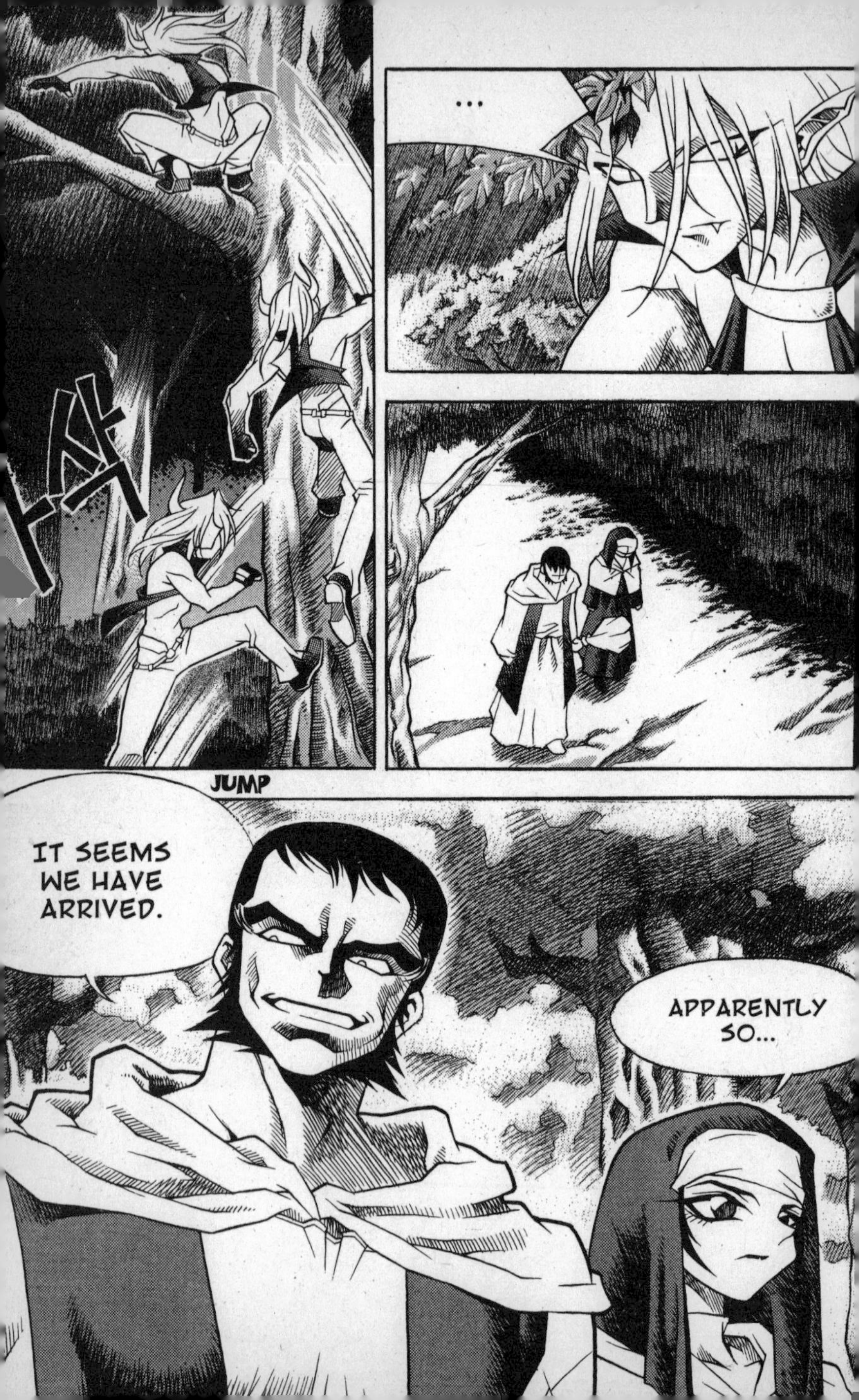
JUMP
...
IT SEEMS WE HAVE ARRIVED.
APPARENTLY SO...

Quest 5

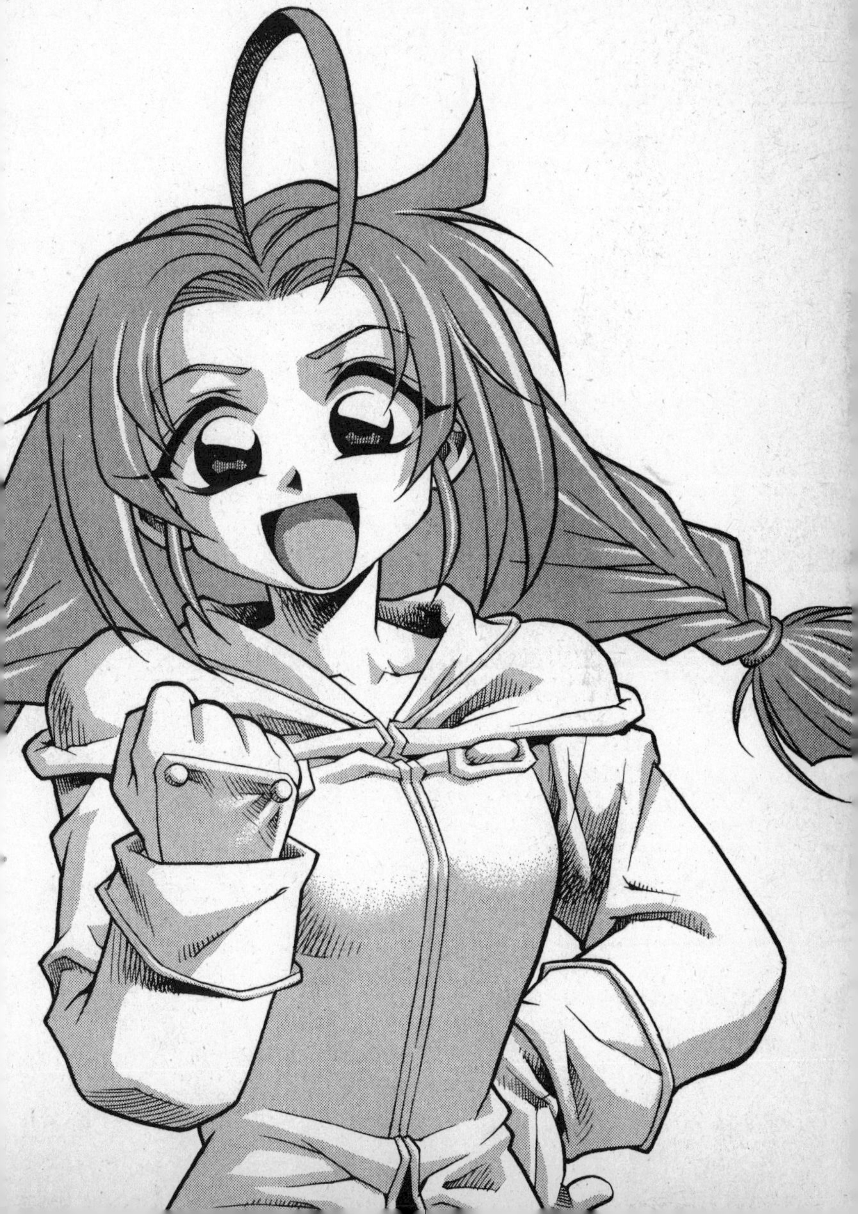

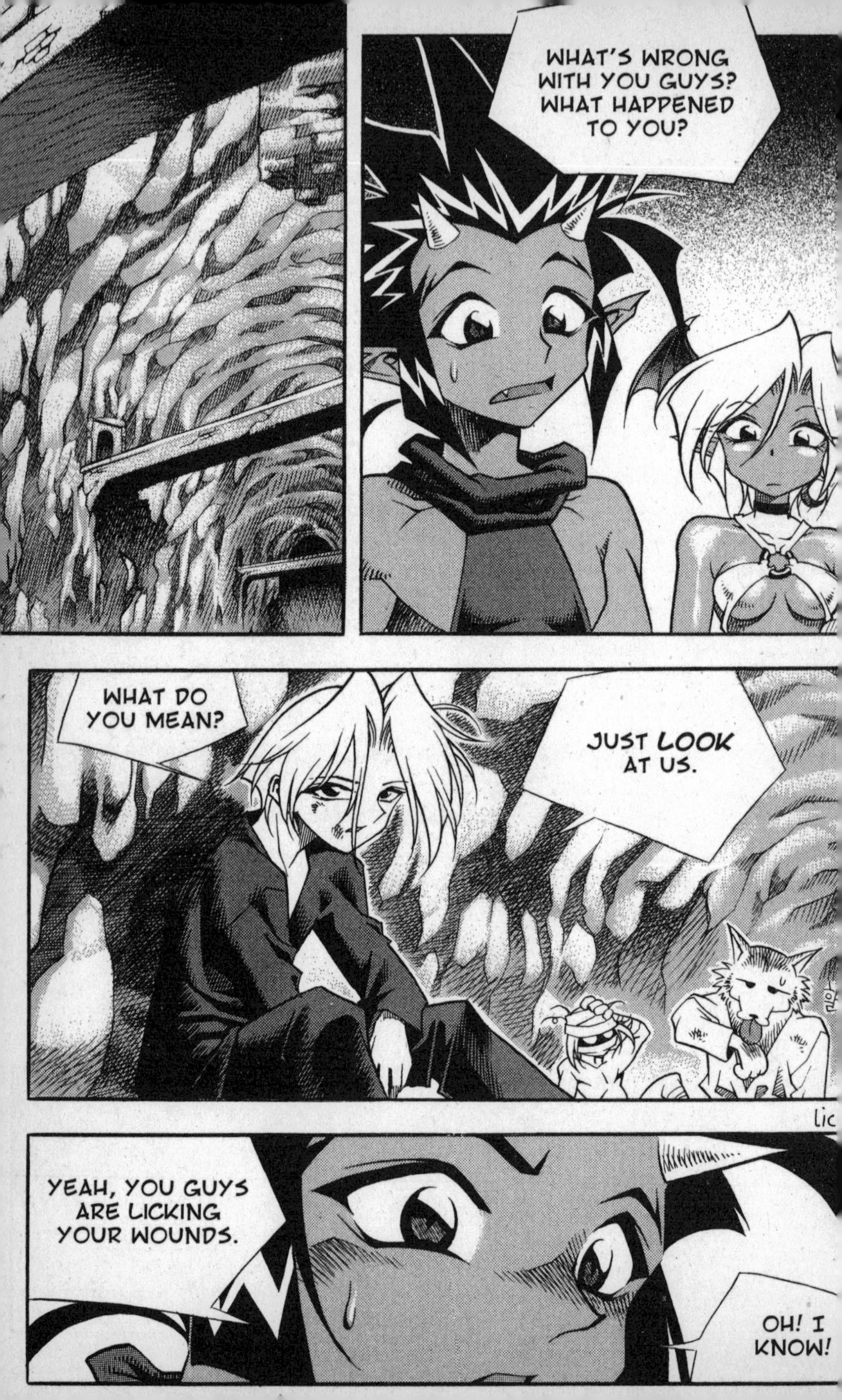
WHAT'S WRONG WITH YOU GUYS? WHAT HAPPENED TO YOU?
WHAT DO YOU MEAN?
JUST LOOK AT US.
lic
YEAH, YOU GUYS ARE LICKING YOUR WOUNDS.
OH! I KNOW!

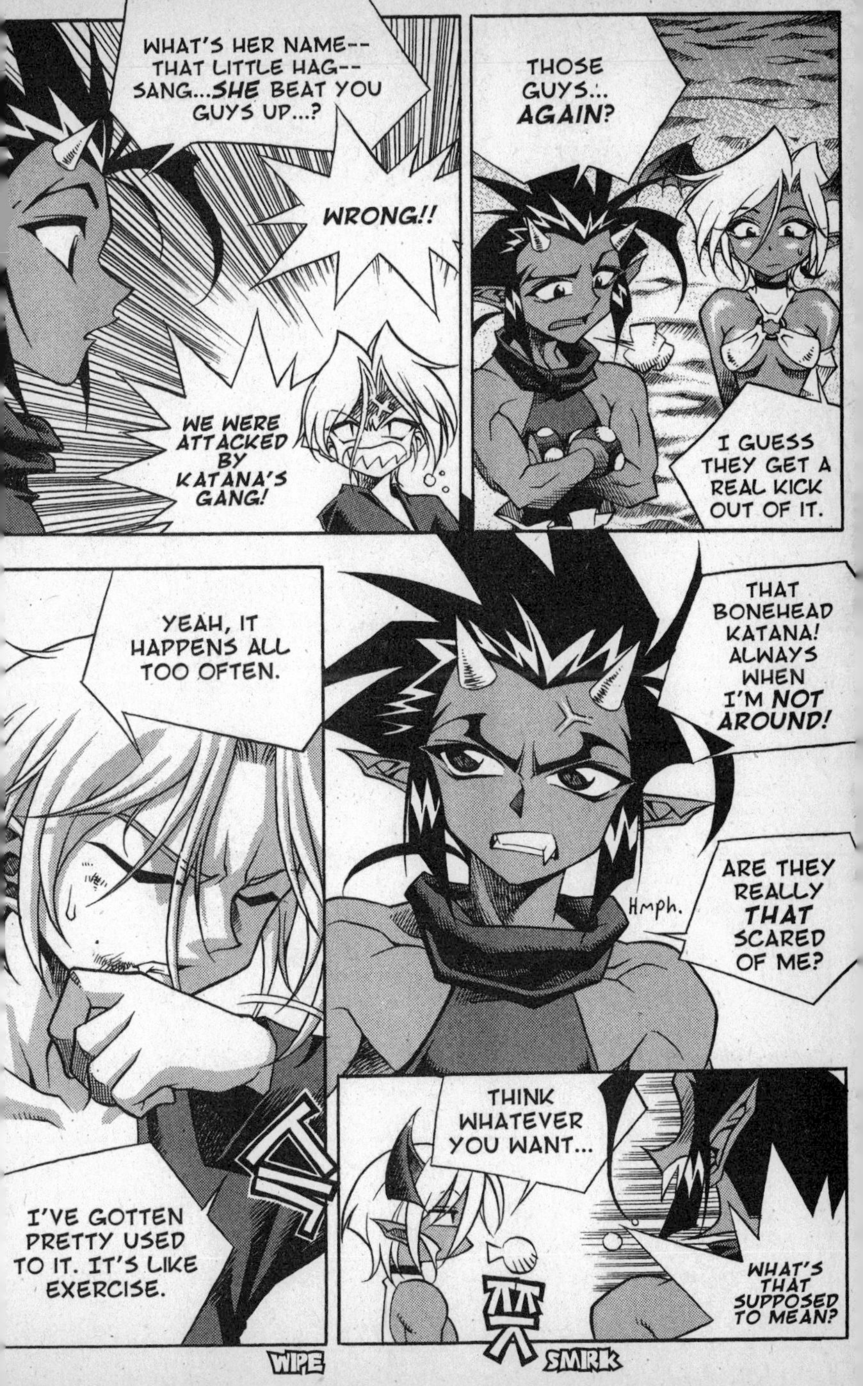
WHAT'S HER NAME-- THAT LITTLE HAG-- SANG...SHE BEAT YOU GUYS UP...?
WRONG!!
WE WERE ATTACKED BY KATANA'S GANG!
THOSE GUYS... AGAIN?
I GUESS THEY GET A REAL KICK OUT OF IT.
YEAH, IT HAPPENS ALL TOO OFTEN.
I'VE GOTTEN PRETTY USED TO IT. IT'S LIKE EXERCISE.
WIPE
THAT BONEHEAD KATANA! ALWAYS WHEN I'M NOT AROUND!
Hmph.
ARE THEY REALLY THAT SCARED OF ME?
THINK WHATEVER YOU WANT...
WHAT'S THAT SUPPOSED TO MEAN?
SMIRK

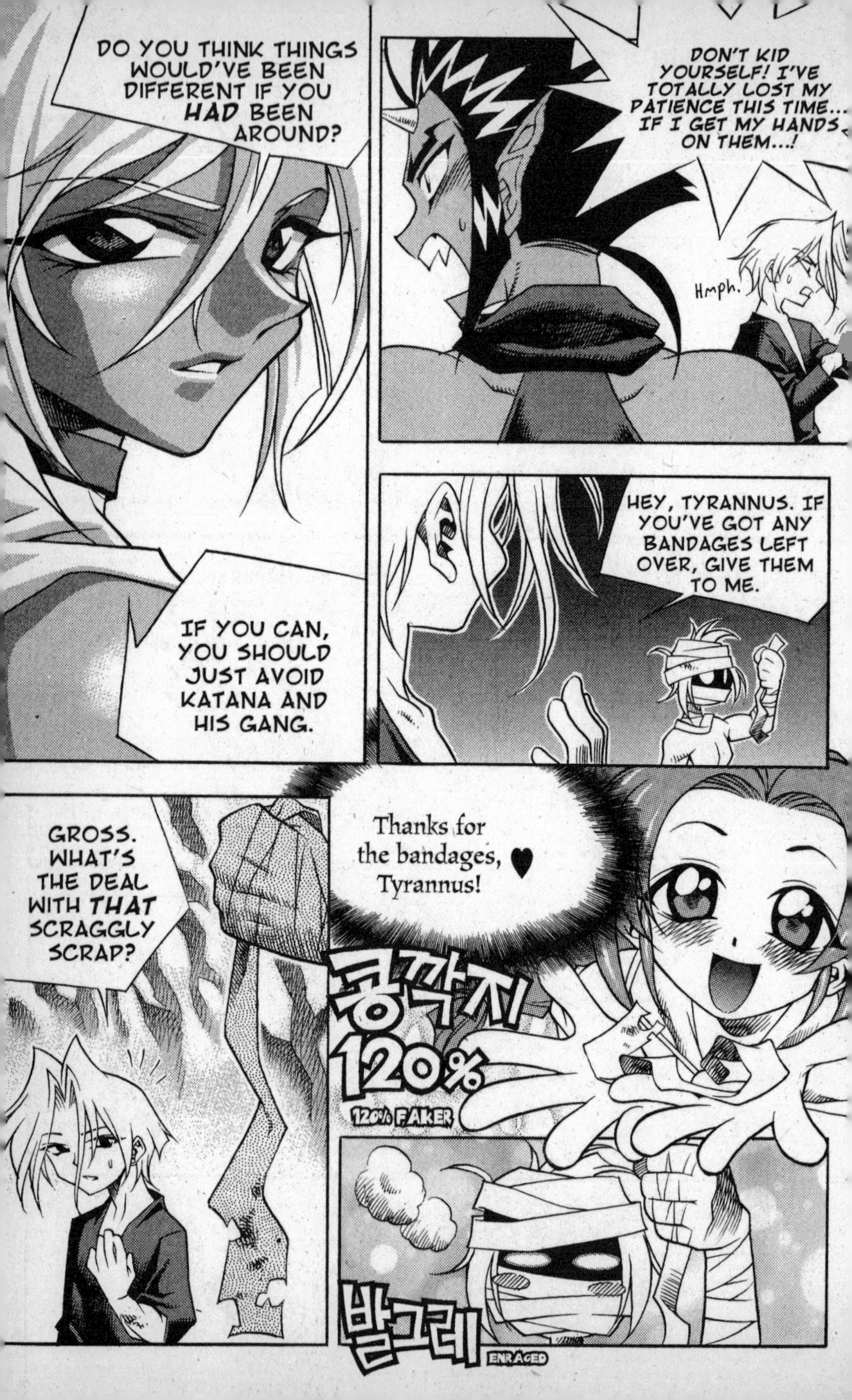
DO YOU THINK THINGS WOULD'VE BEEN DIFFERENT IF YOU **HAD** BEEN AROUND?
IF YOU CAN, YOU SHOULD JUST AVOID KATANA AND HIS GANG.
DON'T KID YOURSELF! I'VE TOTALLY LOST MY PATIENCE THIS TIME... IF I GET MY HANDS ON THEM...!
Hmph.
HEY, TYRANNUS. IF YOU'VE GOT ANY BANDAGES LEFT OVER, GIVE THEM TO ME.
GROSS. WHAT'S THE DEAL WITH **THAT** SCRAGGLY SCRAP?
Thanks for the bandages, ♥ Tyrannus!
콩깍지 120%
120% FAKER
발그레
ENRAGED

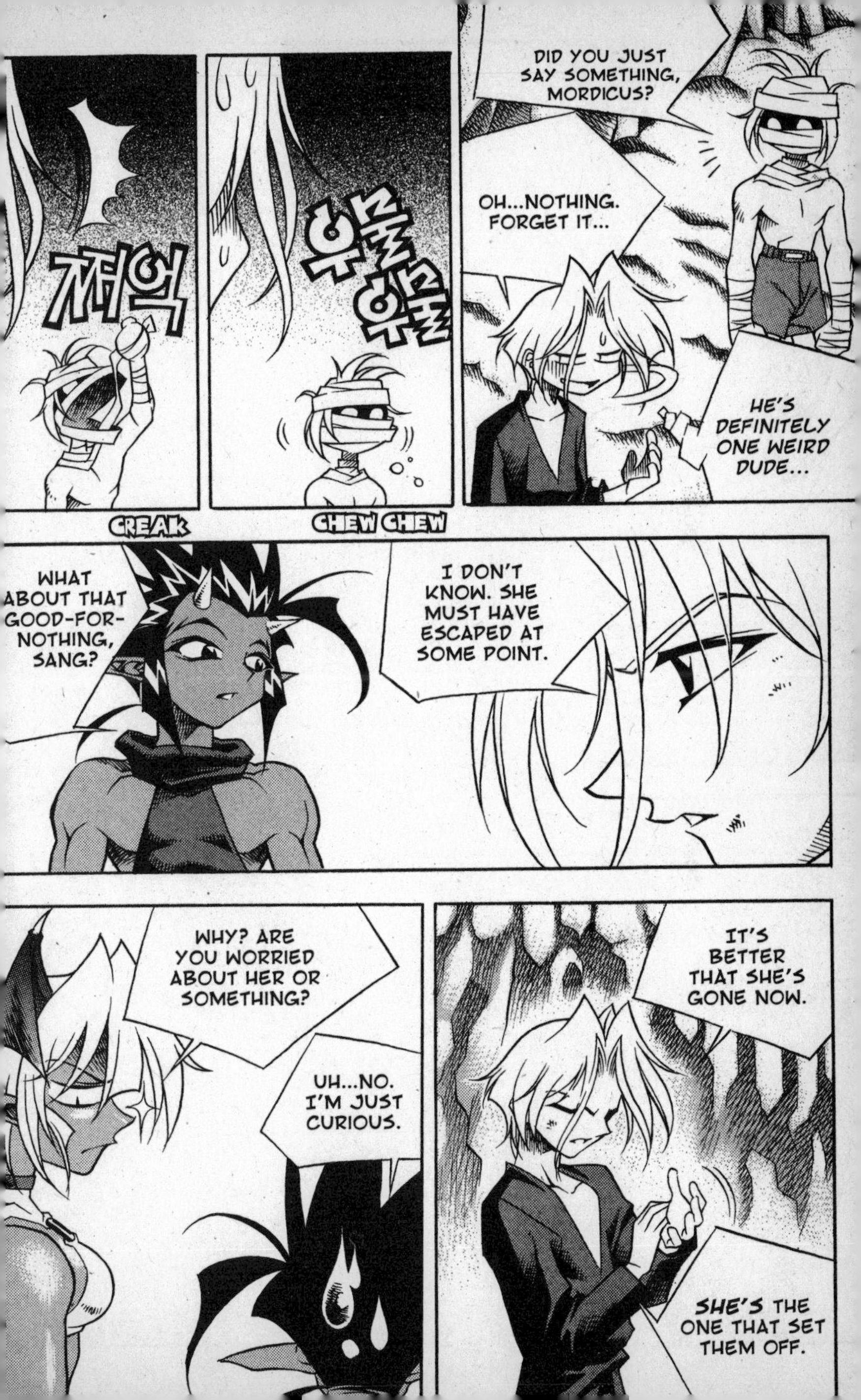

쩌억
CREAK
우물우물
CHEW CHEW
DID YOU JUST SAY SOMETHING, MORDICUS?
OH...NOTHING. FORGET IT...
HE'S DEFINITELY ONE WEIRD DUDE...
WHAT ABOUT THAT GOOD-FOR-NOTHING, SANG?
I DON'T KNOW. SHE MUST HAVE ESCAPED AT SOME POINT.
WHY? ARE YOU WORRIED ABOUT HER OR SOMETHING?
UH...NO. I'M JUST CURIOUS.
IT'S BETTER THAT SHE'S GONE NOW.
SHE'S THE ONE THAT SET THEM OFF.

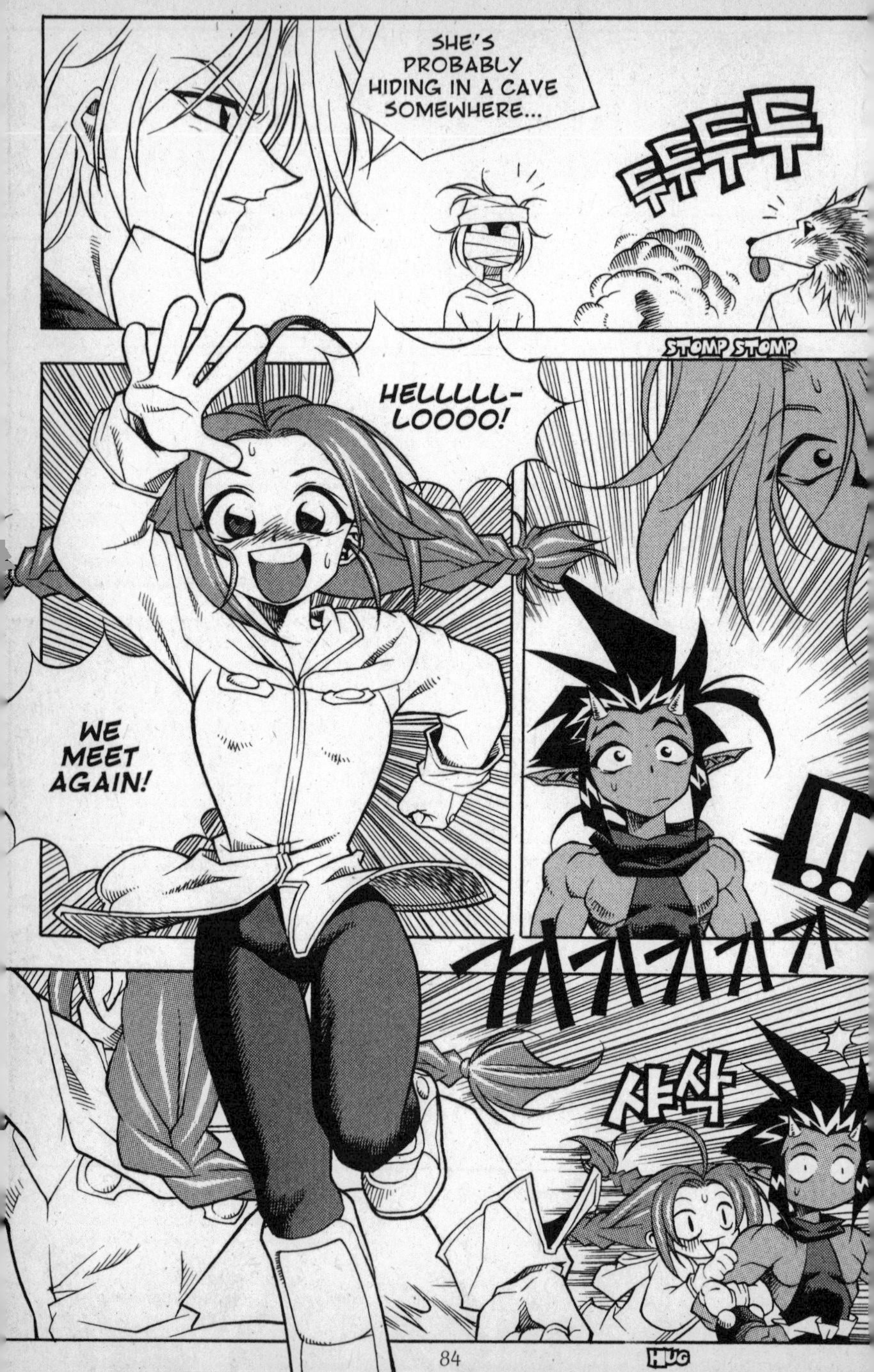

SHE'S PROBABLY HIDING IN A CAVE SOMEWHERE...
두두두두
STOMP STOMP
HELLLLL-LOOOO!
WE MEET AGAIN!
!!
가사가가가가
샤삭
HUG

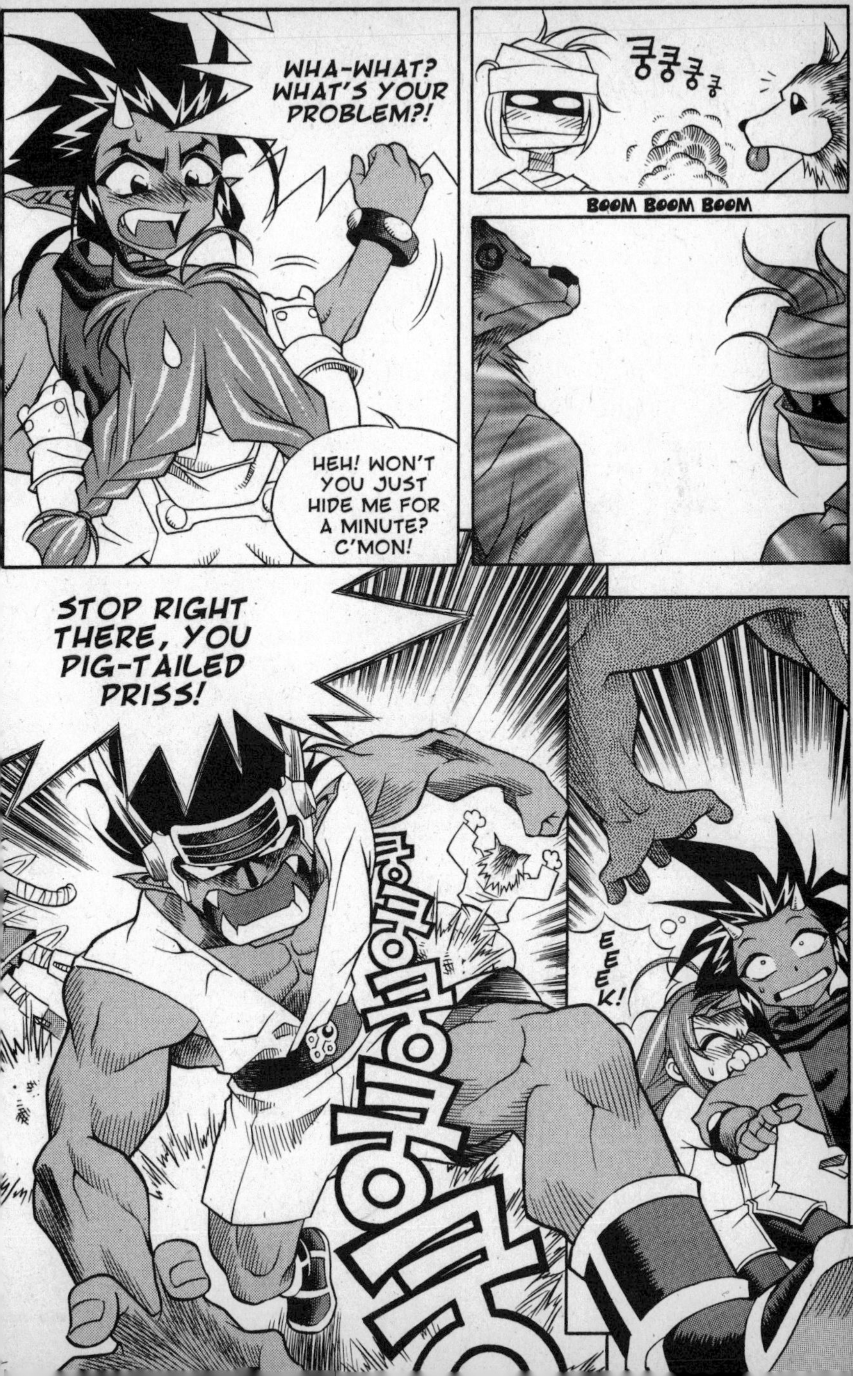
WHA-WHAT? WHAT'S YOUR PROBLEM?!
HEH! WON'T YOU JUST HIDE ME FOR A MINUTE? C'MON!
쿵쿵쿵쿵쿵
BOOM BOOM BOOM
STOP RIGHT THERE, YOU PIG-TAILED PRISS!
EEEK!

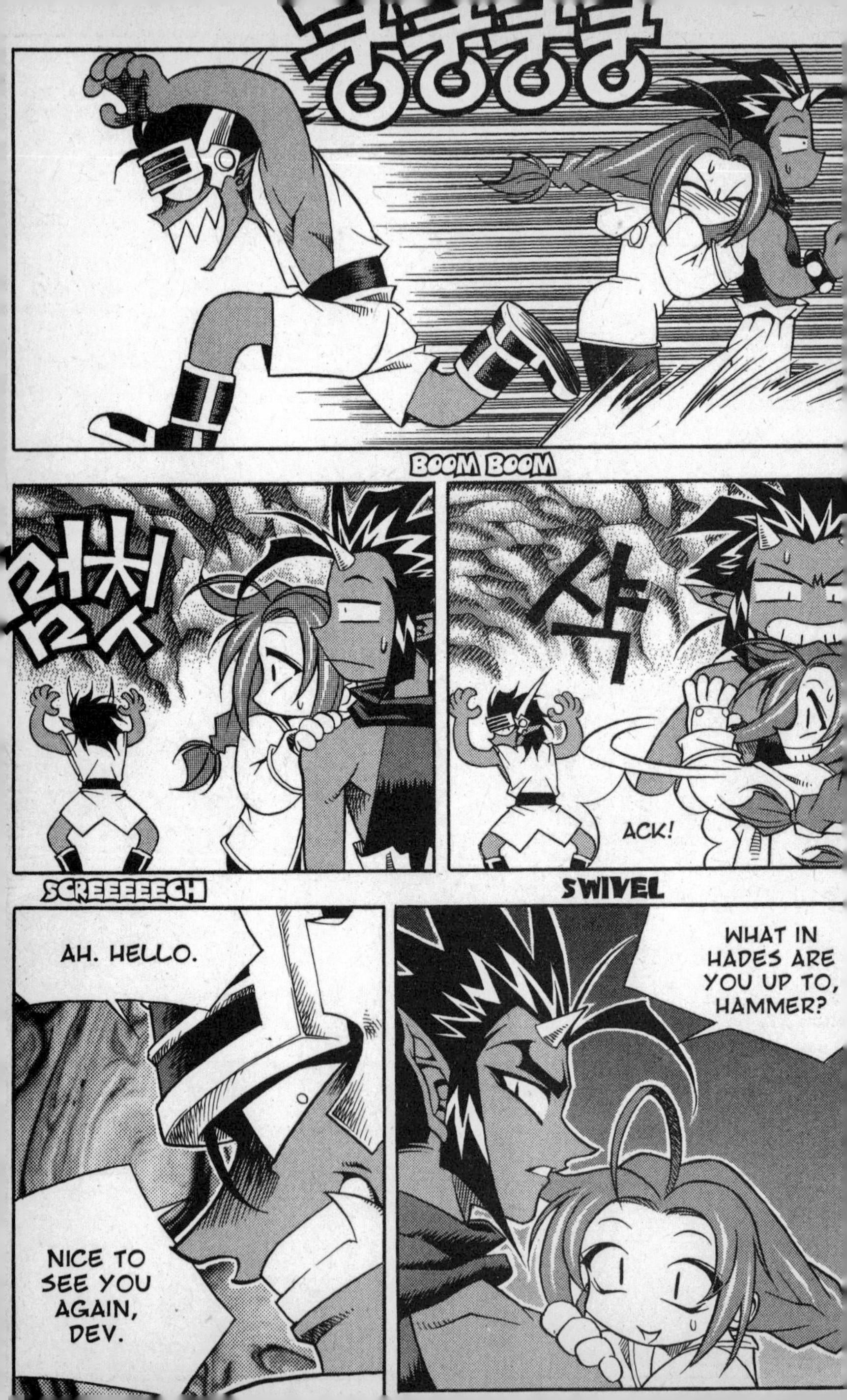
BOOM BOOM
SCREEEEEECH
ACK!
SWIVEL
AH. HELLO.
NICE TO SEE YOU AGAIN, DEV.
WHAT IN HADES ARE YOU UP TO, HAMMER?

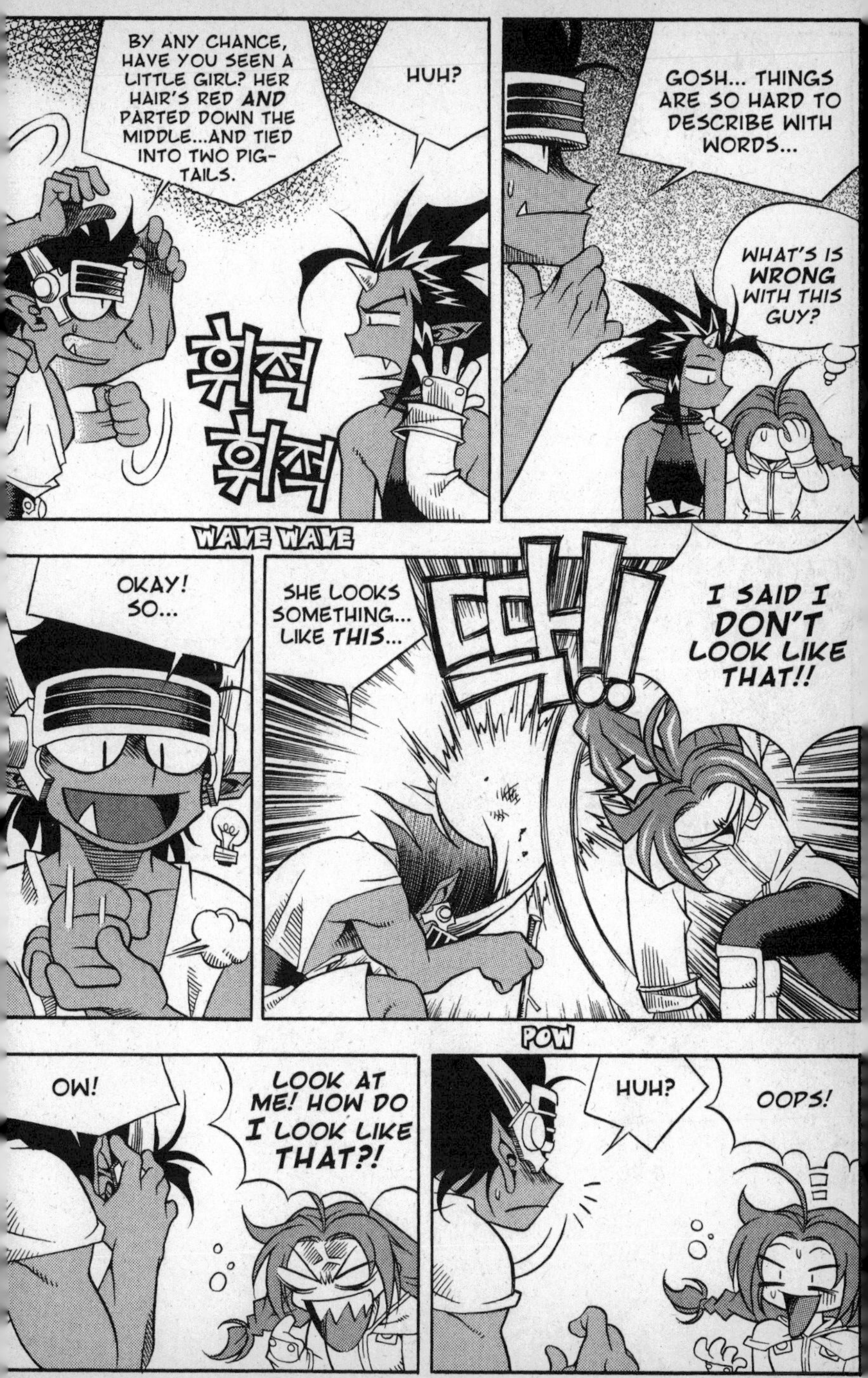
BY ANY CHANCE, HAVE YOU SEEN A LITTLE GIRL? HER HAIR'S RED AND PARTED DOWN THE MIDDLE...AND TIED INTO TWO PIG-TAILS.
HUH?
휘적 휘적
WAVE WAVE
GOSH... THINGS ARE SO HARD TO DESCRIBE WITH WORDS...
WHAT'S IS WRONG WITH THIS GUY?
OKAY! SO...
SHE LOOKS SOMETHING... LIKE THIS...
I SAID I DON'T LOOK LIKE THAT!!
POW
OW!
LOOK AT ME! HOW DO I LOOK LIKE THAT?!
HUH?
OOPS!

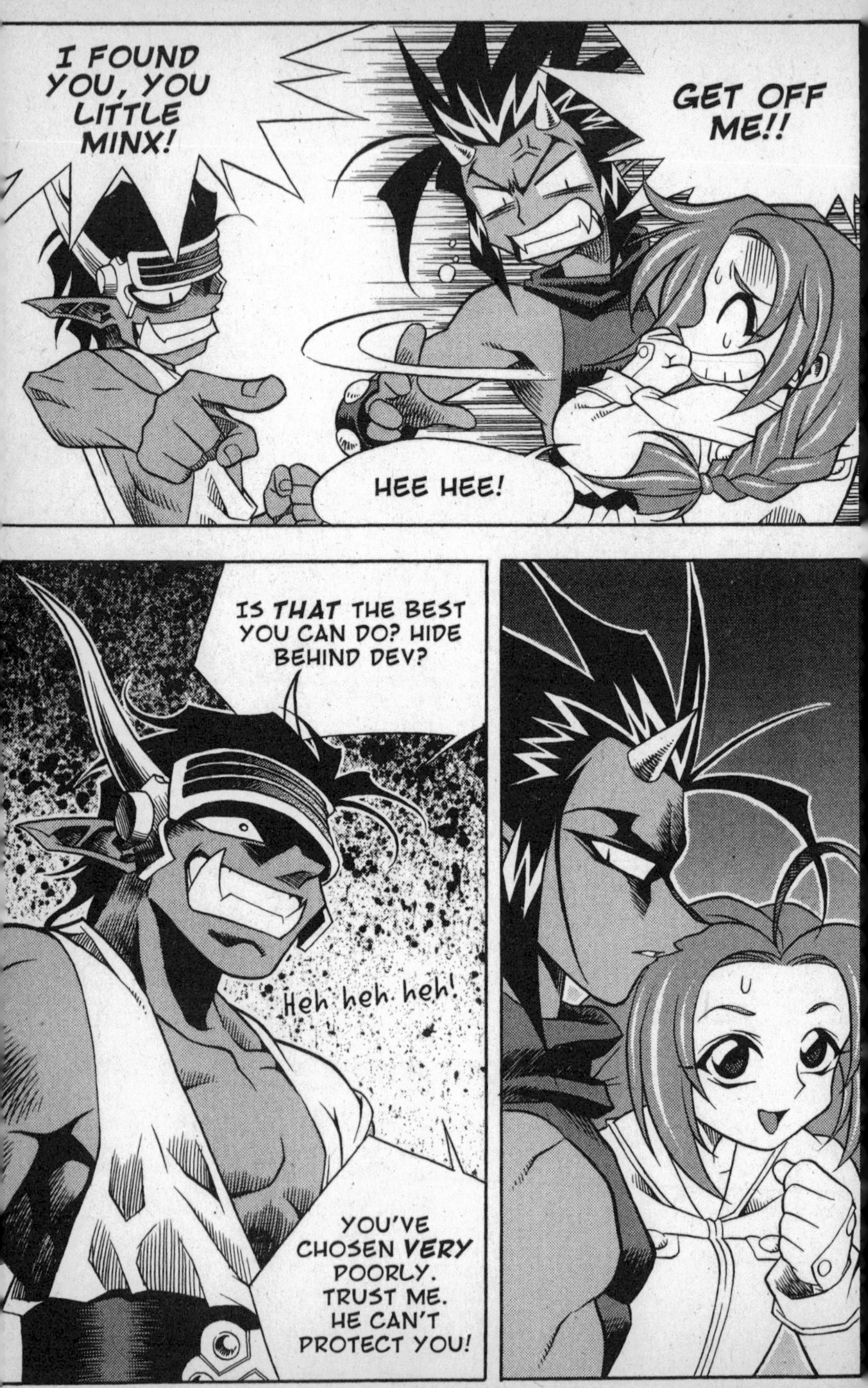
I FOUND YOU, YOU LITTLE MINX!
GET OFF ME!!
HEE HEE!
IS *THAT* THE BEST YOU CAN DO? HIDE BEHIND DEV?
Heh heh heh!
YOU'VE CHOSEN **VERY** POORLY. TRUST ME. HE CAN'T PROTECT YOU!

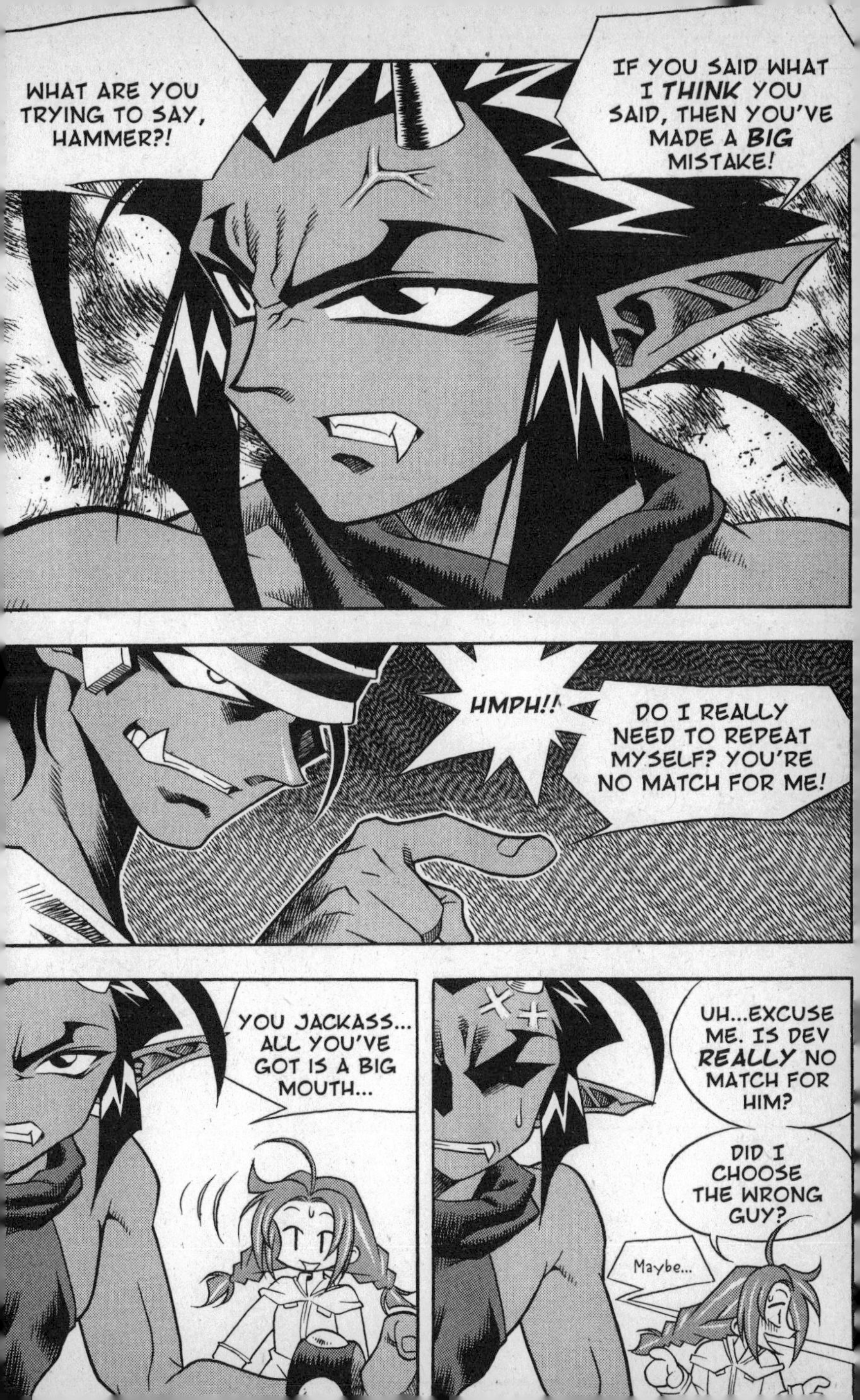
WHAT ARE YOU TRYING TO SAY, HAMMER?!
IF YOU SAID WHAT I THINK YOU SAID, THEN YOU'VE MADE A BIG MISTAKE!
HMPH!!
DO I REALLY NEED TO REPEAT MYSELF? YOU'RE NO MATCH FOR ME!
YOU JACKASS... ALL YOU'VE GOT IS A BIG MOUTH...
UH...EXCUSE ME. IS DEV REALLY NO MATCH FOR HIM?
DID I CHOOSE THE WRONG GUY?
Maybe...

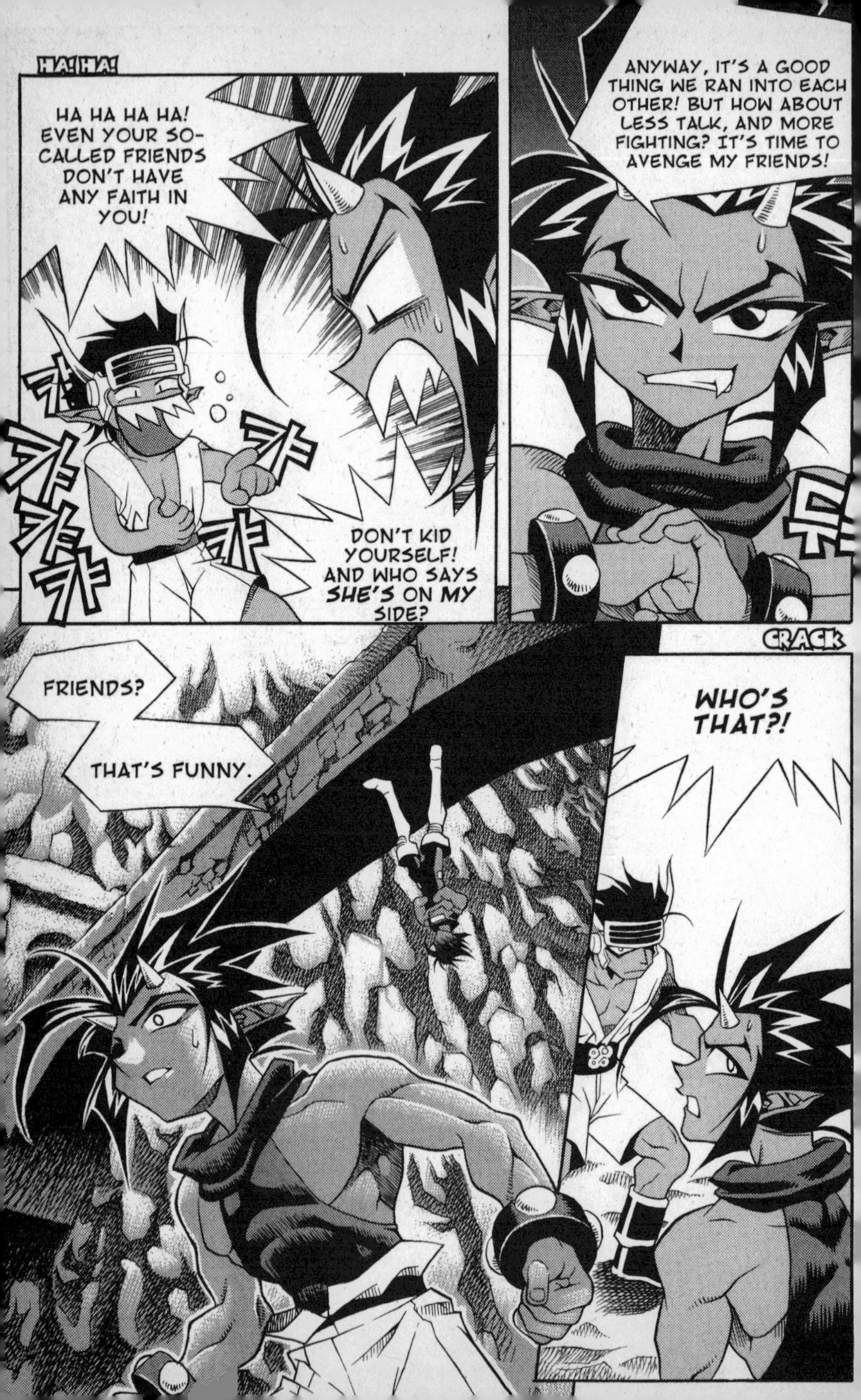
HA! HA!
HA HA HA HA! EVEN YOUR SO-CALLED FRIENDS DON'T HAVE ANY FAITH IN YOU!
DON'T KID YOURSELF! AND WHO SAYS SHE'S ON MY SIDE?
ANYWAY, IT'S A GOOD THING WE RAN INTO EACH OTHER! BUT HOW ABOUT LESS TALK, AND MORE FIGHTING? IT'S TIME TO AVENGE MY FRIENDS!
FRIENDS?
THAT'S FUNNY.
CRACK
WHO'S THAT?!

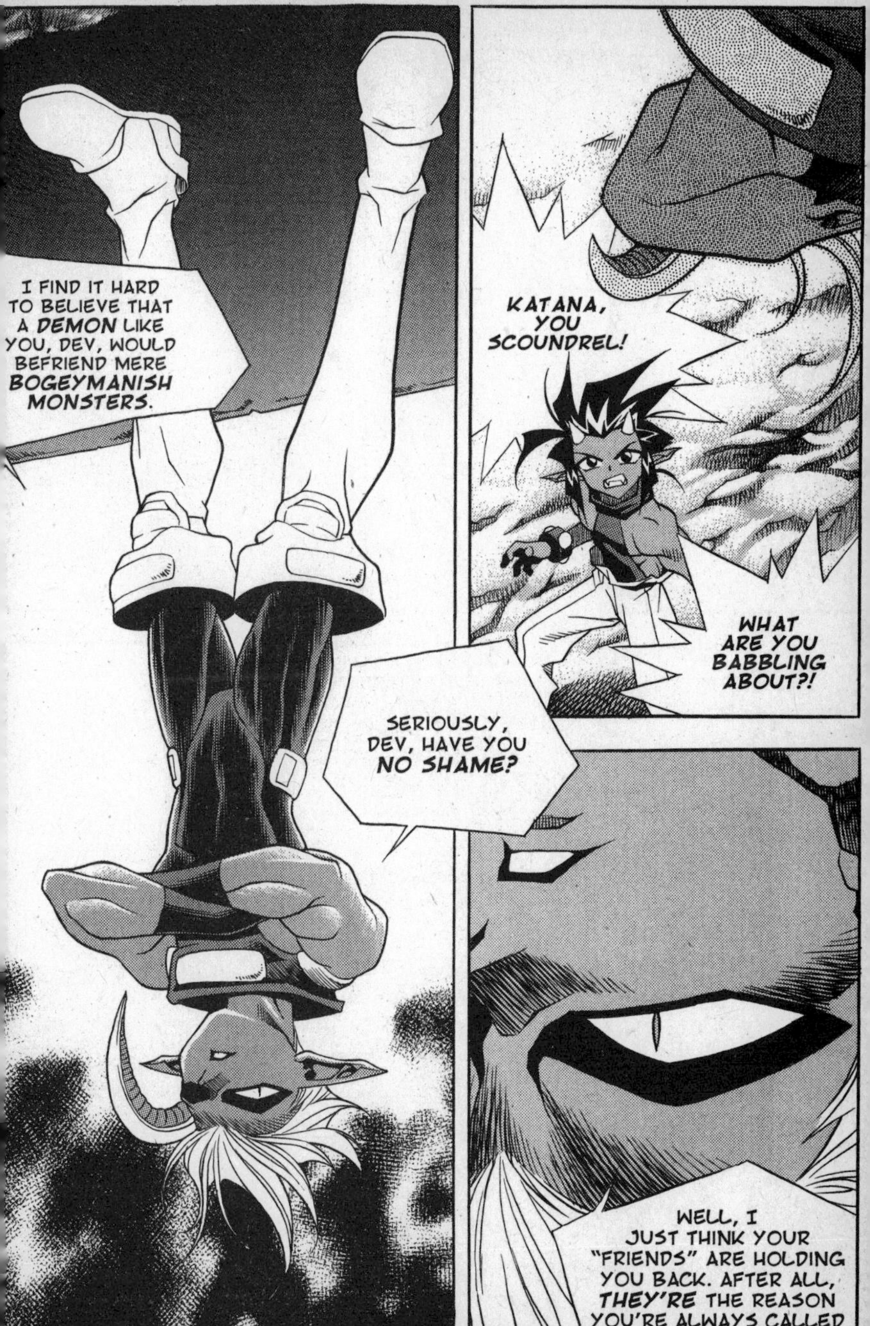
I FIND IT HARD TO BELIEVE THAT A DEMON LIKE YOU, DEV, WOULD BEFRIEND MERE BOGEYMANISH MONSTERS.
SERIOUSLY, DEV, HAVE YOU NO SHAME?
KATANA, YOU SCOUNDREL!
WHAT ARE YOU BABBLING ABOUT?!
WELL, I JUST THINK YOUR "FRIENDS" ARE HOLDING YOU BACK. AFTER ALL, THEY'RE THE REASON YOU'RE ALWAYS CALLED A DROP-OUT DEMON.

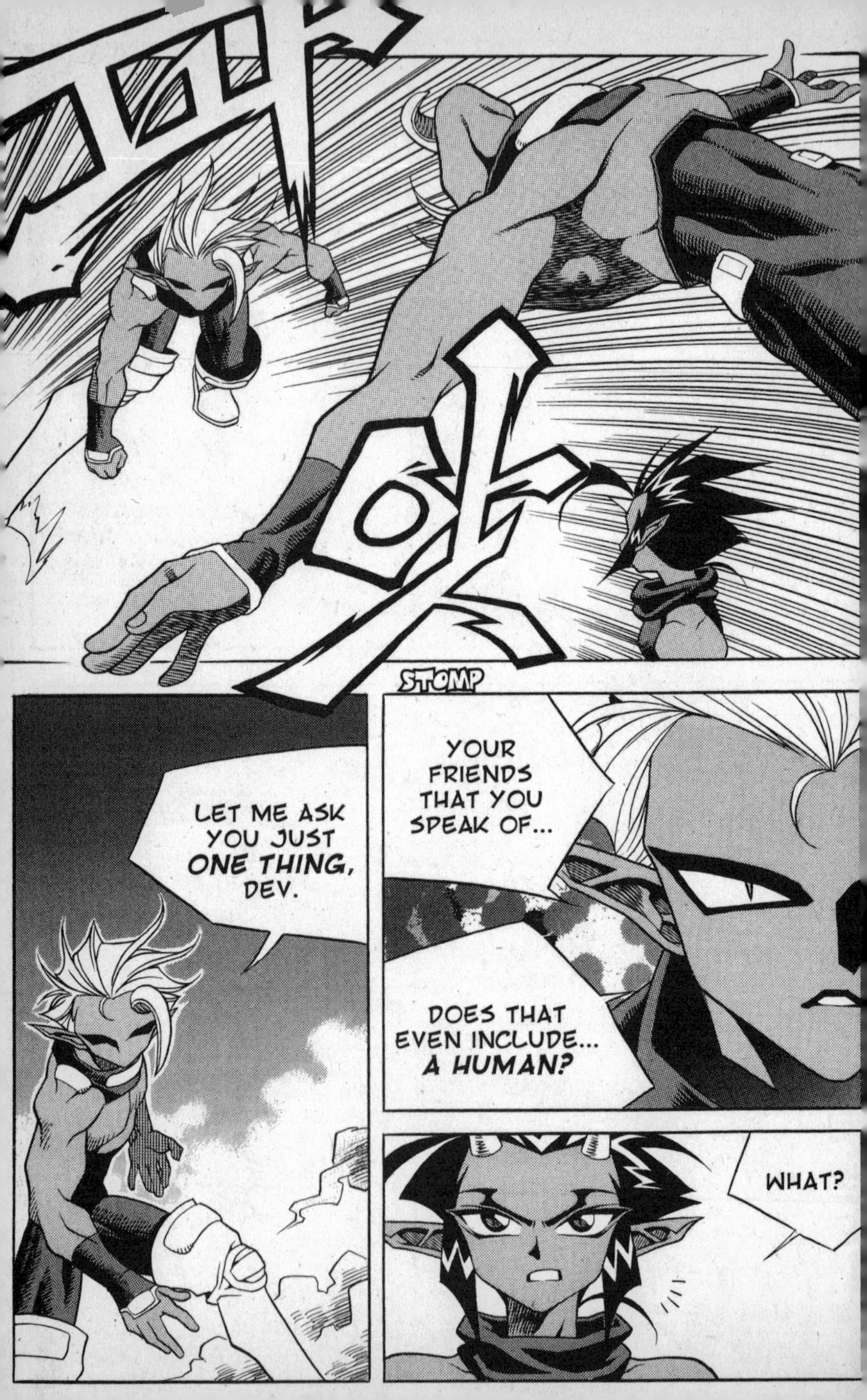
STOMP
LET ME ASK YOU JUST **ONE THING**, DEV.
YOUR FRIENDS THAT YOU SPEAK OF...
DOES THAT EVEN INCLUDE... ***A HUMAN?***
WHAT?

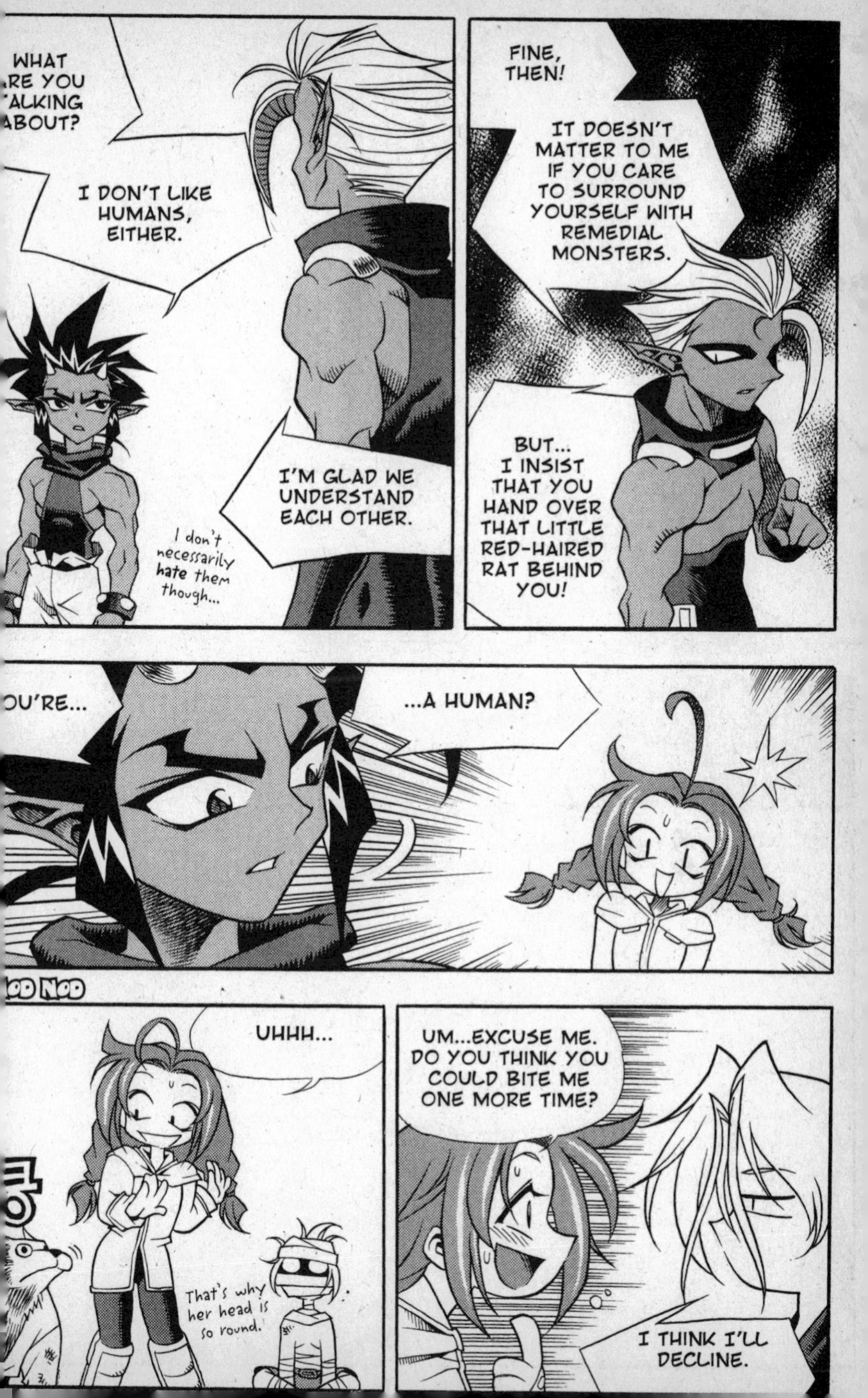
WHAT ARE YOU TALKING ABOUT?
I DON'T LIKE HUMANS, EITHER.
I'M GLAD WE UNDERSTAND EACH OTHER.
I don't necessarily hate them though...
FINE, THEN!
IT DOESN'T MATTER TO ME IF YOU CARE TO SURROUND YOURSELF WITH REMEDIAL MONSTERS.
BUT... I INSIST THAT YOU HAND OVER THAT LITTLE RED-HAIRED RAT BEHIND YOU!
OU'RE...
...A HUMAN?
OD NOD
UHHH...
That's why her head is so round.
UM...EXCUSE ME. DO YOU THINK YOU COULD BITE ME ONE MORE TIME?
I THINK I'LL DECLINE.

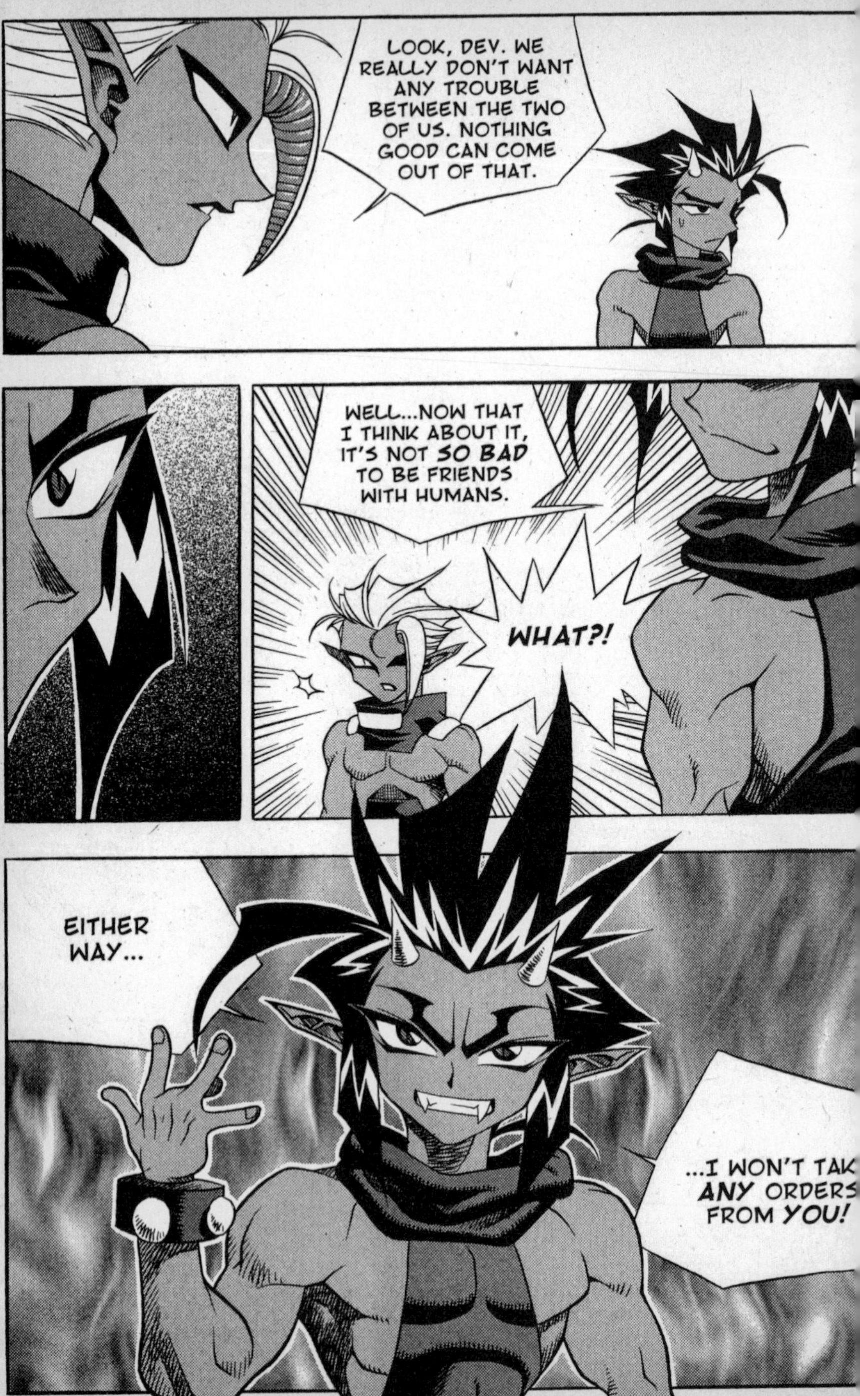
LOOK, DEV. WE REALLY DON'T WANT ANY TROUBLE BETWEEN THE TWO OF US. NOTHING GOOD CAN COME OUT OF THAT.
WELL...NOW THAT I THINK ABOUT IT, IT'S NOT SO BAD TO BE FRIENDS WITH HUMANS.
WHAT?!
EITHER WAY...
...I WON'T TAK ANY ORDERS FROM YOU!

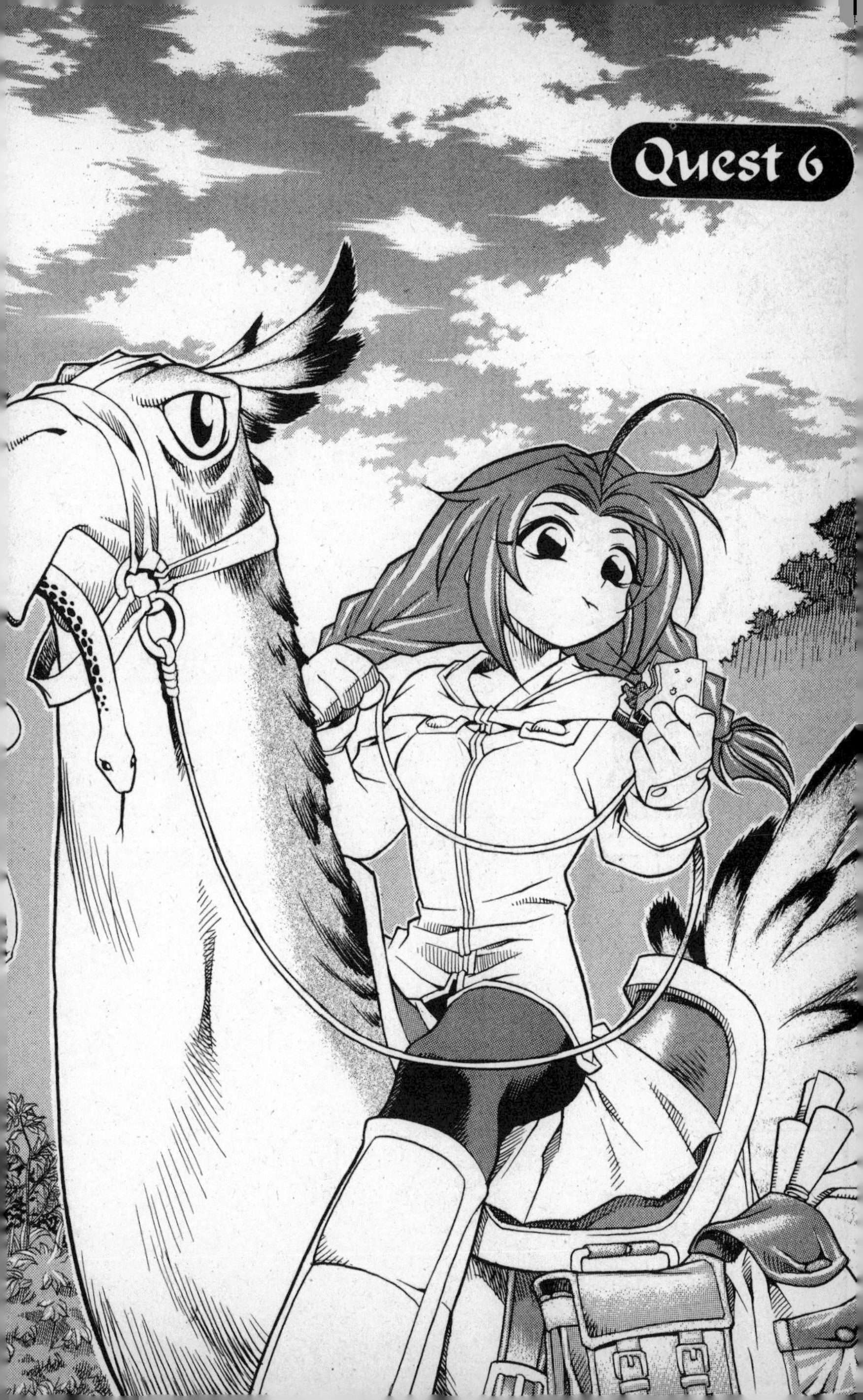
Quest 6

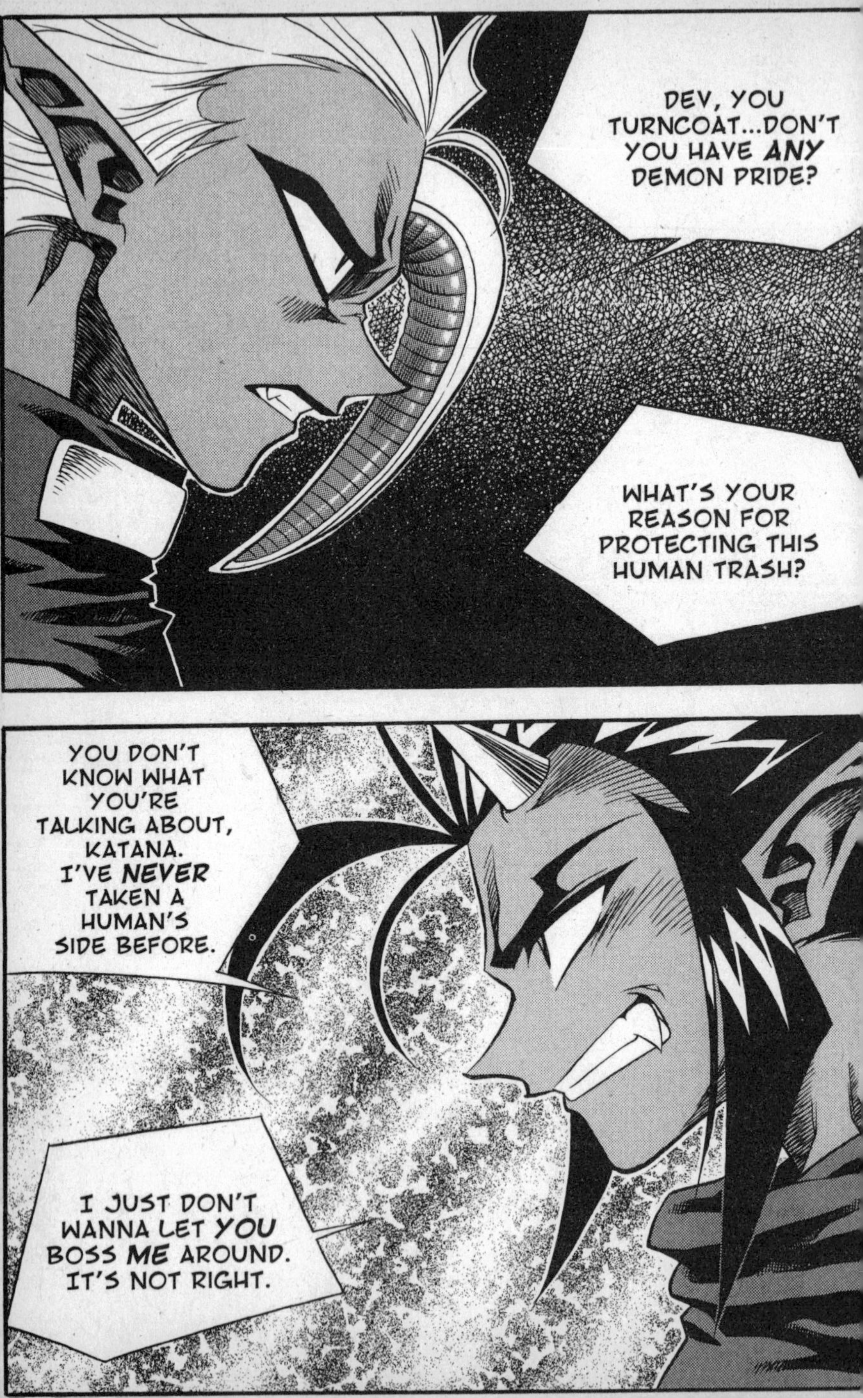
DEV, YOU TURNCOAT...DON'T YOU HAVE ANY DEMON PRIDE?
WHAT'S YOUR REASON FOR PROTECTING THIS HUMAN TRASH?
YOU DON'T KNOW WHAT YOU'RE TALKING ABOUT, KATANA. I'VE NEVER TAKEN A HUMAN'S SIDE BEFORE.
I JUST DON'T WANNA LET YOU BOSS ME AROUND. IT'S NOT RIGHT.

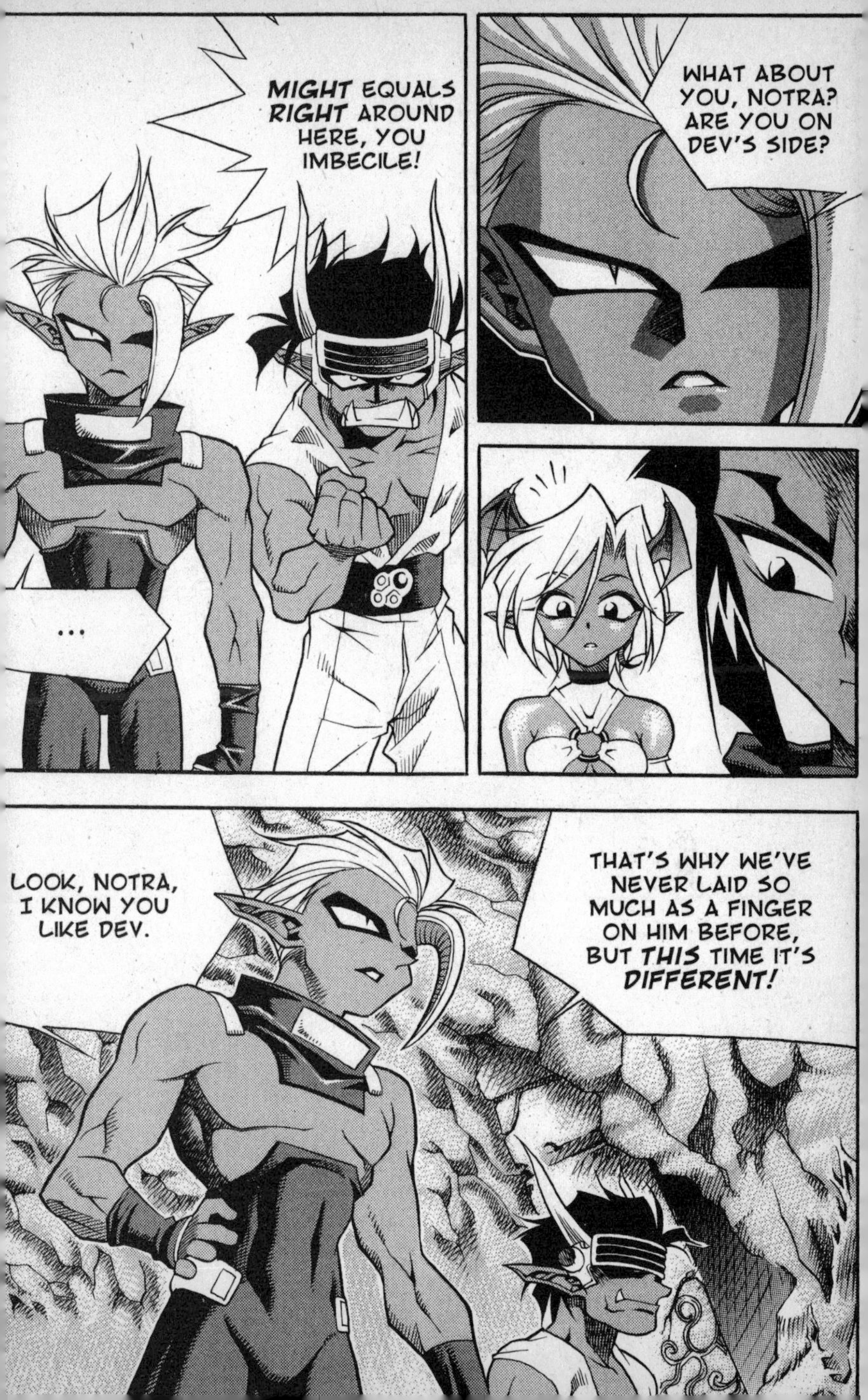
MIGHT EQUALS RIGHT AROUND HERE, YOU IMBECILE!
...
WHAT ABOUT YOU, NOTRA? ARE YOU ON DEV'S SIDE?
LOOK, NOTRA, I KNOW YOU LIKE DEV.
THAT'S WHY WE'VE NEVER LAID SO MUCH AS A FINGER ON HIM BEFORE, BUT THIS TIME IT'S DIFFERENT!

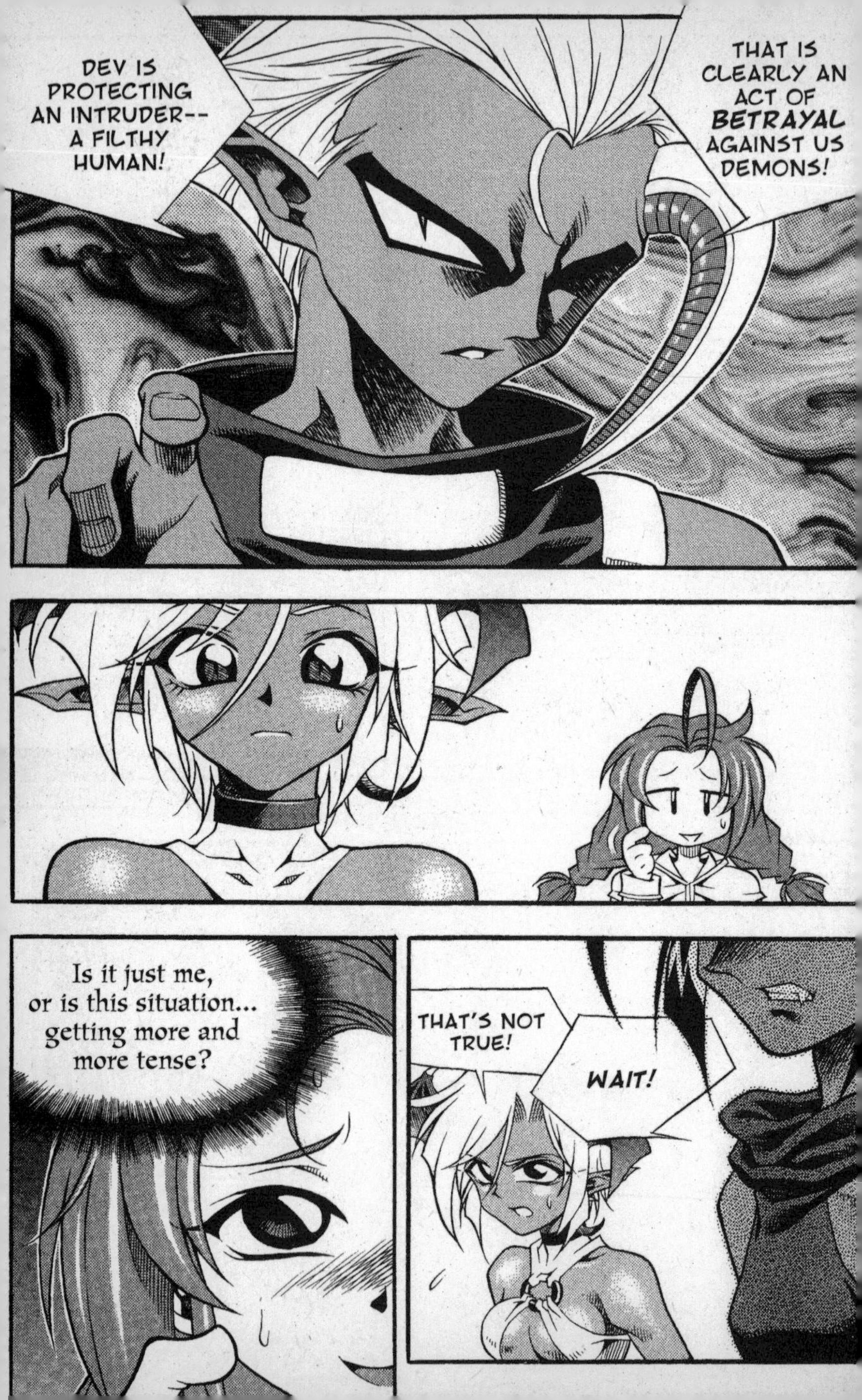
DEV IS PROTECTING AN INTRUDER-- A FILTHY HUMAN!
THAT IS CLEARLY AN ACT OF BETRAYAL AGAINST US DEMONS!
Is it just me, or is this situation... getting more and more tense?
THAT'S NOT TRUE!
WAIT!

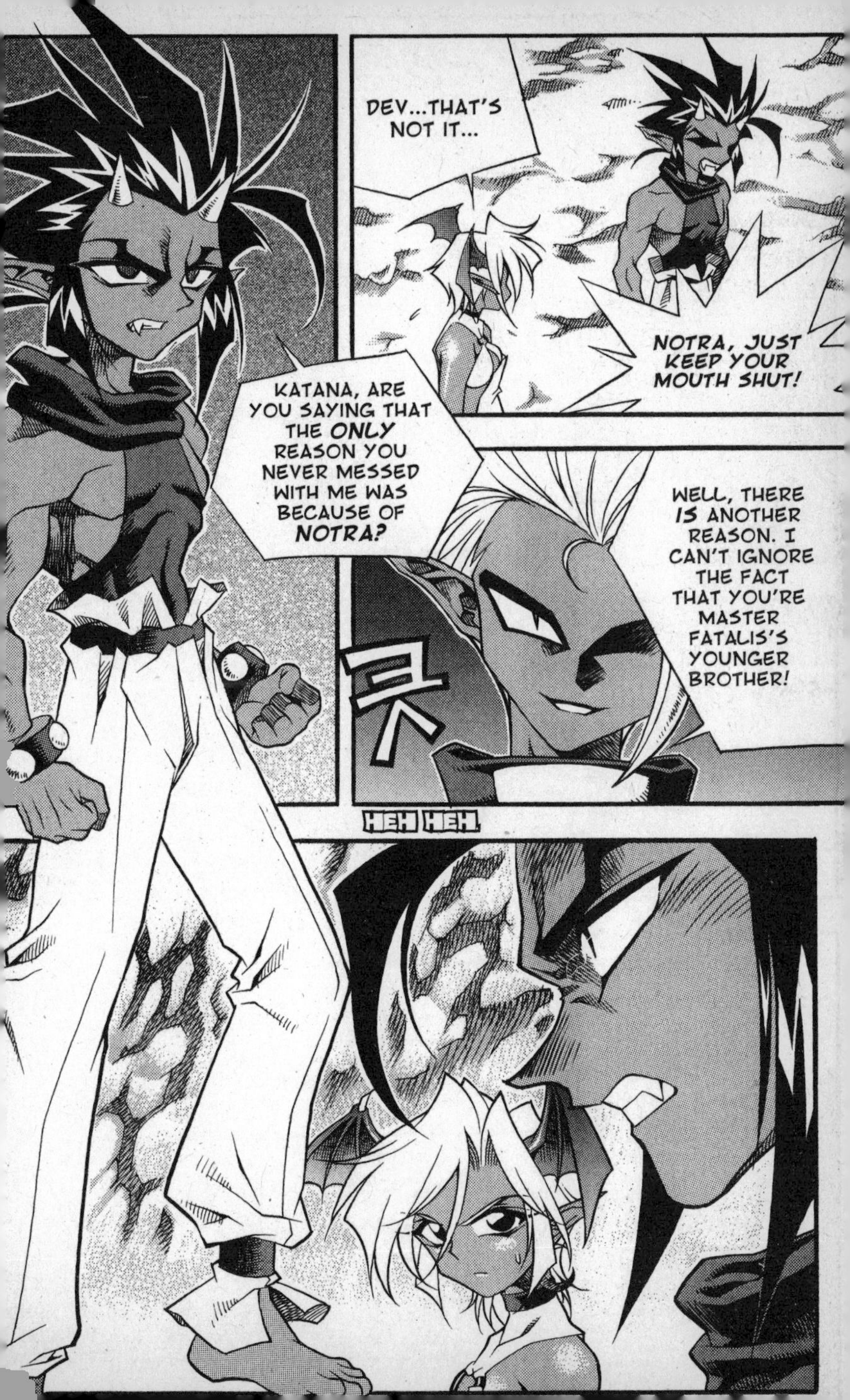
DEV...THAT'S NOT IT...
NOTRA, JUST KEEP YOUR MOUTH SHUT!
KATANA, ARE YOU SAYING THAT THE *ONLY* REASON YOU NEVER MESSED WITH ME WAS BECAUSE OF *NOTRA?*
WELL, THERE *IS* ANOTHER REASON. I CAN'T IGNORE THE FACT THAT YOU'RE MASTER FATALIS'S YOUNGER BROTHER!
큿
HEH HEH.

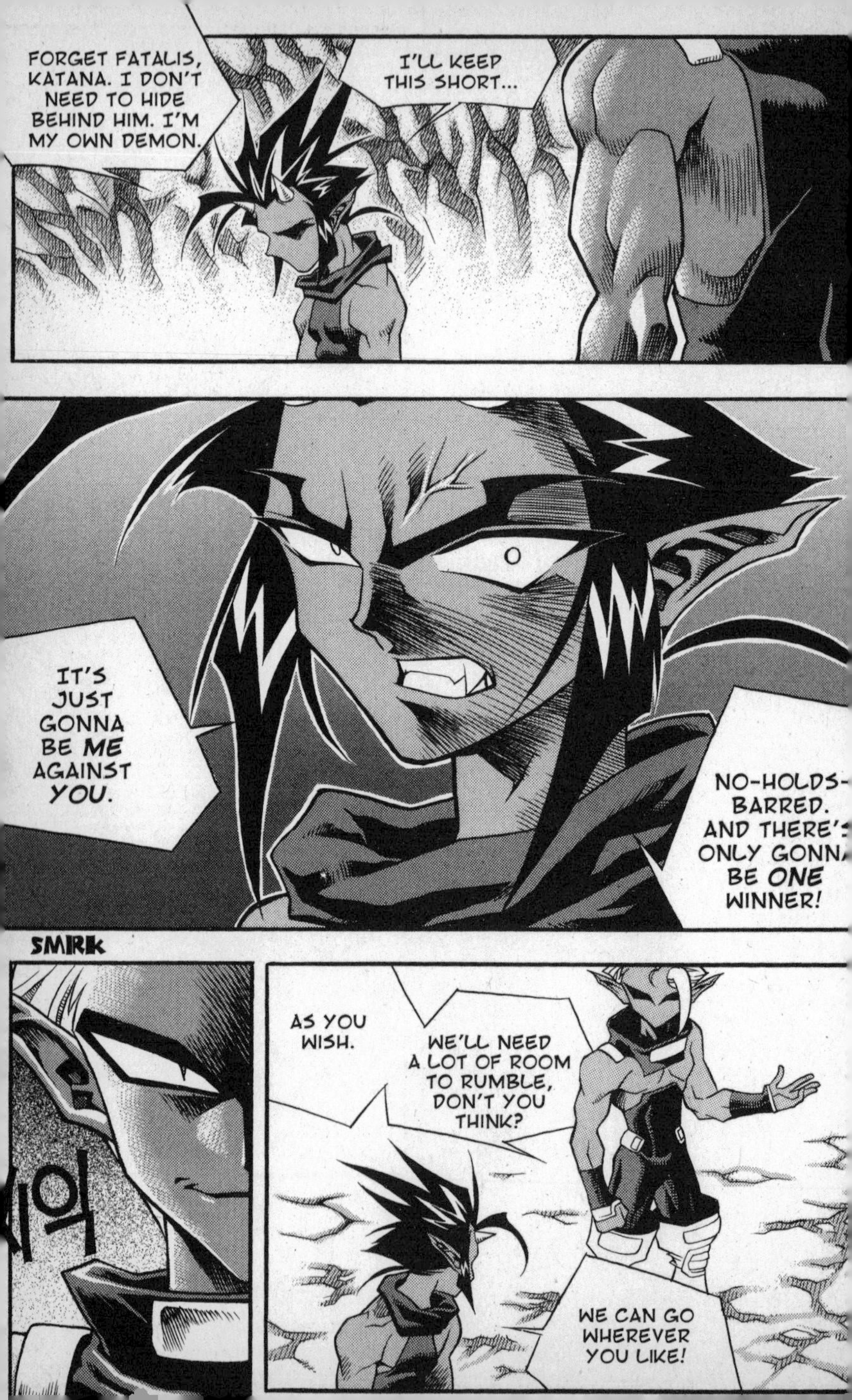
FORGET FATALIS, KATANA. I DON'T NEED TO HIDE BEHIND HIM. I'M MY OWN DEMON.
I'LL KEEP THIS SHORT...
IT'S JUST GONNA BE *ME* AGAINST *YOU*.
NO-HOLDS-BARRED. AND THERE'S ONLY GONNA BE *ONE* WINNER!
SMIRK
AS YOU WISH.
WE'LL NEED A LOT OF ROOM TO RUMBLE, DON'T YOU THINK?
WE CAN GO WHEREVER YOU LIKE!

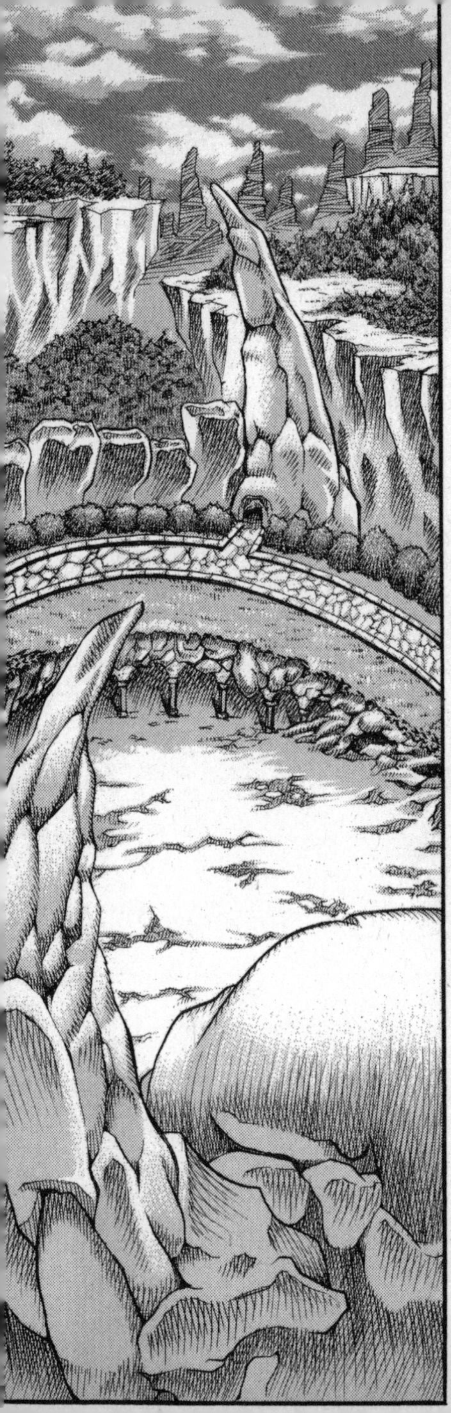

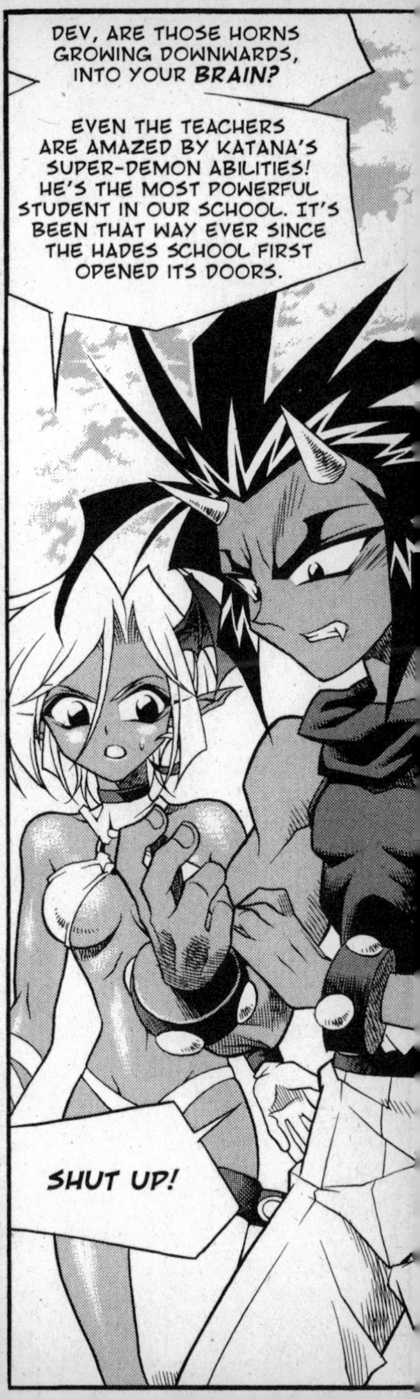
DEV, ARE THOSE HORNS GROWING DOWNWARDS, INTO YOUR BRAIN?
EVEN THE TEACHERS ARE AMAZED BY KATANA'S SUPER-DEMON ABILITIES! HE'S THE MOST POWERFUL STUDENT IN OUR SCHOOL. IT'S BEEN THAT WAY EVER SINCE THE HADES SCHOOL FIRST OPENED ITS DOORS.
SHUT UP!

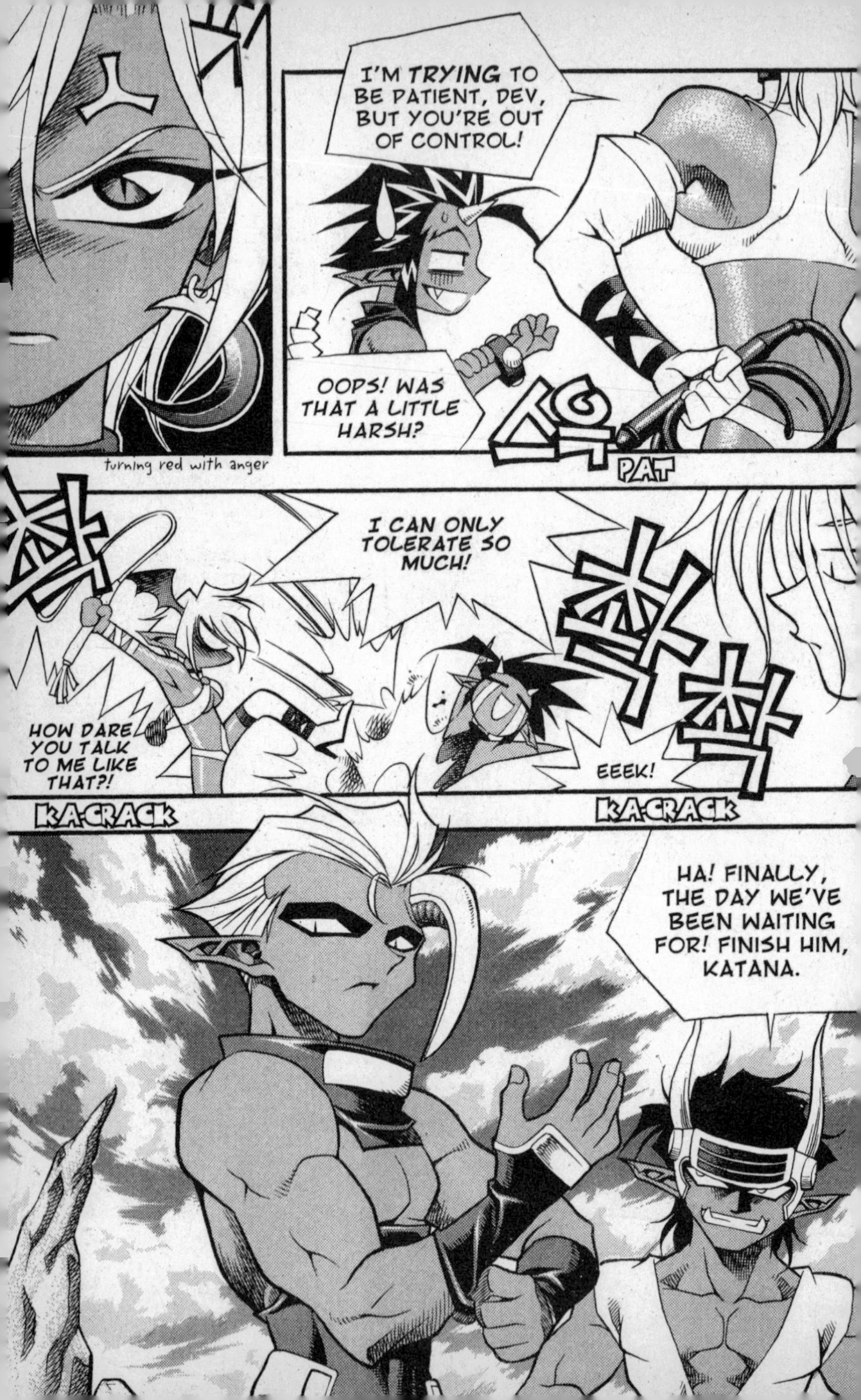
turning red with anger
I'M TRYING TO BE PATIENT, DEV, BUT YOU'RE OUT OF CONTROL!
OOPS! WAS THAT A LITTLE HARSH?
PAT
HOW DARE YOU TALK TO ME LIKE THAT?!
I CAN ONLY TOLERATE SO MUCH!
KA-CRACK
EEEK!
KA-CRACK
HA! FINALLY, THE DAY WE'VE BEEN WAITING FOR! FINISH HIM, KATANA.

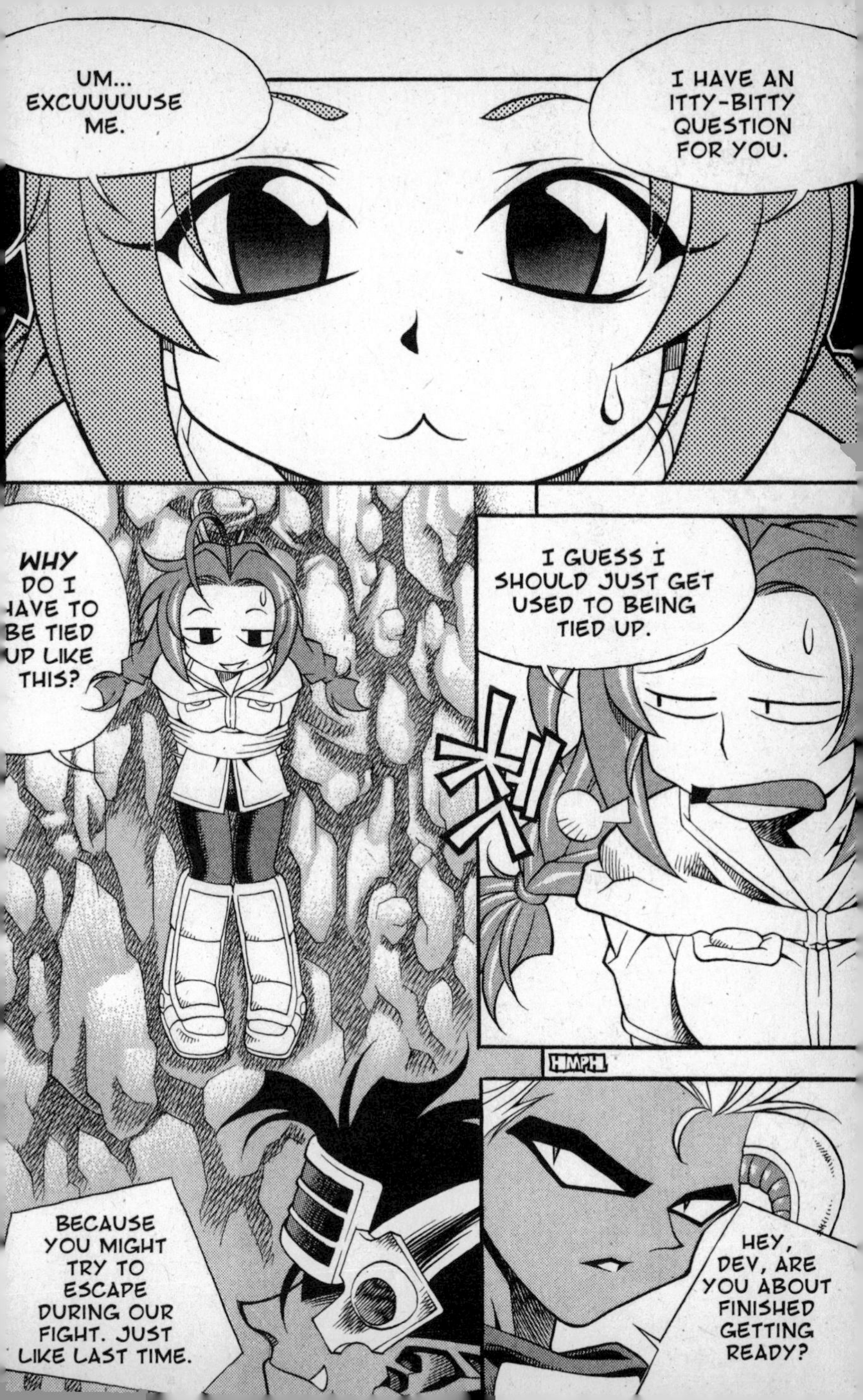
UM... EXCUUUUUSE ME.
I HAVE AN ITTY-BITTY QUESTION FOR YOU.
WHY DO I HAVE TO BE TIED UP LIKE THIS?
BECAUSE YOU MIGHT TRY TO ESCAPE DURING OUR FIGHT. JUST LIKE LAST TIME.
I GUESS I SHOULD JUST GET USED TO BEING TIED UP.
HMPH.
HEY, DEV, ARE YOU ABOUT FINISHED GETTING READY?

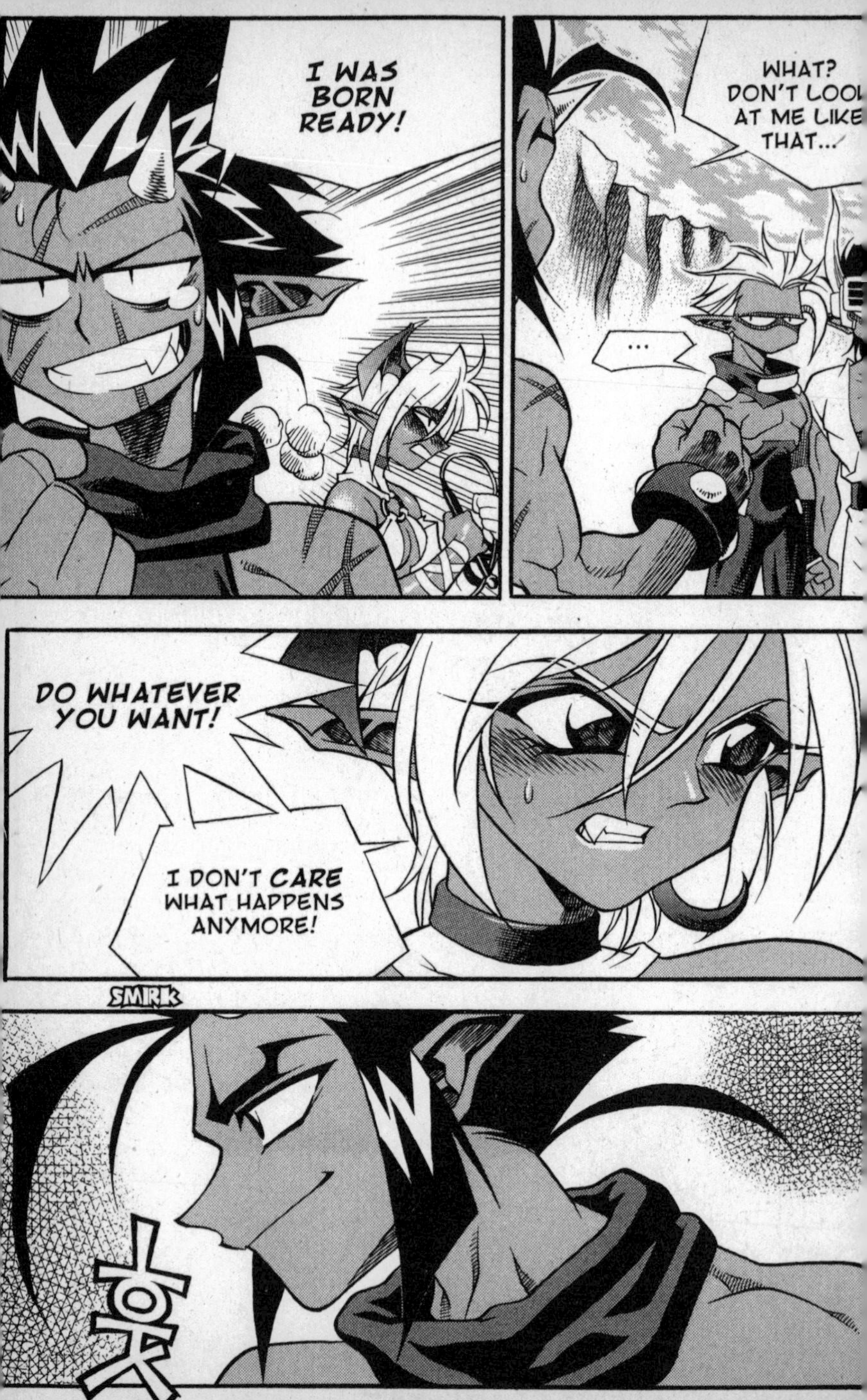
I WAS BORN READY!
WHAT? DON'T LOO AT ME LIKE THAT...
...
DO WHATEVER YOU WANT!
I DON'T CARE WHAT HAPPENS ANYMORE!
SMIRK

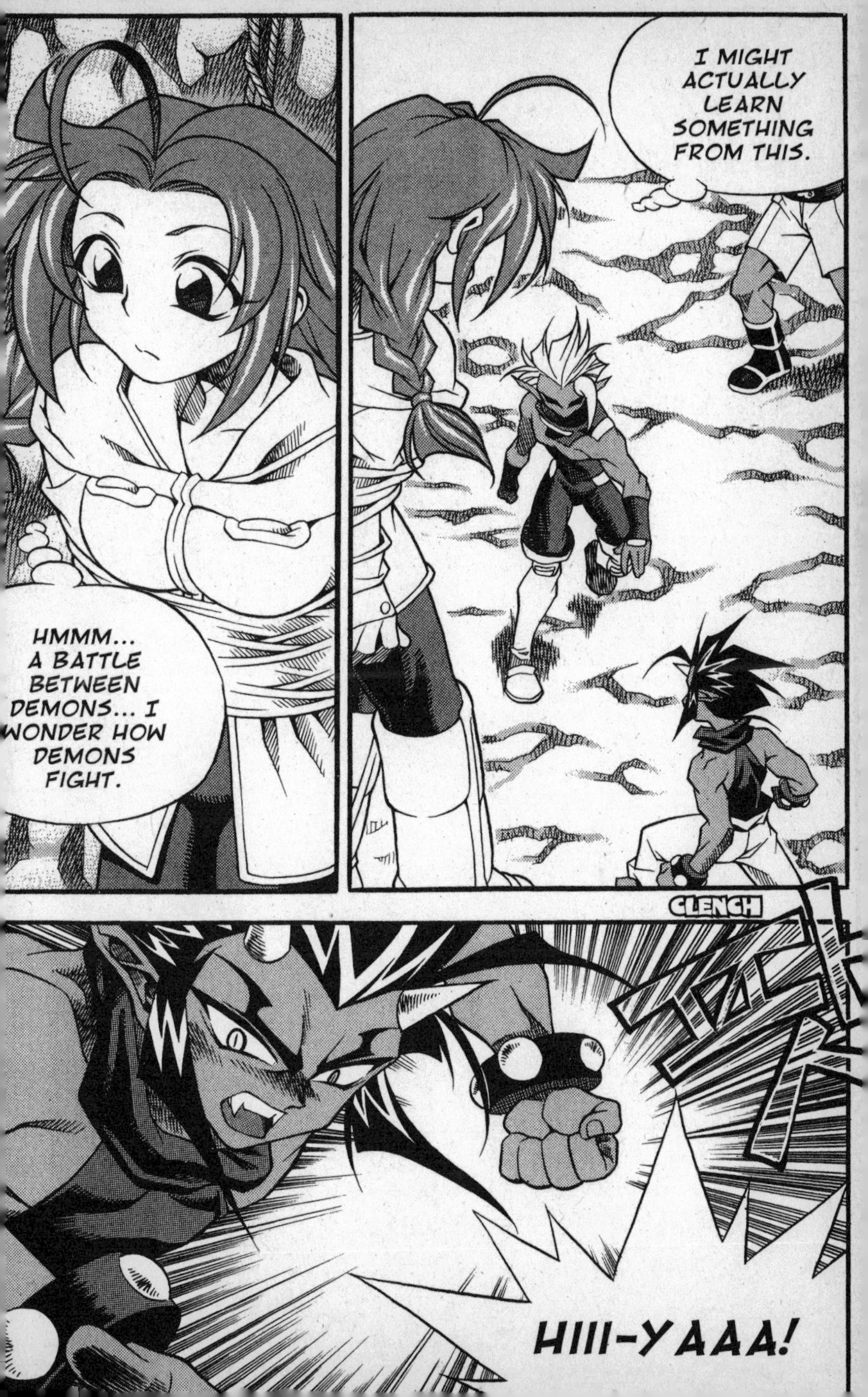
HMMM... A BATTLE BETWEEN DEMONS... I WONDER HOW DEMONS FIGHT.
I MIGHT ACTUALLY LEARN SOMETHING FROM THIS.
CLENCH
HIII-YAAA!

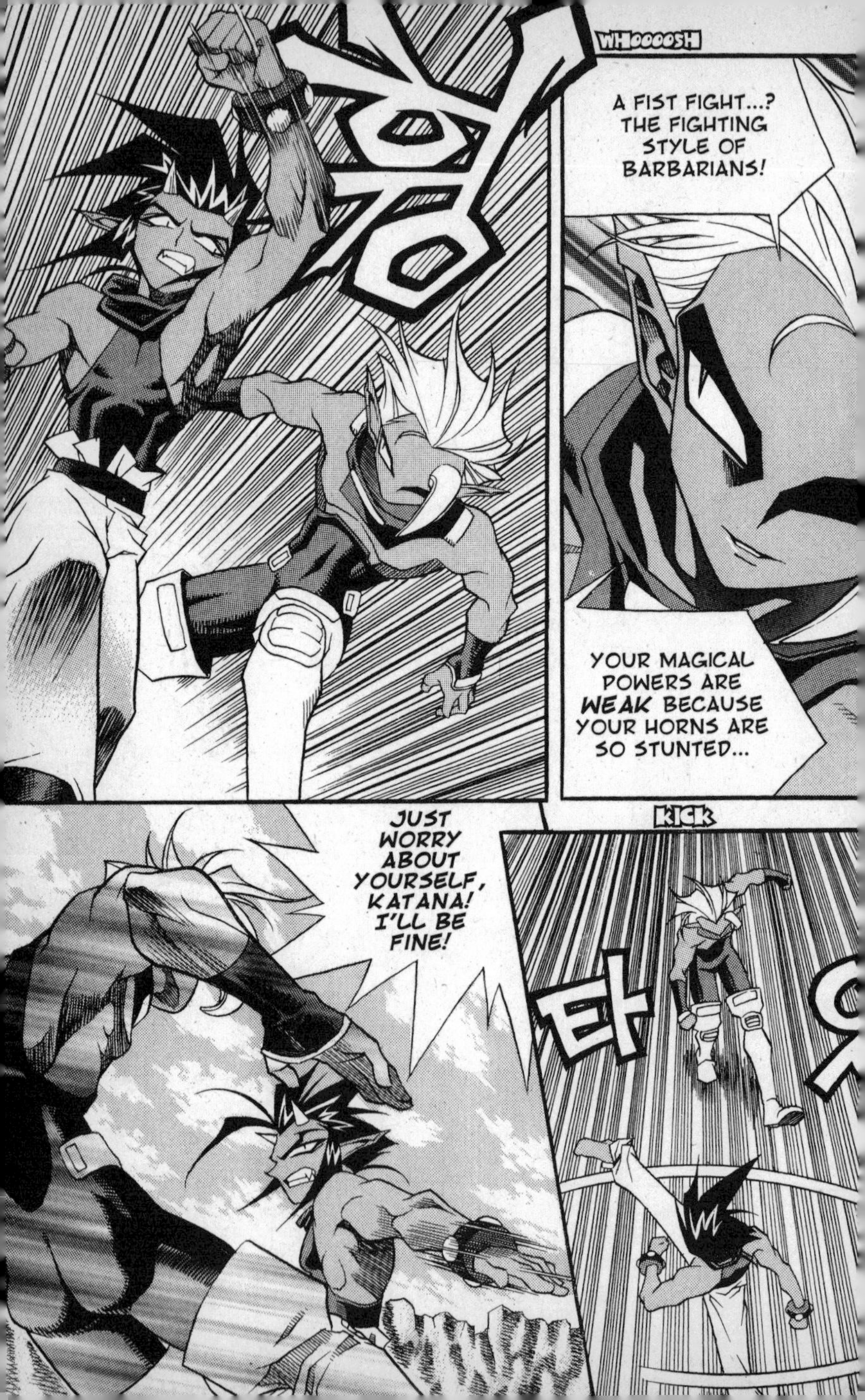
WHOOOOSH
A FIST FIGHT...? THE FIGHTING STYLE OF BARBARIANS!
YOUR MAGICAL POWERS ARE WEAK BECAUSE YOUR HORNS ARE SO STUNTED...
JUST WORRY ABOUT YOURSELF, KATANA! I'LL BE FINE!
KICK
타

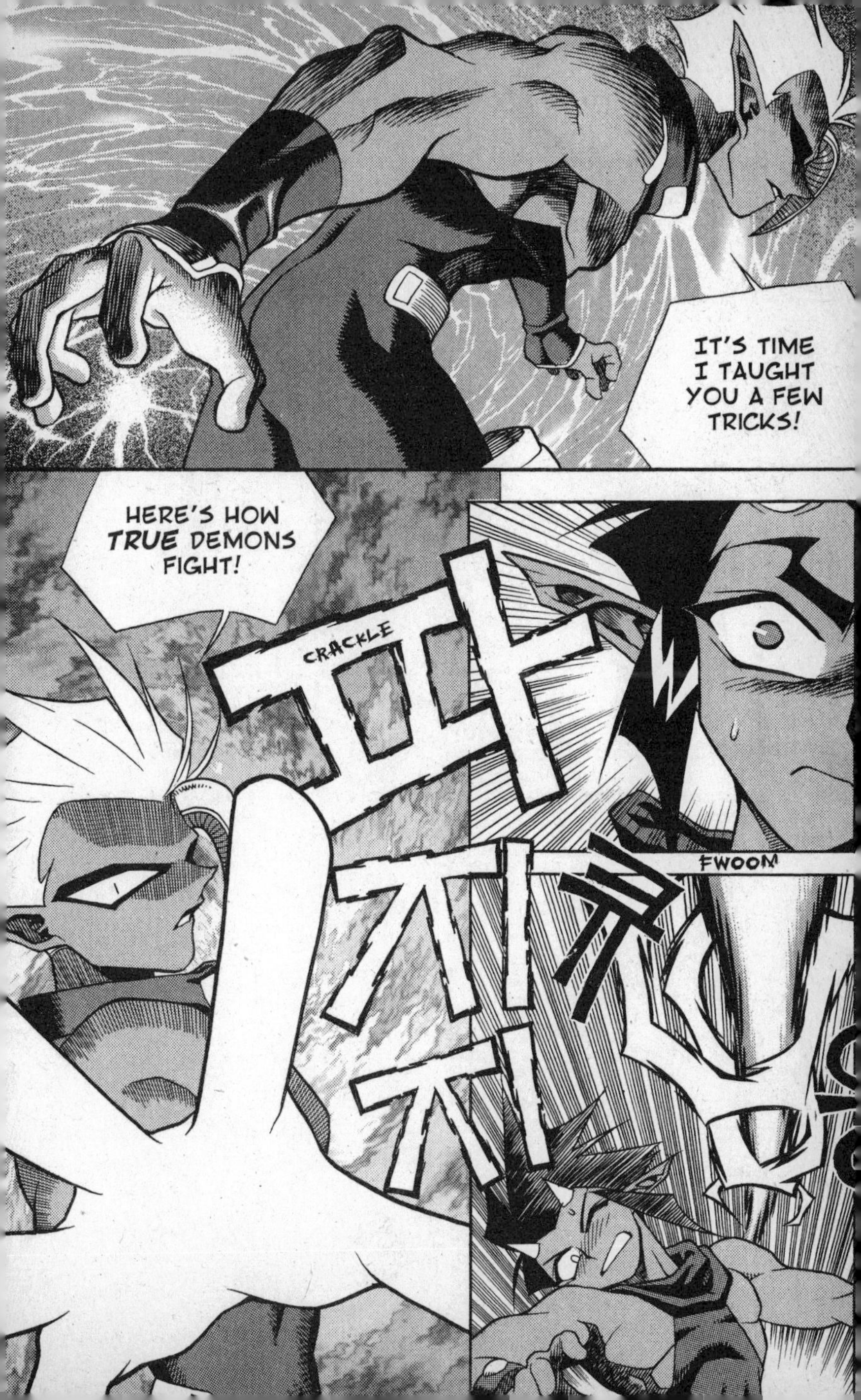
IT'S TIME I TAUGHT YOU A FEW TRICKS!
HERE'S HOW TRUE DEMONS FIGHT!
CRACKLE
FWOOM

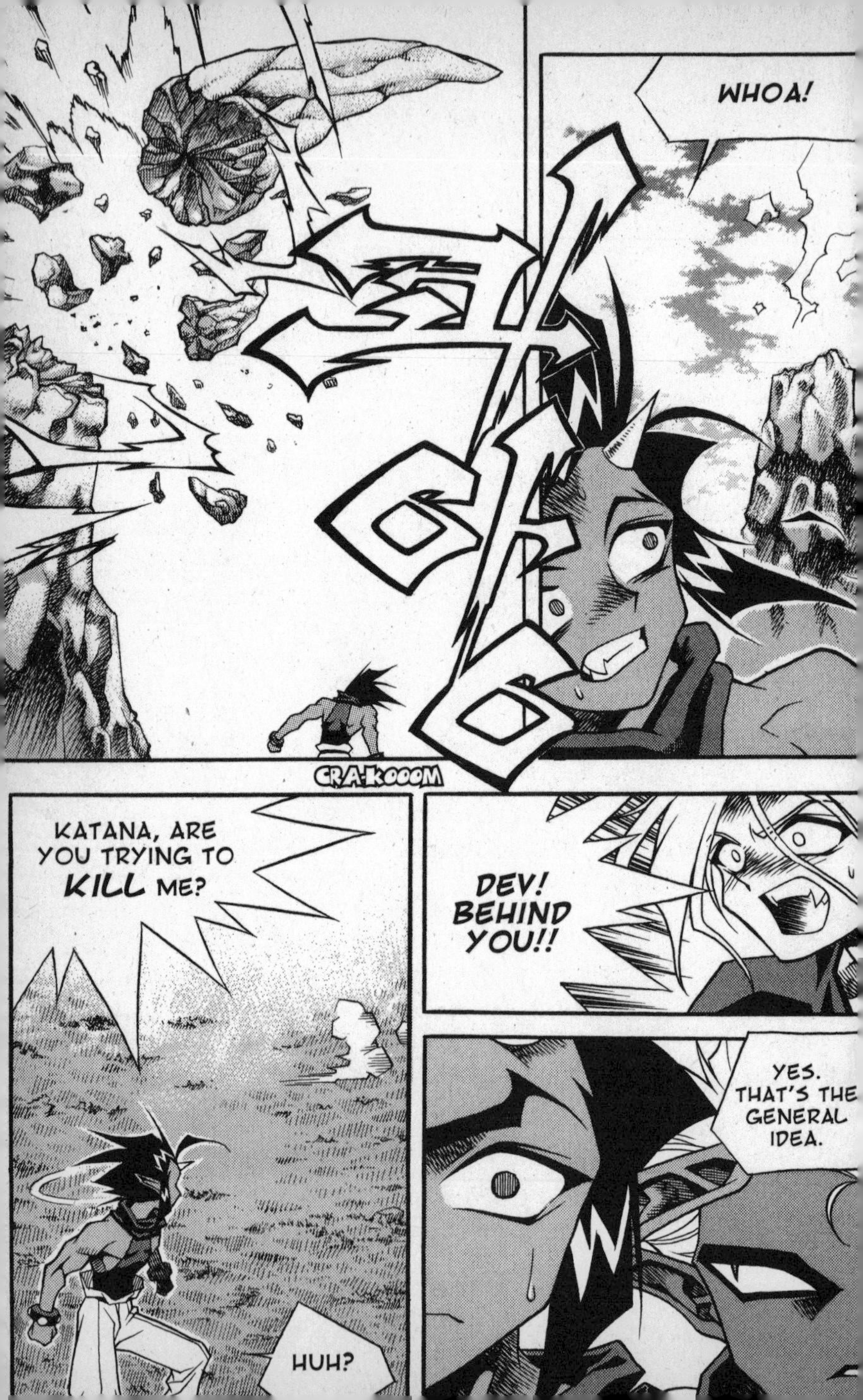
WHOA!
CRA-KOOOM
KATANA, ARE YOU TRYING TO KILL ME?
DEV! BEHIND YOU!!
HUH?
YES. THAT'S THE GENERAL IDEA.

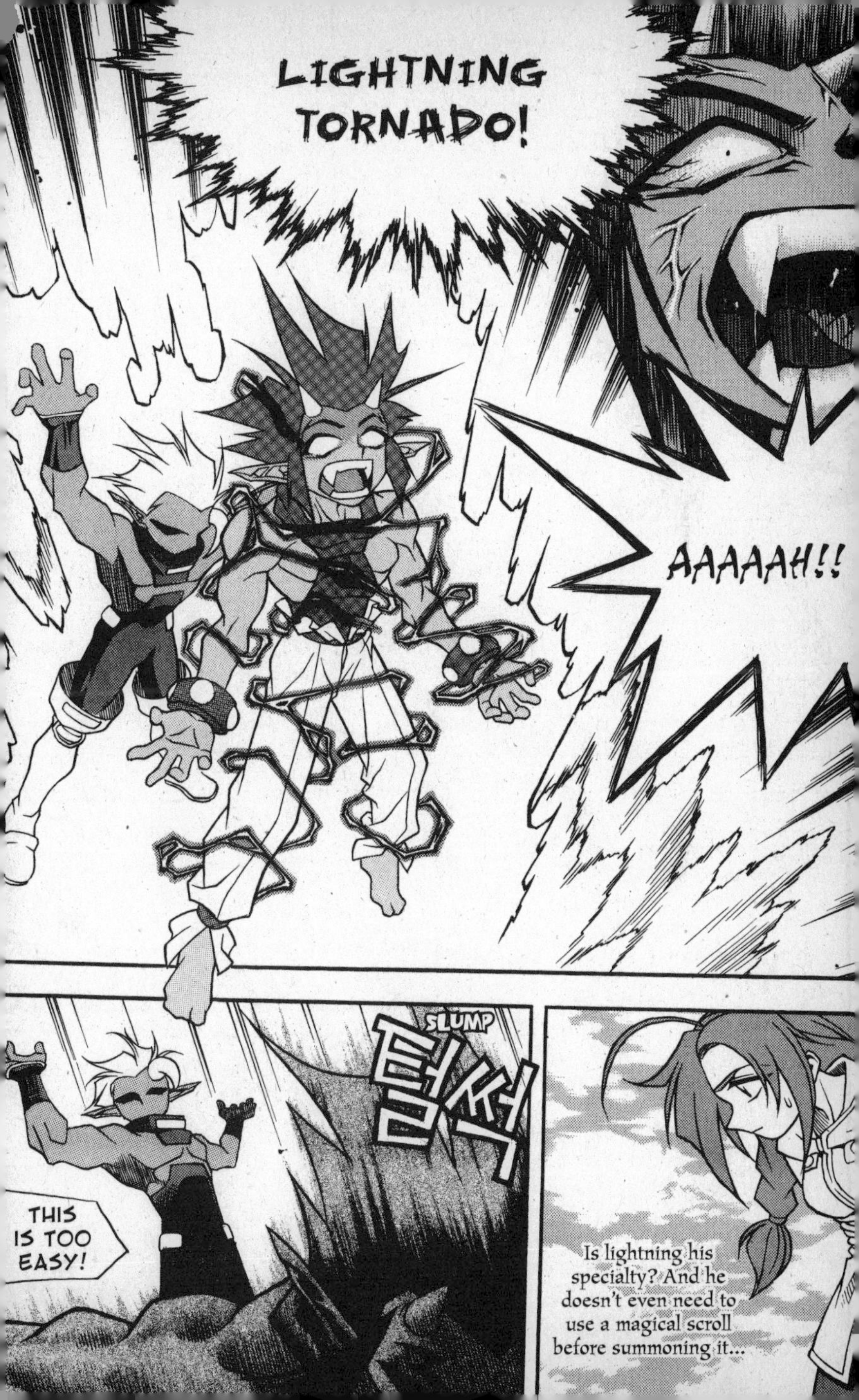
LIGHTNING TORNADO!
AAAAAH!!
SLUMP
THIS IS TOO EASY!
Is lightning his specialty? And he doesn't even need to use a magical scroll before summoning it...

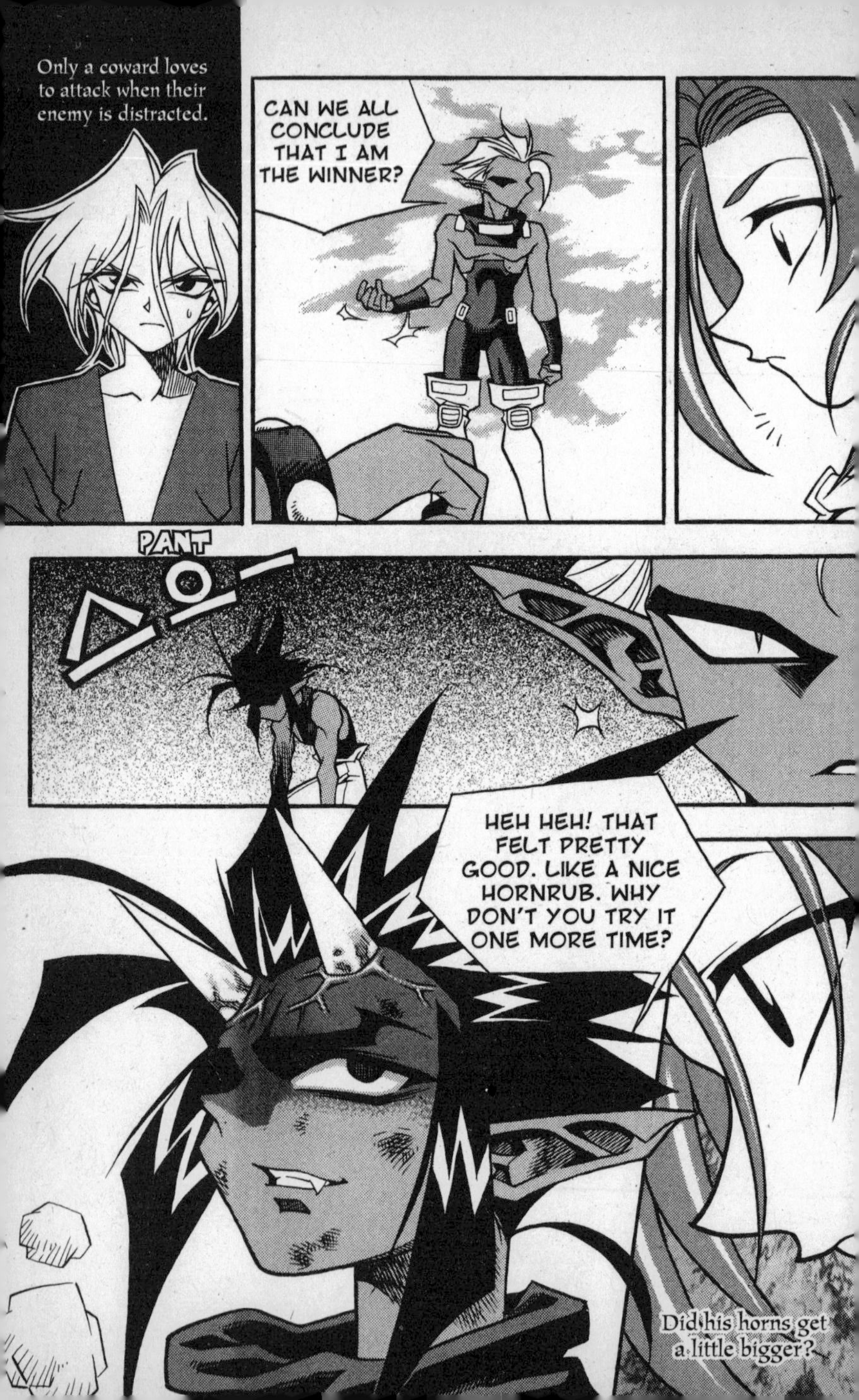

Only a coward loves to attack when their enemy is distracted.
CAN WE ALL CONCLUDE THAT I AM THE WINNER?
PANT
HEH HEH! THAT FELT PRETTY GOOD. LIKE A NICE HORNRUB. WHY DON'T YOU TRY IT ONE MORE TIME?
Did his horns get a little bigger?

Quest 7

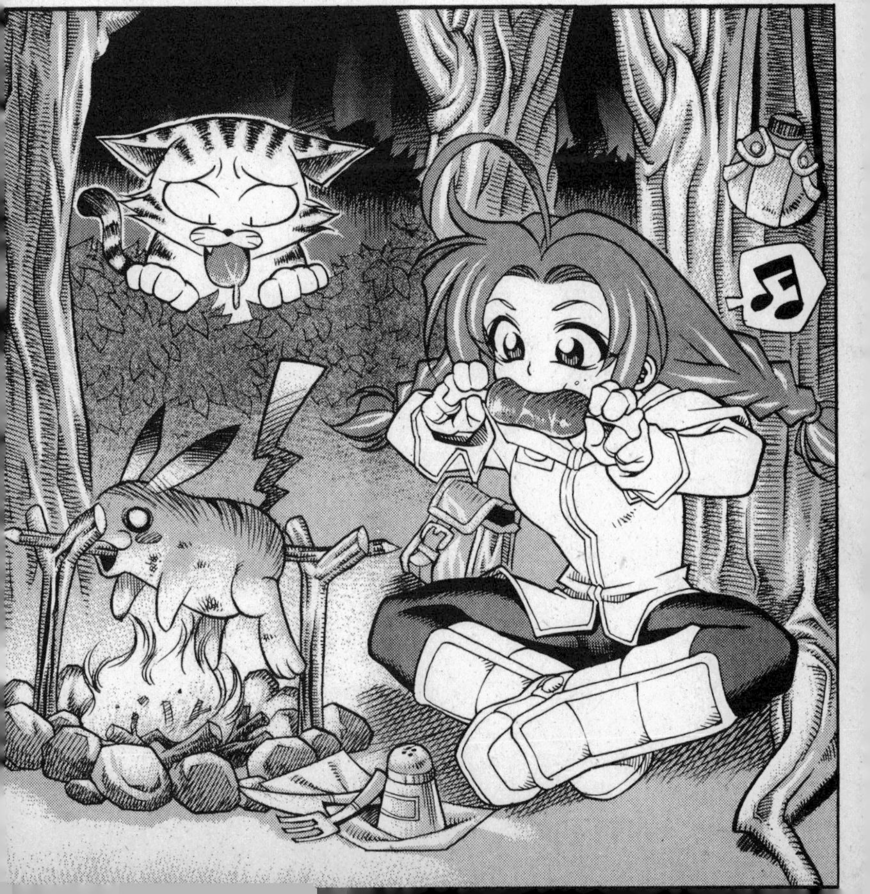

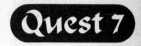

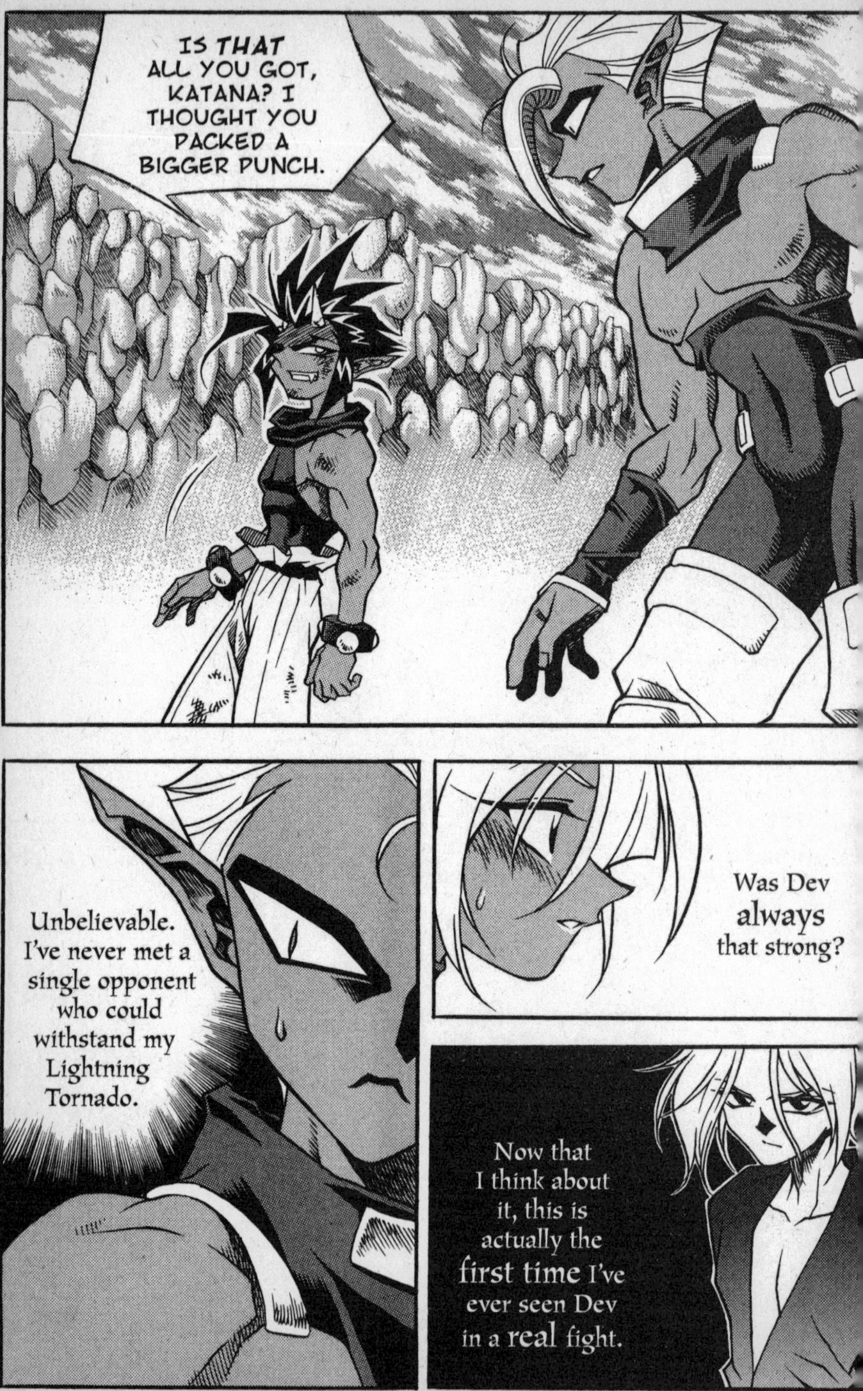
IS *THAT* ALL YOU GOT, KATANA? I THOUGHT YOU PACKED A BIGGER PUNCH.
Unbelievable. I've never met a single opponent who could withstand my Lightning Tornado.
Was Dev always that strong?
Now that I think about it, this is actually the first time I've ever seen Dev in a real fight.

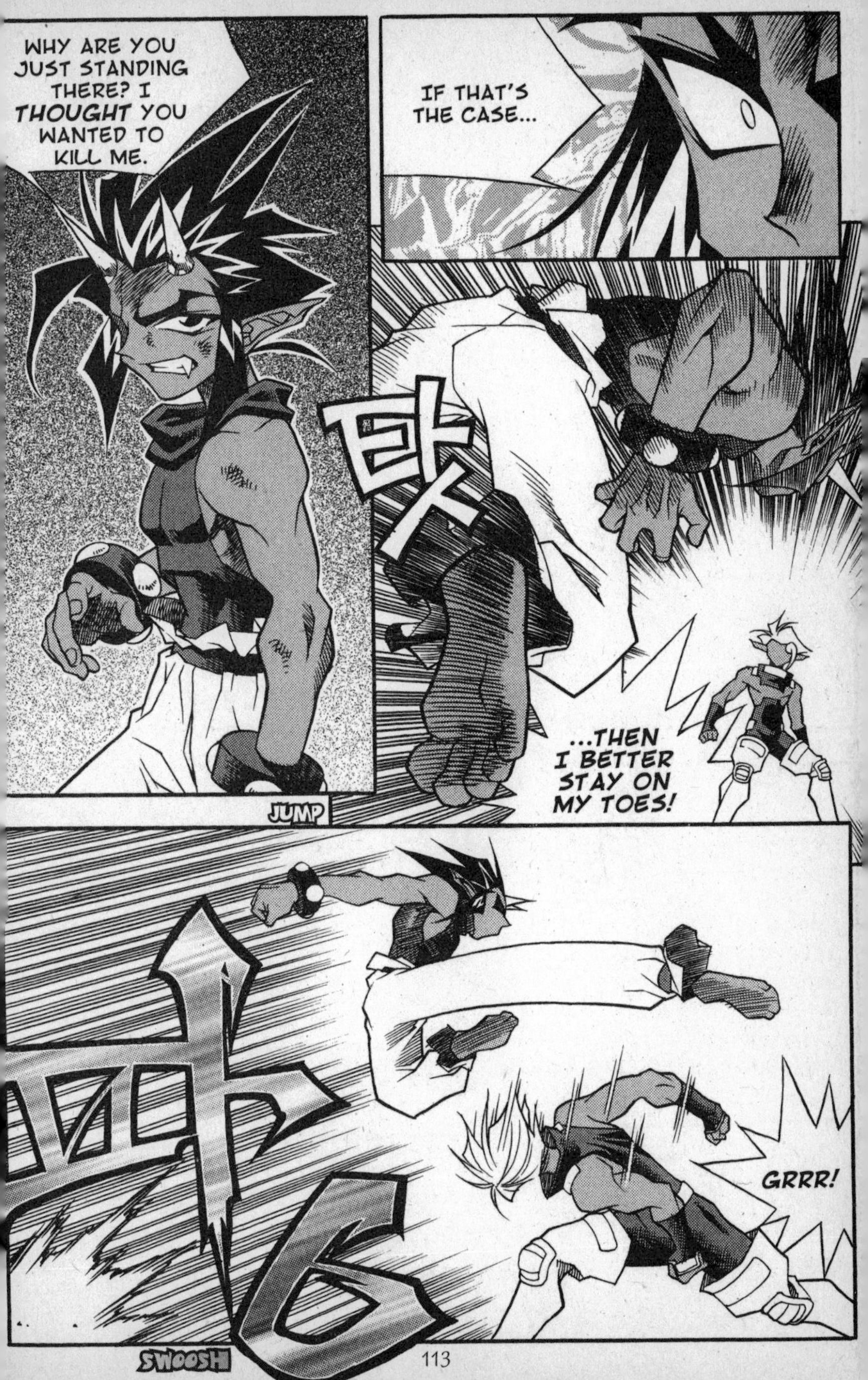
WHY ARE YOU JUST STANDING THERE? I *THOUGHT* YOU WANTED TO KILL ME.
IF THAT'S THE CASE...
JUMP
...THEN I BETTER STAY ON MY TOES!
SWOOSH
GRRR!

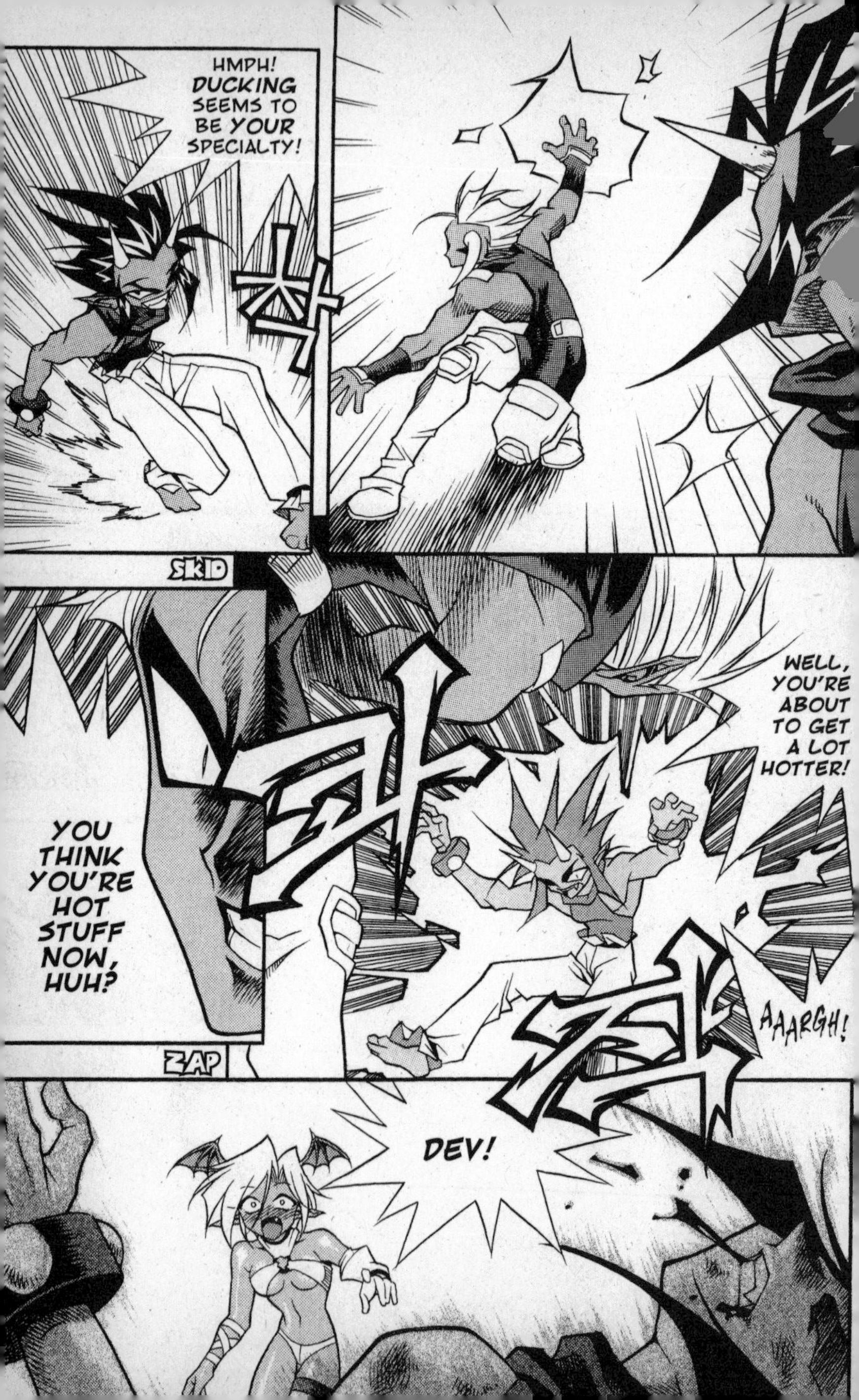
HMPH! DUCKING SEEMS TO BE YOUR SPECIALTY!
SKID
YOU THINK YOU'RE HOT STUFF NOW, HUH?
ZAP
WELL, YOU'RE ABOUT TO GET A LOT HOTTER!
AAARGH!
DEV!

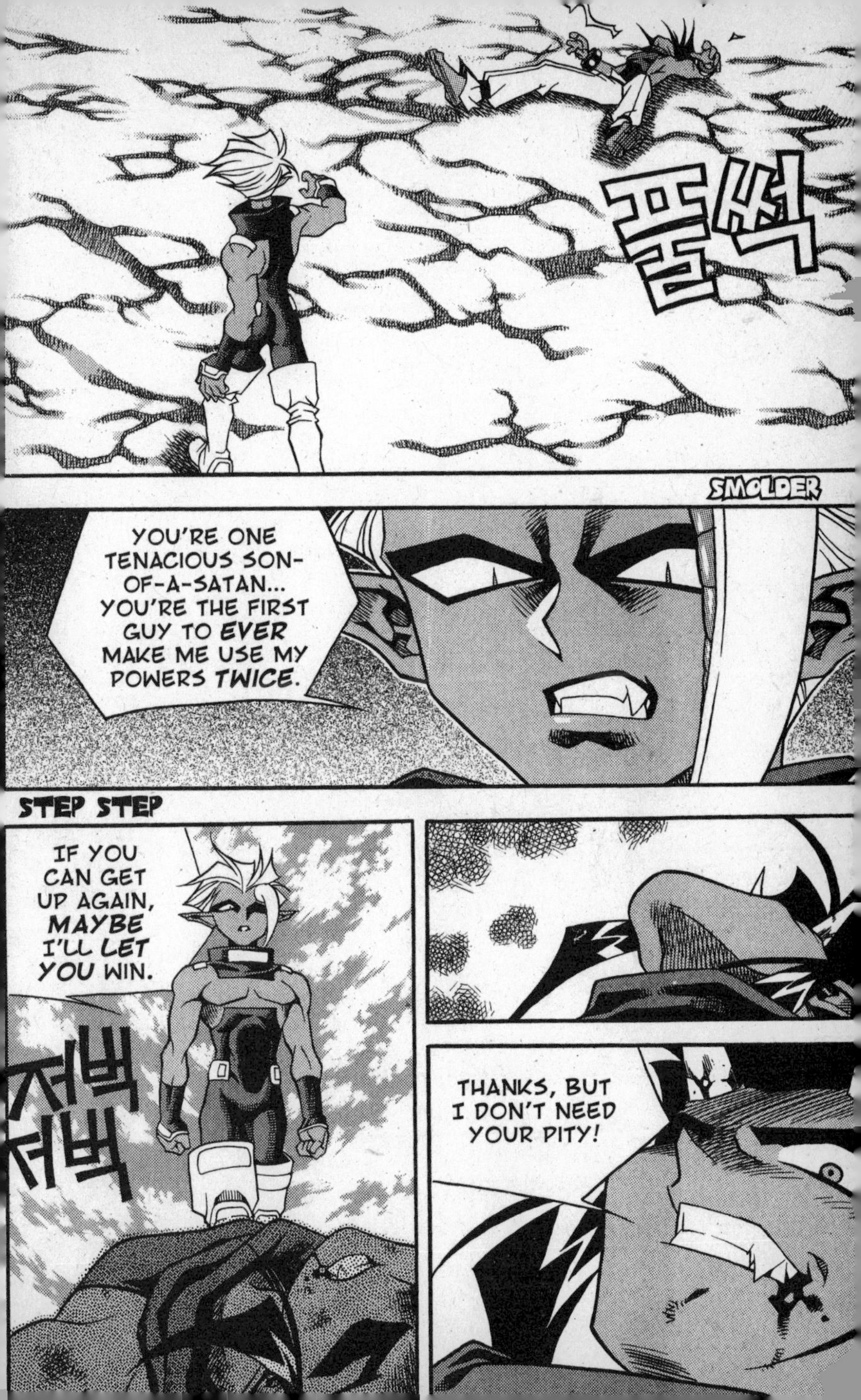

폴썩
SMOLDER
YOU'RE ONE TENACIOUS SON-OF-A-SATAN... YOU'RE THE FIRST GUY TO EVER MAKE ME USE MY POWERS TWICE.
STEP STEP
IF YOU CAN GET UP AGAIN, MAYBE I'LL LET YOU WIN.
저벅 저벅
THANKS, BUT I DON'T NEED YOUR PITY!

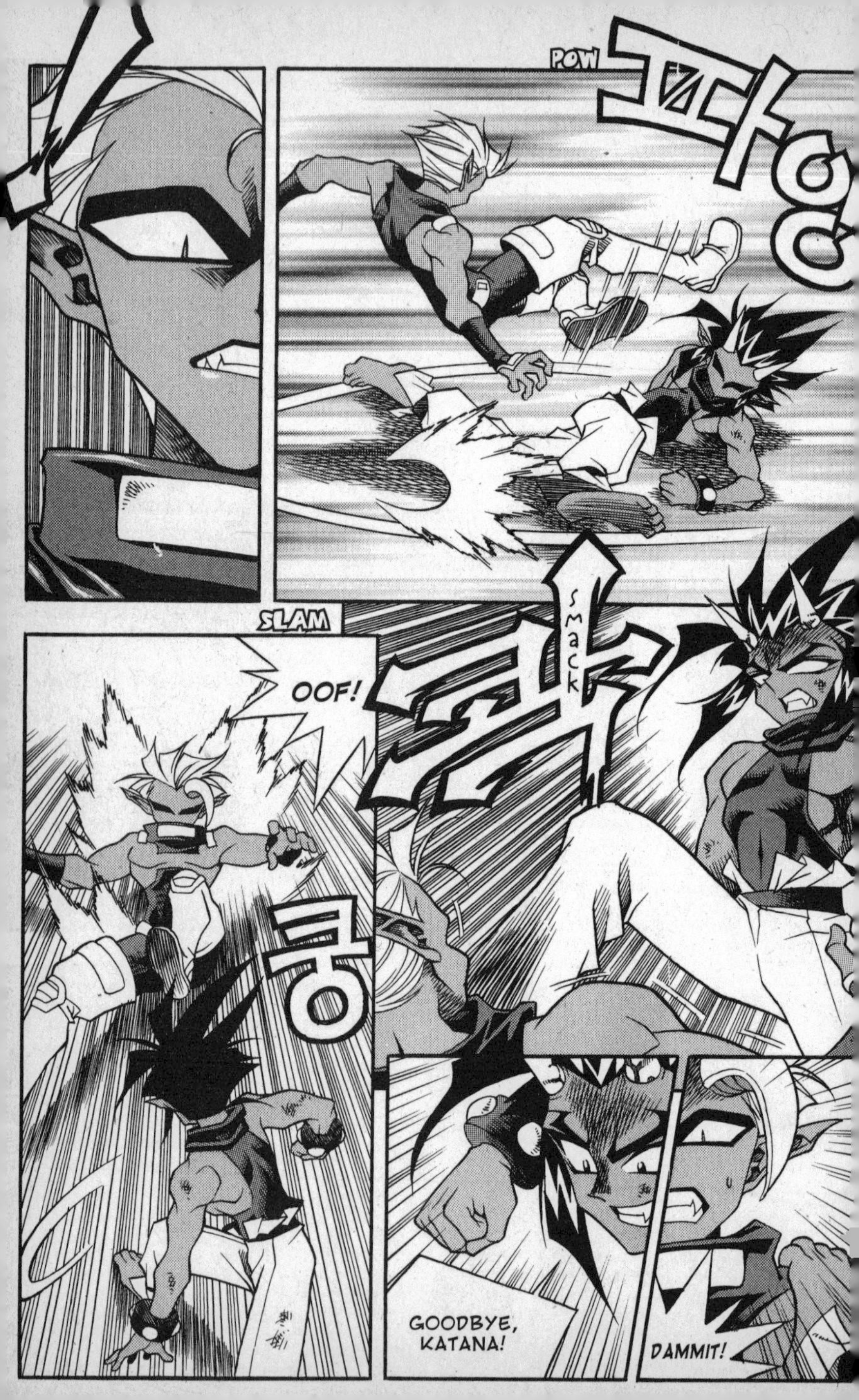
!
POW
SLAM
OOF!
쿵
smack
GOODBYE, KATANA!
DAMMIT!

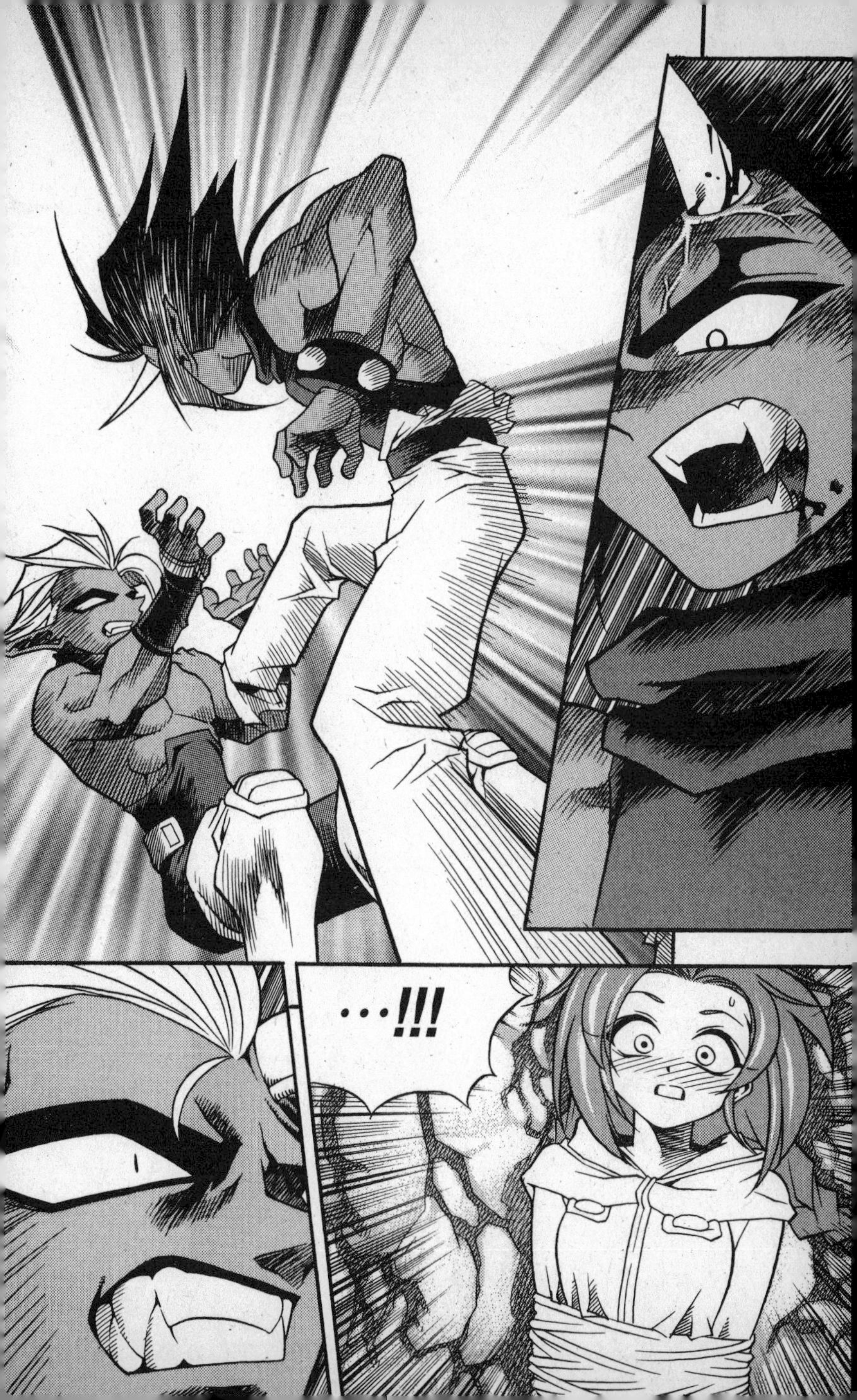
...!!!

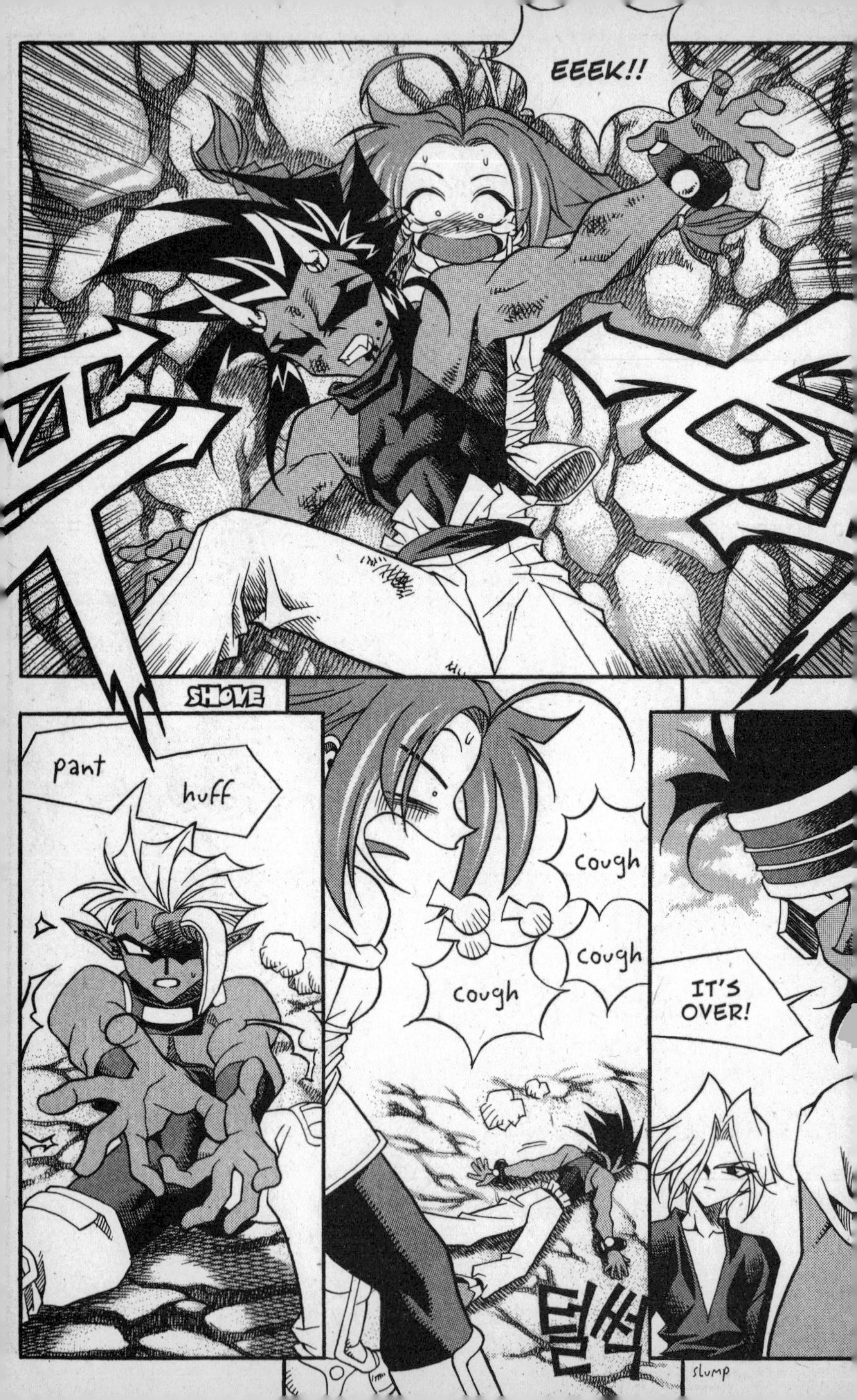
EEEK!!
SHOVE
pant
huff
cough
cough
cough
IT'S OVER!
slump

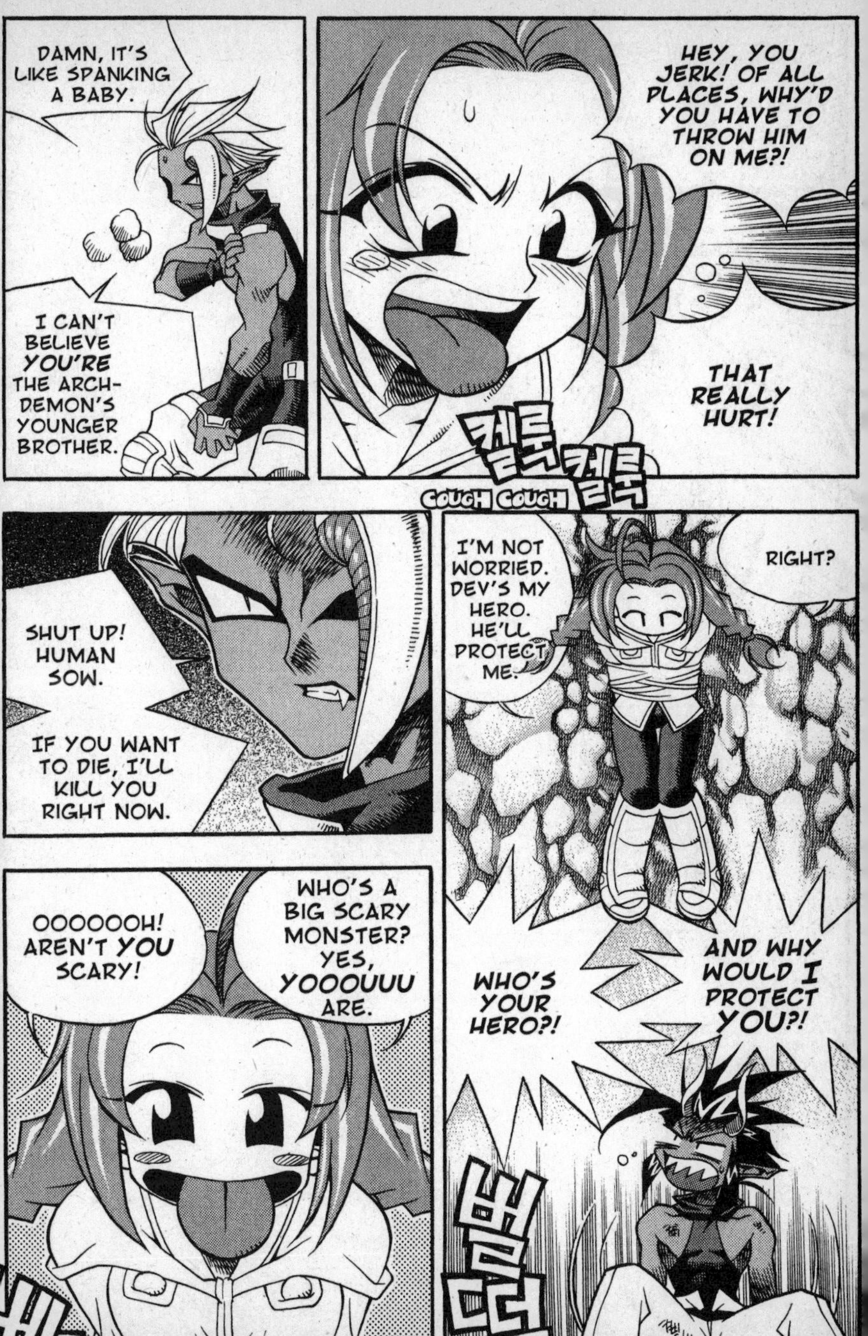
DAMN, IT'S LIKE SPANKING A BABY.
I CAN'T BELIEVE *YOU'RE* THE ARCH-DEMON'S YOUNGER BROTHER.
HEY, YOU JERK! OF ALL PLACES, WHY'D YOU HAVE TO THROW HIM ON ME?!
THAT REALLY HURT!
켈룩 켈룩
COUGH COUGH
SHUT UP! HUMAN SOW.
IF YOU WANT TO DIE, I'LL KILL YOU RIGHT NOW.
OOOOOOH! AREN'T *YOU* SCARY!
WHO'S A BIG SCARY MONSTER? YES, *YOOOUUU* ARE.
PBBBFT
I'M NOT WORRIED. DEV'S MY HERO. HE'LL PROTECT ME.
RIGHT?
WHO'S YOUR HERO?!
AND WHY WOULD *I* PROTECT *YOU*?!
벌떡
sits straight up

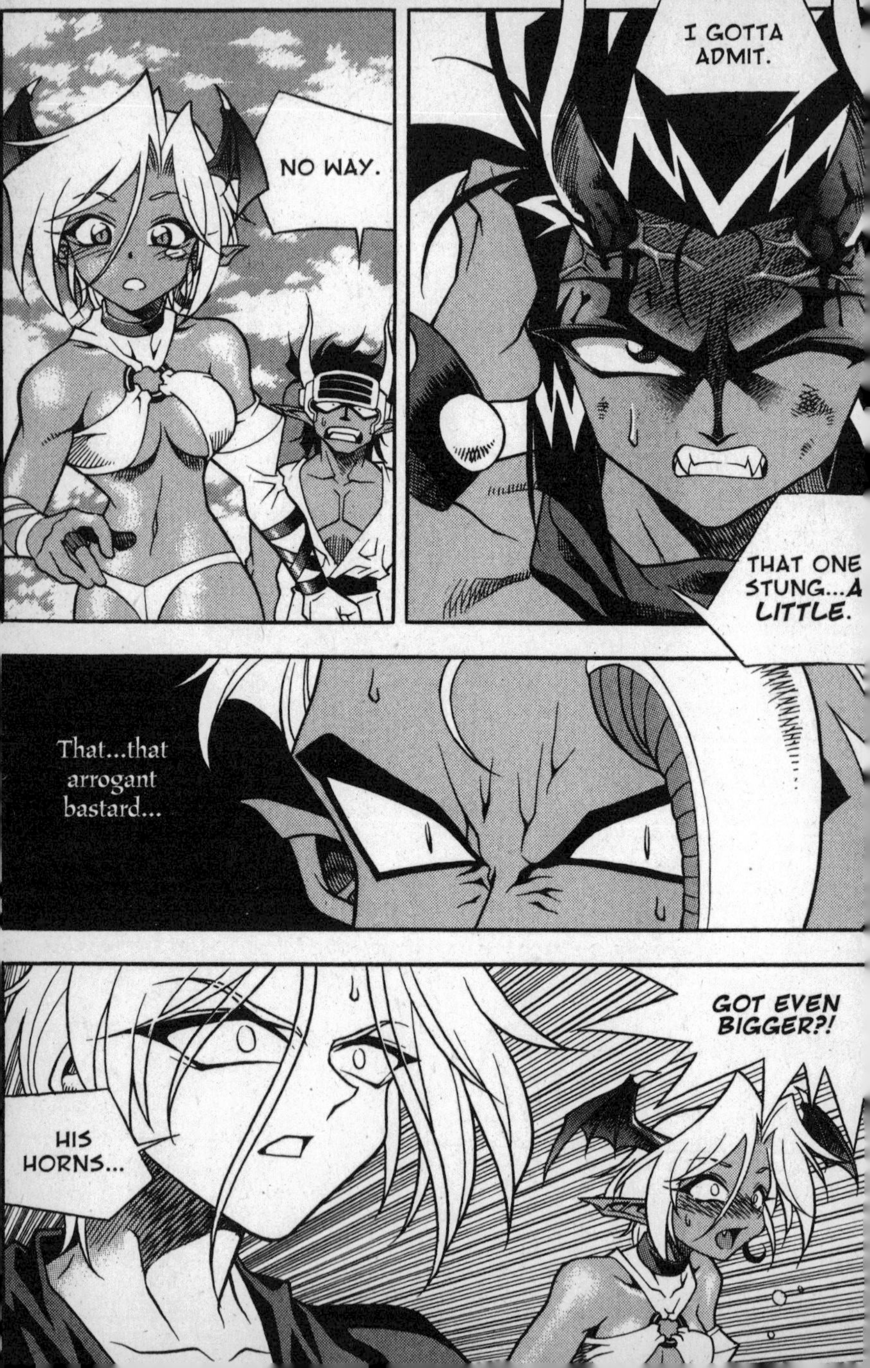
NO WAY.
I GOTTA ADMIT.
THAT ONE STUNG...A LITTLE.
That...that arrogant bastard...
HIS HORNS...
GOT EVEN BIGGER?!

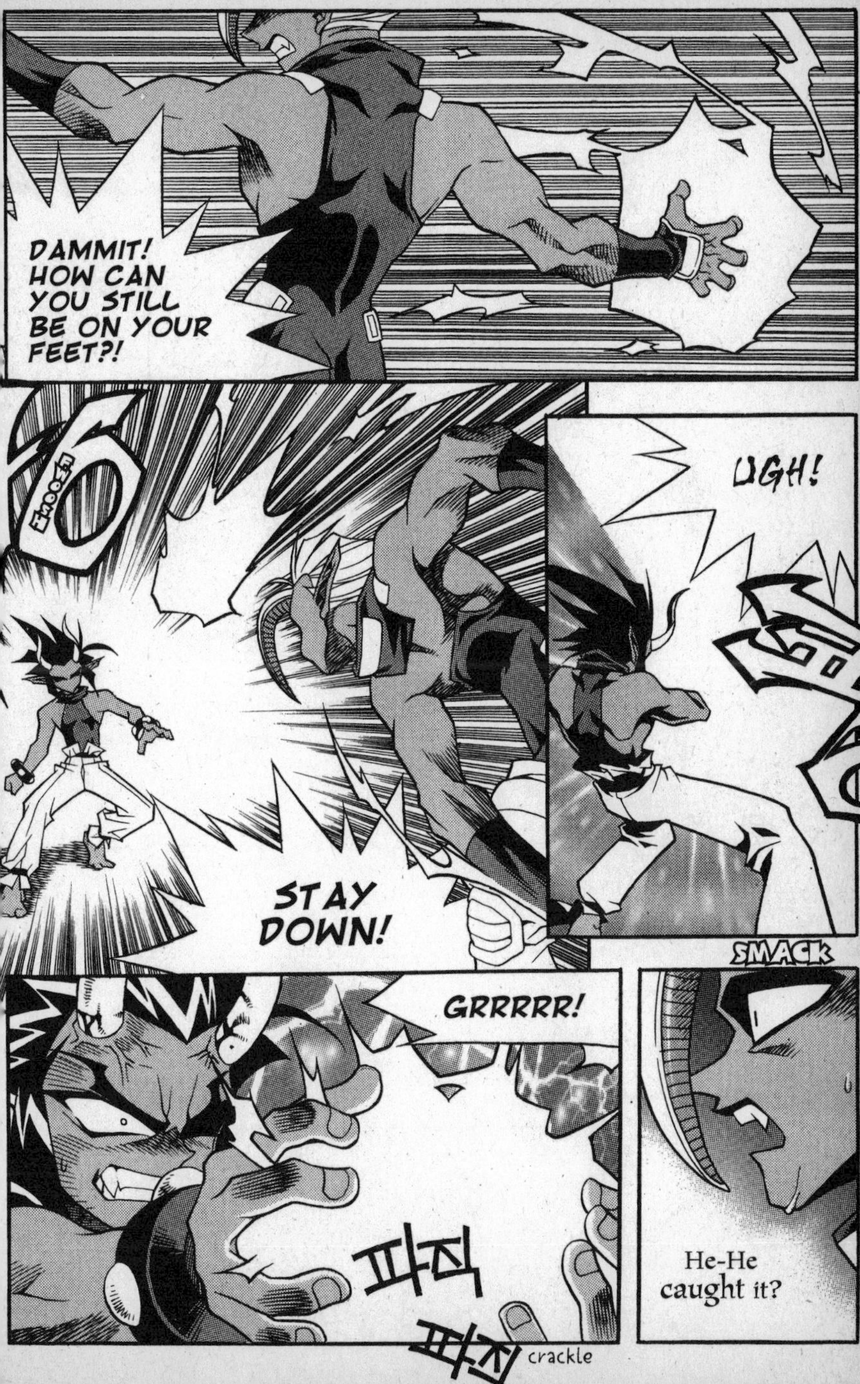
DAMMIT! HOW CAN YOU STILL BE ON YOUR FEET?!
FWOOSH
STAY DOWN!
UGH!
SMACK
GRRRRR!
파직
파직
crackle
He-He caught it?

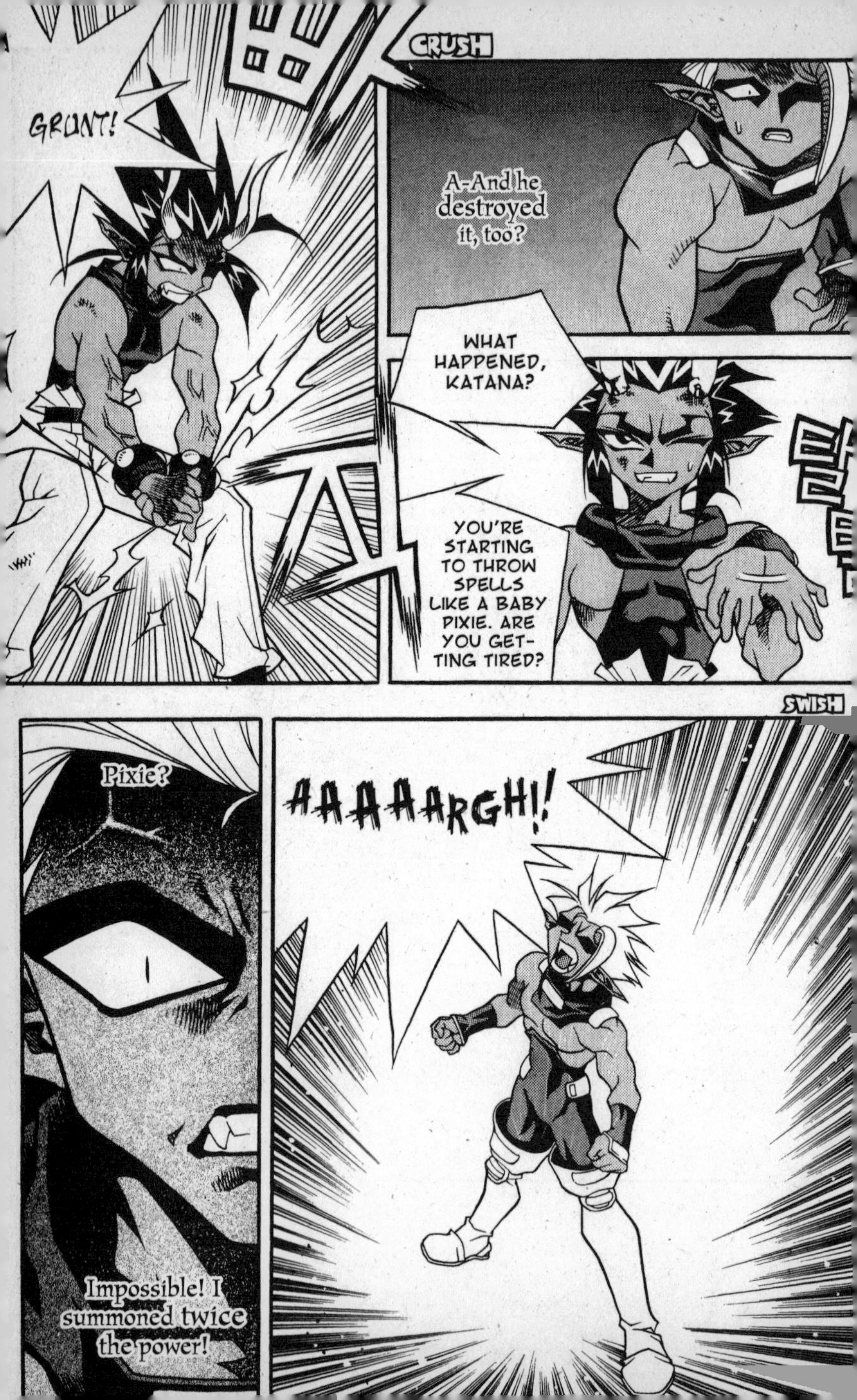
GRUNT!
CRUSH
A-And he destroyed it, too?
WHAT HAPPENED, KATANA?
YOU'RE STARTING TO THROW SPELLS LIKE A BABY PIXIE. ARE YOU GET-TING TIRED?
Pixie?
Impossible! I summoned twice the power!
SWISH
AAAAARGH!!

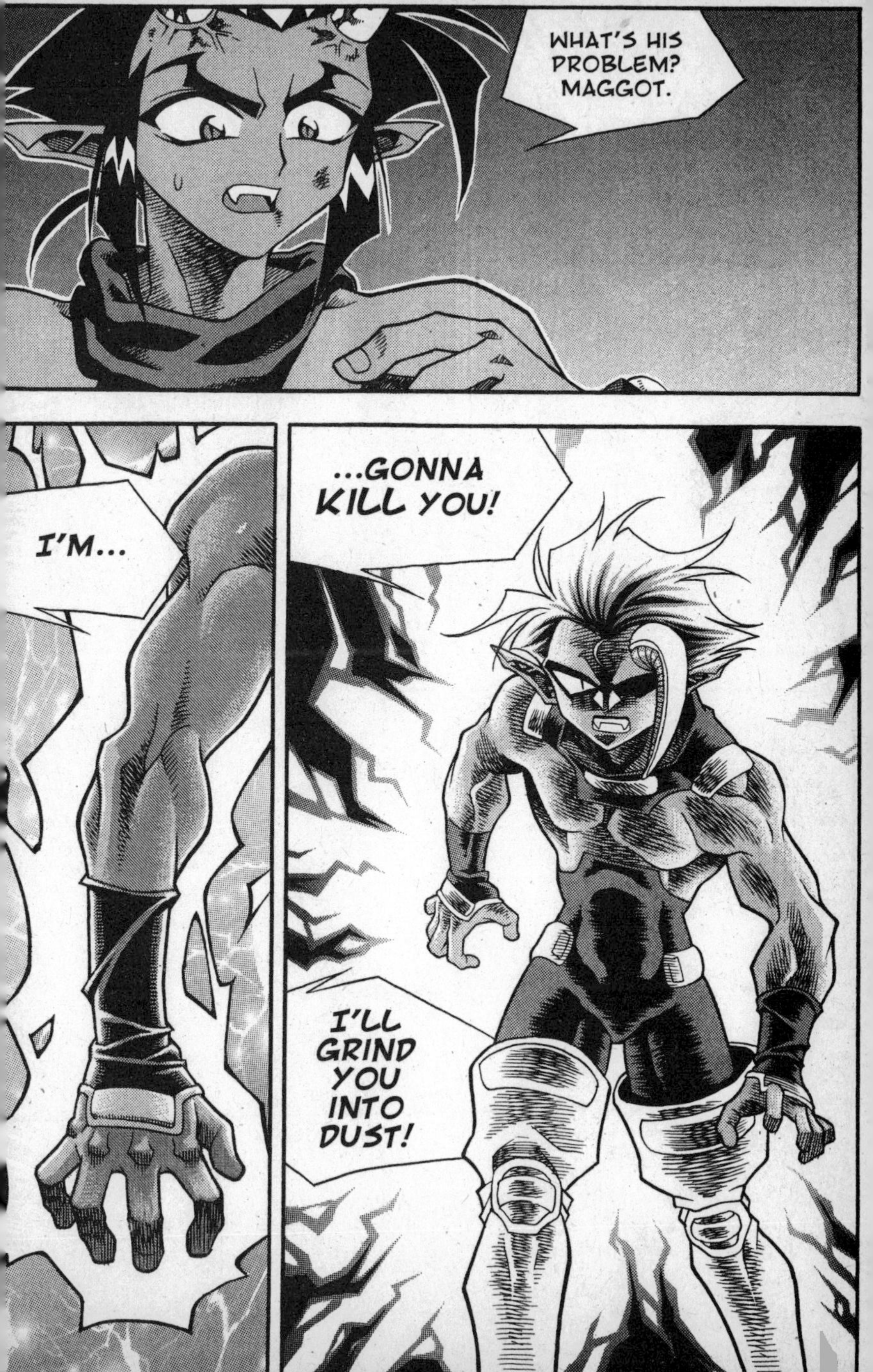
WHAT'S HIS PROBLEM? MAGGOT.
I'M...
...GONNA KILL YOU!
I'LL GRIND YOU INTO DUST!

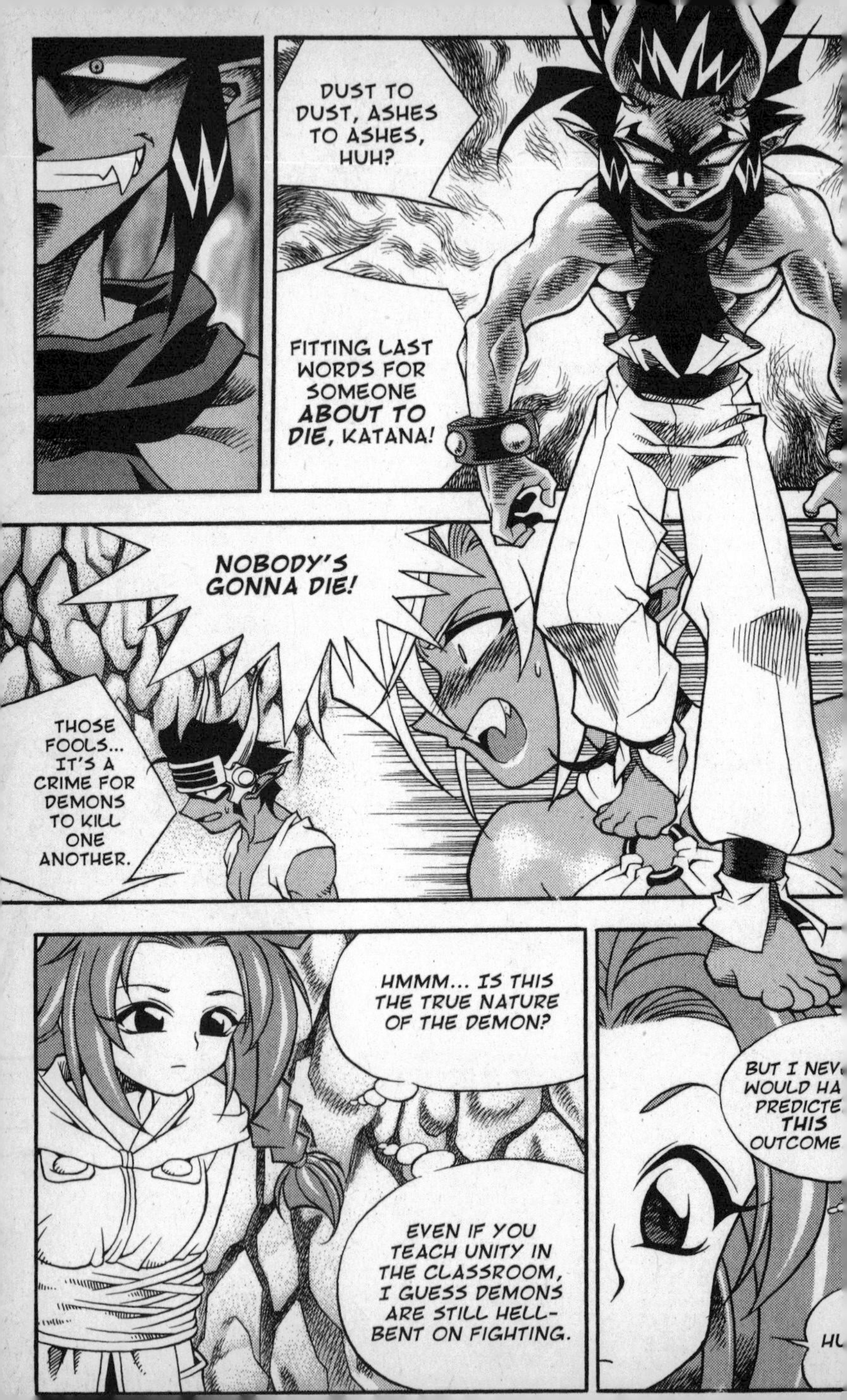
DUST TO DUST, ASHES TO ASHES, HUH?
FITTING LAST WORDS FOR SOMEONE **ABOUT TO DIE**, KATANA!
NOBODY'S GONNA DIE!
THOSE FOOLS... IT'S A CRIME FOR DEMONS TO KILL ONE ANOTHER.
HMMM... IS THIS THE TRUE NATURE OF THE DEMON?
EVEN IF YOU TEACH UNITY IN THE CLASSROOM, I GUESS DEMONS ARE STILL HELL-BENT ON FIGHTING.
BUT I NEV WOULD HA PREDICTE **THIS** OUTCOME
HU

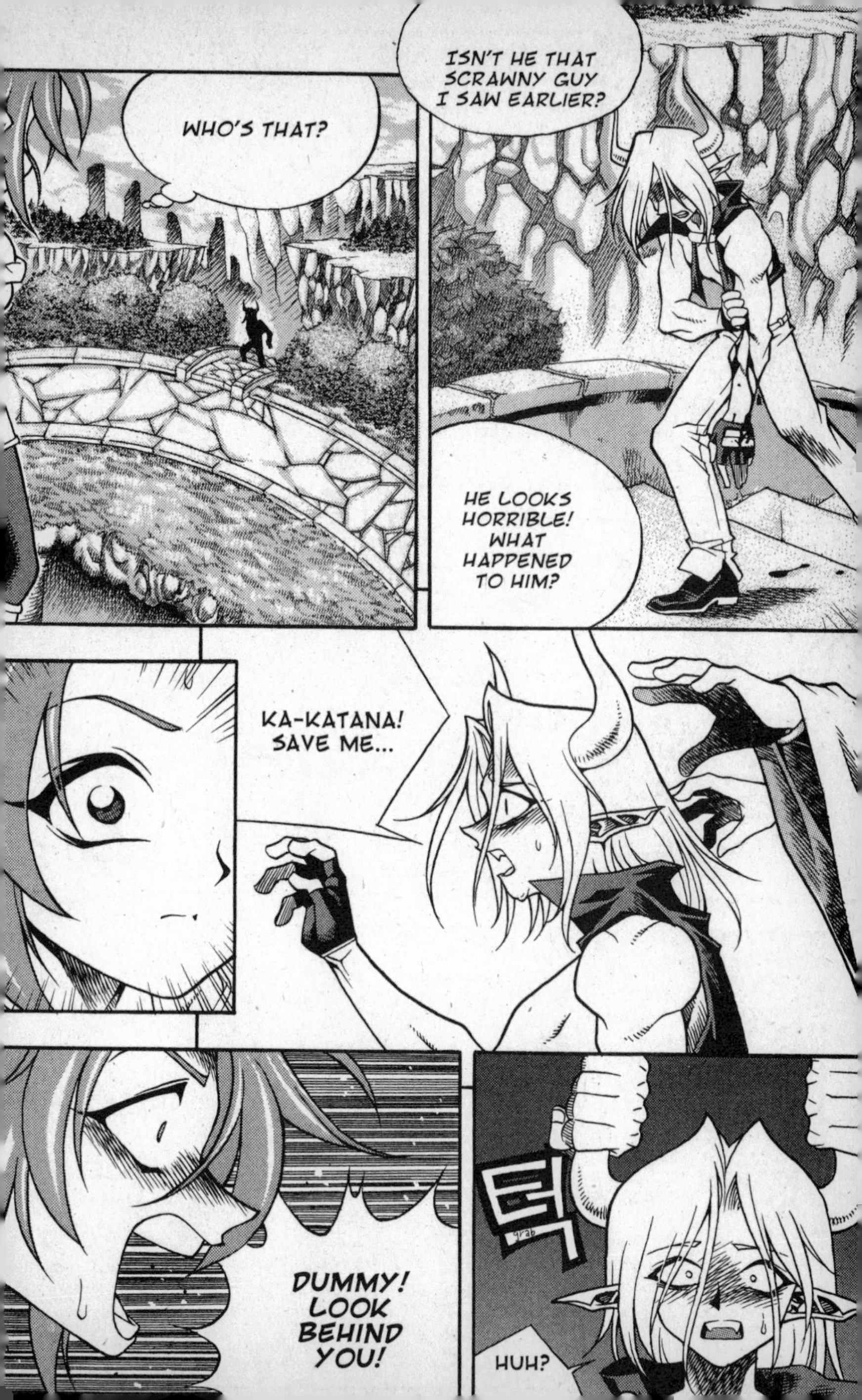
WHO'S THAT?
ISN'T HE THAT SCRAWNY GUY I SAW EARLIER?
HE LOOKS HORRIBLE! WHAT HAPPENED TO HIM?
KA-KATANA! SAVE ME...
DUMMY! LOOK BEHIND YOU!
grab
HUH?

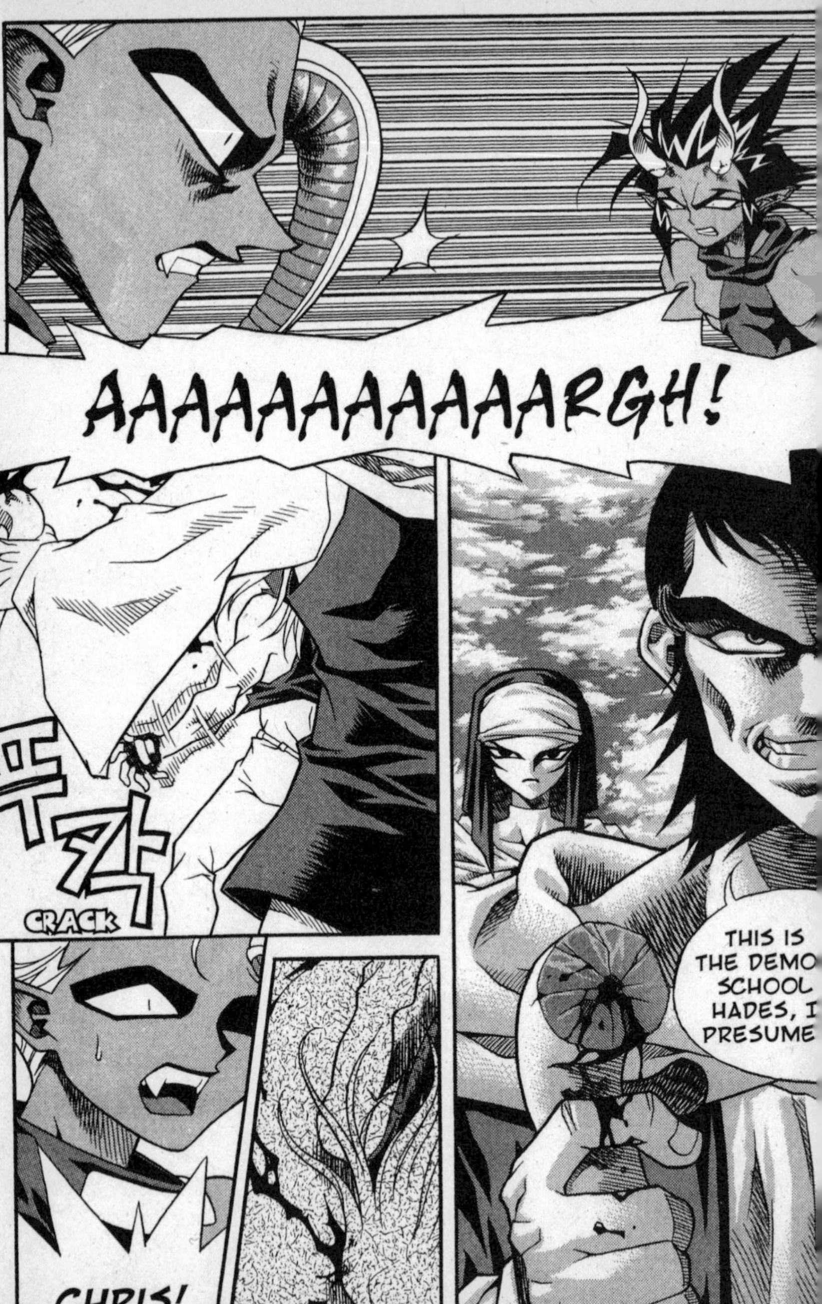
AAAAAAAAAAAARGH!
CRACK
THIS IS THE DEMO SCHOOL HADES, I PRESUME
CHRIS!

Quest 8

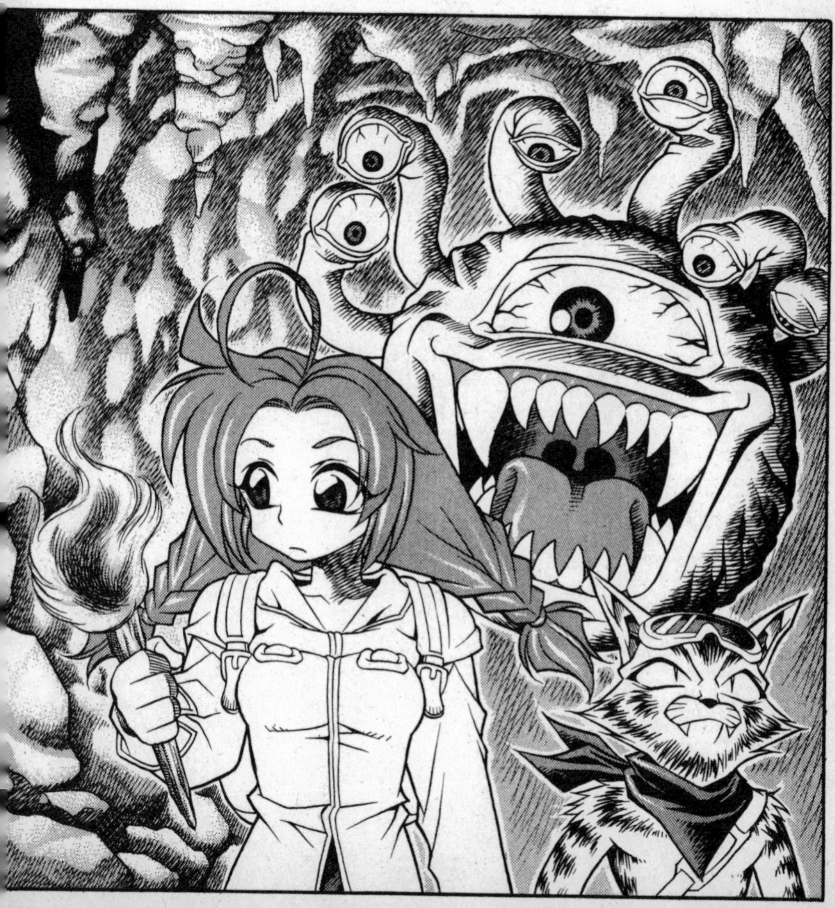

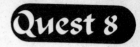

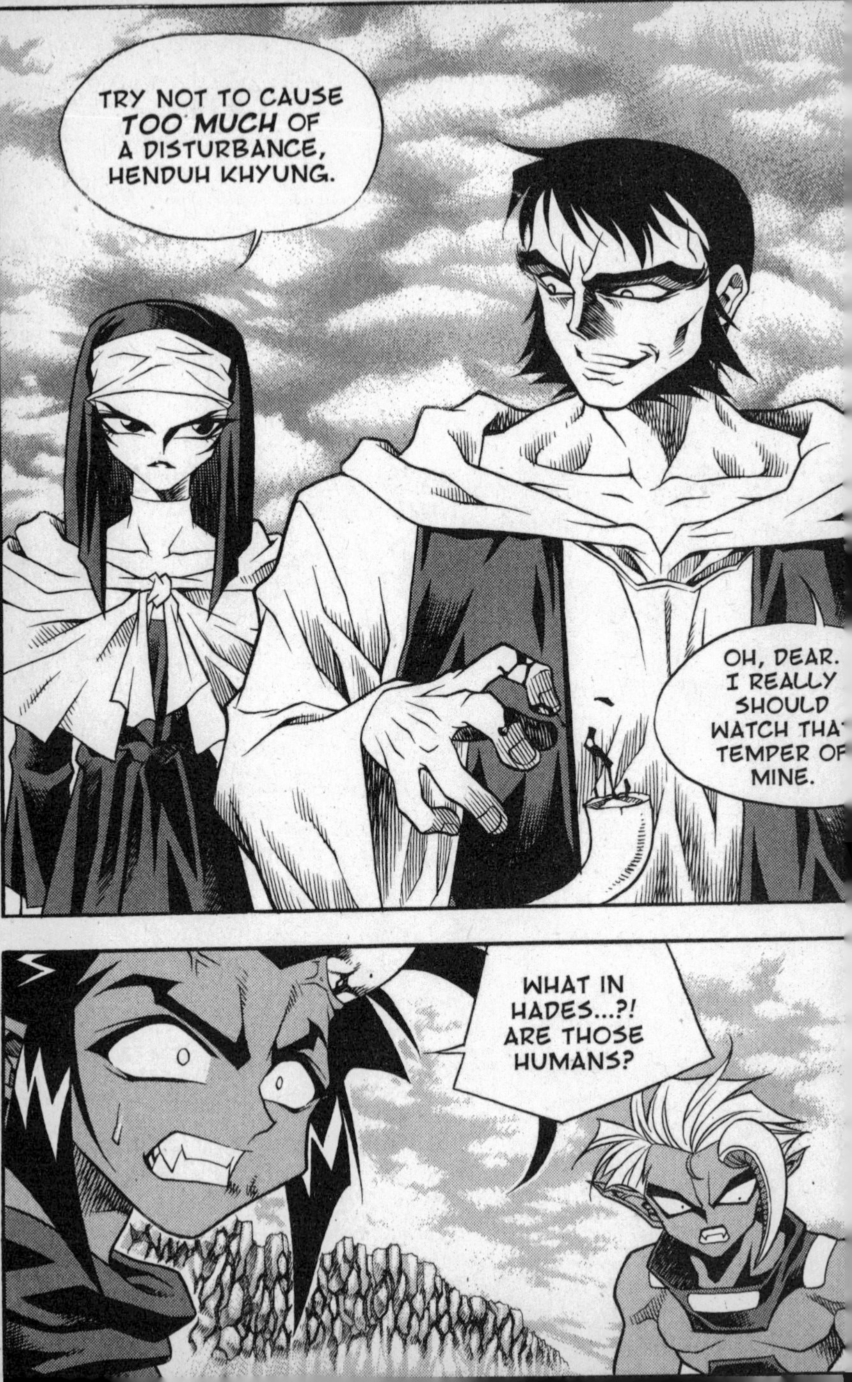
TRY NOT TO CAUSE *TOO MUCH* OF A DISTURBANCE, HENDUH KHYUNG.
OH, DEAR. I REALLY SHOULD WATCH THA TEMPER OF MINE.
WHAT IN HADES...?! ARE THOSE HUMANS?

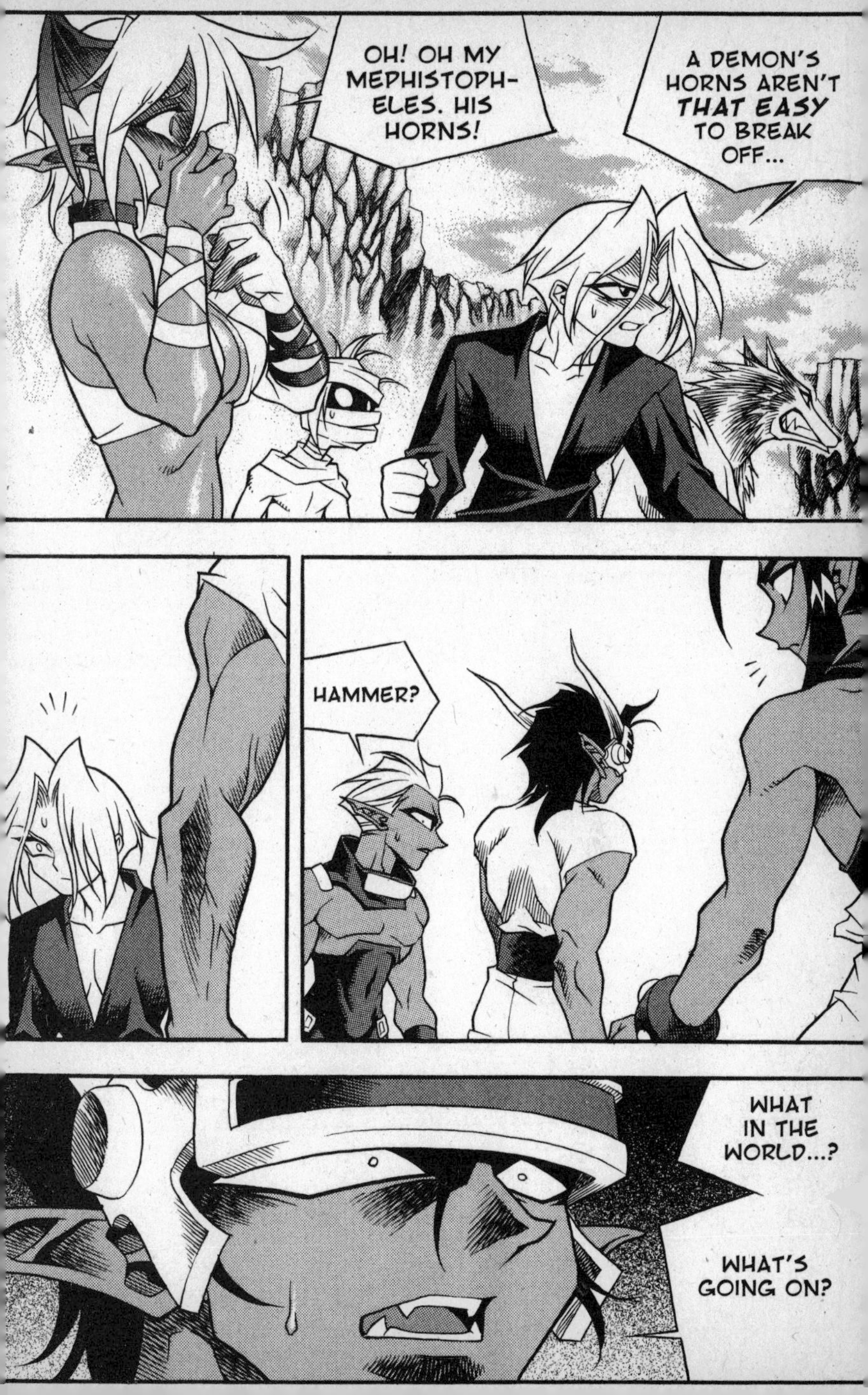
OH! OH MY MEPHISTOPHELES. HIS HORNS!
A DEMON'S HORNS AREN'T THAT EASY TO BREAK OFF...
HAMMER?
WHAT IN THE WORLD...?
WHAT'S GOING ON?

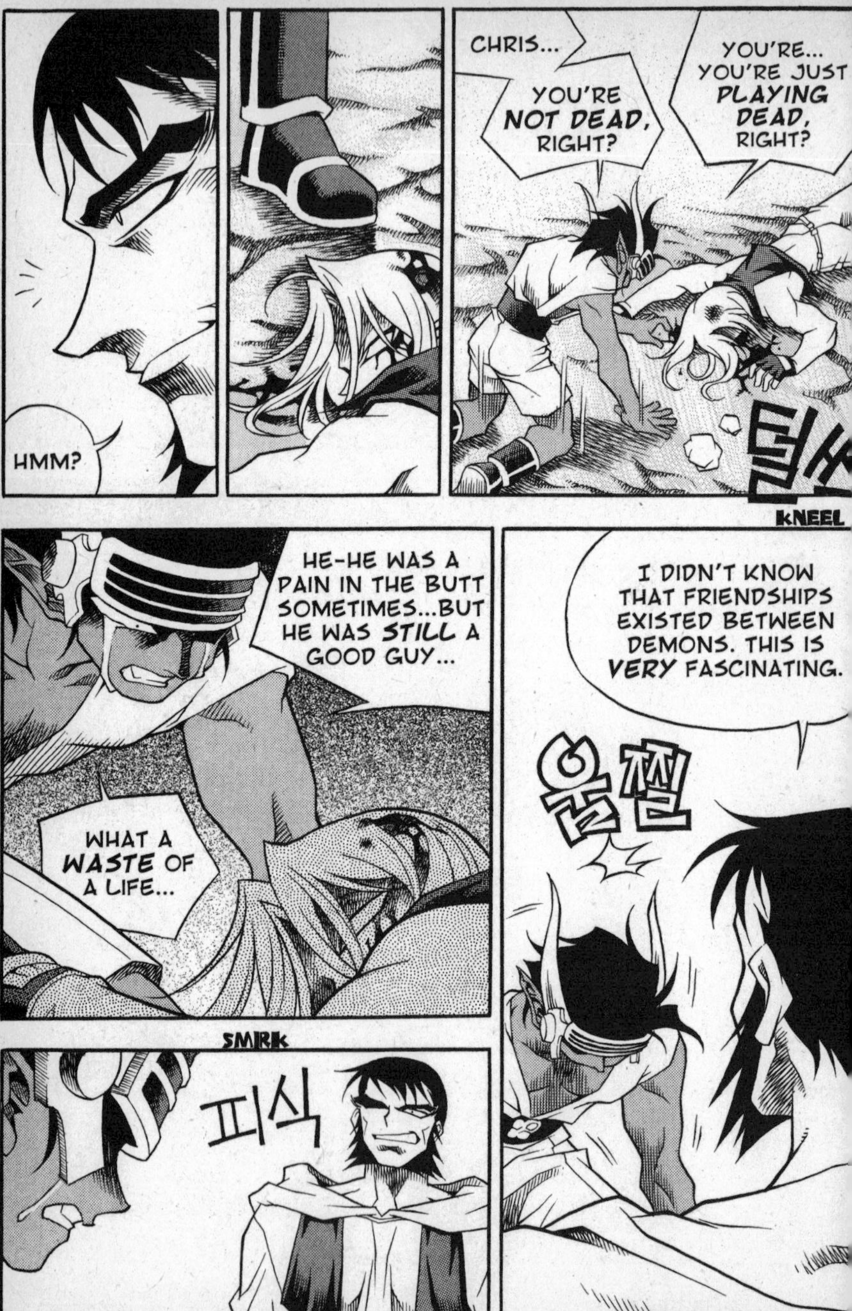
HMM?
CHRIS...
YOU'RE NOT DEAD, RIGHT?
YOU'RE... YOU'RE JUST PLAYING DEAD, RIGHT?
KNEEL
HE-HE WAS A PAIN IN THE BUTT SOMETIMES...BUT HE WAS STILL A GOOD GUY...
WHAT A WASTE OF A LIFE...
SMIRK
피식
I DIDN'T KNOW THAT FRIENDSHIPS EXISTED BETWEEN DEMONS. THIS IS VERY FASCINATING.
움찔
FREEZE

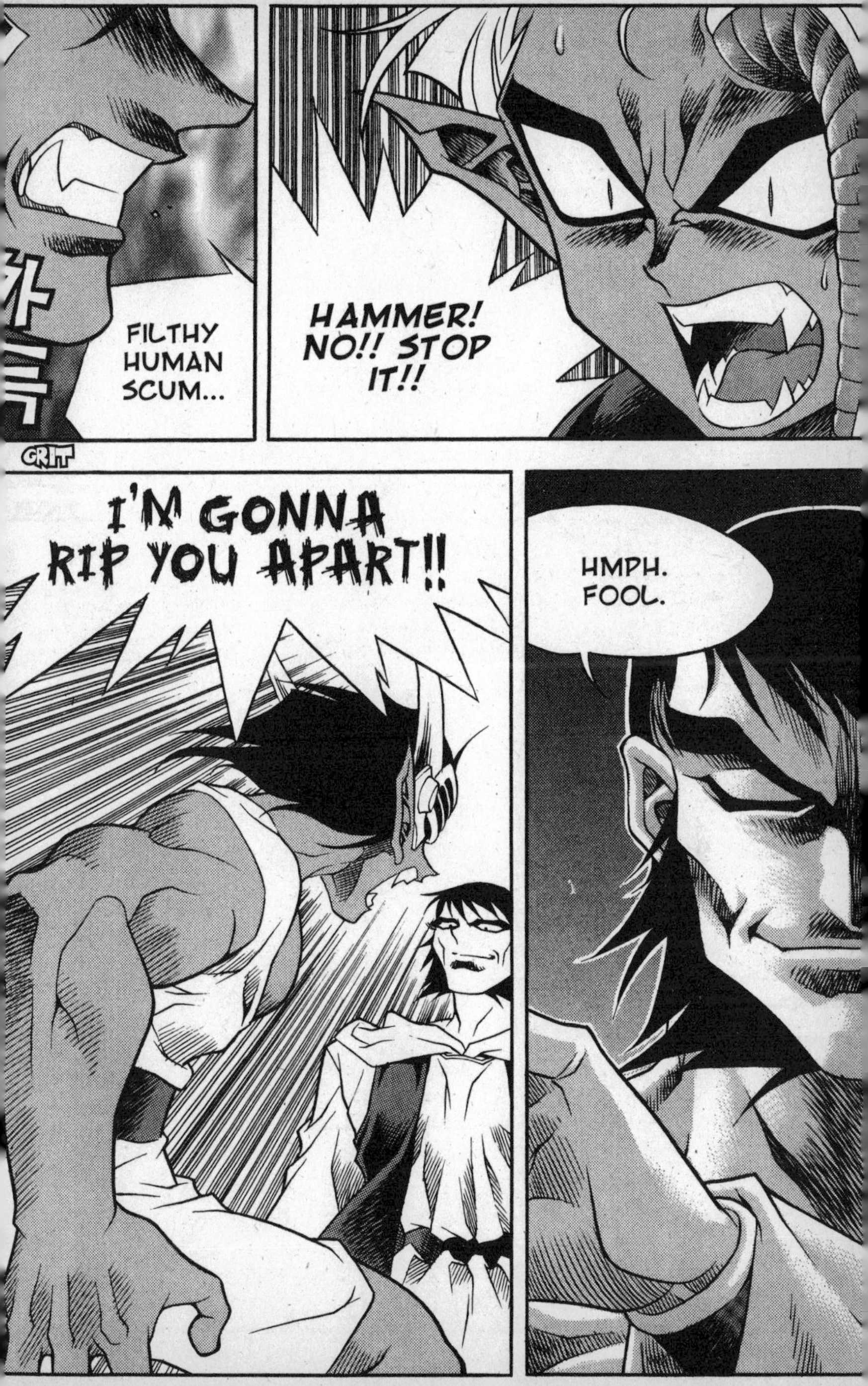

FILTHY HUMAN SCUM...
HAMMER! NO!! STOP IT!!
GRIT
I'M GONNA RIP YOU APART!!
HMPH. FOOL.

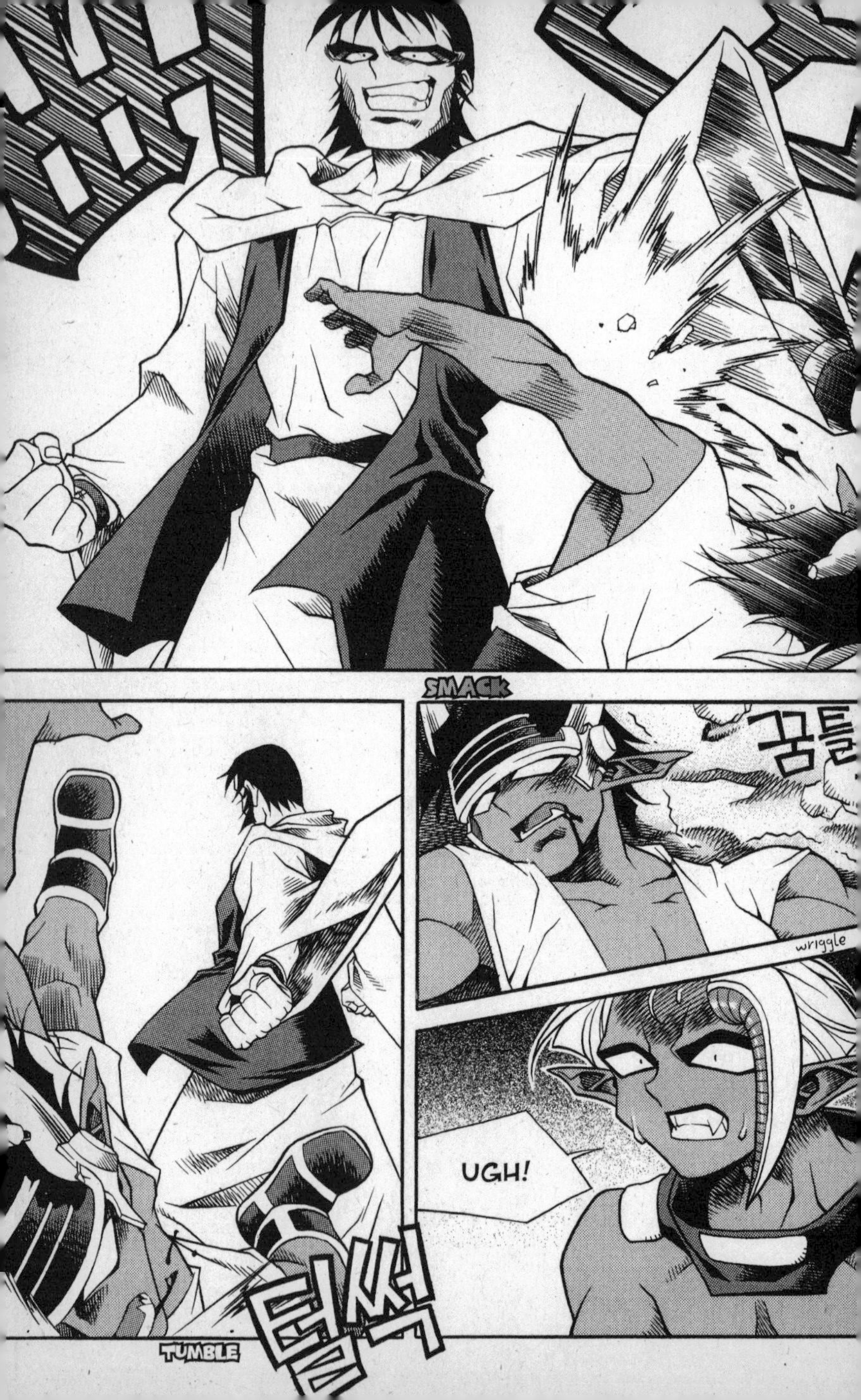
SMACK
털썩
TUMBLE
꿈틀
wriggle
UGH!

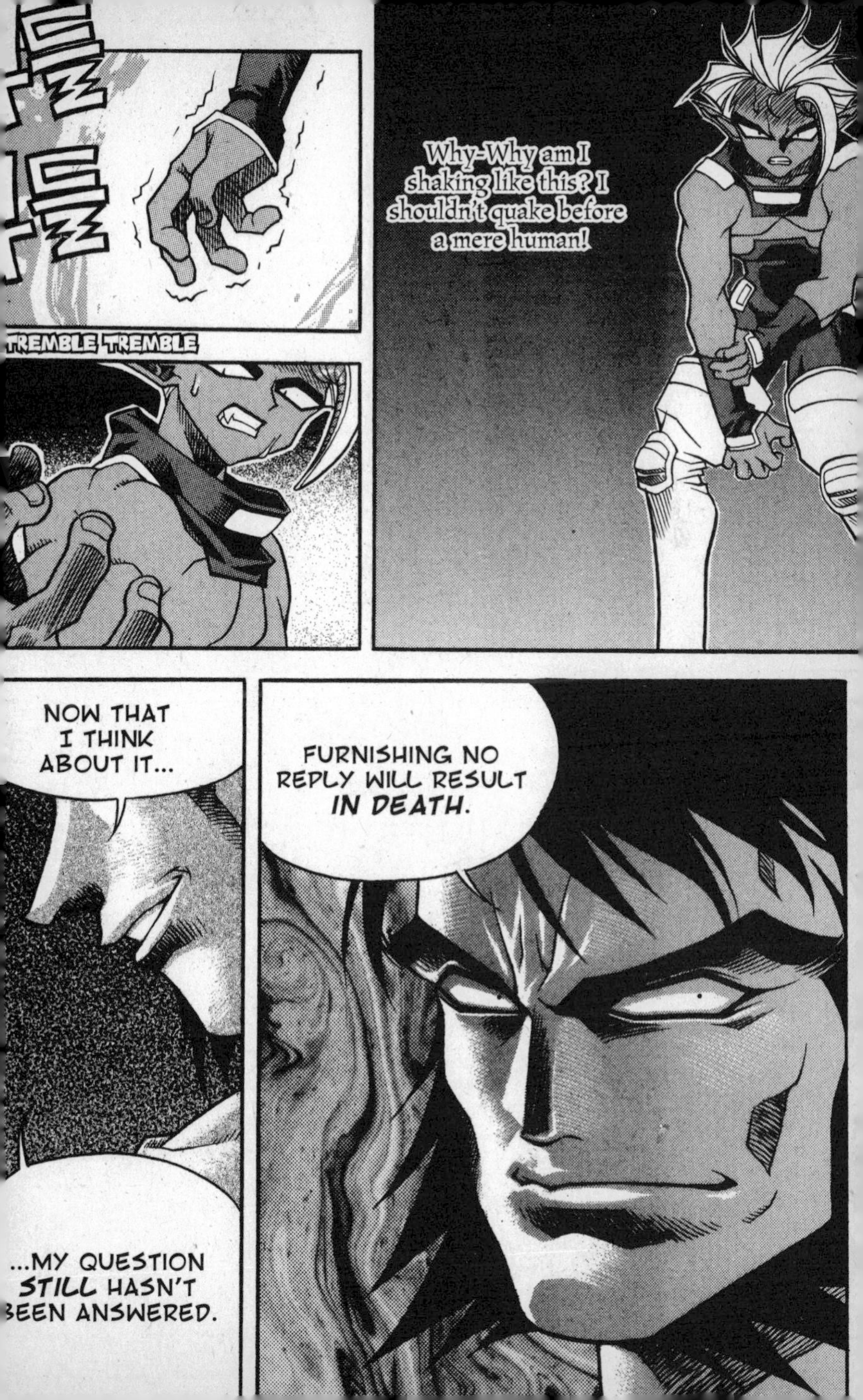
TREMBLE TREMBLE
Why-Why am I shaking like this? I shouldn't quake before a mere human!
NOW THAT I THINK ABOUT IT...
...MY QUESTION STILL HASN'T BEEN ANSWERED.
FURNISHING NO REPLY WILL RESULT IN DEATH.

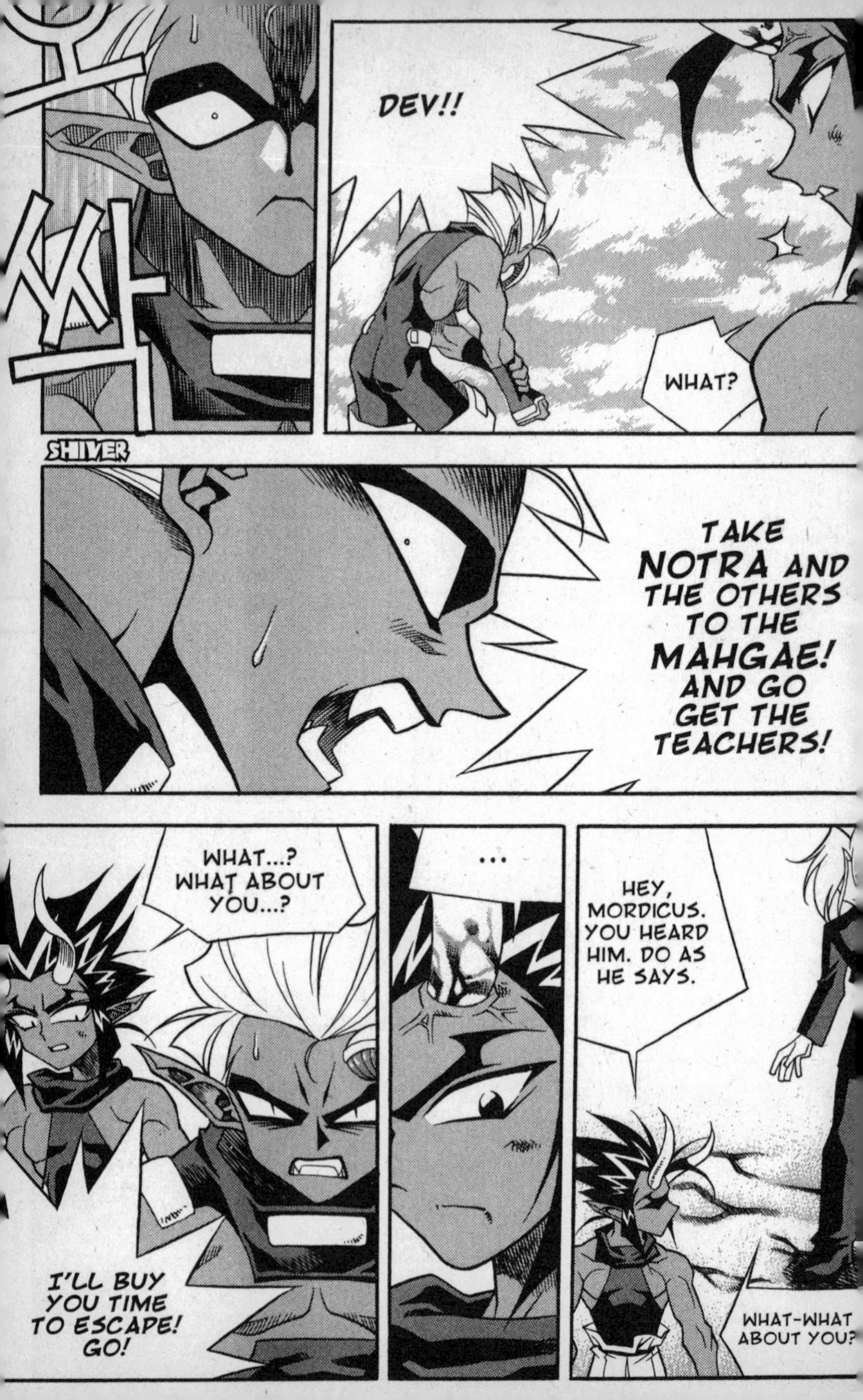
DEV!!
WHAT?
SHIVER
TAKE NOTRA AND THE OTHERS TO THE MAHGAE! AND GO GET THE TEACHERS!
WHAT...? WHAT ABOUT YOU...?
I'LL BUY YOU TIME TO ESCAPE! GO!
...
HEY, MORDICUS. YOU HEARD HIM. DO AS HE SAYS.
WHAT-WHAT ABOUT YOU?

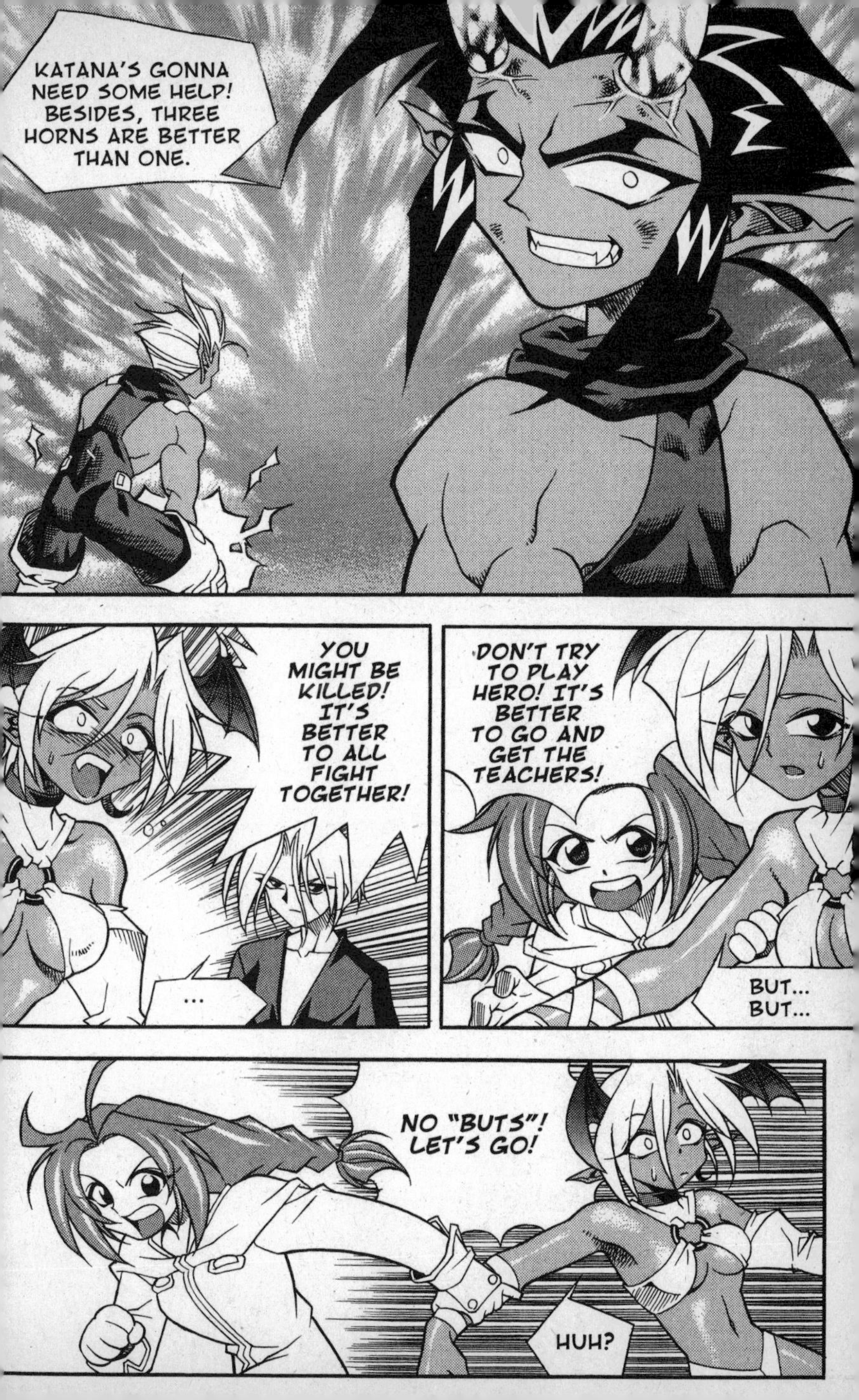
KATANA'S GONNA NEED SOME HELP! BESIDES, THREE HORNS ARE BETTER THAN ONE.
YOU MIGHT BE KILLED! IT'S BETTER TO ALL FIGHT TOGETHER!
...
DON'T TRY TO PLAY HERO! IT'S BETTER TO GO AND GET THE TEACHERS!
BUT... BUT...
NO "BUTS"! LET'S GO!
HUH?

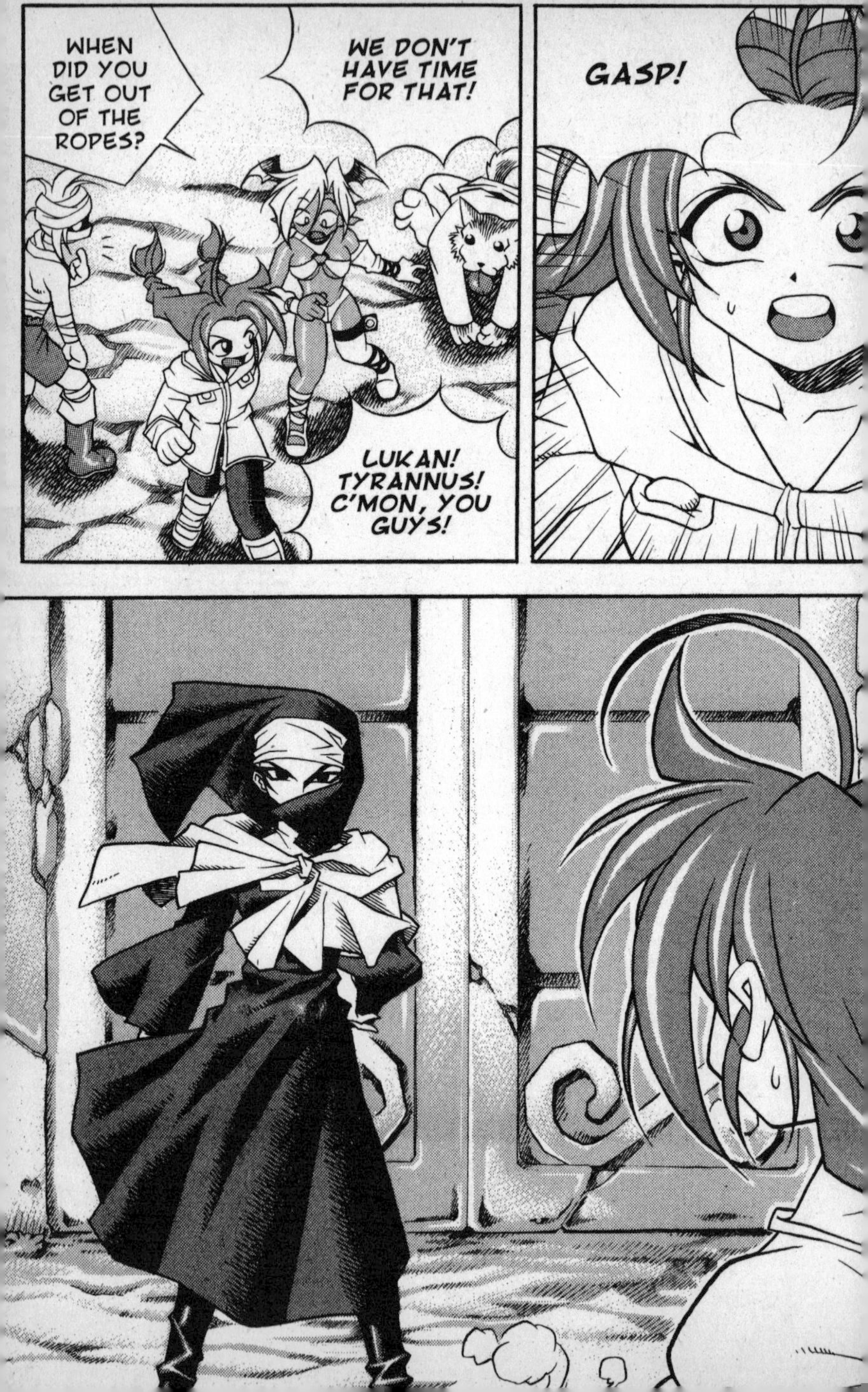
WHEN DID YOU GET OUT OF THE ROPES?
WE DON'T HAVE TIME FOR THAT!
LUKAN! TYRANNUS! C'MON, YOU GUYS!
GASP!

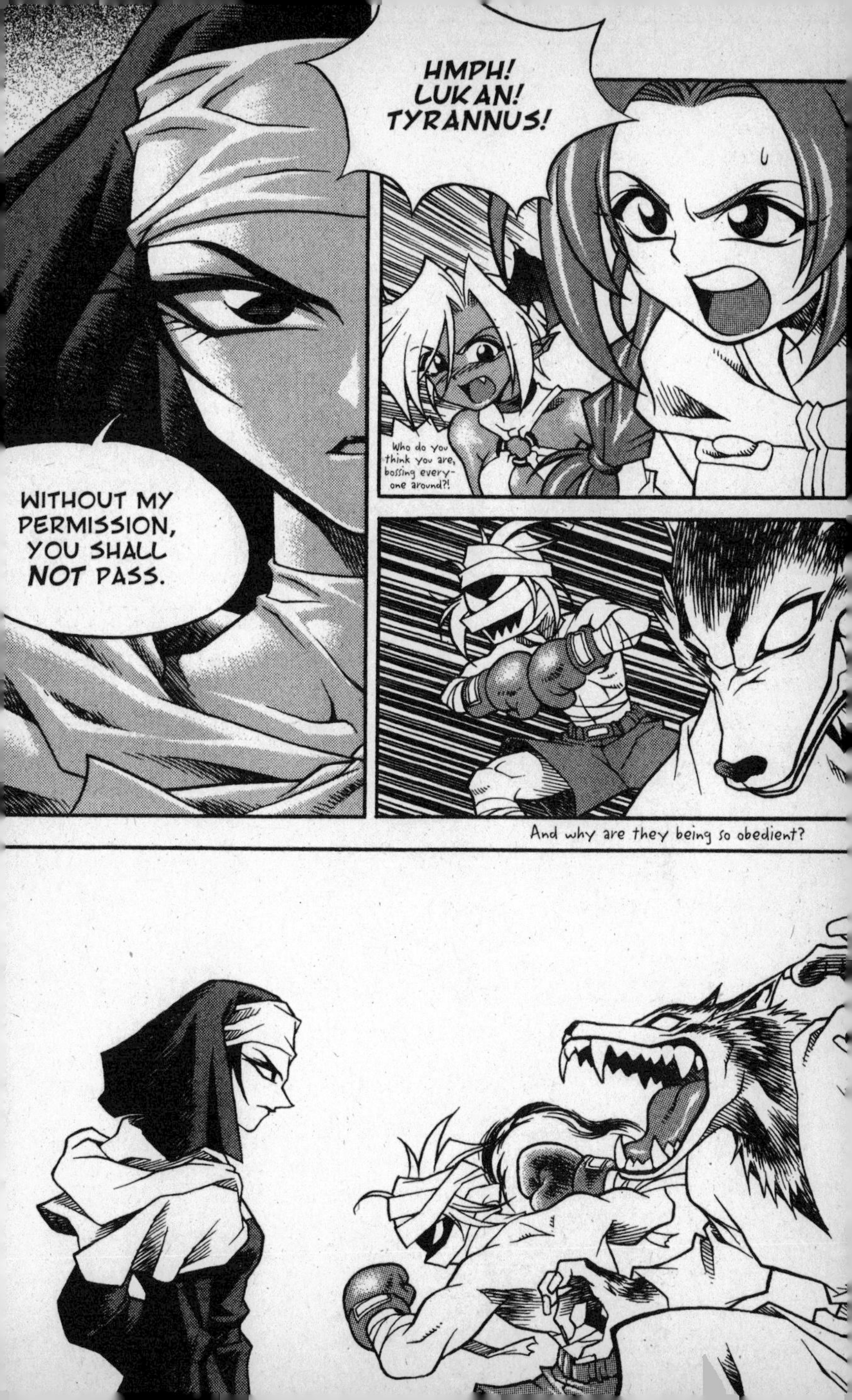
WITHOUT MY PERMISSION, YOU SHALL NOT PASS.
HMPH! LUKAN! TYRANNUS!
Who do you think you are, bossing every-one around?!
And why are they being so obedient?

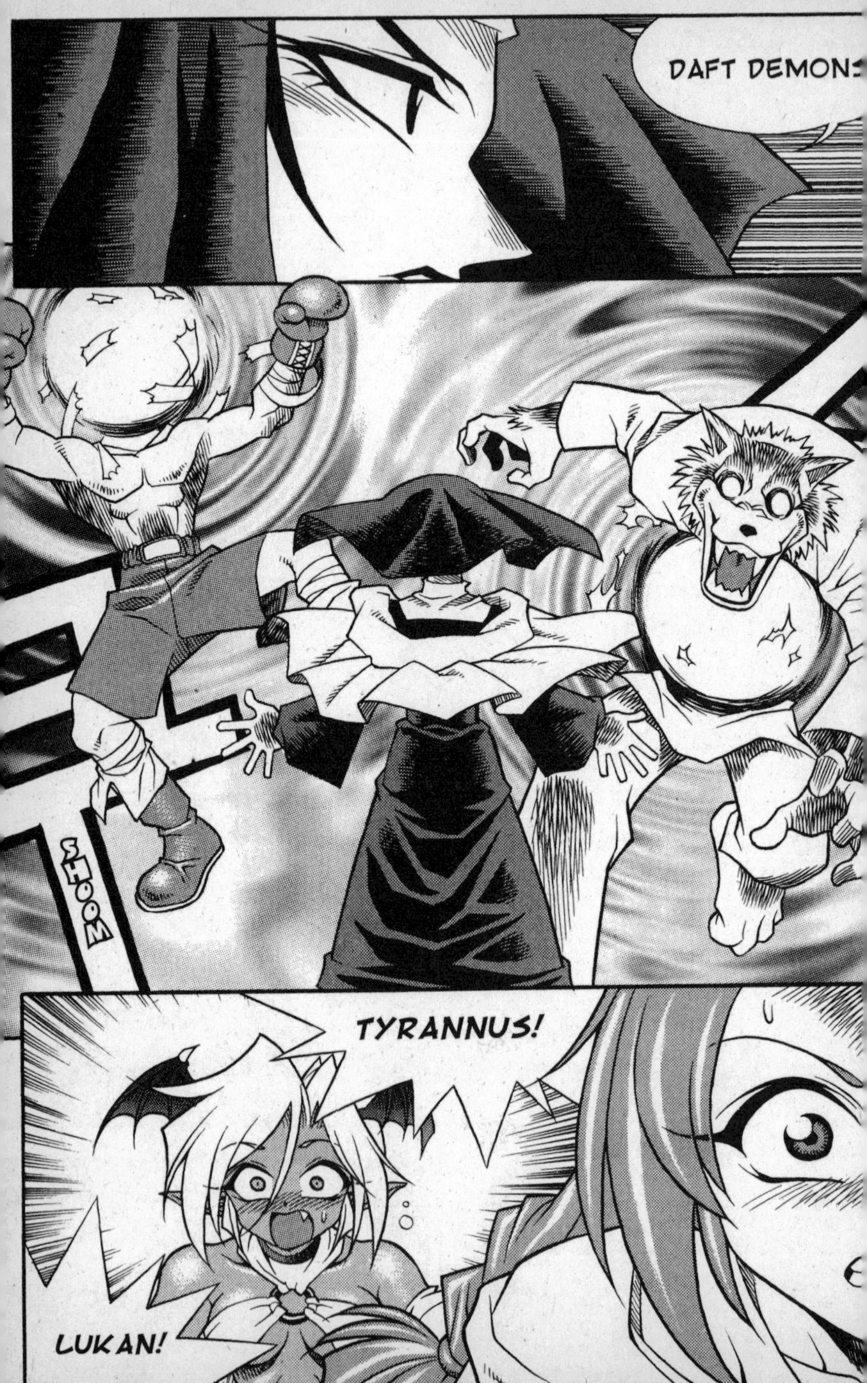
DAFT DEMONS
SHOOOM
TYRANNUS!
LUKAN!

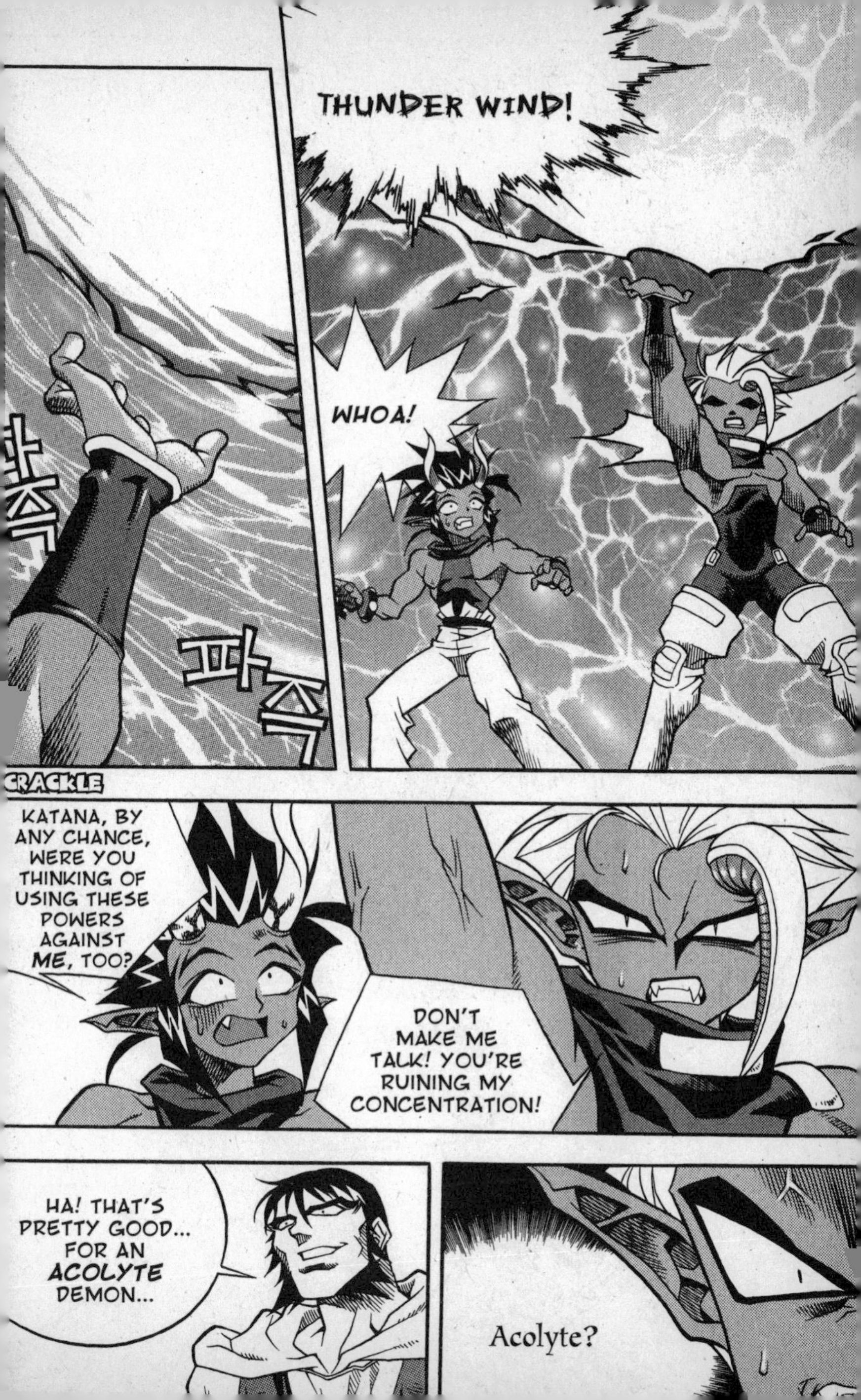
파직
파직
CRACKLE
THUNDER WIND!
WHOA!
KATANA, BY ANY CHANCE, WERE YOU THINKING OF USING THESE POWERS AGAINST ME, TOO?
DON'T MAKE ME TALK! YOU'RE RUINING MY CONCENTRATION!
HA! THAT'S PRETTY GOOD... FOR AN ACOLYTE DEMON...
Acolyte?

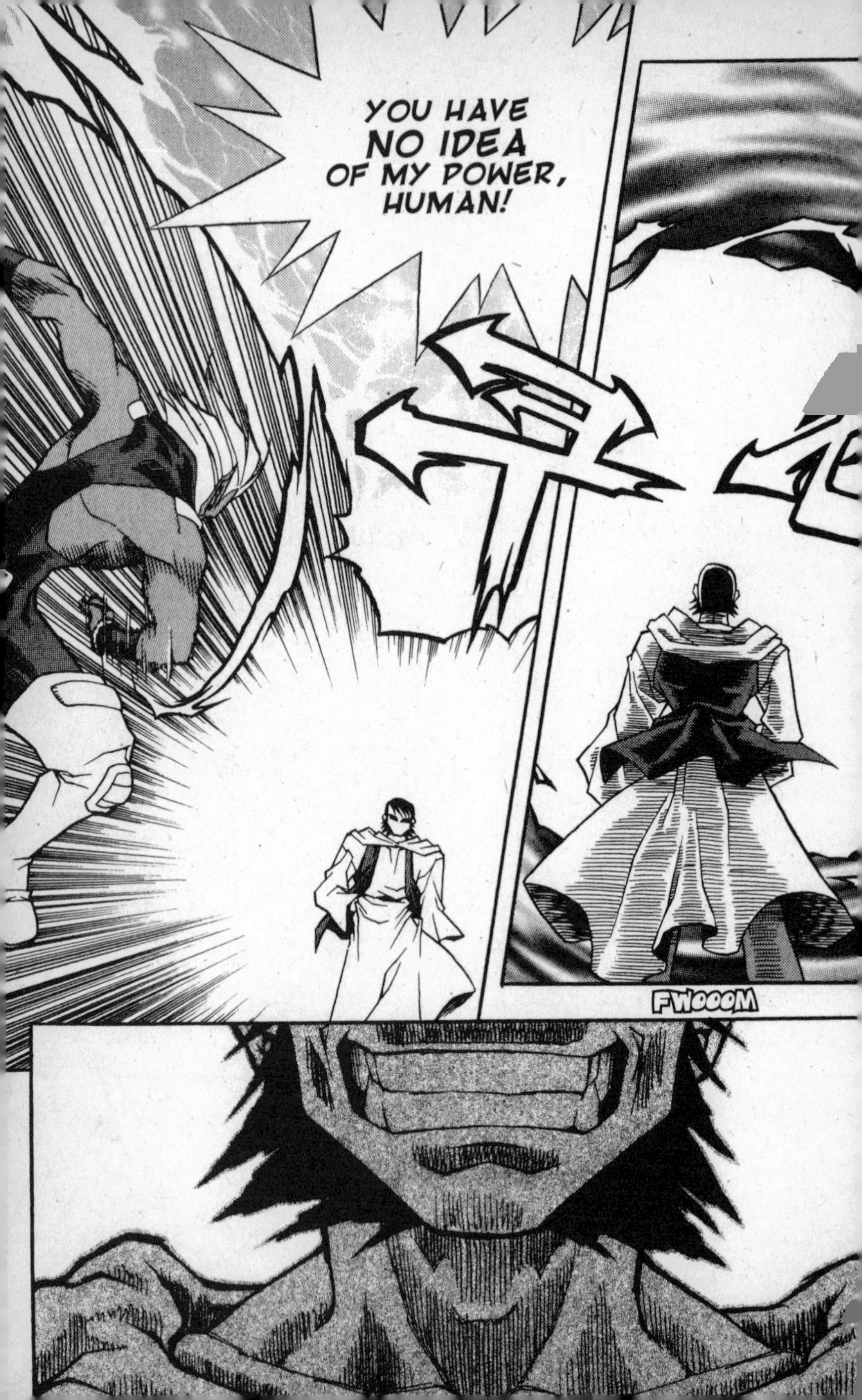
YOU HAVE NO IDEA OF MY POWER, HUMAN!
FWOOOM

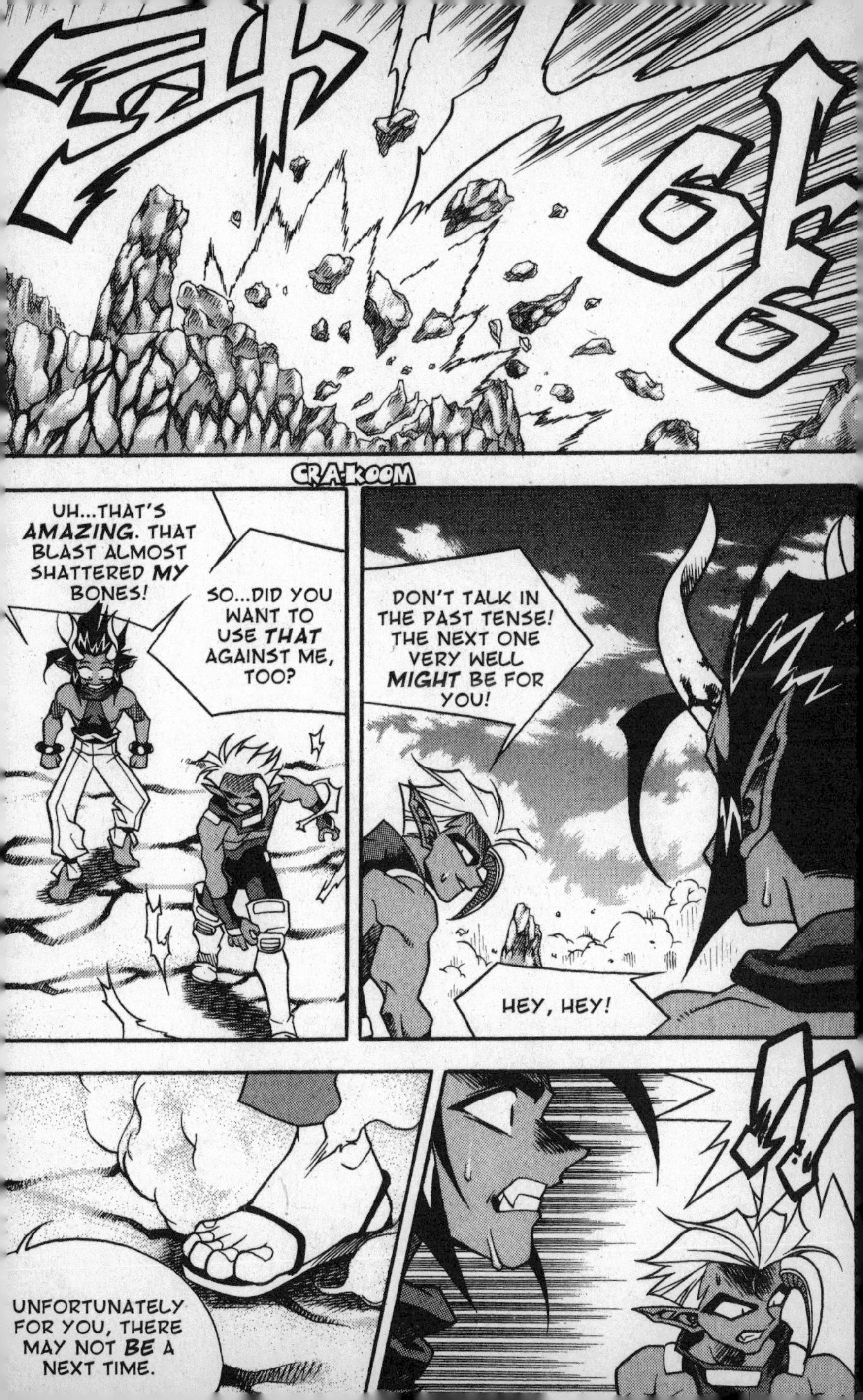
CRA-KOOM
UH...THAT'S AMAZING. THAT BLAST ALMOST SHATTERED MY BONES!
SO...DID YOU WANT TO USE THAT AGAINST ME, TOO?
DON'T TALK IN THE PAST TENSE! THE NEXT ONE VERY WELL MIGHT BE FOR YOU!
HEY, HEY!
UNFORTUNATELY FOR YOU, THERE MAY NOT BE A NEXT TIME.

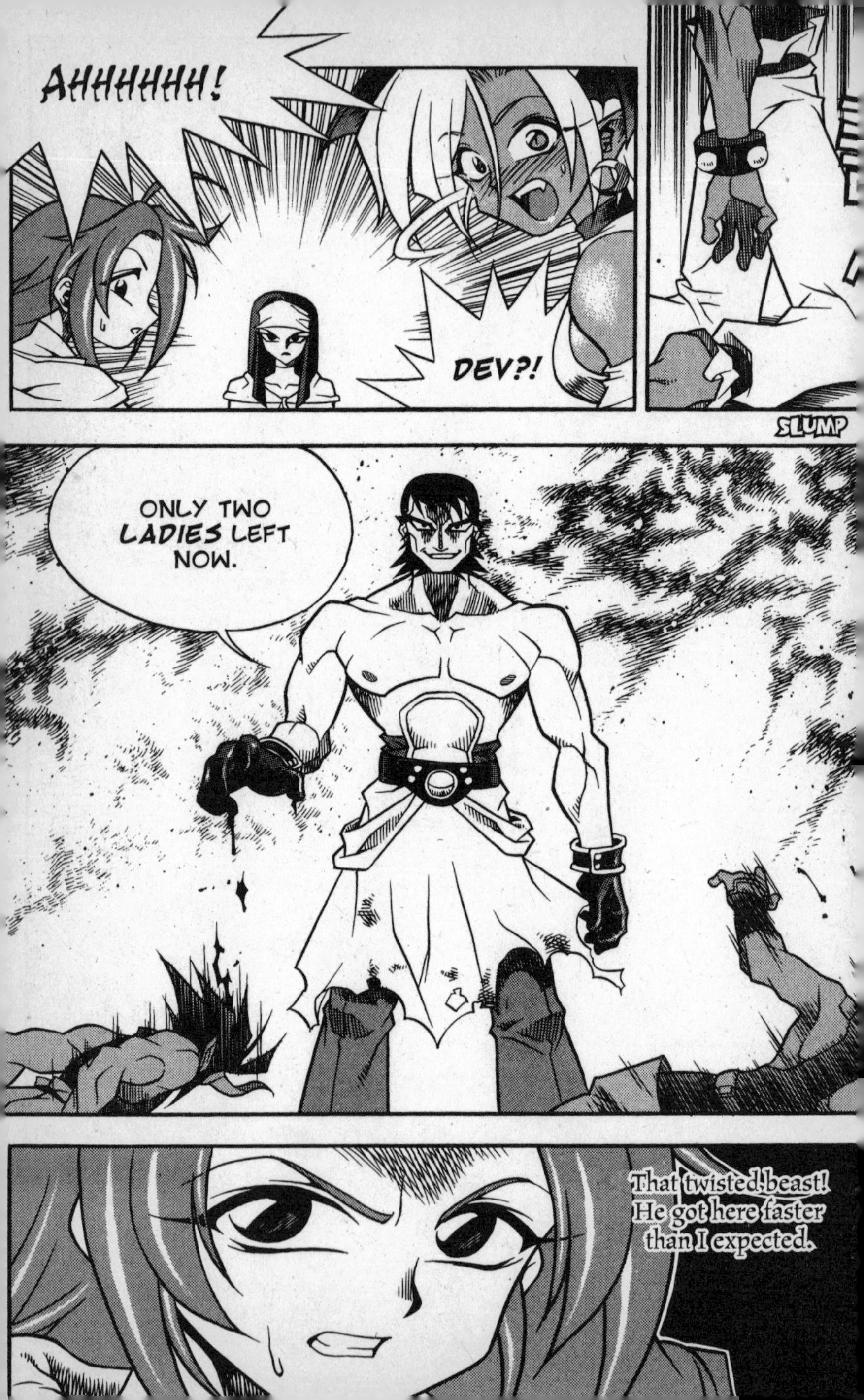
AHHHHHH!
DEV?!
SLUMP
ONLY TWO LADIES LEFT NOW.
That twisted beast! He got here faster than I expected.

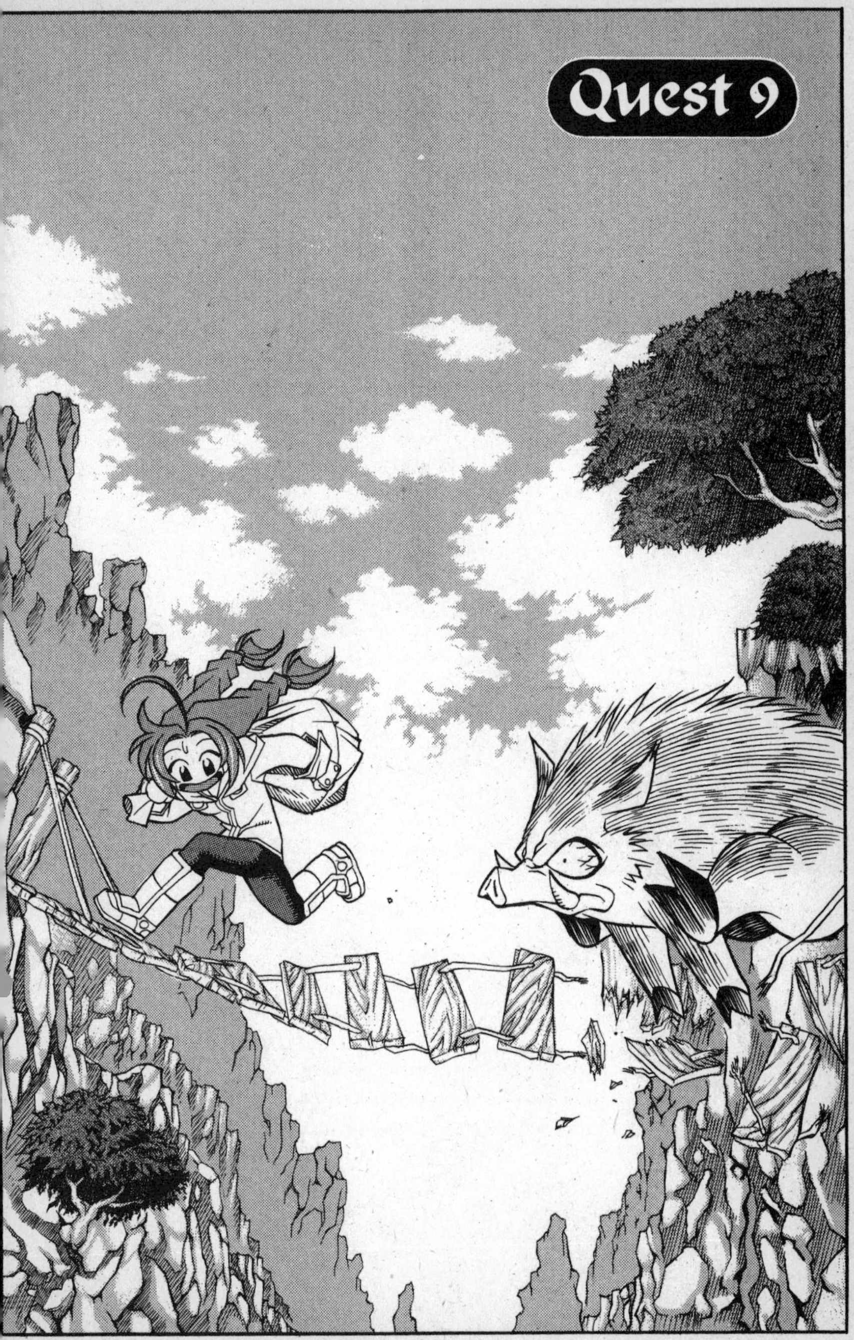
Quest 9

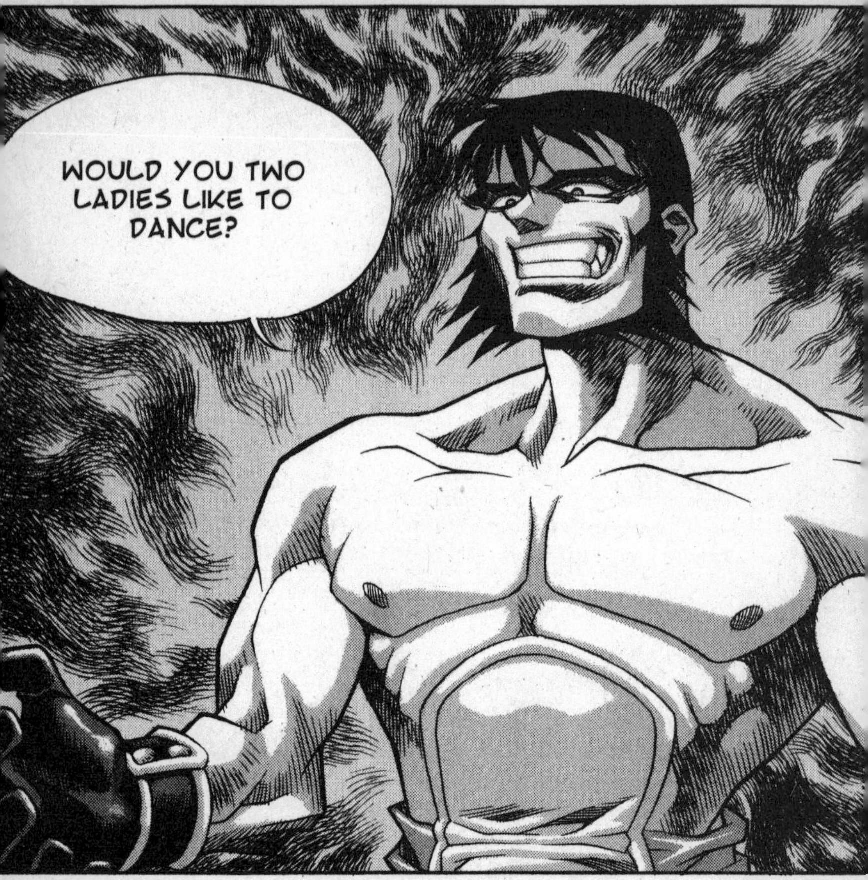
WOULD YOU TWO LADIES LIKE TO DANCE?

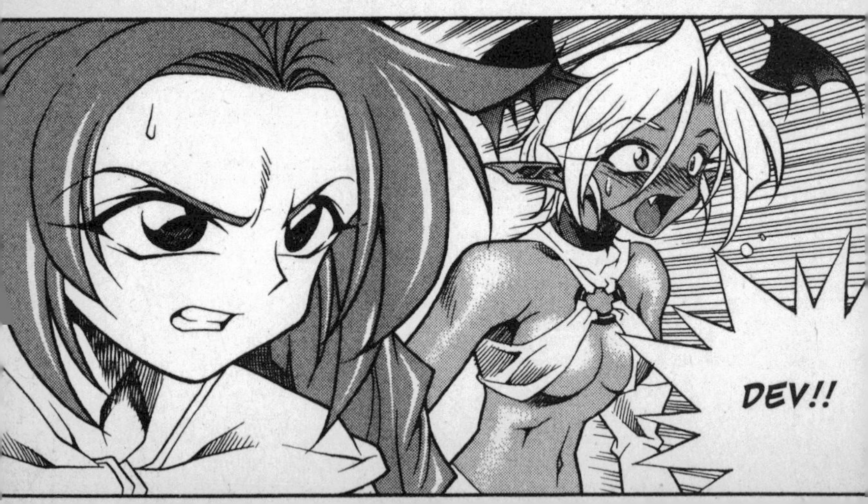
DEV!!

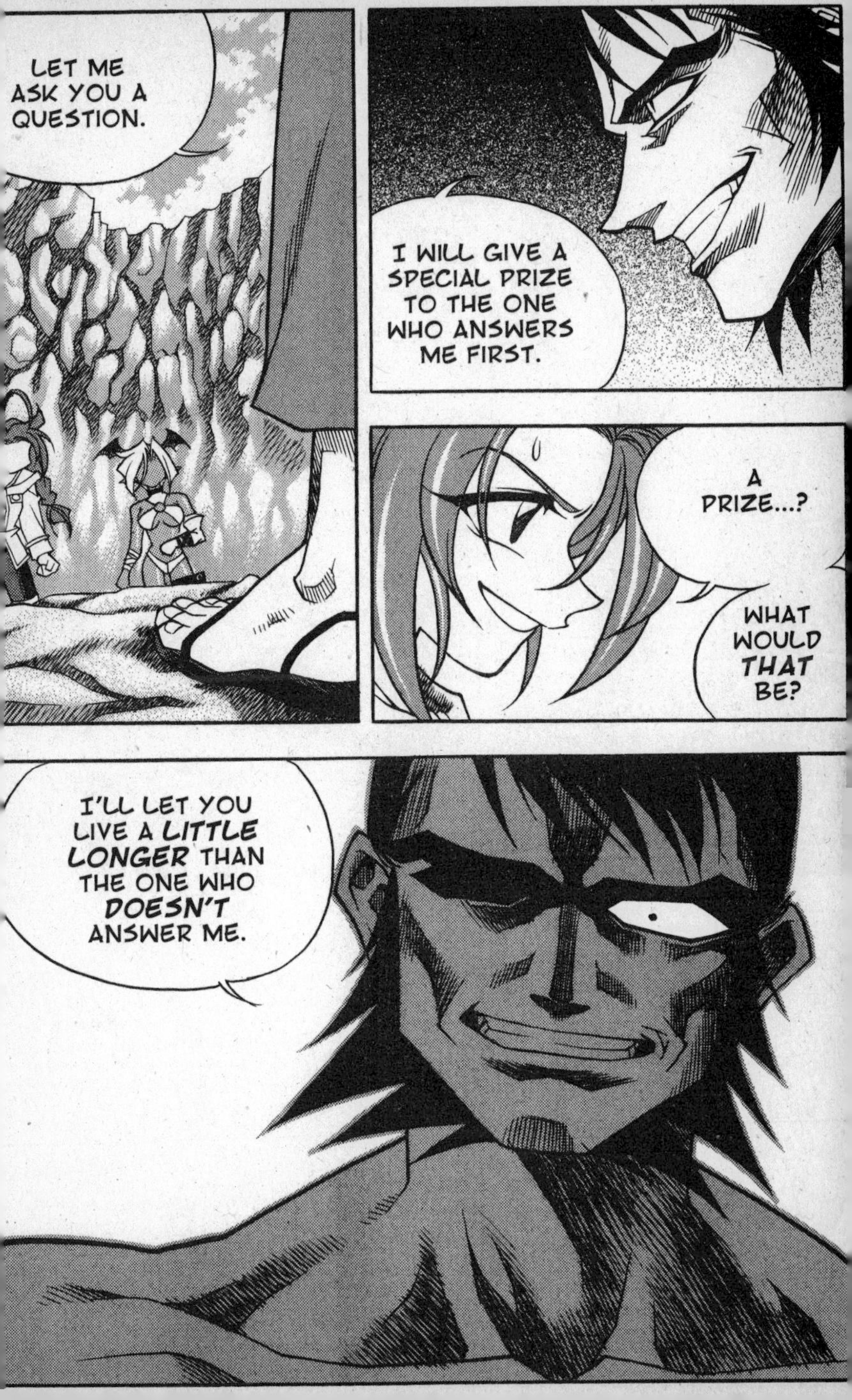
LET ME ASK YOU A QUESTION.
I WILL GIVE A SPECIAL PRIZE TO THE ONE WHO ANSWERS ME FIRST.
A PRIZE...?
WHAT WOULD *THAT* BE?
I'LL LET YOU LIVE A ***LITTLE LONGER*** THAN THE ONE WHO ***DOESN'T*** ANSWER ME.

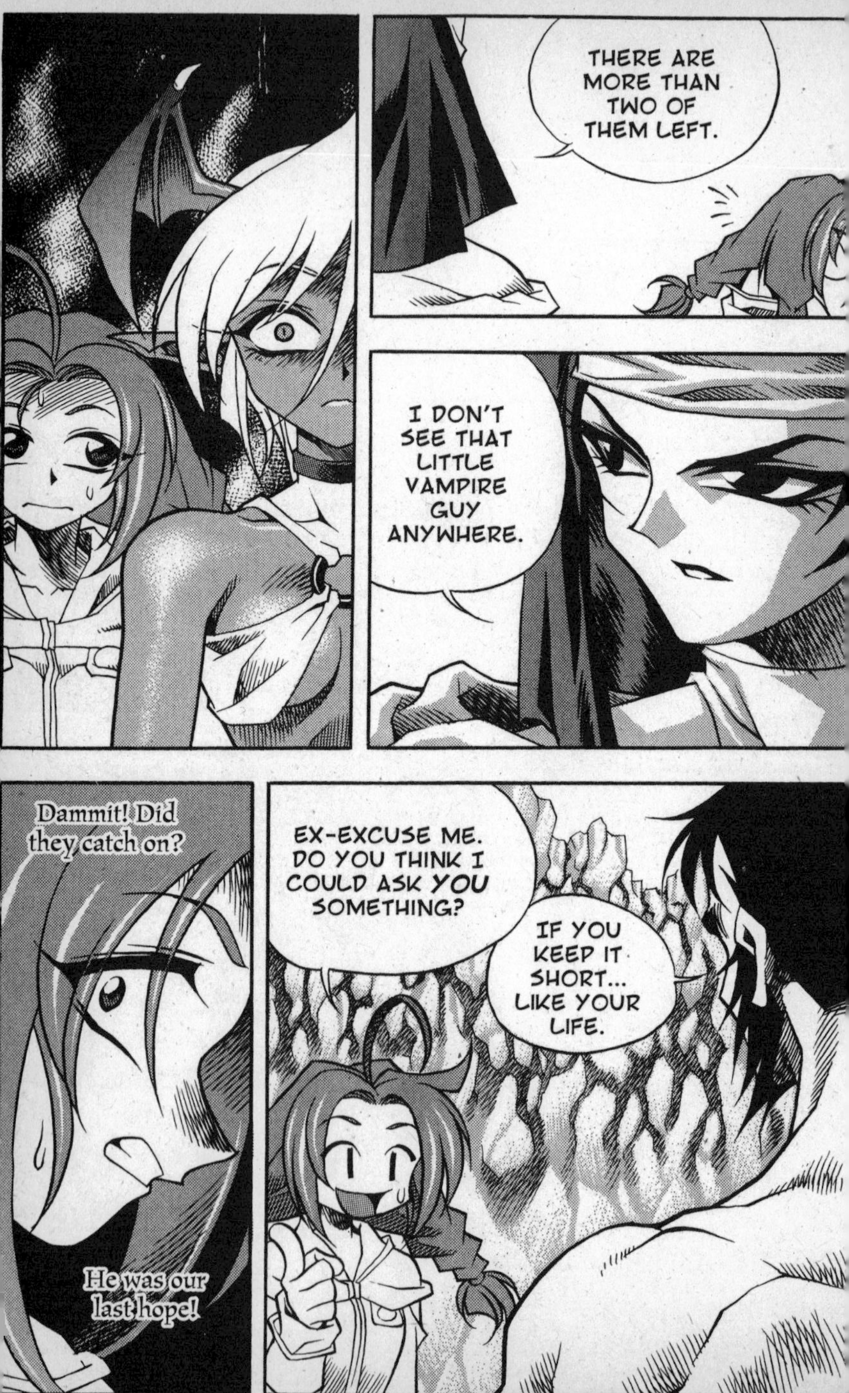
THERE ARE MORE THAN TWO OF THEM LEFT.
I DON'T SEE THAT LITTLE VAMPIRE GUY ANYWHERE.
Dammit! Did they catch on?
He was our last hope!
EX-EXCUSE ME. DO YOU THINK I COULD ASK YOU SOMETHING?
IF YOU KEEP IT SHORT... LIKE YOUR LIFE.

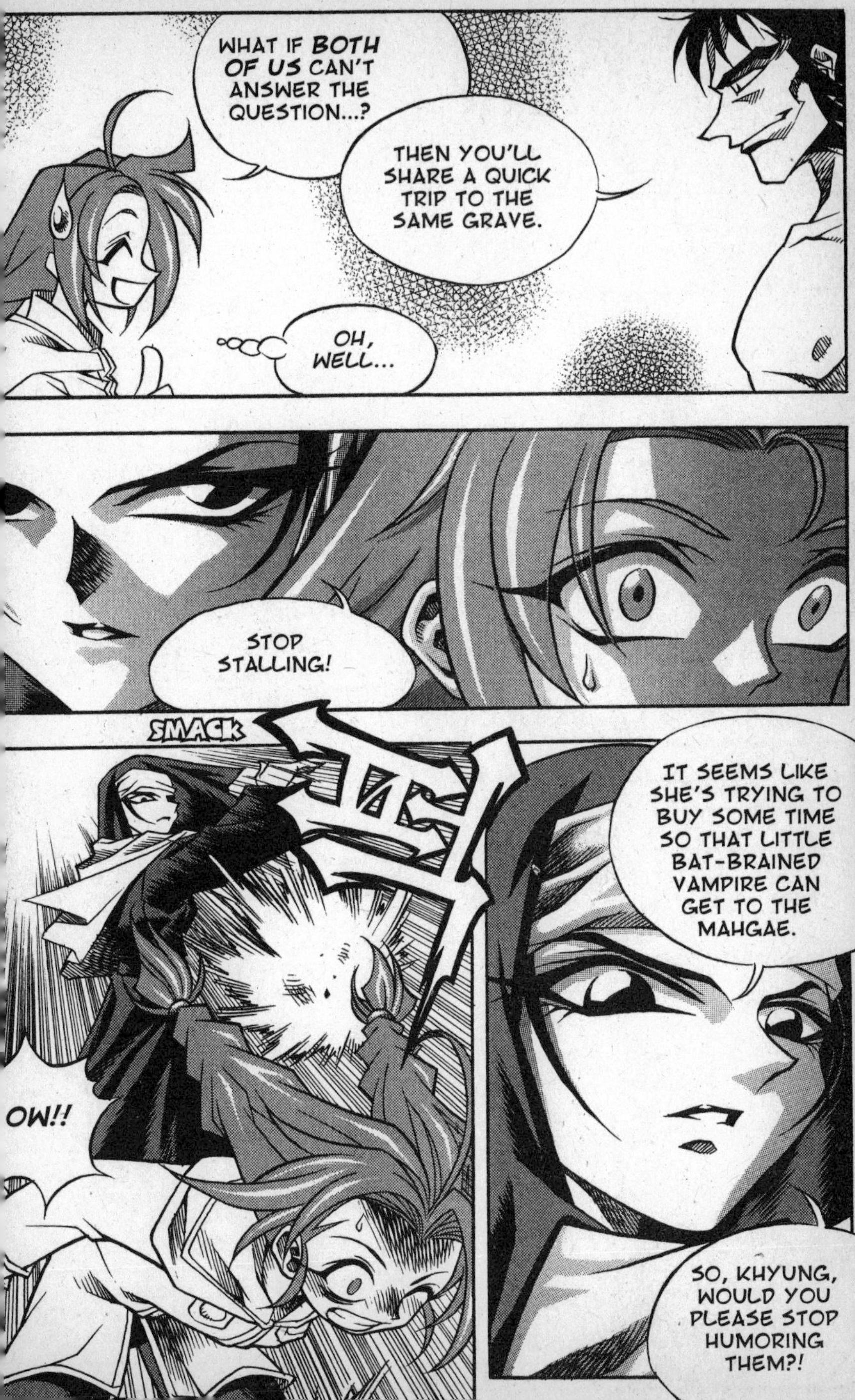

WHAT IF BOTH OF US CAN'T ANSWER THE QUESTION...?
THEN YOU'LL SHARE A QUICK TRIP TO THE SAME GRAVE.
OH, WELL...
STOP STALLING!
SMACK
OW!!
IT SEEMS LIKE SHE'S TRYING TO BUY SOME TIME SO THAT LITTLE BAT-BRAINED VAMPIRE CAN GET TO THE MAHGAE.
SO, KHYUNG, WOULD YOU PLEASE STOP HUMORING THEM?!

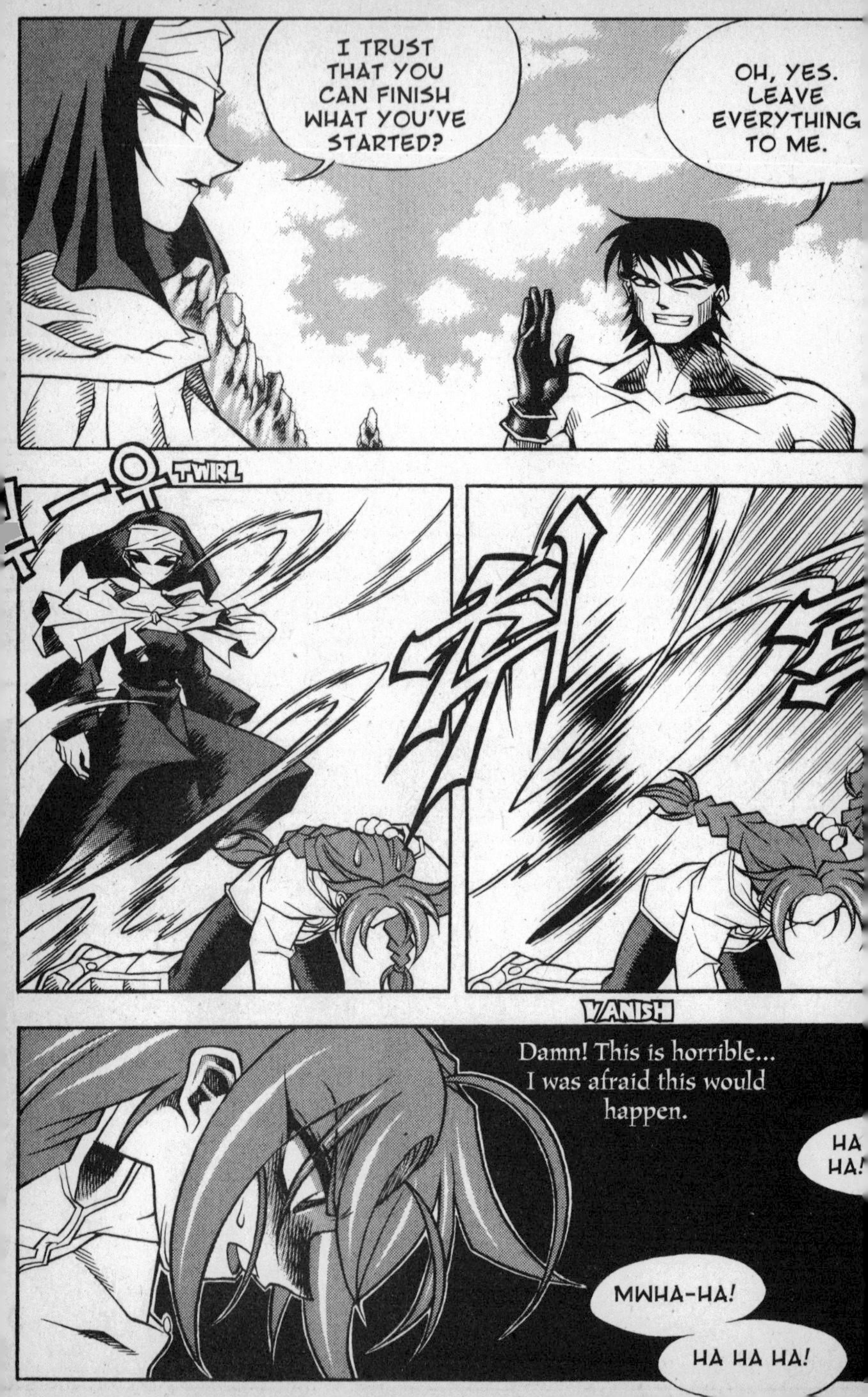
I TRUST THAT YOU CAN FINISH WHAT YOU'VE STARTED?
OH, YES. LEAVE EVERYTHING TO ME.
TWIRL
VANISH
Damn! This is horrible... I was afraid this would happen.
HA HA!
MWHA-HA!
HA HA HA!

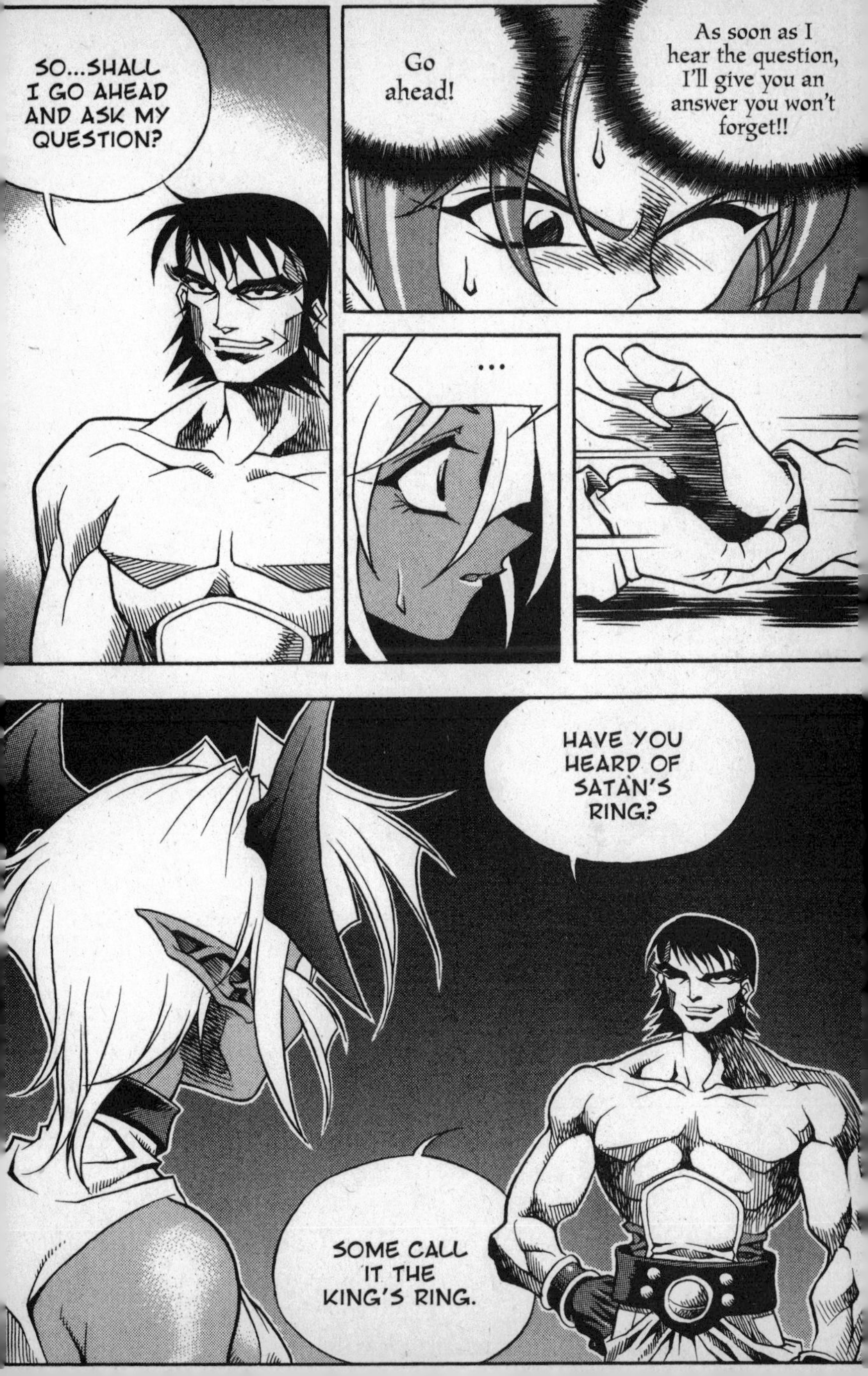
SO...SHALL I GO AHEAD AND ASK MY QUESTION?
Go ahead!
As soon as I hear the question, I'll give you an answer you won't forget!!
...
HAVE YOU HEARD OF SATAN'S RING?
SOME CALL IT THE KING'S RING.

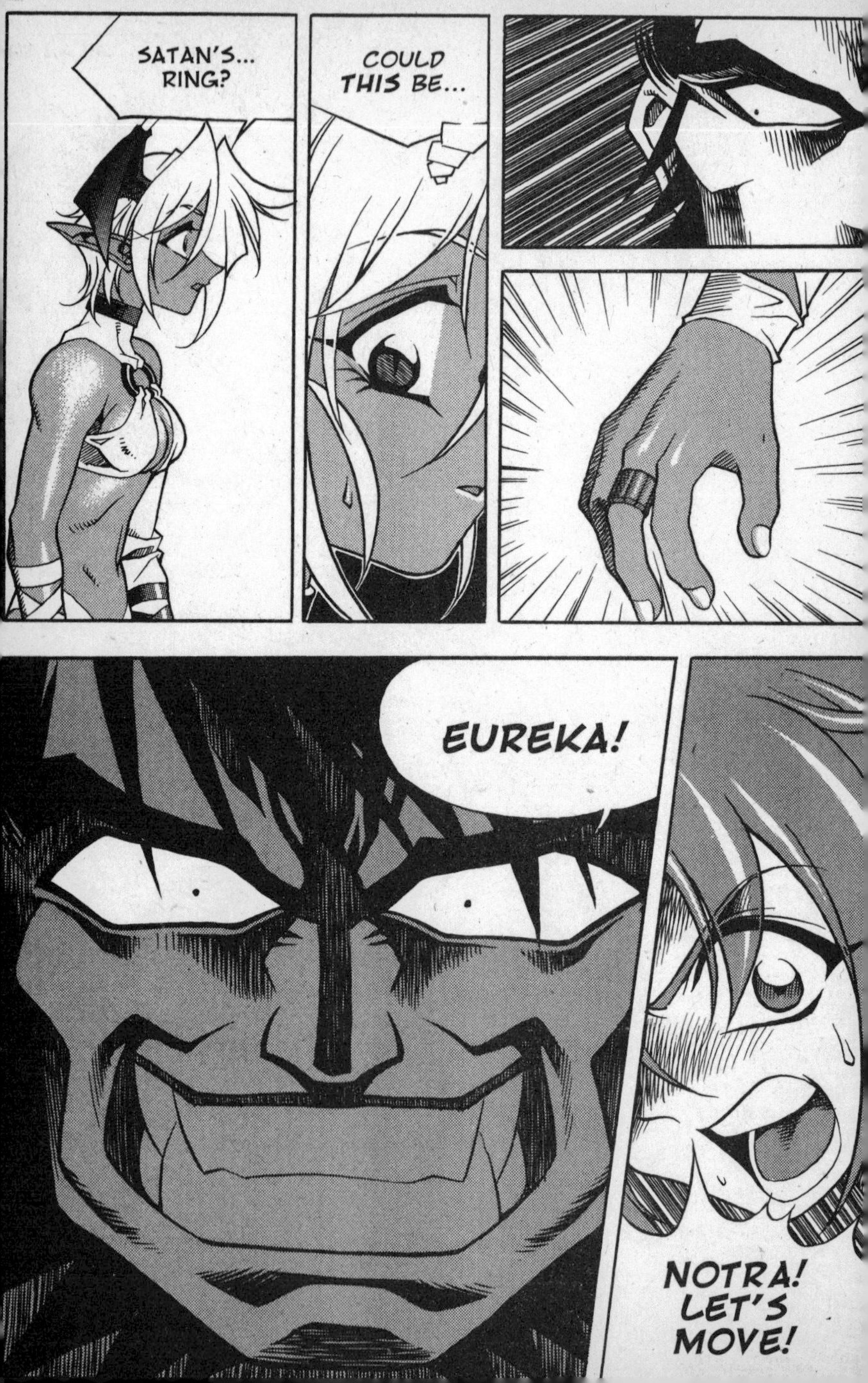
SATAN'S... RING?
COULD THIS BE...
EUREKA!
NOTRA! LET'S MOVE!

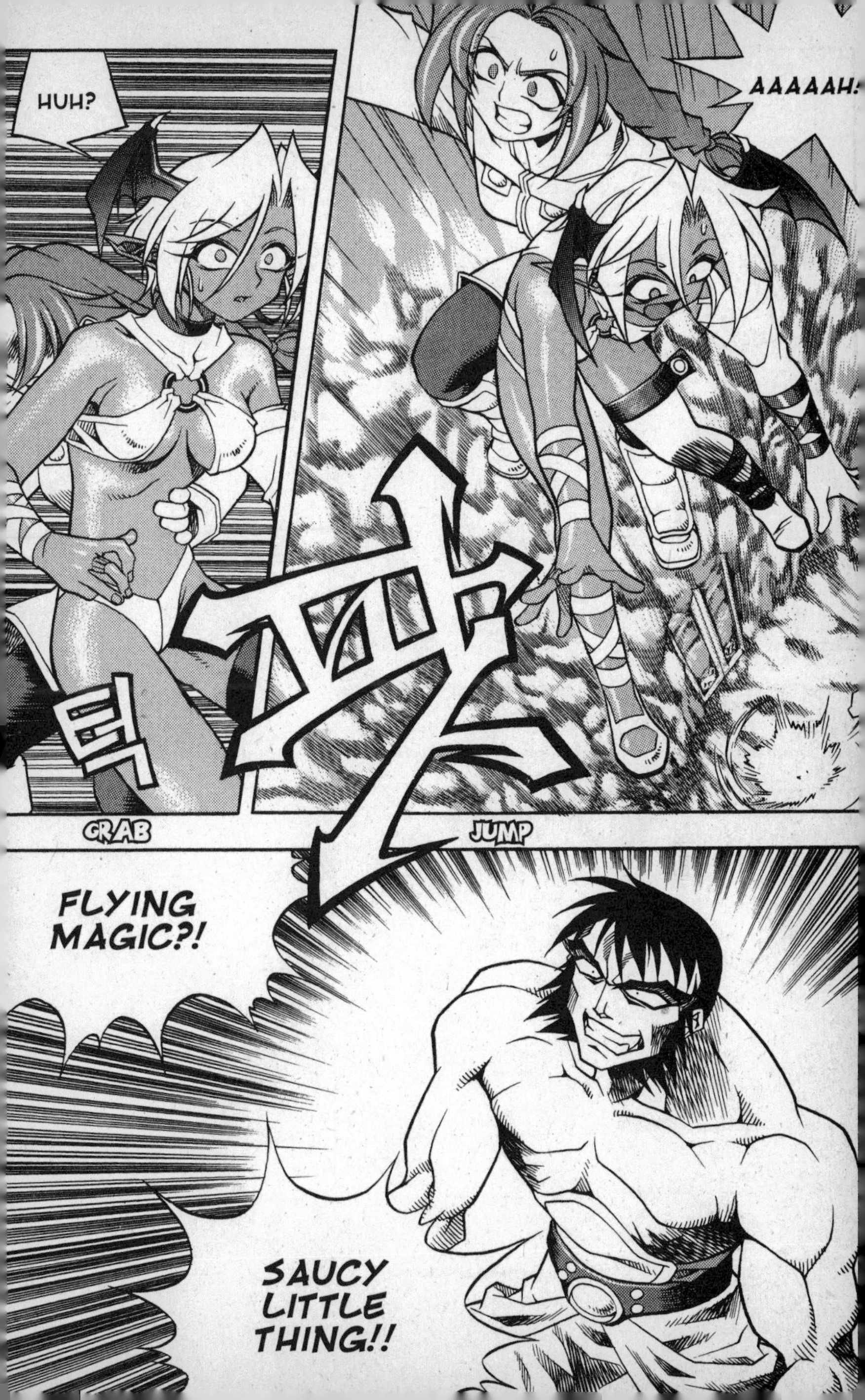
HUH?
AAAAAH!
GRAB
JUMP
FLYING MAGIC?!
SAUCY LITTLE THING!!

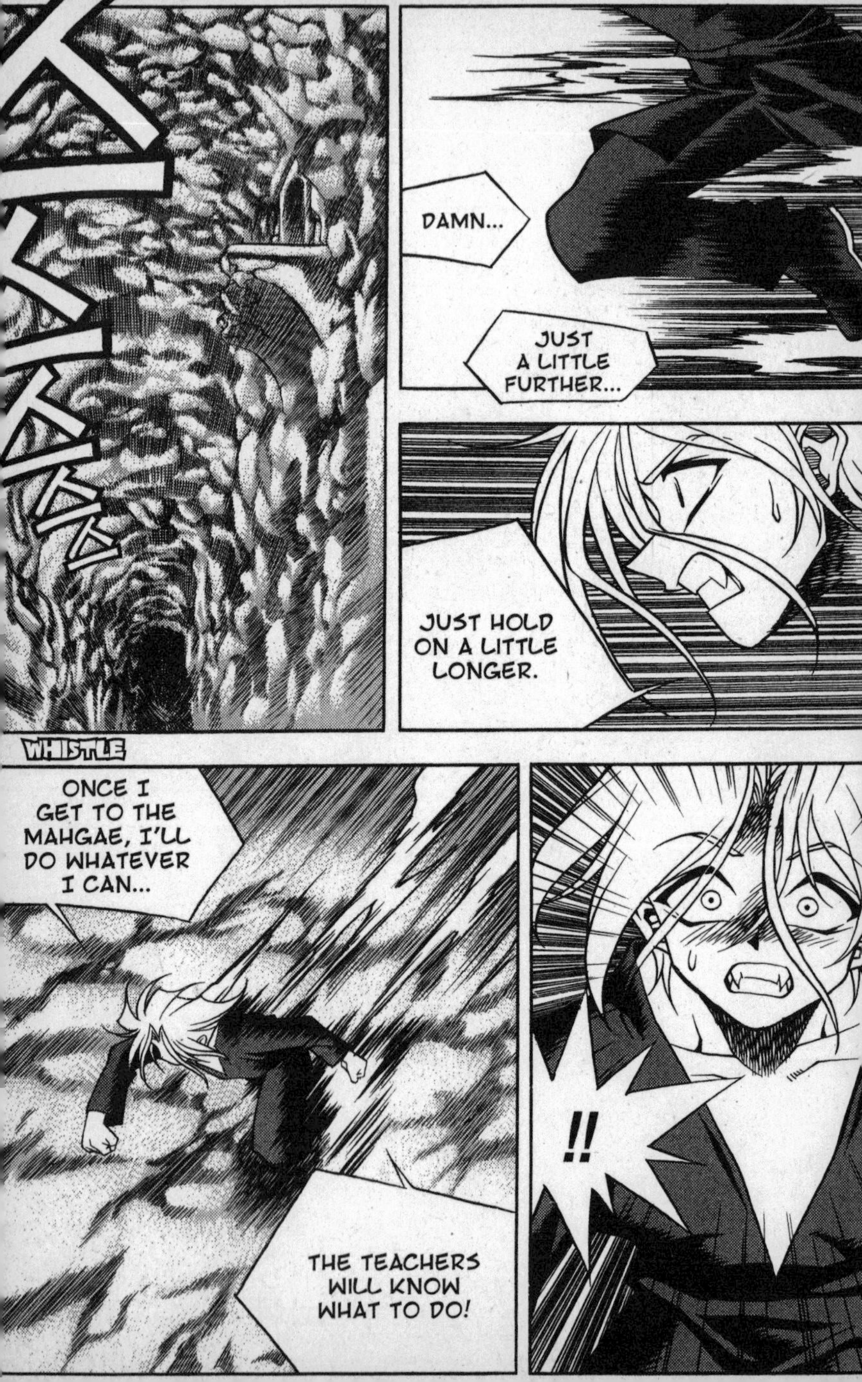
DAMN...
JUST A LITTLE FURTHER...
JUST HOLD ON A LITTLE LONGER.
WHISTLE
ONCE I GET TO THE MAHGAE, I'LL DO WHATEVER I CAN...
THE TEACHERS WILL KNOW WHAT TO DO!
!!

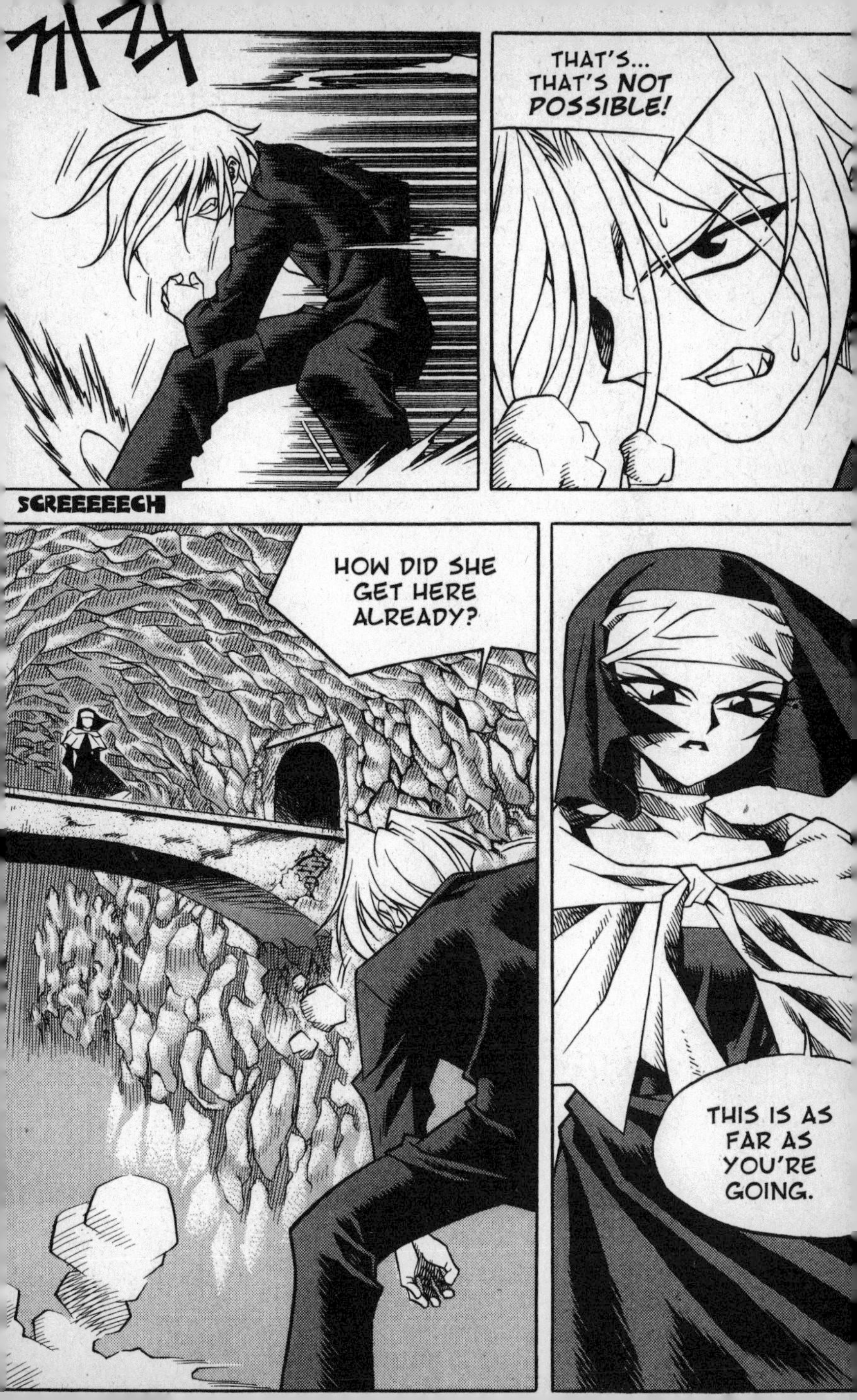
THAT'S... THAT'S NOT POSSIBLE!
SCREEEEECH
HOW DID SHE GET HERE ALREADY?
THIS IS AS FAR AS YOU'RE GOING.

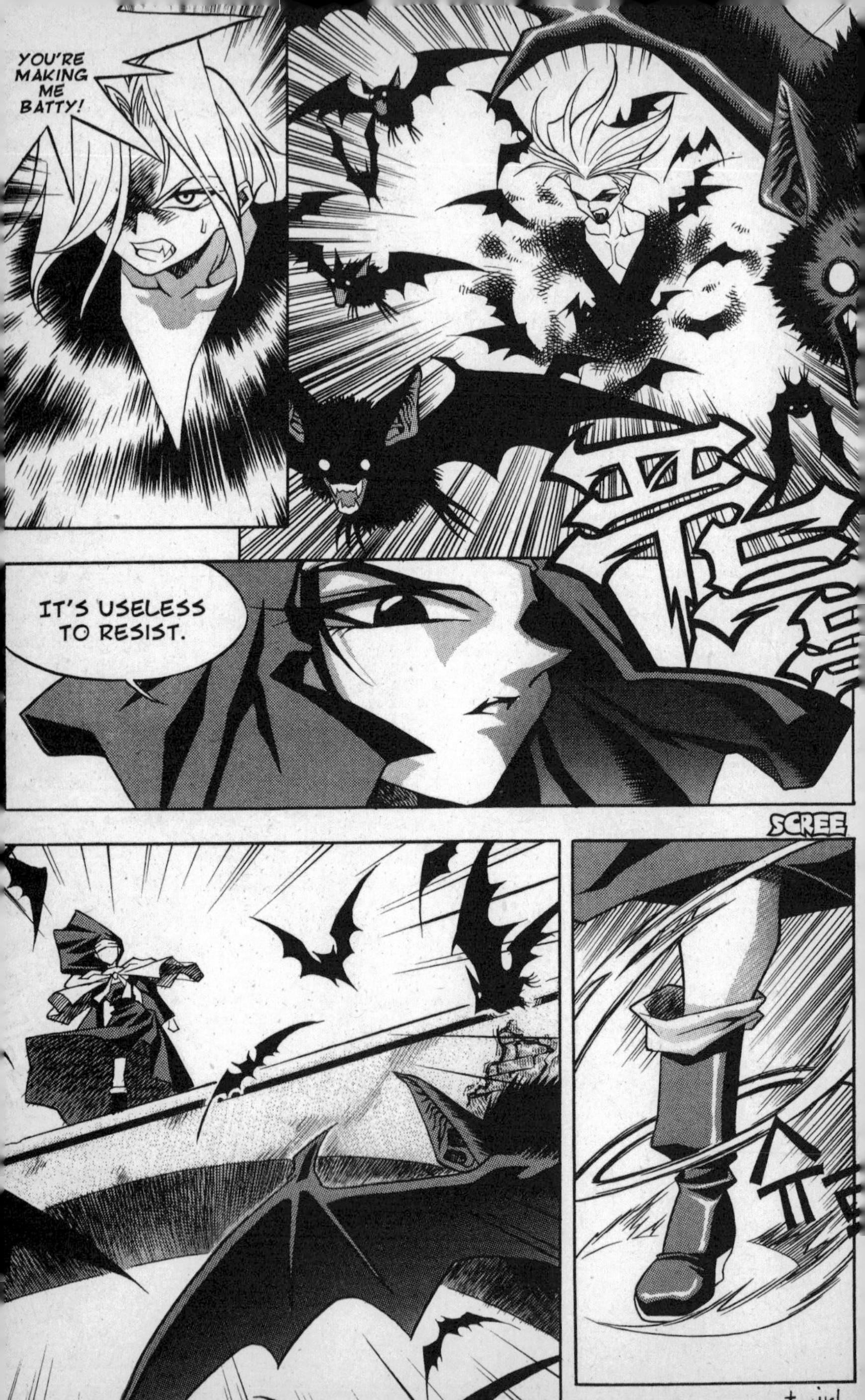
YOU'RE MAKING ME BATTY!
IT'S USELESS TO RESIST.
SCREE

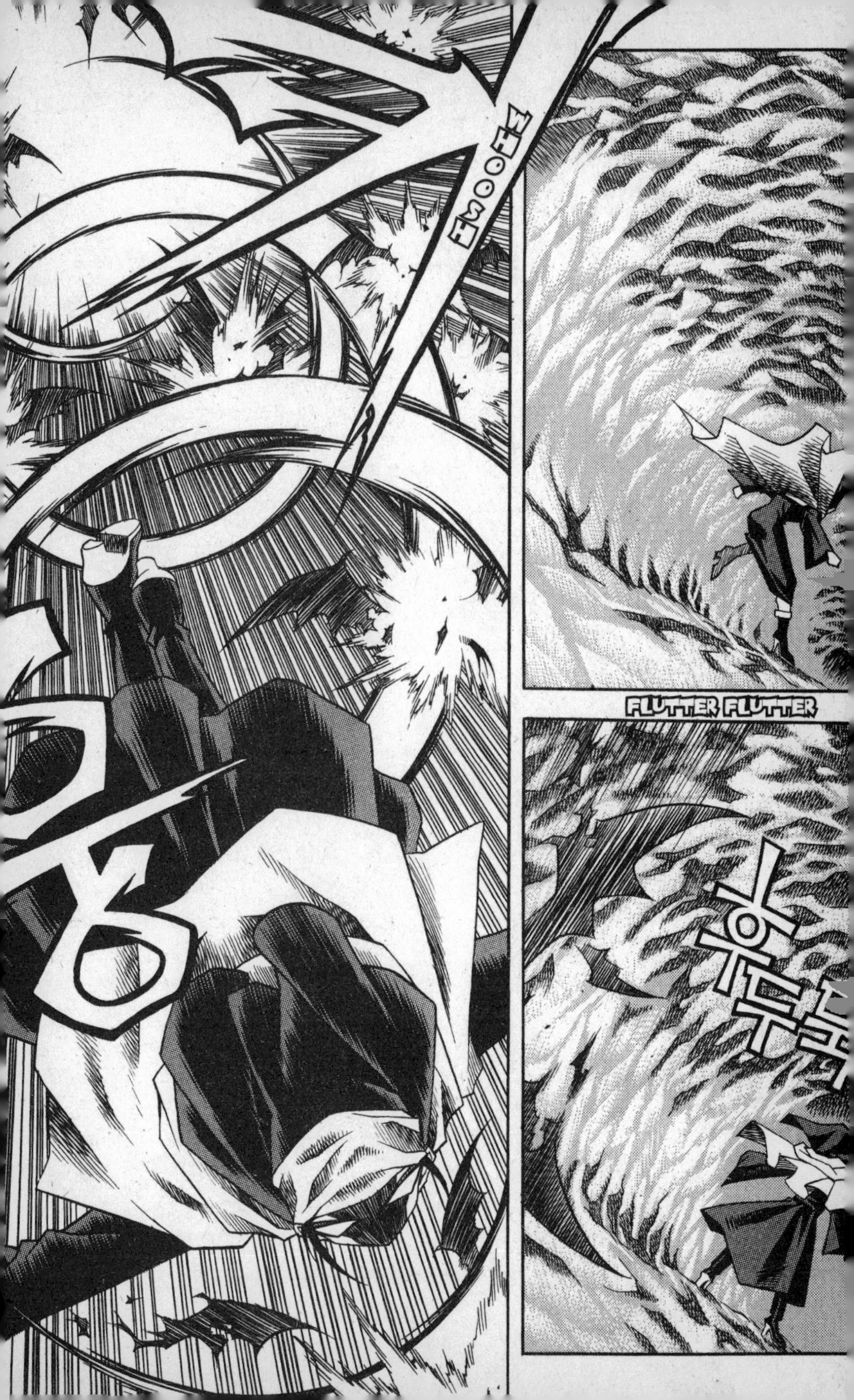
WHOOSH
FLUTTER FLUTTER

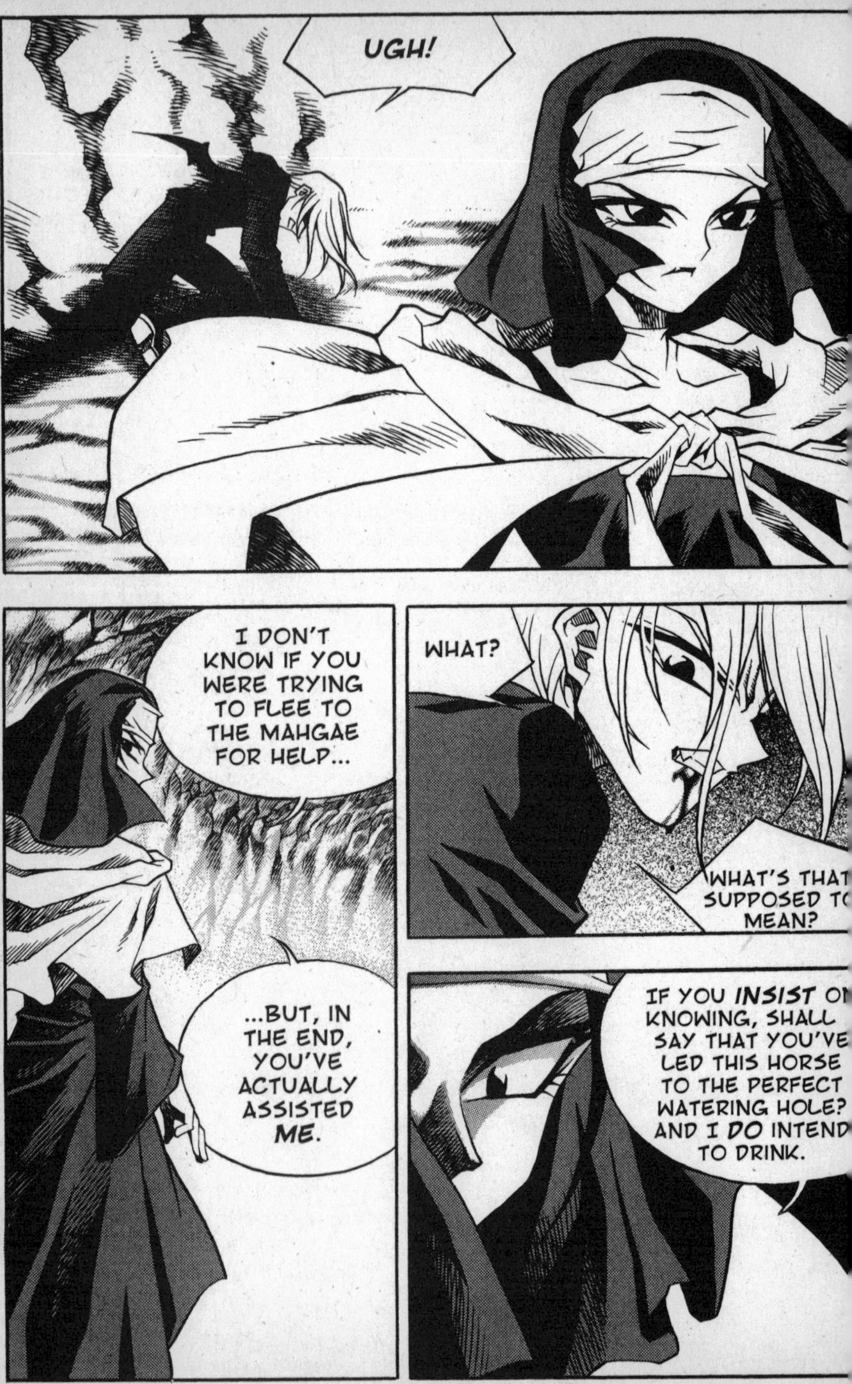
UGH!
I DON'T KNOW IF YOU WERE TRYING TO FLEE TO THE MAHGAE FOR HELP...
...BUT, IN THE END, YOU'VE ACTUALLY ASSISTED ME.
WHAT?
WHAT'S THAT SUPPOSED TO MEAN?
IF YOU INSIST ON KNOWING, SHALL SAY THAT YOU'VE LED THIS HORSE TO THE PERFECT WATERING HOLE? AND I DO INTEND TO DRINK.

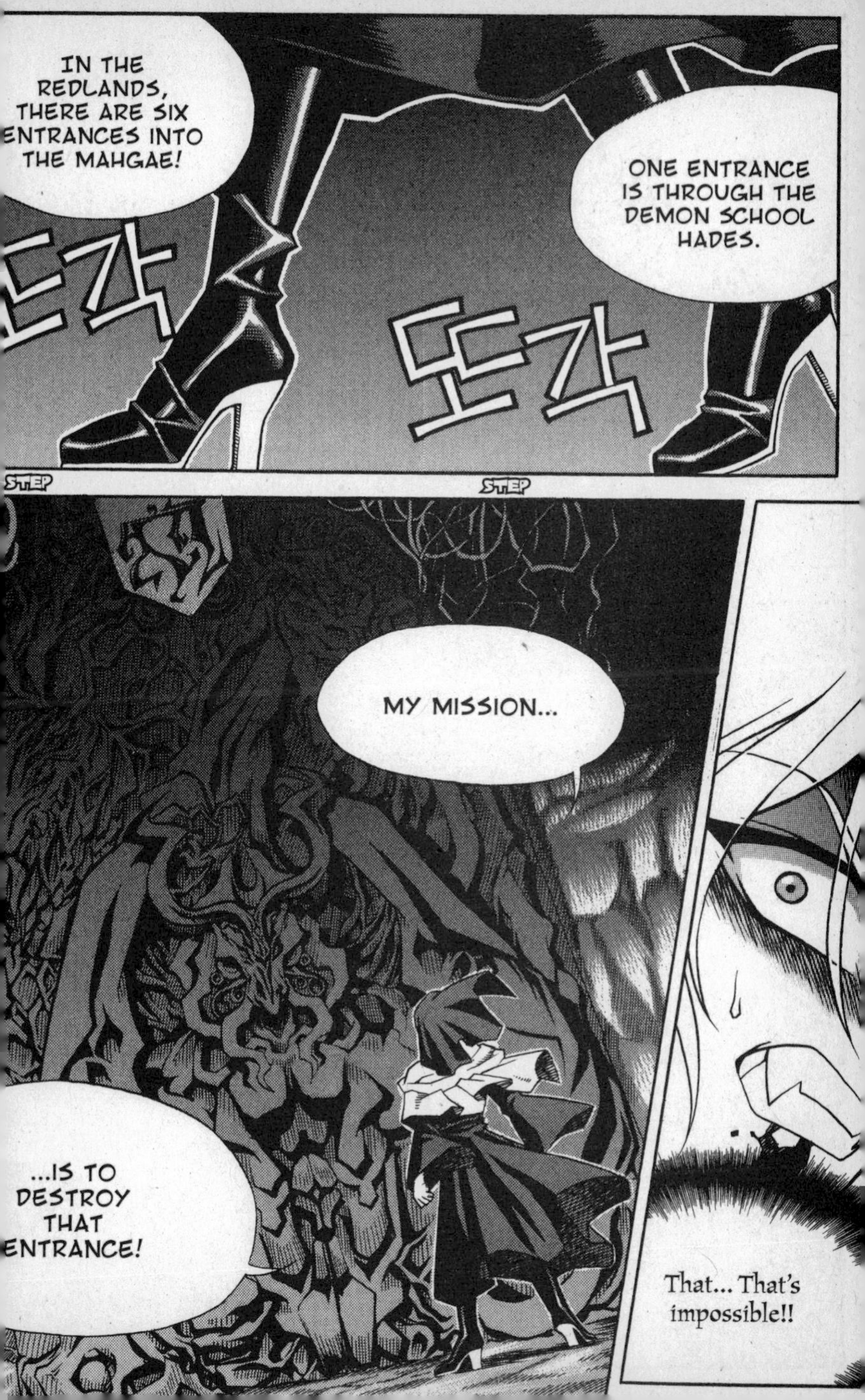
IN THE REDLANDS, THERE ARE SIX ENTRANCES INTO THE MAHGAE!
또각
STEP
ONE ENTRANCE IS THROUGH THE DEMON SCHOOL HADES.
또각
STEP
MY MISSION...
...IS TO DESTROY THAT ENTRANCE!
That... That's impossible!!

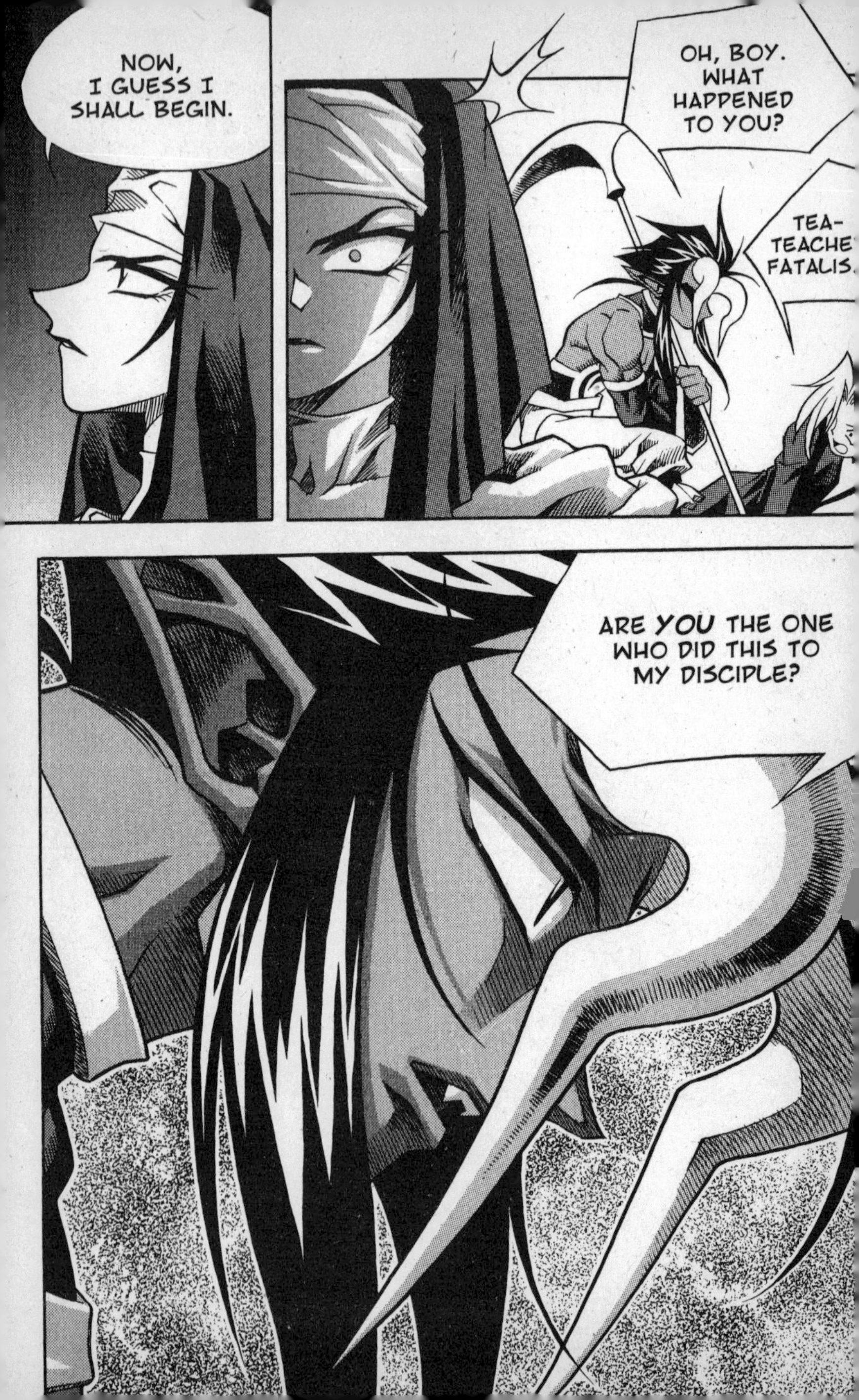
NOW, I GUESS I SHALL BEGIN.
OH, BOY. WHAT HAPPENED TO YOU?
TEA- TEACHE FATALIS.
ARE YOU THE ONE WHO DID THIS TO MY DISCIPLE?

Quest 10

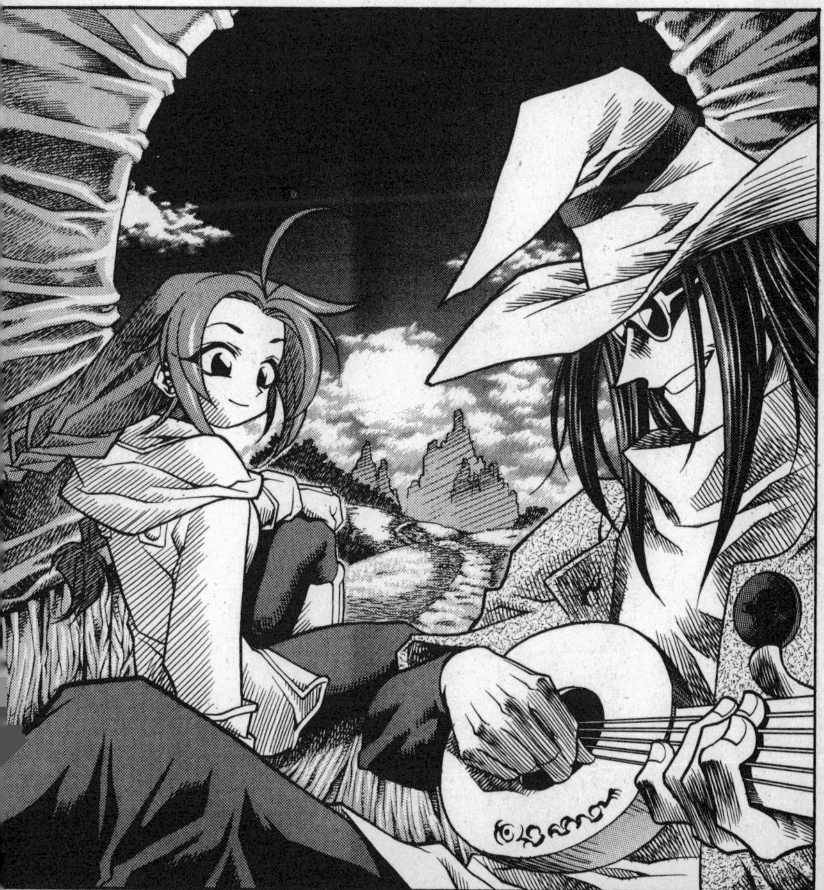

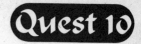

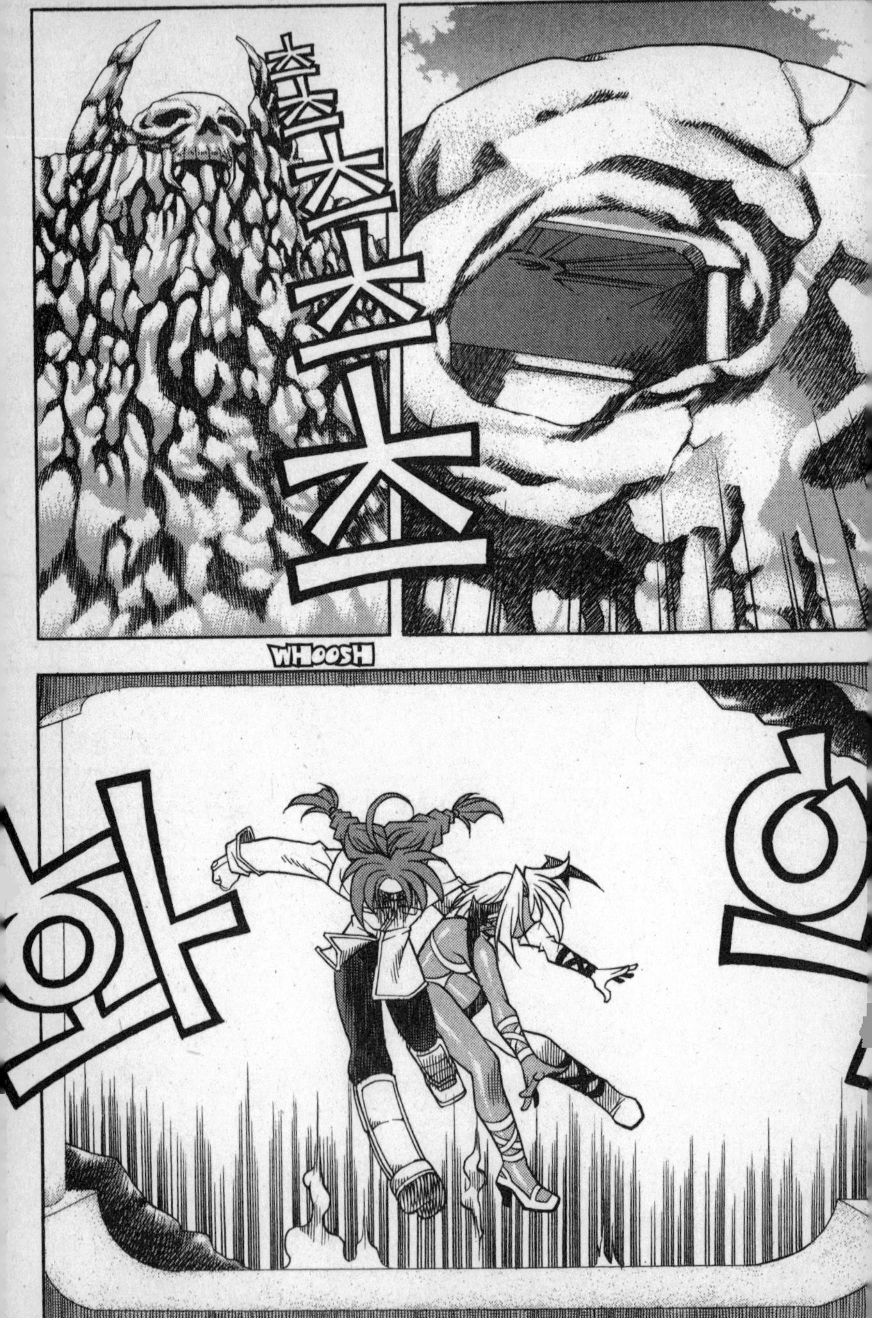
WHOOSH
FWOOSH

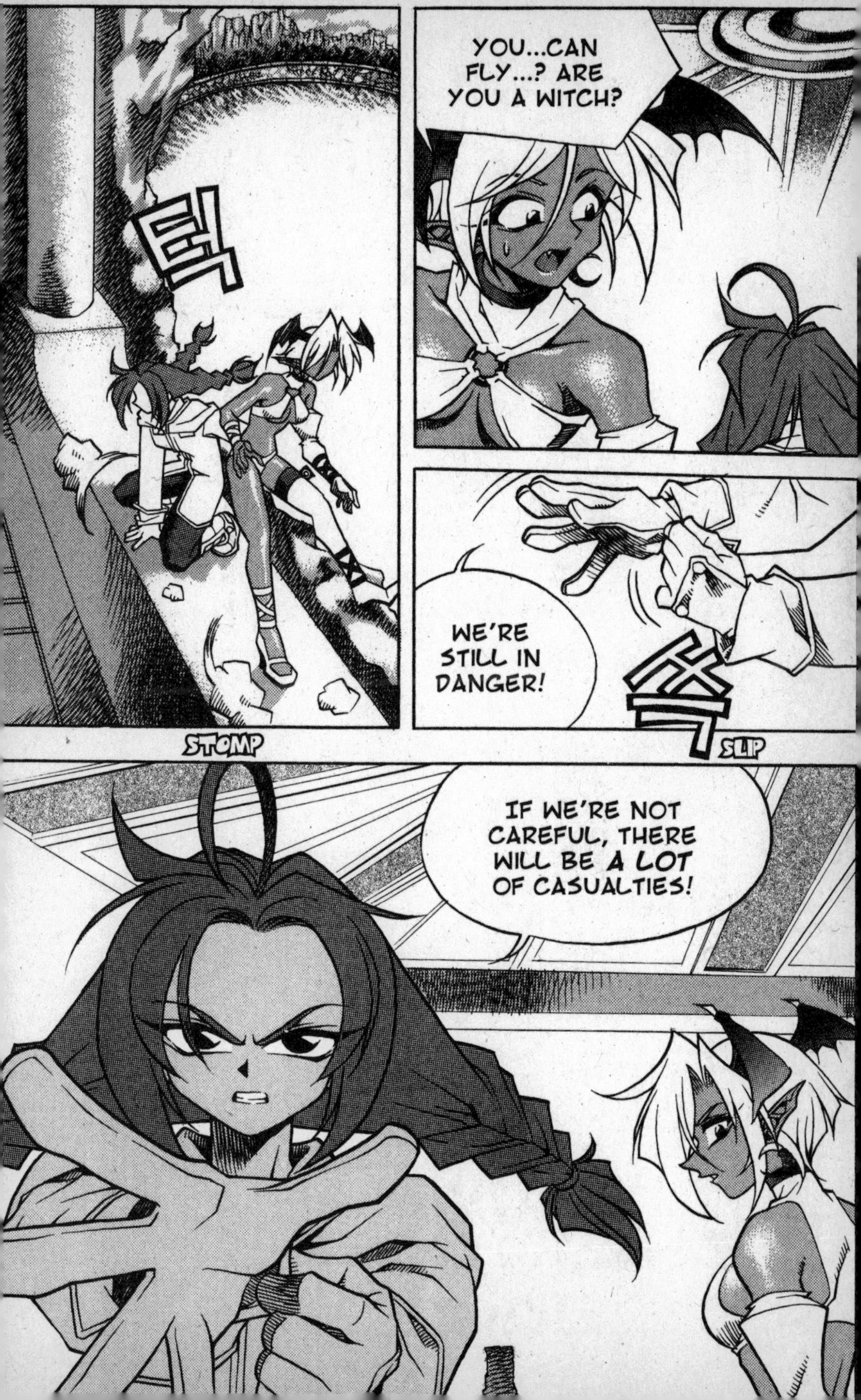
STOMP
YOU...CAN FLY...? ARE YOU A WITCH?
WE'RE STILL IN DANGER!
SLIP
IF WE'RE NOT CAREFUL, THERE WILL BE A LOT OF CASUALTIES!

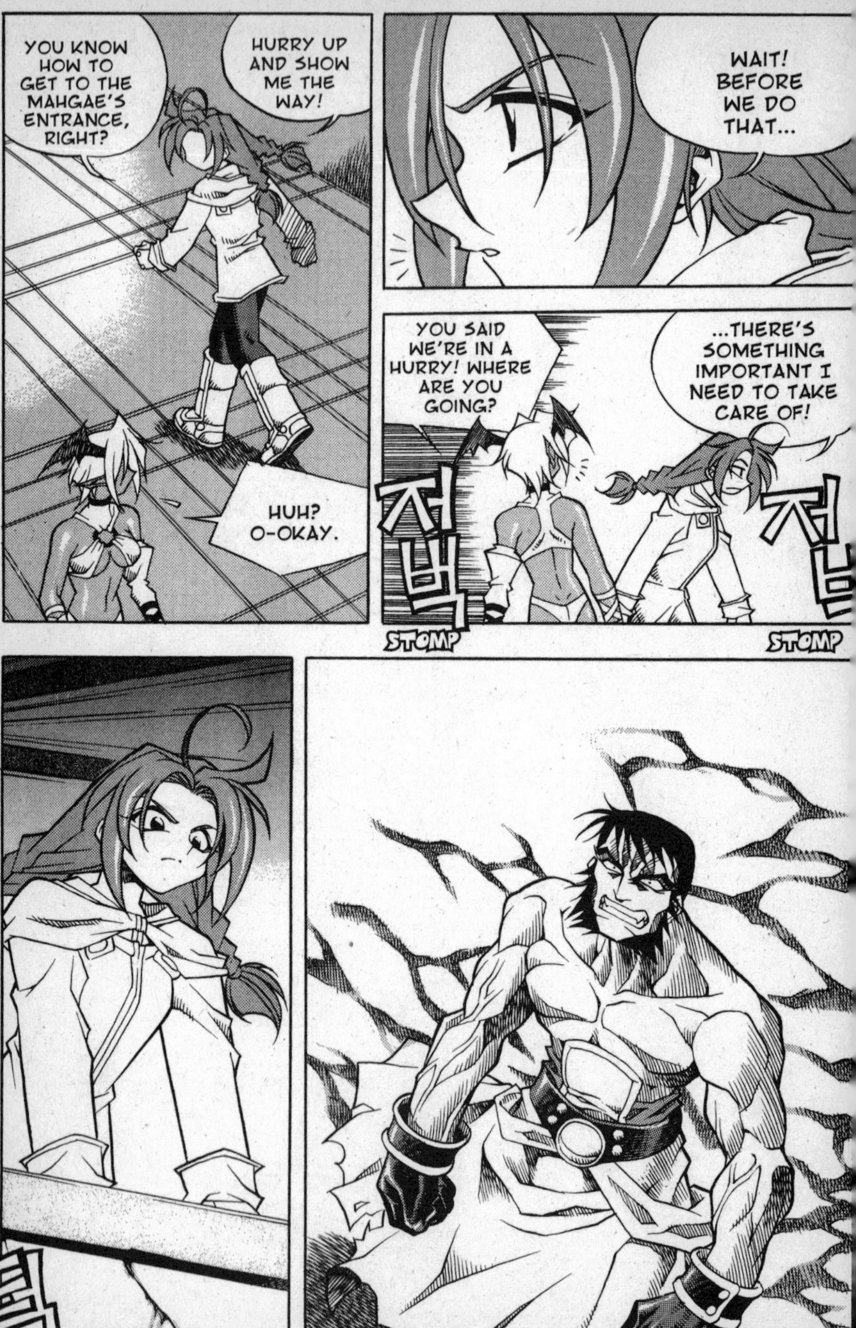
YOU KNOW HOW TO GET TO THE MAHGAE'S ENTRANCE, RIGHT?
HURRY UP AND SHOW ME THE WAY!
HUH? O-OKAY.
WAIT! BEFORE WE DO THAT...
YOU SAID WE'RE IN A HURRY! WHERE ARE YOU GOING?
...THERE'S SOMETHING IMPORTANT I NEED TO TAKE CARE OF!
STOMP
STOMP
GLARE

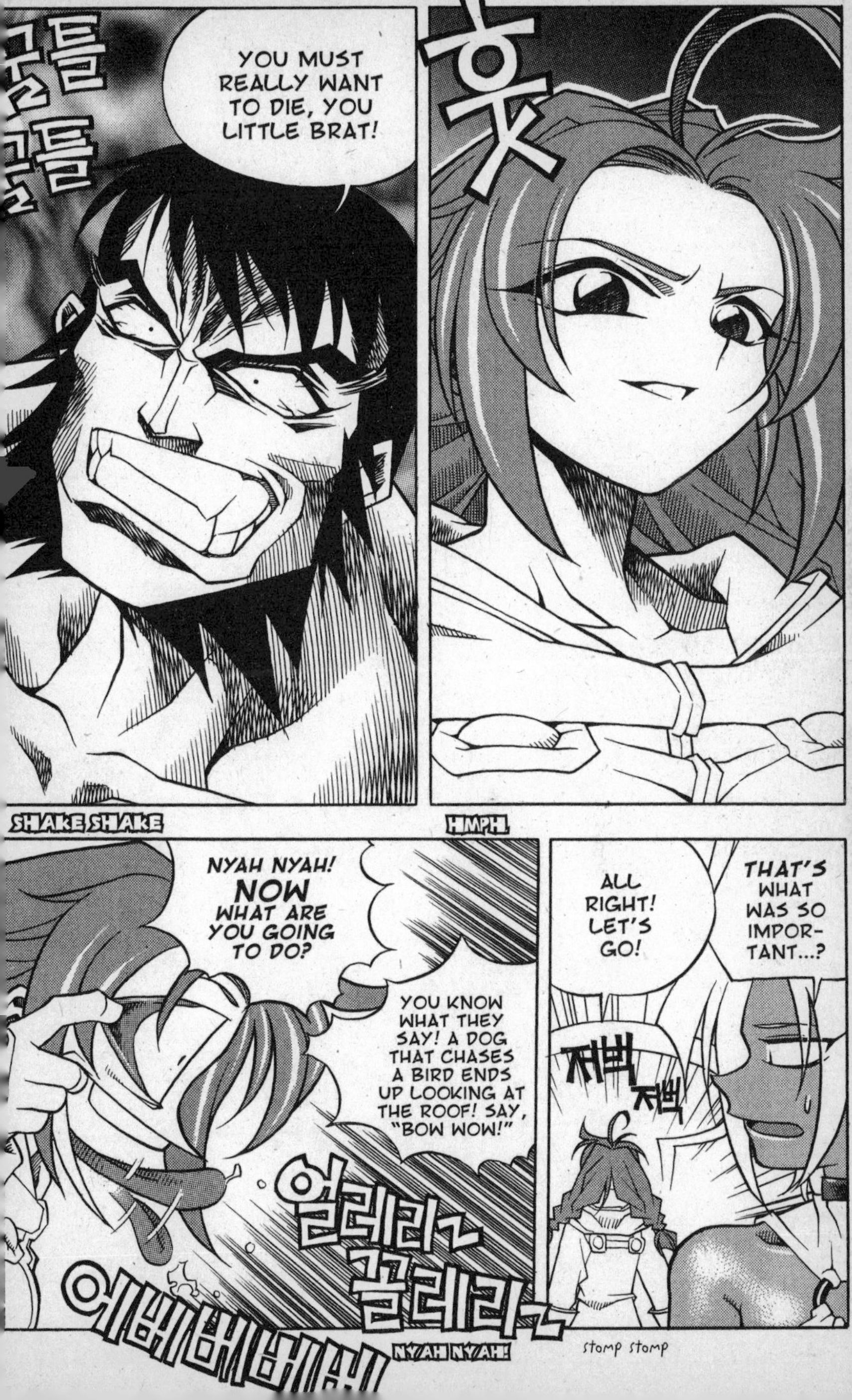

YOU MUST REALLY WANT TO DIE, YOU LITTLE BRAT!
SHAKE SHAKE
흥
HMPH
NYAH NYAH! NOW WHAT ARE YOU GOING TO DO?
YOU KNOW WHAT THEY SAY! A DOG THAT CHASES A BIRD ENDS UP LOOKING AT THE ROOF! SAY, "BOW WOW!"
얼레리~ 꼴레리~
에베베베!
NYAH NYAH!
ALL RIGHT! LET'S GO!
THAT'S WHAT WAS SO IMPOR-TANT...?
저벅 저벅
stomp stomp

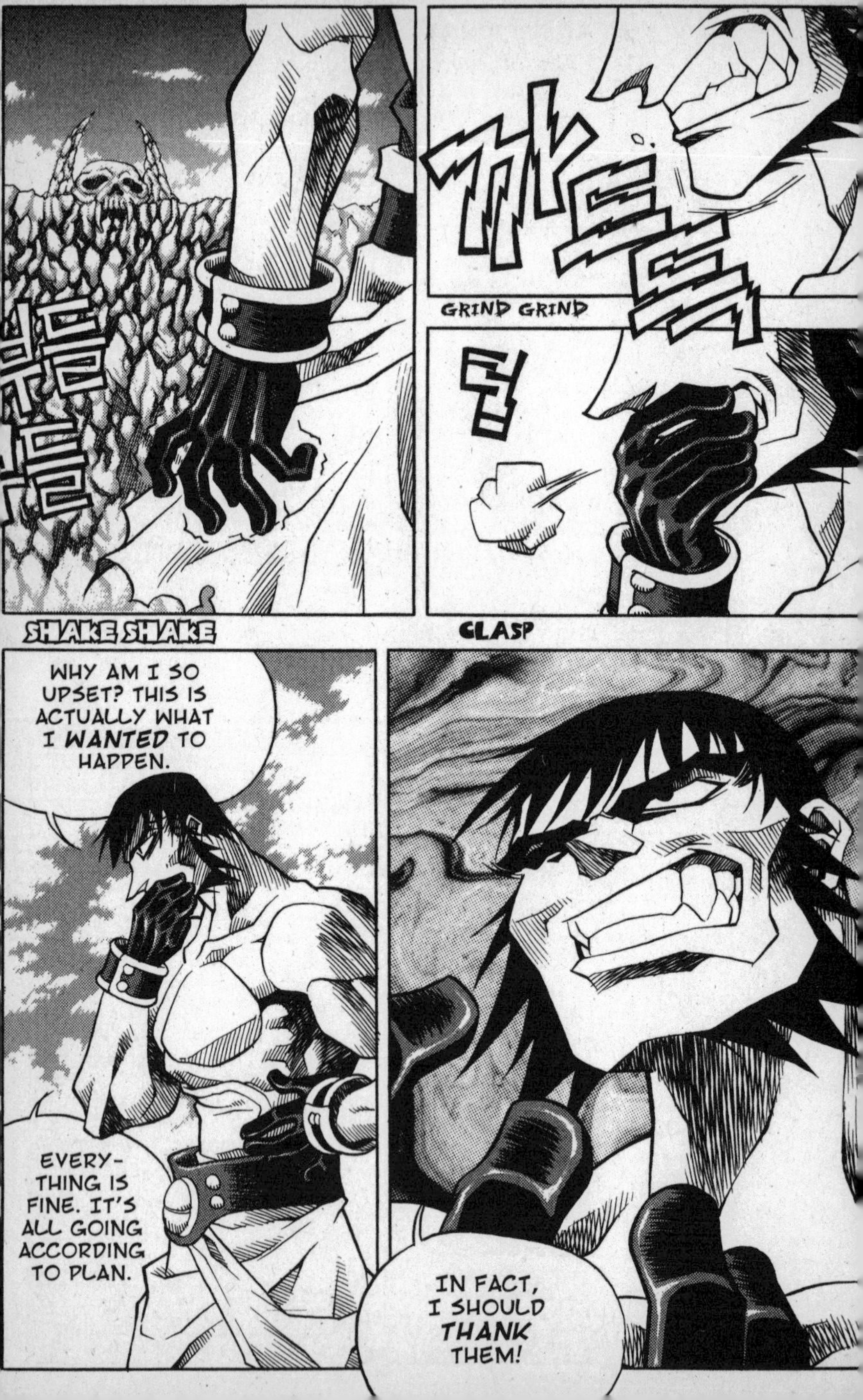
SHAKE SHAKE
까드득
GRIND GRIND
CLASP
WHY AM I SO UPSET? THIS IS ACTUALLY WHAT I WANTED TO HAPPEN.
EVERY-THING IS FINE. IT'S ALL GOING ACCORDING TO PLAN.
IN FACT, I SHOULD THANK THEM!

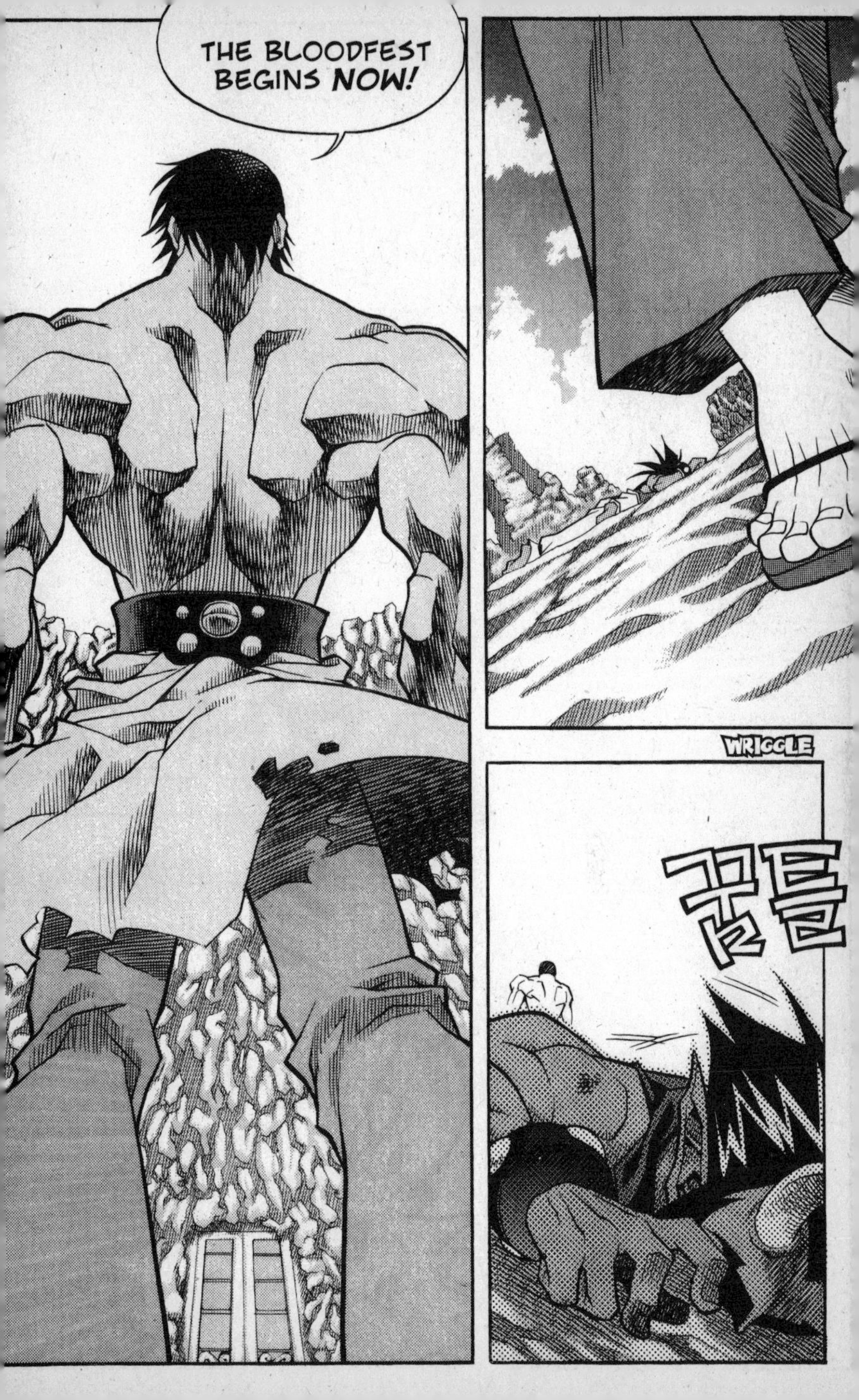
THE BLOODFEST BEGINS NOW!
WRIGGLE

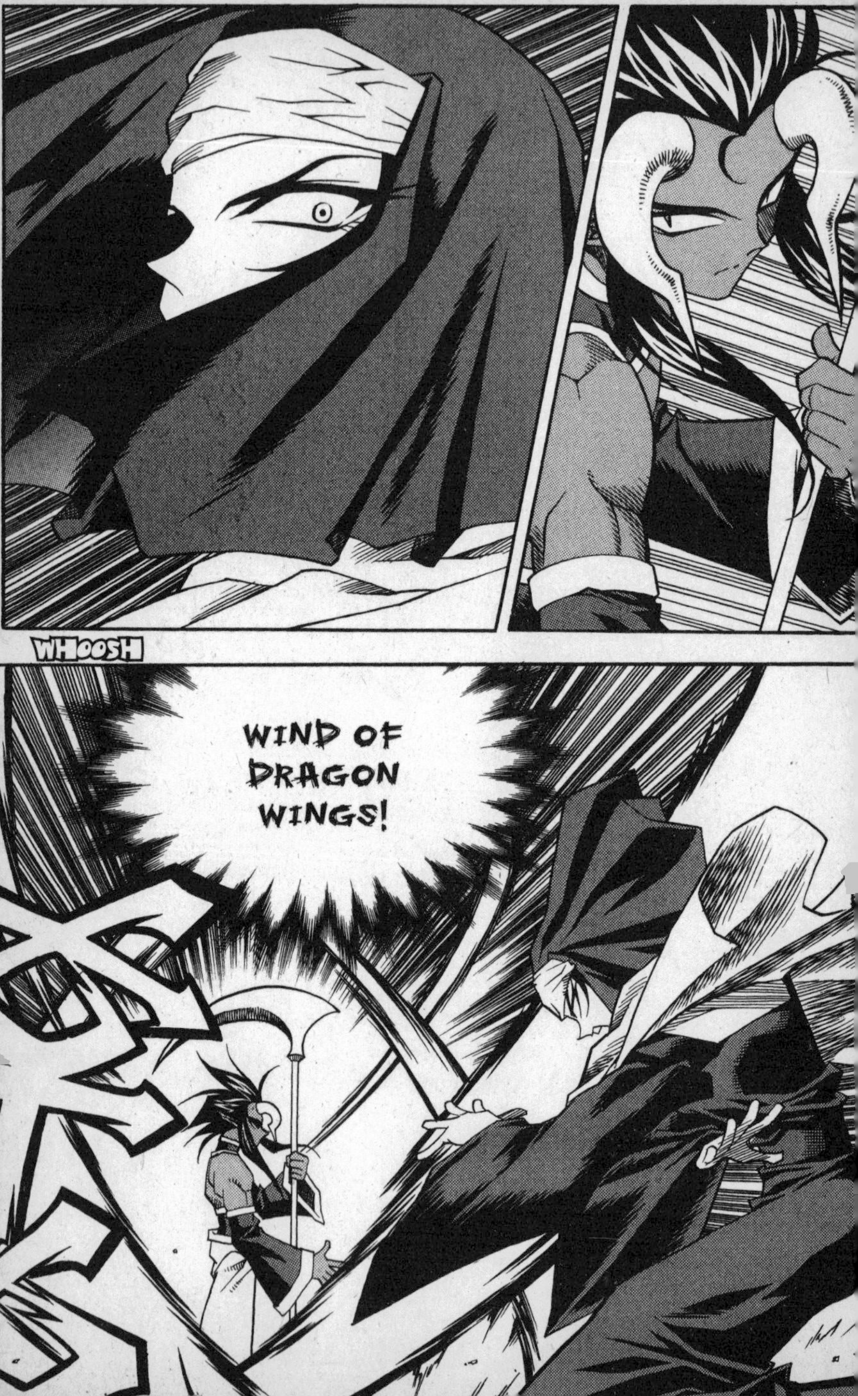
WHOOSH
WIND OF DRAGON WINGS!

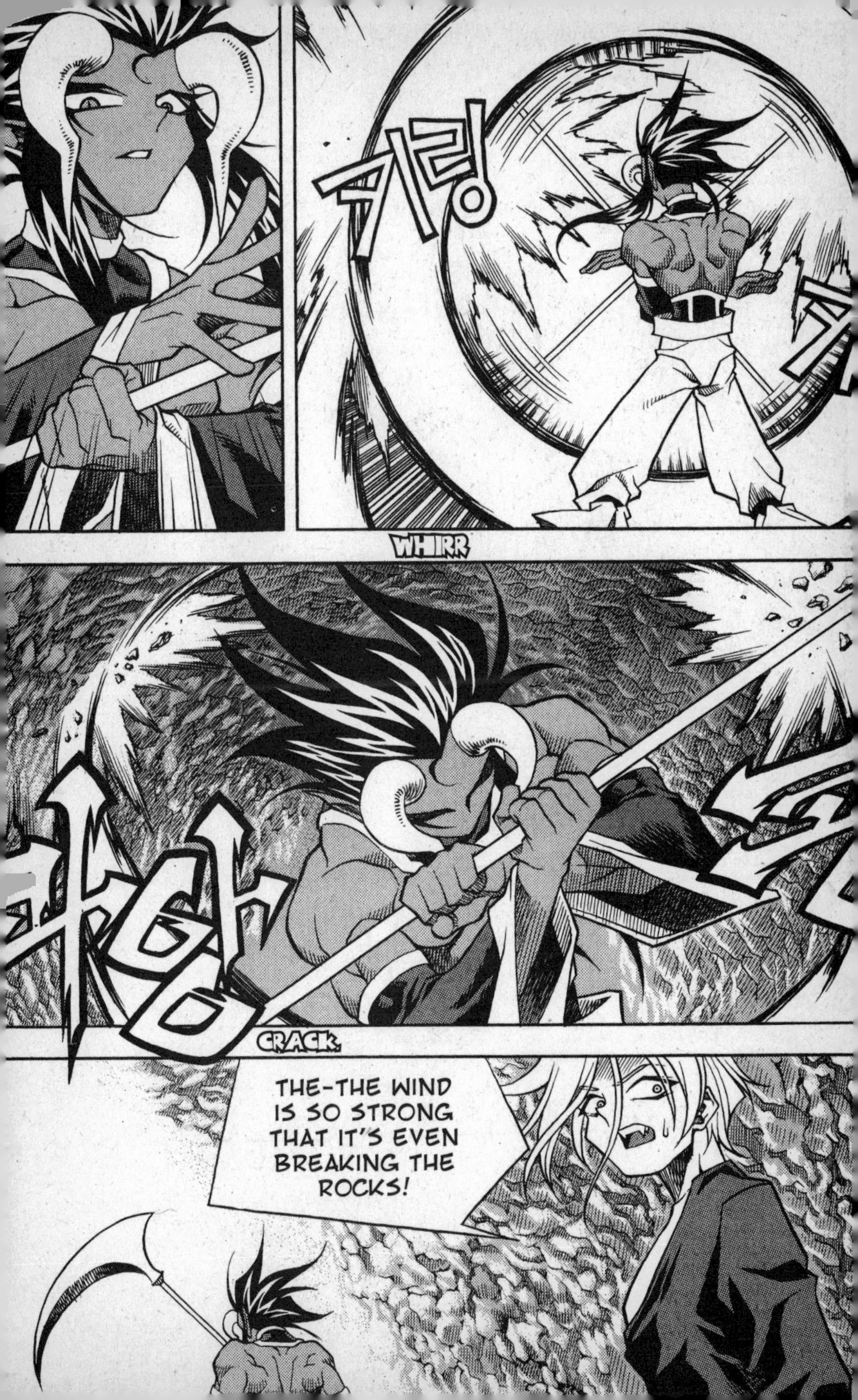
WHIRR
CRACK
THE-THE WIND IS SO STRONG THAT IT'S EVEN BREAKING THE ROCKS!

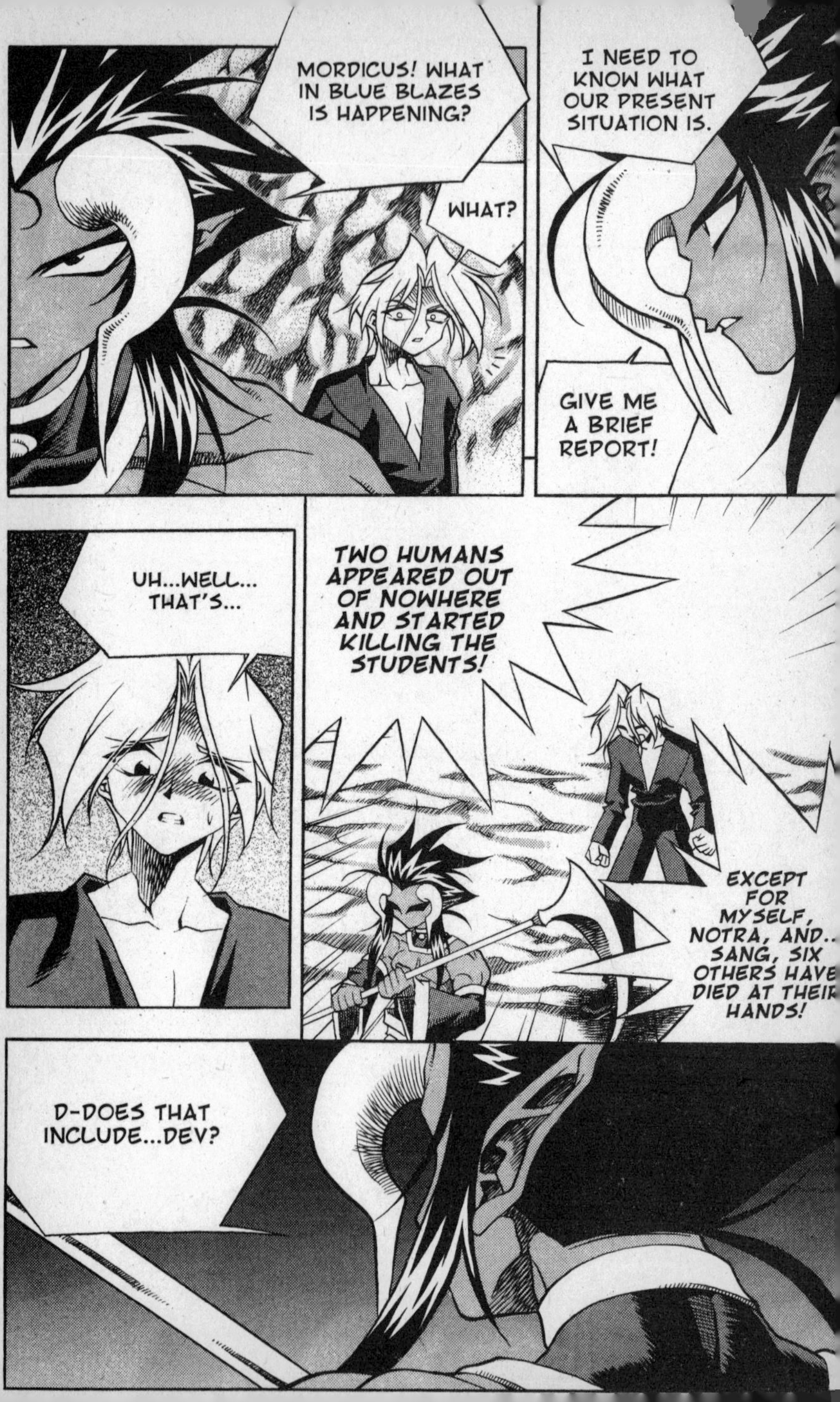
MORDICUS! WHAT IN BLUE BLAZES IS HAPPENING?
WHAT?
I NEED TO KNOW WHAT OUR PRESENT SITUATION IS.
GIVE ME A BRIEF REPORT!
UH...WELL... THAT'S...
TWO HUMANS APPEARED OUT OF NOWHERE AND STARTED KILLING THE STUDENTS!
EXCEPT FOR MYSELF, NOTRA, AND... SANG, SIX OTHERS HAVE DIED AT THEIR HANDS!
D-DOES THAT INCLUDE...DEV?

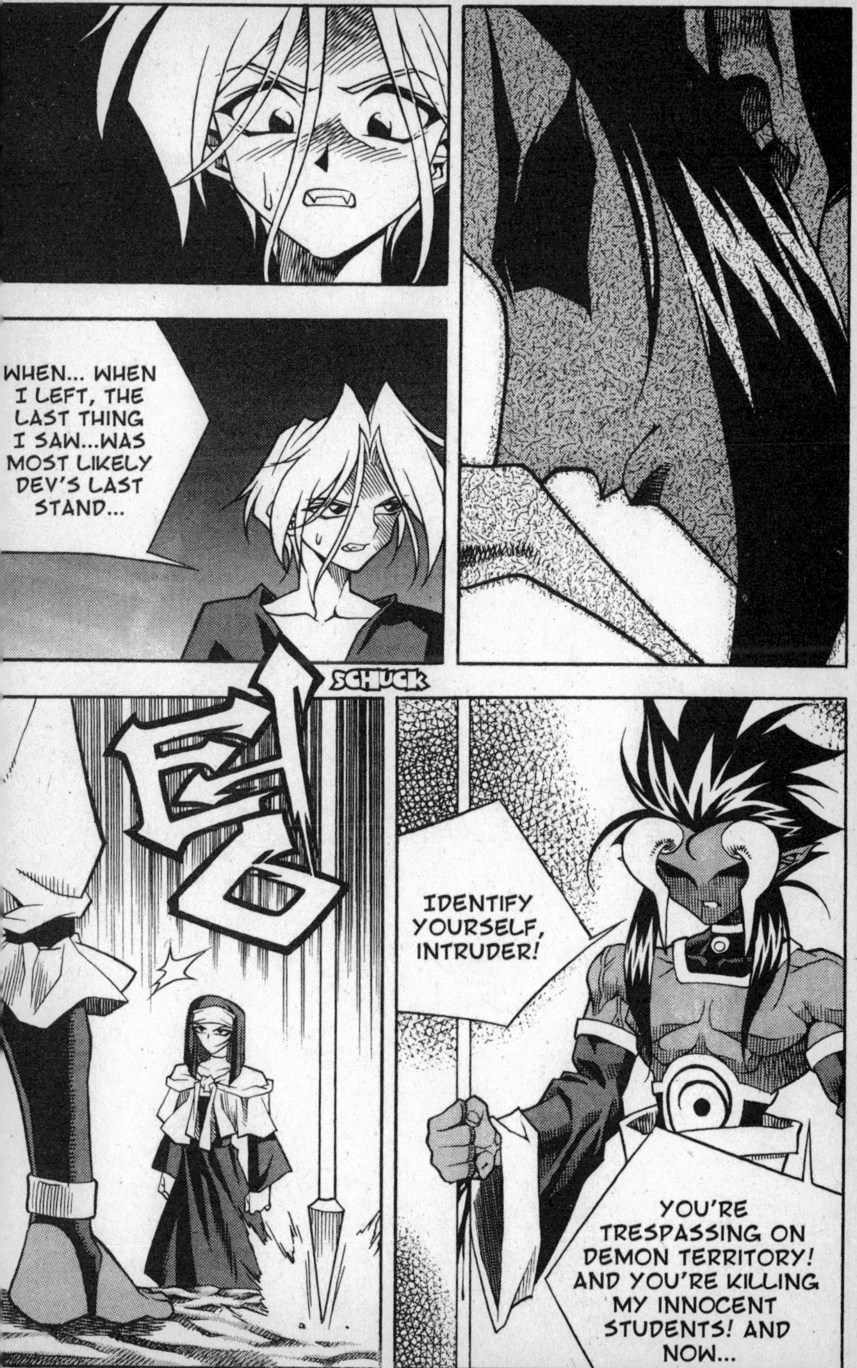
WHEN... WHEN I LEFT, THE LAST THING I SAW...WAS MOST LIKELY DEV'S LAST STAND...
SCHUCK
IDENTIFY YOURSELF, INTRUDER!
YOU'RE TRESPASSING ON DEMON TERRITORY! AND YOU'RE KILLING MY INNOCENT STUDENTS! AND NOW...

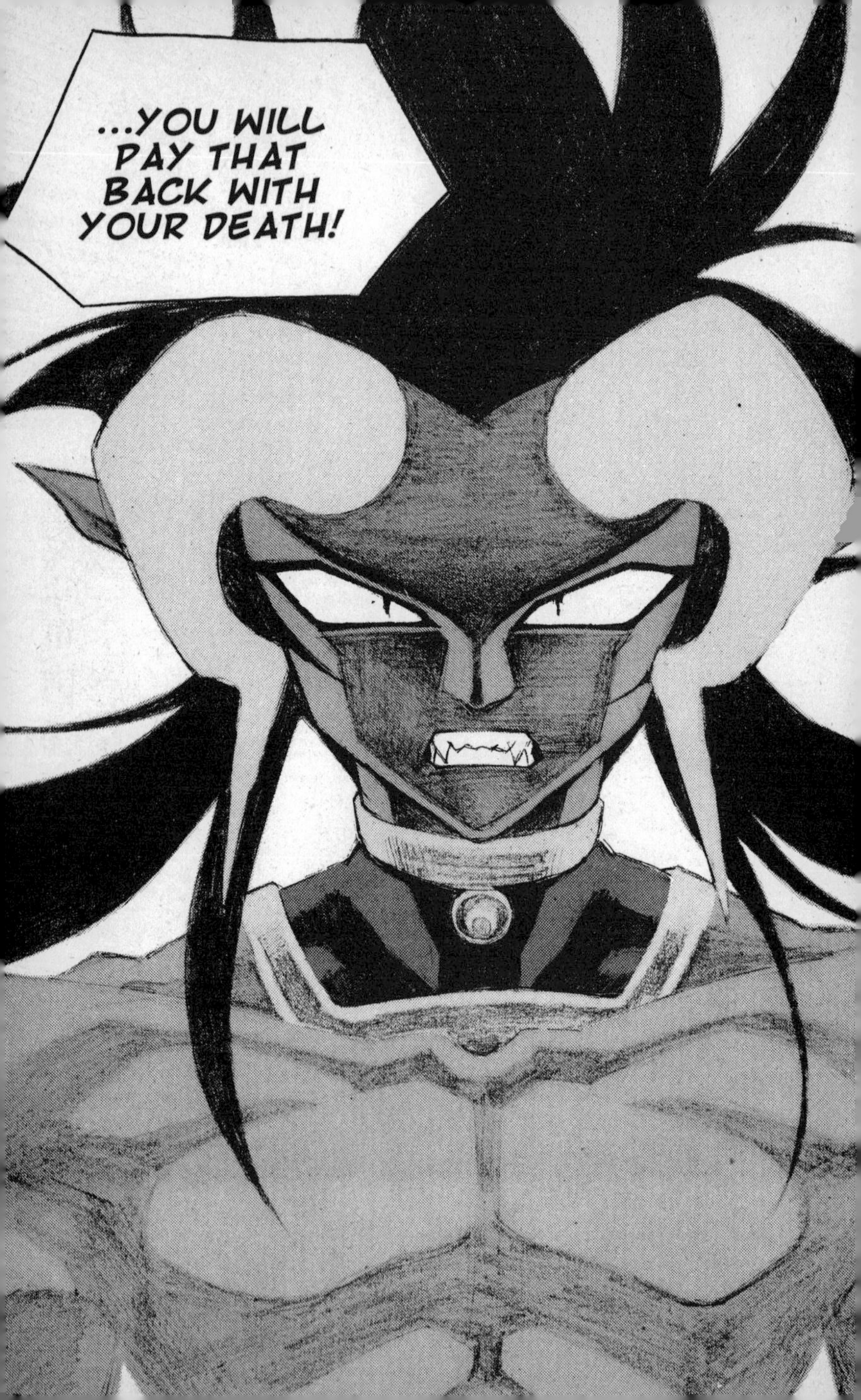
...YOU WILL PAY THAT BACK WITH YOUR DEATH!

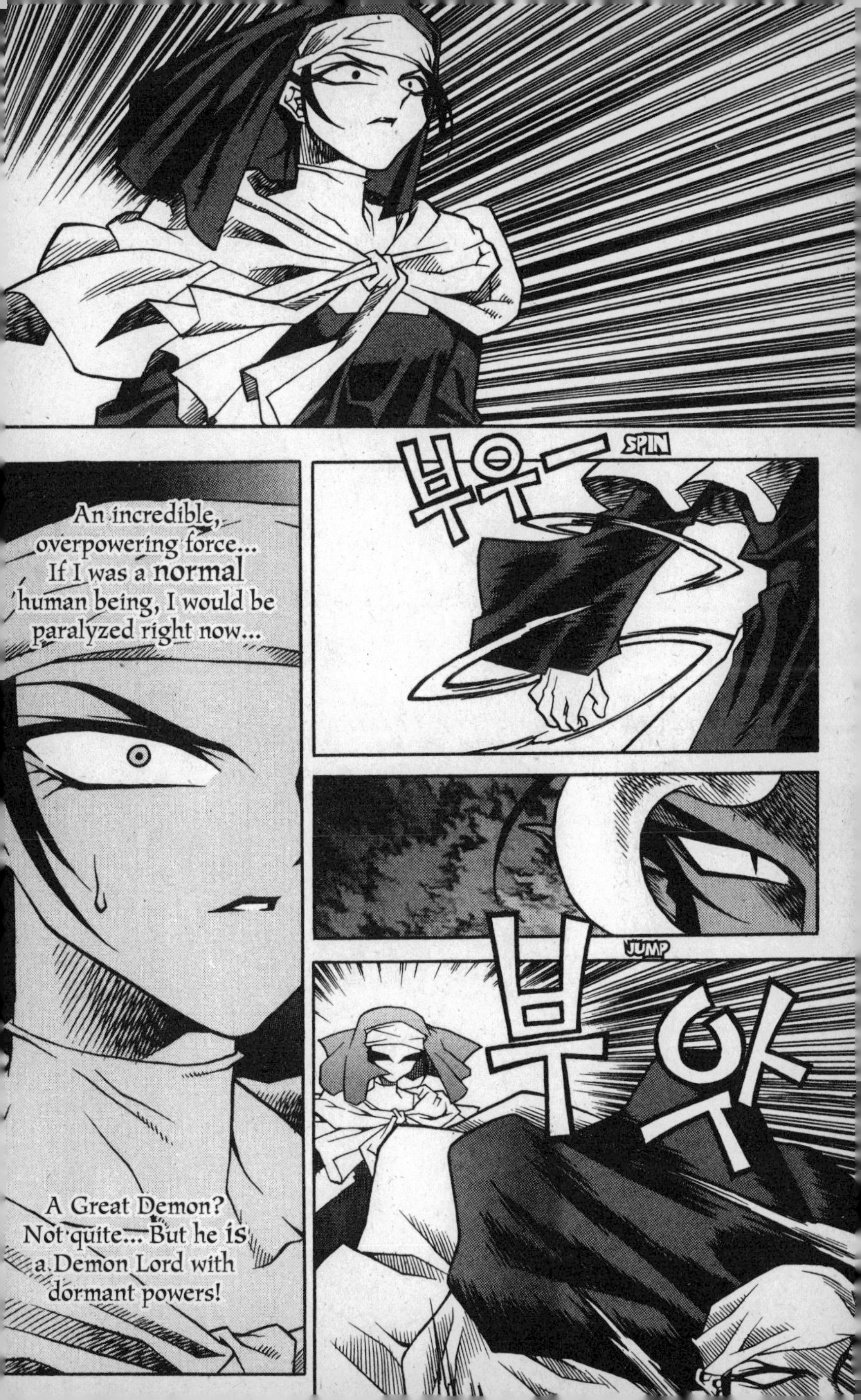

An incredible, overpowering force... If I was a normal human being, I would be paralyzed right now...
A Great Demon? Not quite... But he is a Demon Lord with dormant powers!
부우ー
SPIN
붕
JUMP
앗

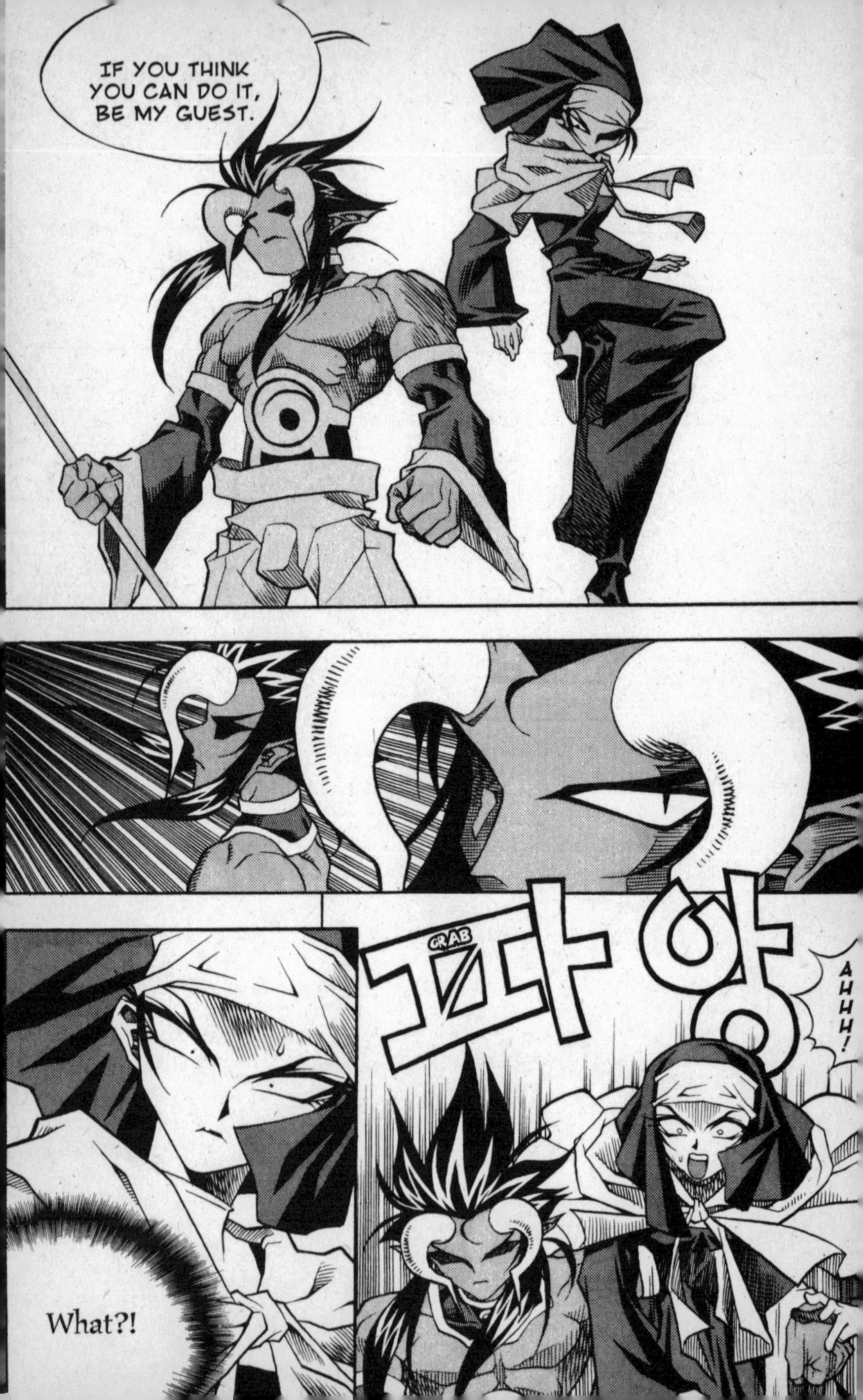
IF YOU THINK YOU CAN DO IT, BE MY GUEST.
What?!
GRAB
AHHHH!

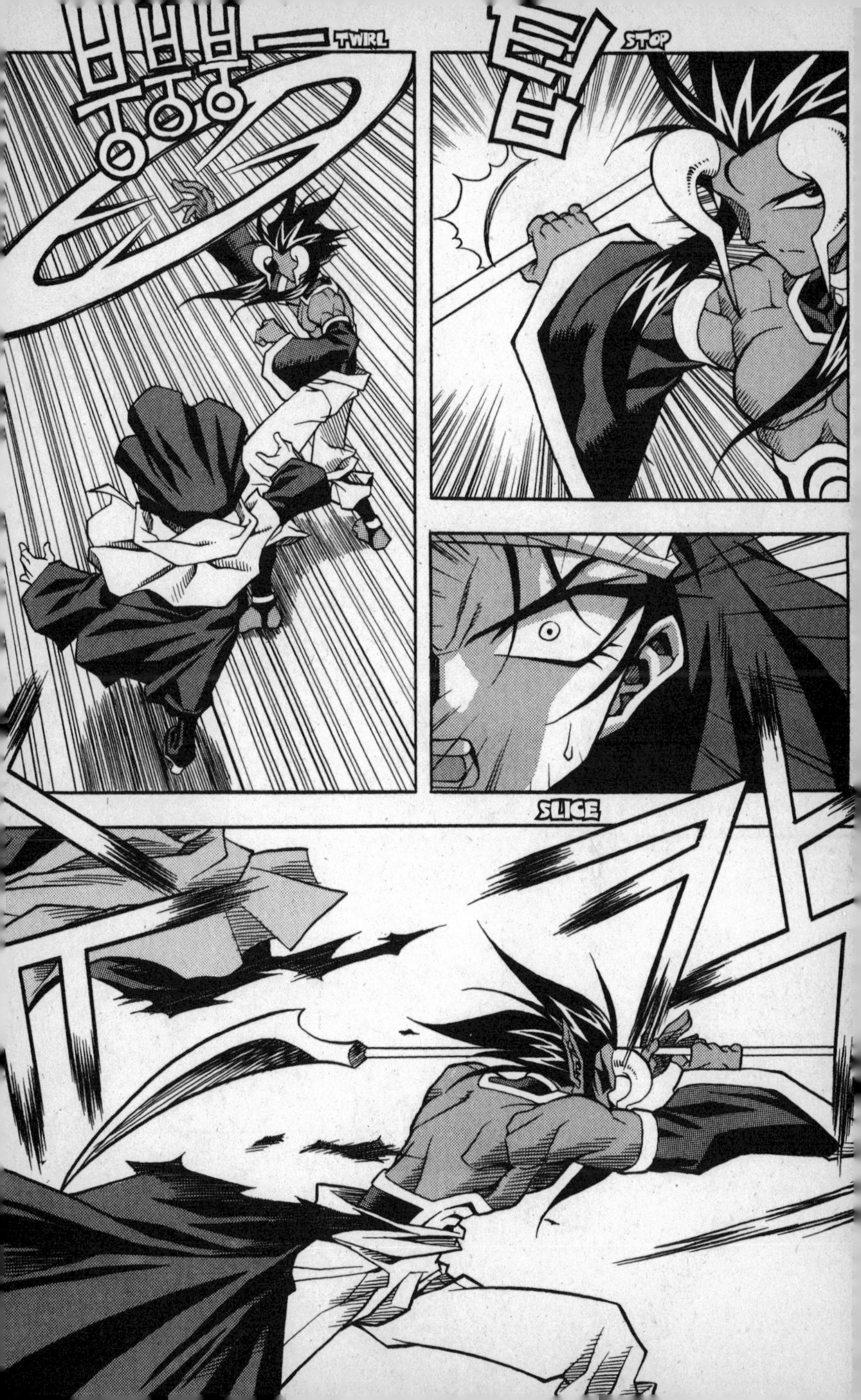
TWIRL
STOP
SLICE

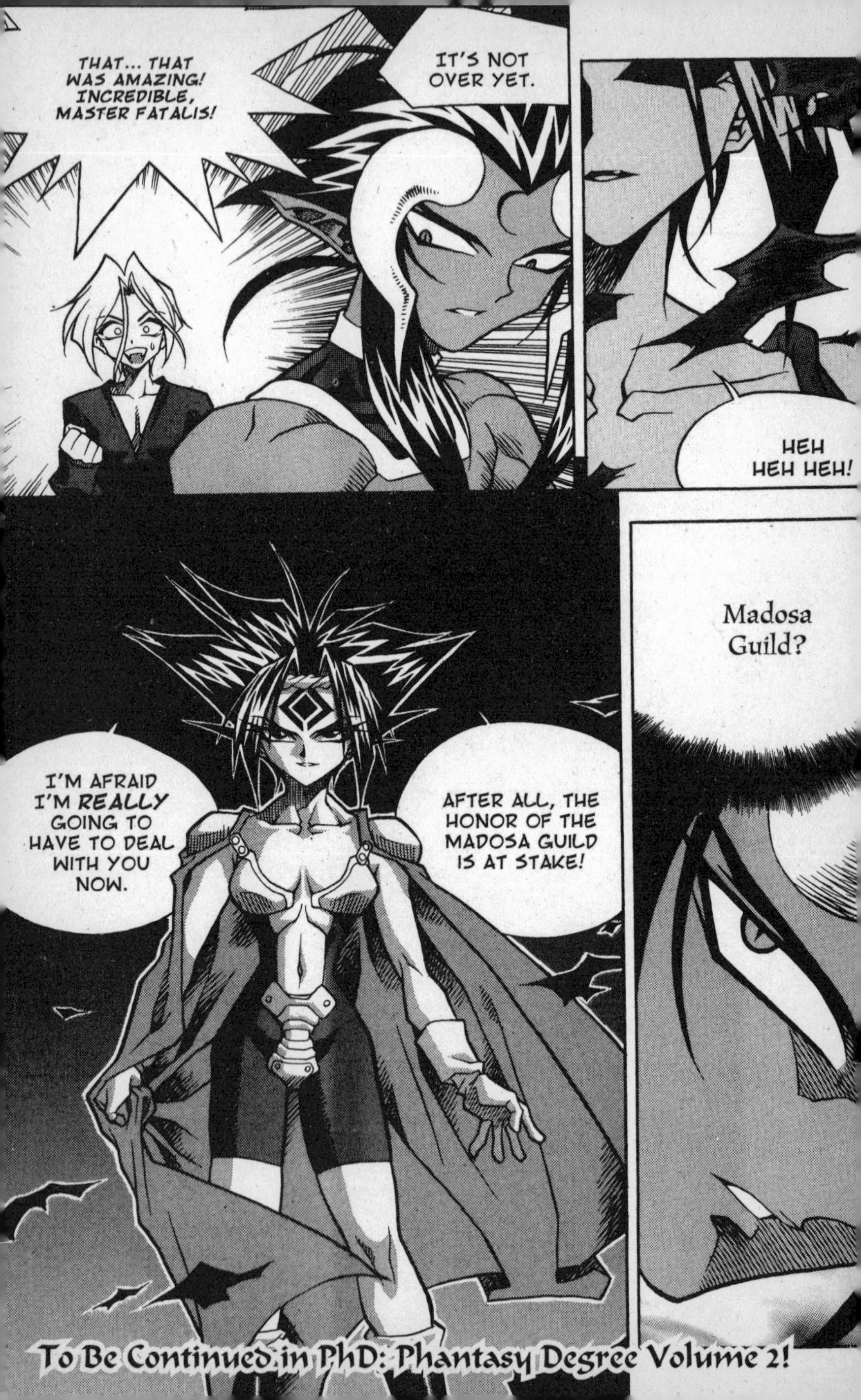
THAT... THAT WAS AMAZING! INCREDIBLE, MASTER FATALIS!
IT'S NOT OVER YET.
HEH HEH HEH!
I'M AFRAID I'M REALLY GOING TO HAVE TO DEAL WITH YOU NOW.
AFTER ALL, THE HONOR OF THE MADOSA GUILD IS AT STAKE!
Madosa Guild?
To Be Continued in PhD: Phantasy Degree Volume 2!

In the Next Volume of...

PHD

PHANTASY DEGREE

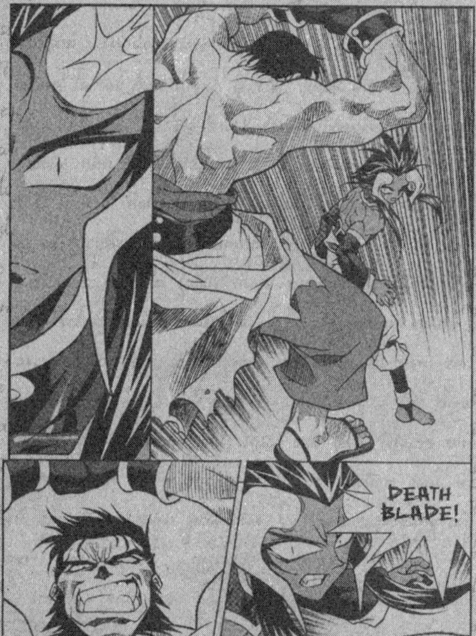
DEATH BLADE!
NEVER TURN YOUR BACK ON ME!

The battle continues to rage between the delinquent denizens of the Demon School Hades and the human members of the mysterious Madosa Guild. Sang, Mordicus, Notra and Fatalis try valiantly to keep the gates to the Mahgae open, while their friends and classmates are mercilessly slain. But, luckily, there might just be an afterlife--even if you reside in Hades. Fallen comrades are seemingly resurrected, transformed into more powerful versions of their former selves!

GRROAAWWR!
HUH-WOOF?
HEY, LUKAN, ARE YOU AWAKE, TOO?
Grrr!
MUZZLE IT, DUMMY. IT'S ME. TYRANNUS!
THIS IS VERY STRANGE.
I WAS ABSOLUTELY CERTAIN THAT WE DIED...

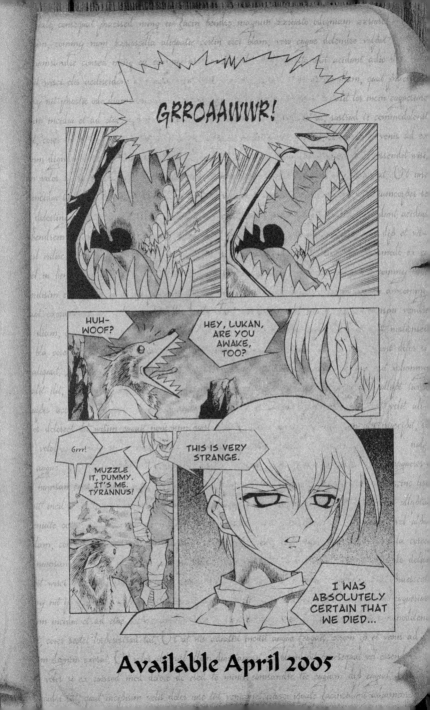

Available April 2005

PhD

PHANTASY DEGREE

Greetings, beloved readers! It is my great honor and privilege to chronicle Sang's exciting adventures! As with many tales and legends, this one has been handed down through the ages. With the passage of time, however, many such tales are slightly altered. For example, the Romans called the Greek god Zeus, the supreme ruler of Mount Olympus, "Jupiter." Similarly, a few characters featured in "PhD" have undergone some name changes, and the next few pages will explain these alterations. Oh, and speaking of "Olympus," in some faraway lands, "PhD: Phantasy Degree" is called "Master School Olympus." What and where is this Master School Olympus, you ask? Well, keep following Sang's quest and you will eventually find out! Safe journeys!

- Paul Morrissey, Editor

Dev and Fatalis

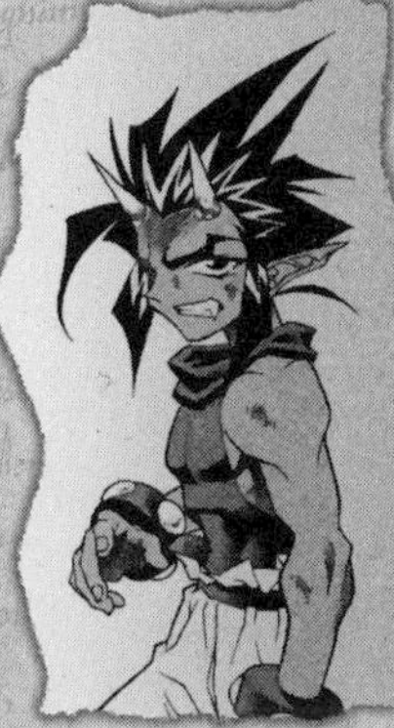
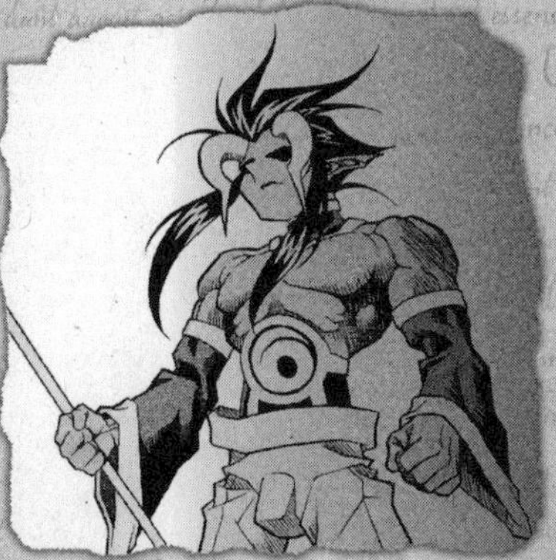

In some circles (or is that pentagrams?), Dev was originally known as "Des." So, why call him Dev? Well, in Persian mythology, "Dev" is a ruthless demon of incredible power. Of course, Dev's brother, Fatalis, is probably the most powerful demon in Hades. In some translations, Fatalis is known rather plainly as "Deadly." But if you know Latin, you'd realize that Fatalis is the perfect name change, since it actually means "deadly" or "fatal."

Mordicus

In Latin, Mordicus means "with teeth" or "biting." What a perfectly fitting name for a vampire! It's arguably creepier and more menacing than his original name, "Hyo."

Pannus Tyrannus

We can't keep Pannus Tyrannus' original name under wraps any longer. It was simply "Tyrant." Again, Latin comes to the renaming rescue. Pannus means "rag" or "piece of cloth" and Tyrannus is Latin for--you guessed it--"tyrant."

Lukan

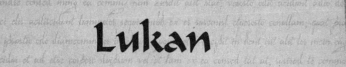

In some packs, Lukan is known as "Hook." In the West, however, "Hook" evokes a certain Pirate Captain in search of Peter Pan and the Lost Boys. Perhaps some would refer to him as "Fang," but in this version of Sang's adventures, he is known as Lukan. If your Latin is rusty, maybe you should try your Greek. Lukan is short for "lukanthropos," which means wolf.

Henduh Khyung

This menacing villain's name is often translated as "Henduh Kyung." Granted, adding the "h" is a very subtle change, but it gives the character some interesting depth. In Korean, the word "Khyung" is used as a term of nobility, similar to "Lord" or "Sir." Interestingly, the Khyung is also a mythical, magical Tibetan bird. Speaking of magic, Khyung is a member of the Madosa Guild--and in Korean, the word "Madosa" refers to wizards and magic users.

ALSO AVAILABLE FROM ✿TOKYOPOP®

MANGA

.HACK//LEGEND OF THE TWILIGHT
@LARGE
ABENOBASHI: MAGICAL SHOPPING ARCADE
A.I. LOVE YOU
AI YORI AOSHI
ANGELIC LAYER
ARM OF KANNON
BABY BIRTH
BATTLE ROYALE
BATTLE VIXENS
BOYS BE...
BRAIN POWERED
BRIGADOON
B'TX
CANDIDATE FOR GODDESS, THE
CARDCAPTOR SAKURA
CARDCAPTOR SAKURA - MASTER OF THE CLOW
CHOBITS
CHRONICLES OF THE CURSED SWORD
CLAMP SCHOOL DETECTIVES
CLOVER
COMIC PARTY
CONFIDENTIAL CONFESSIONS
CORRECTOR YUI
COWBOY BEBOP
COWBOY BEBOP: SHOOTING STAR
CRAZY LOVE STORY
CRESCENT MOON
CROSS
CULDCEPT
CYBORG 009
D•N•ANGEL
DEMON DIARY
DEMON ORORON, THE
DEUS VITAE
DIABOLO
DIGIMON
DIGIMON TAMERS
DIGIMON ZERO TWO
DOLL
DRAGON HUNTER
DRAGON KNIGHTS
DRAGON VOICE
DREAM SAGA
DUKLYON: CLAMP SCHOOL DEFENDERS
EERIE QUEERIE!
ERICA SAKURAZAWA: COLLECTED WORKS
ET CETERA
ETERNITY
EVIL'S RETURN
FAERIES' LANDING
FAKE
FLCL
FLOWER OF THE DEEP SLEEP, THE
FORBIDDEN DANCE
FRUITS BASKET

G GUNDAM
GATEKEEPERS
GETBACKERS
GIRL GOT GAME
GRAVITATION
GTO
GUNDAM SEED ASTRAY
GUNDAM WING
GUNDAM WING: BATTLEFIELD OF PACIFISTS
GUNDAM WING: ENDLESS WALTZ
GUNDAM WING: THE LAST OUTPOST (G-UNIT)
HANDS OFF!
HAPPY MANIA
HARLEM BEAT
HYPER RUNE
I.N.V.U.
IMMORTAL RAIN
INITIAL D
INSTANT TEEN: JUST ADD NUTS
ISLAND
JING: KING OF BANDITS
JING: KING OF BANDITS - TWILIGHT TALES
JULINE
KARE KANO
KILL ME, KISS ME
KINDAICHI CASE FILES, THE
KING OF HELL
KODOCHA: SANA'S STAGE
LAMENT OF THE LAMB
LEGAL DRUG
LEGEND OF CHUN HYANG, THE
LES BIJOUX
LOVE HINA
LOVE OR MONEY
LUPIN III
LUPIN III: WORLD'S MOST WANTED
MAGIC KNIGHT RAYEARTH I
MAGIC KNIGHT RAYEARTH II
MAHOROMATIC: AUTOMATIC MAIDEN
MAN OF MANY FACES
MARMALADE BOY
MARS
MARS: HORSE WITH NO NAME
MINK
MIRACLE GIRLS
MIYUKI-CHAN IN WONDERLAND
MODEL
MOURYOU KIDEN: LEGEND OF THE NYMPHS
NECK AND NECK
ONE
ONE I LOVE, THE
PARADISE KISS
PARASYTE
PASSION FRUIT
PEACH GIRL
PEACH GIRL: CHANGE OF HEART
PET SHOP OF HORRORS
PITA-TEN

07.15.04T

ALSO AVAILABLE FROM TOKYOPOP

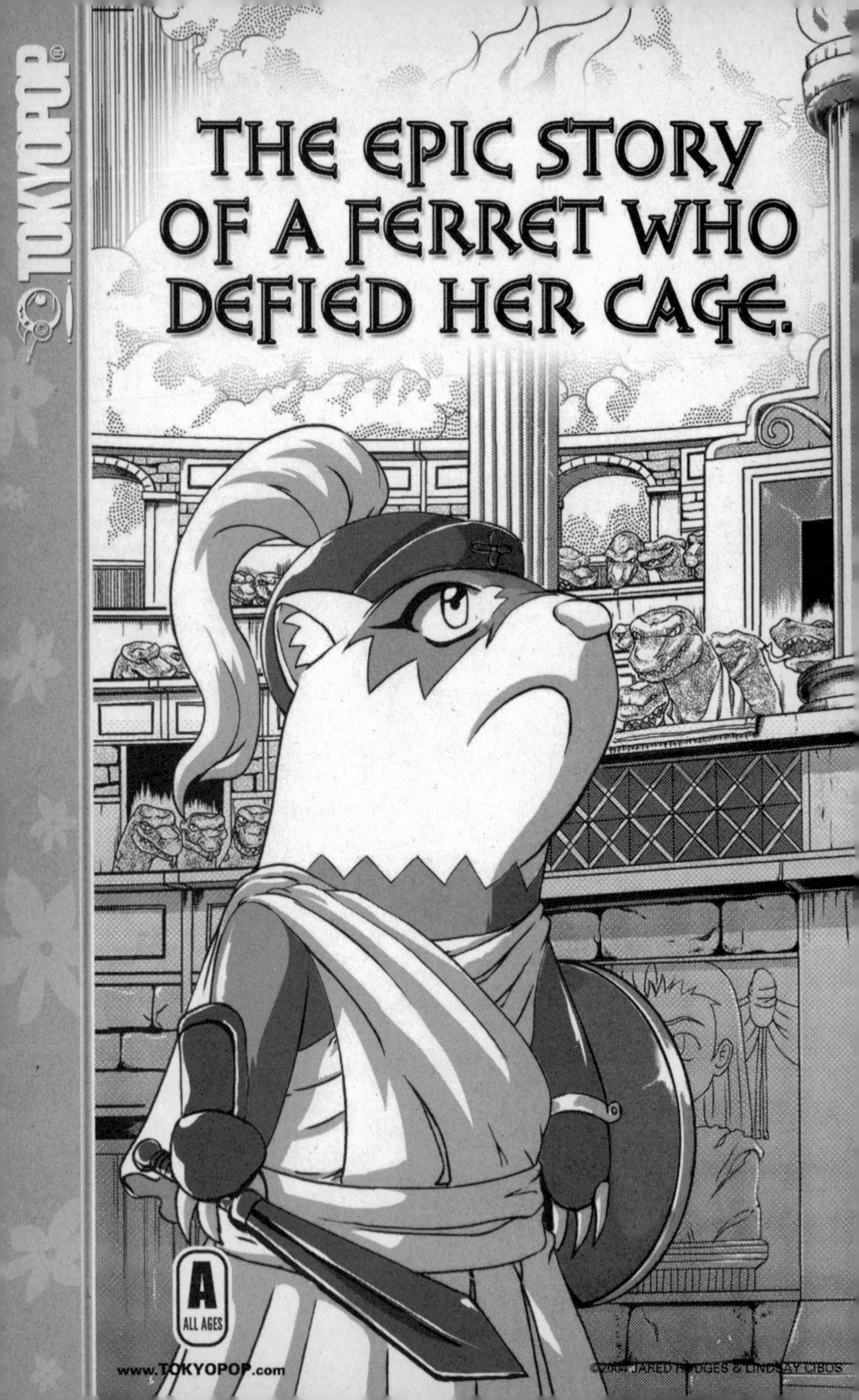
TOKYOPOP
THE EPIC STORY OF A FERRET WHO DEFIED HER CAGE.
A
ALL AGES
www.TOKYOPOP.com
©2004 JARED HODGES & LINDSAY CIBOS

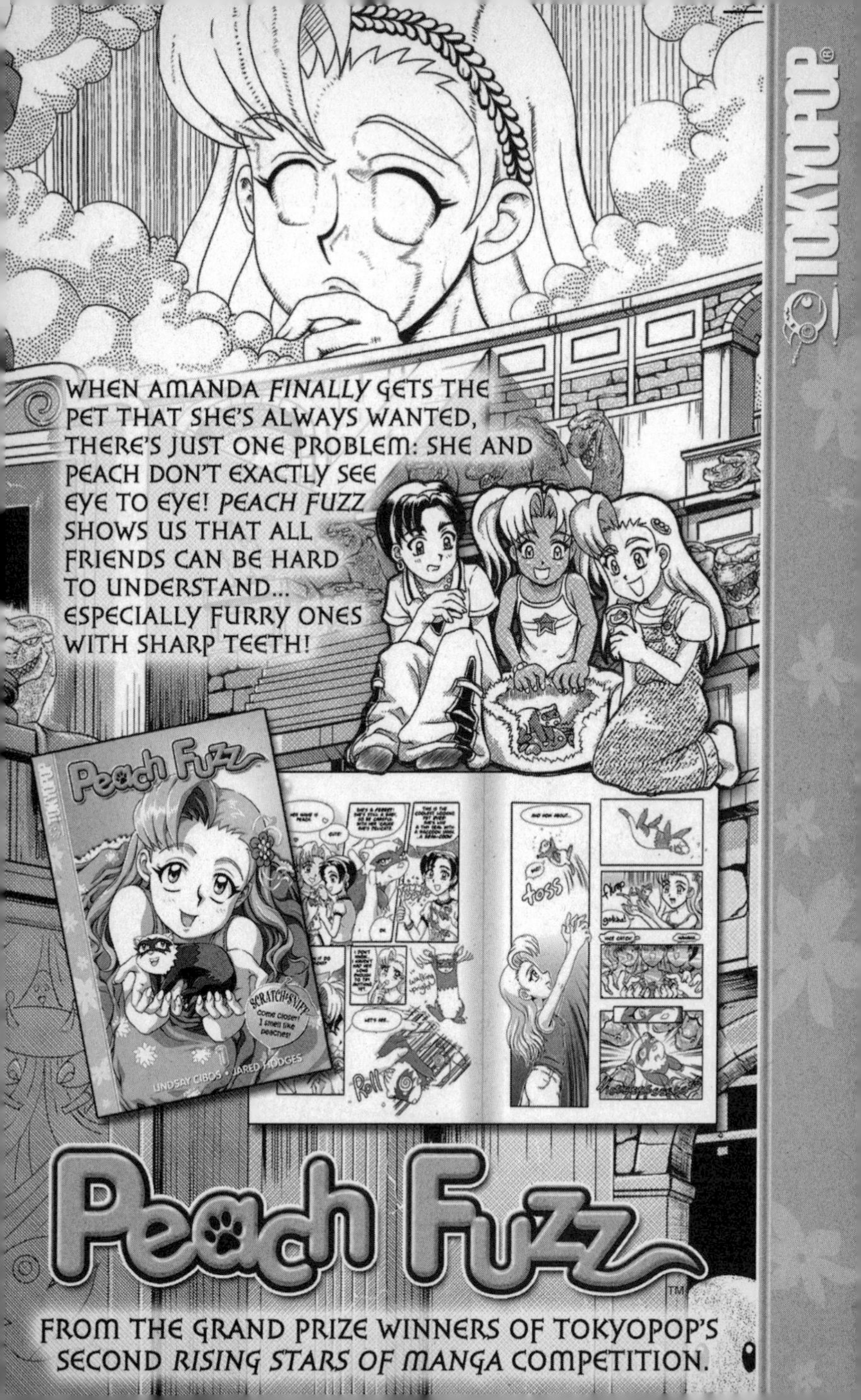
TOKYOPOP
WHEN AMANDA *FINALLY* GETS THE PET THAT SHE'S ALWAYS WANTED, THERE'S JUST ONE PROBLEM: SHE AND PEACH DON'T EXACTLY SEE EYE TO EYE! *PEACH FUZZ* SHOWS US THAT ALL FRIENDS CAN BE HARD TO UNDERSTAND... ESPECIALLY FURRY ONES WITH SHARP TEETH!
Peach Fuzz
SCRATCH & SNIFF
Come closer! I smell like peaches!
LINDSAY CIBOS • JARED HODGES
toss
Roll
Peach Fuzz™
FROM THE GRAND PRIZE WINNERS OF TOKYOPOP'S SECOND *RISING STARS OF MANGA* COMPETITION.

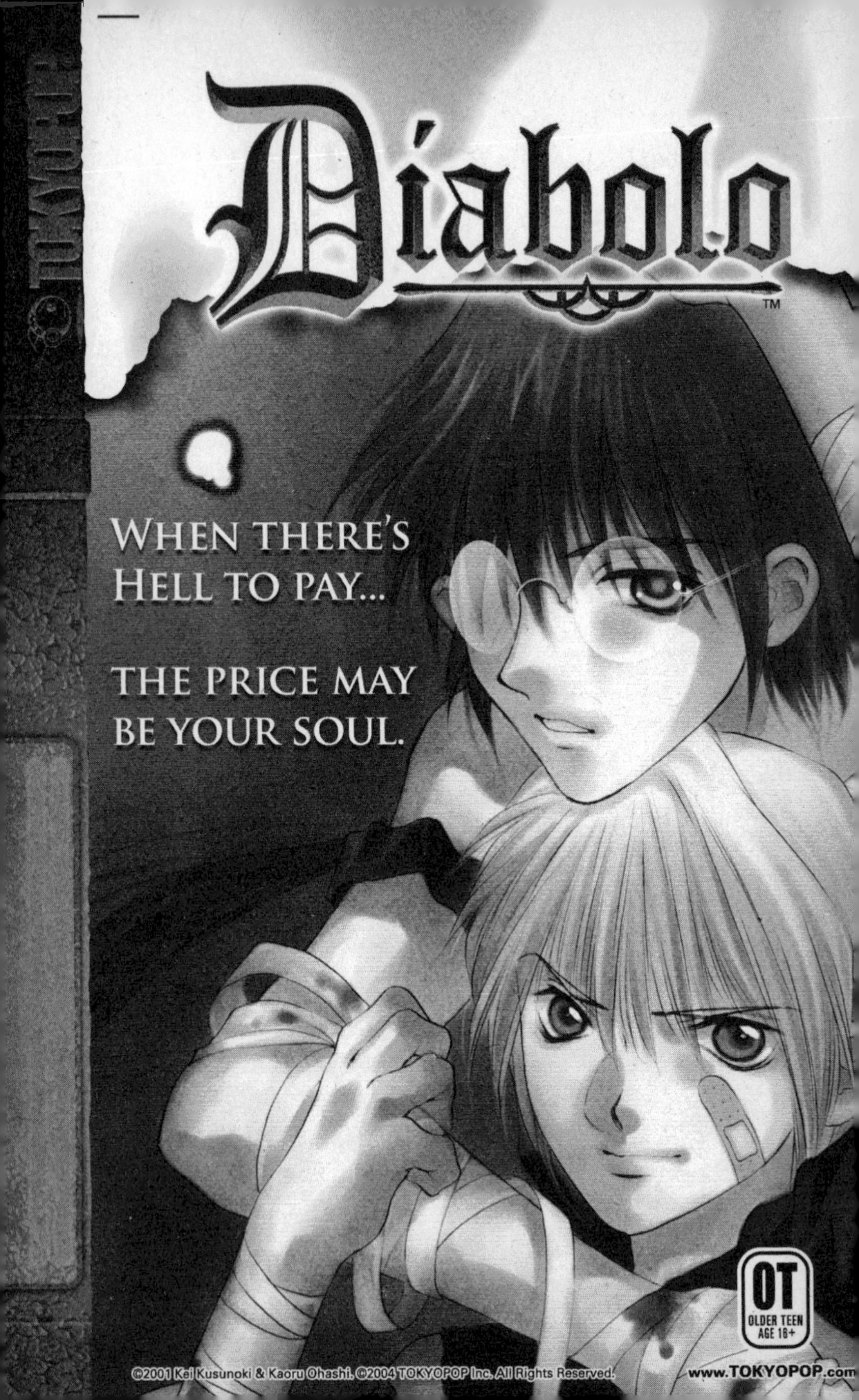
TOKYOPOP
Diabolo™
WHEN THERE'S HELL TO PAY...
THE PRICE MAY BE YOUR SOUL.
OT
OLDER TEEN
AGE 16+
©2001 Kei Kusunoki & Kaoru Ohashi. ©2004 TOKYOPOP Inc. All Rights Reserved.
www.TOKYOPOP.com

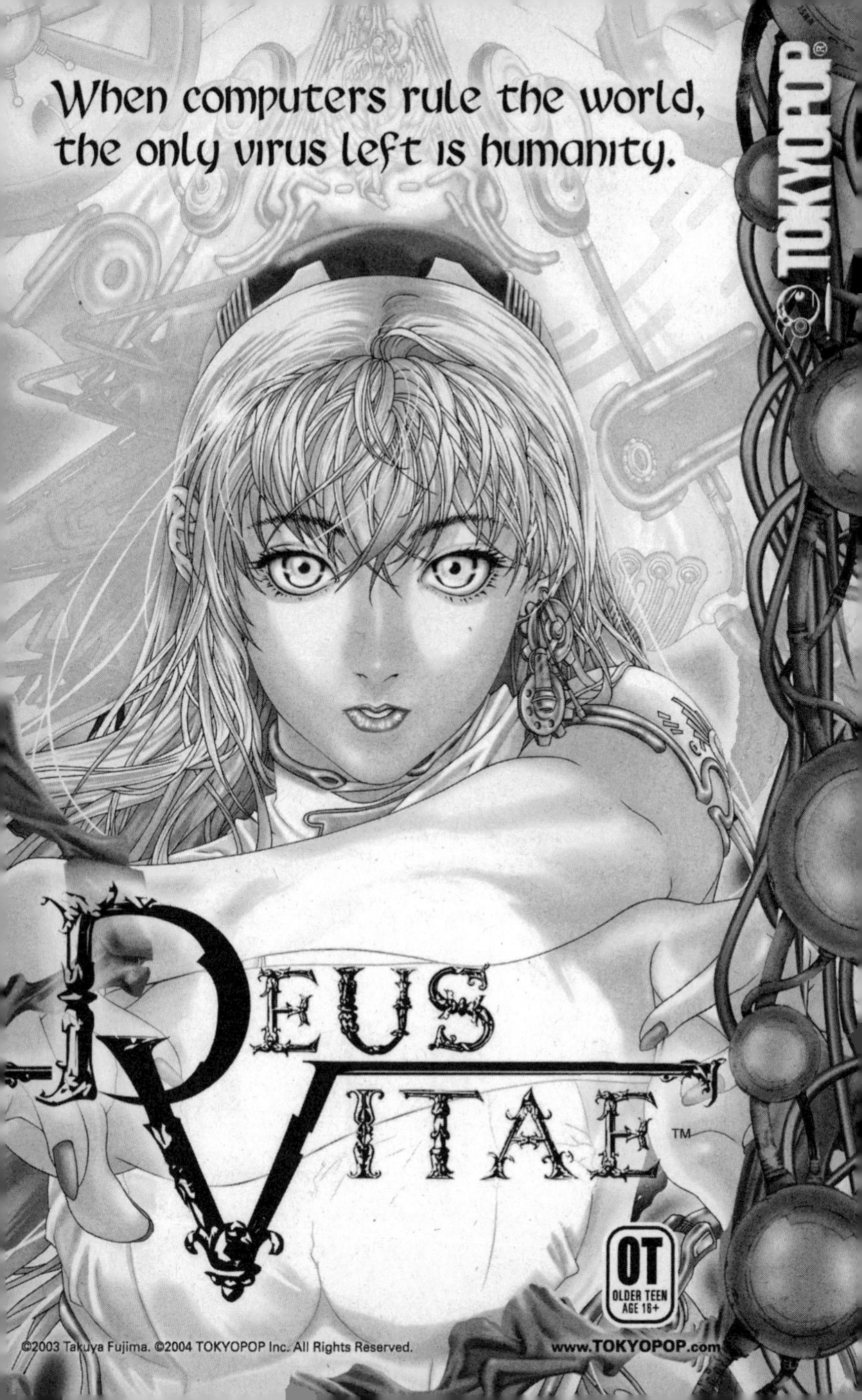
When computers rule the world, the only virus left is humanity.
TOKYOPOP
DEUS VITAE™
OT
OLDER TEEN
AGE 16+
©2003 Takuya Fujima. ©2004 TOKYOPOP Inc. All Rights Reserved.
www.TOKYOPOP.com